J. T. FRASER

Time, Conflict, and Human Values

University of Illinois Press

URBANA AND CHICAGO

Manufactured in the
United States of America
∞ This book is printed on acid-free paper.

Library of Congress Cataloging-in-Publication Data
Fraser, J. T. (Julius Thomas), 1923–
Time, conflict, and human values / J. T. Fraser.
p.   cm.
Includes bibliographical references and index.
ISBN 0-252-02476-1 (cloth : alk. paper)
1. Time. 2. Values. 3. Conflict (Psychology)
4. Truth. 5. Good and evil. I. Title.
BD638.F68   1999
115—dc21   98-58033
CIP

1 2 3 4 5 C P 5 4 3 2 1

For Thomas,

Anne-Marie, and

Margaret

Ruin hath taught me thus to ruminate—
That Time will come and take my love away.
    This thought is as a death, which cannot choose
    But weep to have that which it fears to lose.
    —Shakespeare

Sound, sound the clarion, fill the fife!
    To all the sensual world proclaim,
One crowded hour of glorious life
    Is worth an age without a name.
    —Sir Walter Scott

Things are seldom as they seem
Skim milk masquerades as cream.
    —Gilbert and Sullivan

CONTENTS

TIME, CONFLICT, AND HUMAN VALUES

THE PERUVIAN LABORATORY

In Thornton Wilder's masterpiece *The Bridge of San Louis Rey*, Brother Juniper traces the lives of five people who died together at noon on Friday, 20 July 1714, when the finest bridge in all Peru broke and precipitated them into the gulf below. The little red-haired Franciscan from northern Italy was approaching the bridge when he heard the ropes snap and saw the bridge divide and fling five gesticulating ants to their deaths.

Brother Juniper was an empiricist. He believed that theology should take its place among the exact, experimental sciences. He has been intending to place it there by demonstrating the workings of Providence through clear and unambiguous examples. He was never short of material, because his charges often met with calamity:

> spiders had stung them; their lungs had been touched; their houses had burned down and things happened to their children from which one averts one's mind. But these occasions of human woe had never been quite fit for scientific examination. They had lacked what our good savants were later to call proper control. The accident had been dependent on human error, for example, or had contained elements of probability. But this collapse of the bridge of San Luis Rey was a sheer Act of God. It afforded a perfect laboratory. Here at least one could surprise His intentions in a pure state.[1]

Brother Juniper could now demonstrate the wisdom of God's providence in his ways with man if he could explain why the tragedy happened to *those* five out of the hundreds of men, women, and children who crossed the bridge daily. "If there were any plans in the universe at all, if there were any pattern to human life, surely it could be discovered mysteriously latent in these lives so suddenly cut off. Either we live by accident and die by accident, or live by plan and die by plan."[2]

The friar spent the next six years reconstructing the lives of the three men and two women. He tabulated his data and compiled an enormous book. But the book was pronounced heretical by the judges of a court and was ordered burned in the square, together with its author.

Brother Juniper's story is a powerful allegory. The means for establishing, maintaining, or changing beliefs about what is true and what is untrue are often brutal. The same may be said about ideas and practices pertaining to what is good and right and, in subtle and not so subtle ways, about judgments concerning what is to be regarded as beautiful and what as ugly.

The three types of qualitative judgments, the true, the good, and the beautiful, serving respectively as guidelines to beliefs, conduct, and the management of emotions, constitute the family of human values.

As the twenty-first century begins, 5.5 billion people are crossing a cultural bridge. It connects social institutions appropriate for an earth on which human groups could interact only very slowly, if at all, to an earth on which all social institutions interact instantaneously and continuously. The time compactness of the globe promotes the sharing of the material and spiritual aspirations of all people, but it also reveals in image, word, and quality of life the unequal means and skills available for the support of those aspirations. The broad recognition of the difference between hopes and reality finds expression in challenges to all received teachings about human values and a struggle to decide what standards and ideas of the true, the good, and the beautiful are best suited to the needs and dreams of a cyberspaced humanity.

Beneath the achievements of our epoch, beyond the vast drama of historical transformations, Brother Juniper's puzzlement over the patterns of human fate remains very much alive. But unlike the red-haired Franciscan, most men and women of our age would agree with the first-century B.C. Latin poet Lucretius that nature is uncontrolled by proud masters and runs the universe by itself, without the aid of the gods. They would add only that nature includes us, people. In this mind-set and because of our rapidly changing understanding of man and the world, many old answers to some even older questions about human values demand reconsideration.

Using the allegory of Brother Juniper's rope bridge, one may ask several questions: Why have people of all ages been so eager to cross so many bridges in the pursuit of goals that were not related to their immediate biological needs? Why did they do so even though they knew that the ropes would give way under their weights? Why have men and women been so ready to suffer for the benefit of people long dead or not yet conceived? Why have so many people been so ready to cut the ropes of their brethren's bridges, intending to fling them to their deaths? This book seeks answers to these and related questions by examining the origins and evolutionary roles of human values.

Opinions about what specifically constitutes the true, the good, and the beautiful and about how to test for them vary from culture to culture, epoch to epoch, and person to person. Still, as forms of knowledge, they have been seen as conservative influences that promote permanence, continuity, and balance in the affairs of mind, heart, and society.

Such views may sometimes be valid in the short term. For the long, historical term, however, the role of human values has not been that of revealing eternal verities through truth, taming destructive passions by advocating the right and the good, or offering glimpses of the timeless through whatever is judged beautiful. On the contrary, these values have been and remain revolutionary forces that promote change. They give rise to and maintain certain unresolvable conflicts rooted in the human awareness of passage and dream of timelessness. It is here that an understanding of time's genesis and evolutionary structure permits a novel understanding of the dynamics of human values: seeking the true, trying to do what is right, and admiring what is beautiful perpetuate the chronic insecurity of the time-knowing species and drive its remarkable creativity and frightening destructiveness.

The reasoning is presented in six chapters:

1. a natural history of biological and human values,
2. a natural philosophy of time in terms of which the inquiry will be carried out,
3. a critique of truths as guidelines to beliefs,
4. a critique of good and evil as guidelines to conduct,
5. a critique of the beautiful and the ugly as guidelines to the management of emotions, and
6. a discussion of the ferment of human values on the time-compact globe.

CHAPTER ONE

Perspectives on a Strange Walker

Twenty-five centuries ago Sophocles identified the hallmarks of humankind in words that are as valid today as they must have been for our ancestors forty or fifty thousand years ago.[1]

> Many the wonders but nothing walks stranger than man. . . .
> This thing crosses the sea in winter's storm,
> making his path through the roaring waves. . . .
>
> Language, and thought like the wind
> and the feelings that make the town,
> he has taught himself. . . .
>
> He faces no future helpless. There's only death
> that he cannot find escape from. . . .
>
> Clever beyond all dreams
> the inventive craft he has
> which may drive him one time or another to well or ill.
> When he honors the laws of the land and the gods' sworn right
> high indeed is his city; but stateless the man
> who dares to dwell with dishonor. Not by my fire,
> never to share my thoughts. . . .[2]

With the help of evolutionary biology and psychology, this chapter offers a sketch of the strange walker. It claims that his virtuoso performance, including a measure of cosmic arrogance and a slight shiver, are made possible by the unbounded imaginative powers of his mind and that human values, working through symbols, serve as collectively developed guidelines to the control of that imagination.

1.1   Life, Time, and Mortality

In ordinary wisdom no less than in the works of sages, poets, and scientists, time is seen to relate to life through the inevitability of aging and death. That broadly held opinion is untenable. This section suggests an understanding that is defensible and that permits a joint interpretation of time, life, self-awareness, and death by aging.

Life, Time, and Death by Aging

Life is about 3.5 billion years old, as is death, for all living organisms may be killed. But death as the final and necessary result of senescence is only a billion years old or even less. It follows that time cannot relate to life through the inevitability of death by aging, as in "Golden lads and girls all must / As chimney sweepers come to dust." Instead, I will argue, time relates to life through the nature of the organic present.

With very few exceptions,[3] the literature tacitly assumes that the history of life consists of two phases. First, life emerged (through steps so far not completely understood); later, living systems began to internalize external cycles and generate some of their own. Henceforth the cyclic complement of organic behavior came to assist in the enterprise of living.

The internalization of external cycles through natural selection is a convincing proposition, but it is a mistake to assume that the coming about of life predated its rhythmic processes. Such an assumption is analogous to claiming that the sounds of instruments assist the orchestra in making music. Those sounds do not assist in making music; they constitute music, provided they are kept correlated from instant to instant according to stable principles. Likewise, the many physical and chemical oscillations present in all living organisms do not merely *assist* them in their adaptive endeavors. Rather, they *constitute* the process of life, provided they are maintained in mutually supportive rather than destructive relationships. It is this inner synchronization that defines the organic present (which I discuss in sec. 2.2, on the nature of time). Life may then be seen as the capacity of a system to secure its integrity by maintaining its organic present against internal and external perturbations.

This proposal represents a way of reasoning that is traditional to natural science: it sets the background for the understanding of a process in a manner that is independent of, and is uncommitted to, any of its specific manifestations. It is possible, for instance, to imagine life forms that use silicon instead of carbon, but it is not possible to imagine living organisms that do not maintain their organic presents.

Death by aging, then, is not a necessary feature of life. It is only an evolutionary development, an improvement in the methods available for maintaining the continuity of life, one that came about some 3 billion years after the emergence of life.

The earliest forms of life replicated; they reproduced asexually, for example, by fission. In that process, although the parent cell ceases to exist, there is no dead body left over, and hence the cell may be called deathless. This understanding of the origin of life is consistent with the best guesses available at this time as to the origin of life, namely, the postulate that our nearest nonliving ancestors resembled crystals: crystals "reproduce" by growing and then splitting (see appendix A, "Time and the Origin of Life").

In the replication of living organisms, new individuals can differ from their parents only by chance mutations. It is reasonable to assume that as life flourished, the environment to which species had to adapt came to include a substantial sampling of life and that the living targets of adaptation changed more rapidly than did the inanimate environment. This condition made life subject to a Malthusian principle in evolutionary rates: species that could adapt more rapidly began to gain advantages over their slower competitors. Many evolutionary biologists believe that it was the need for faster adaptive change that helped to select for sexual reproduction.

In sexual reproduction genetic contributions from two different individual combine to form a new individual with genes from both parents and hence different from both. The result is an increased pool of phenotypes based on continuously reshuffled genes. The development of different phenotypes in different environments then creates the immense variety of different individuals among which the environment may select. Sexual reproduction thus provides a degree of adaptive flexibility unavailable through asexual reproduction, a feat that involves a division of labor in securing life's continuity.

The task of passing on the know-how of synchronization (the skill of maintaining the organic present) became that of the germ cells; these replicate asexually and remain deathless in the previously explained sense of the term. Caring for the germ cells became the task of the soma, a multicellular assembly that possesses much greater flexibility than do the germ cells. But the soma ages and dies by aging. Death by aging was thus the price paid for the increased speed of adaptation and a necessary condition for securing the continuity of advanced forms of life.

7

A useful perspective on the change from replication to reproduction—on the coming about of death by aging—is a principle formulated by the mathematician John von Neumann. According to that principle, any system must reach a certain threshold of complexity before it can produce others of its own kind that possess equal or increased complexity and higher potentialities.[4] Only after a species has reached a certain level of complexity will it become advantageous for the species to reproduce through heirs that develop and die by aging instead of replicating through identical heirs and remaining, in a sense, undying.[5]

If humans reproduced through fission, Socrates could not have held that a man who devotes his life to philosophy should be cheerful in the face of death. Instead he would have had to say that a philosopher should be cheerful when contemplating splitting into two daughters; for her, time and life would not be correlated through death by aging. Symbolic funerals and baby showers would then have been one and the same celebration. Would they have been sad or happy?

Sexual reproduction and death by aging, being complementary aspects of the same evolutionary change, are fatefully inscribed on the biology of multicellular organisms and can easily fire human imagination. Plato tells us in his *Symposium* that Zeus sliced our four-legged, bisexual ancestors in half as one would slice an egg with a hair.[6] Since that slicing operation, the two halves that made up each original creature have been seeking each other. Whenever they meet, the original unity prevails and new life is conceived. Saint Paul failed to see the joy of that act and preferred to assert that the wages of sin is death, an idea that came to be incorporated in the doctrine of Original Sin. Nineteen centuries after St. Paul, Freudian thought detected in the mind of man a consciousness of time and hence of the inevitability of death, together with unconscious processes that Freud described as "timeless" in that they are not ordered temporally and have no reference to time.

Plato, St. Paul, and Freud articulated some of the peculiar consequences of the division of reproductive labor invented by organic evolution a billion years earlier.

I believe that in all cultures time, life, aging, and death by aging form a single constellation of ideas. This is understandable because humans, the creators of those cultures, all age and all die. Biologists might be able to make a duck that lives for eighty-five years or modify a woman so that she may deliver her great-grandson at the age of 110, but unless our species is reengineered to reproduce by fission, time, the self, and death by aging will remain a single fateful triad at the foundations of human values. This should not make us forget that, except for advanced species, time does not relate to life through aging and consequent death but through the unique and necessary capacity of maintaining an organic present against internal and external perturbations.

Self-Awareness and the Human Sense of Time

In the course of organic evolution, the behavior of advanced species became less rigid and hence less predictable in its details. But in the world of our immediate humanoid ancestors, there was an object that remained their permanent companion. As our ancestors walked, that companion made birds fly away and tigers attack. Obviously it shared the external world with those birds and tigers, which is why they could react to it as they did. But this companion differed from all other external objects in that, unlike them, it was able to feel pleasure and pain. The neurologist Gerald Edelman remarked that "the appearance of the biological individual allowed the development of a neurally based self-nonself distinction that was to a certain degree independent of environmental change."[7] In its simplest form, that permanent companion is the biological individual; in its most sophisticated form, it is the human self.

One of Wallace Stegner's masterful short stories is about a traveler lost at night in an empty winter landscape. He comes upon a lonely ranch where a boy helps him. The boy, who is tending to a dying old man, is himself in need of help. The traveler leaves the house to get that help. "Along a road he had never driven he went swiftly towards an unknown farm and an unknown town, to distribute according to some wise law part of the burden of the boy's emergency and his own; but he bore in his mind, bright as moonlight over snow, a vivid wonder, almost an awe. For from the most chronic and incurable of ills, identity, he had looked outward and for one unmistakable instant recognized himself."[8] This is what seems to have happened to our distant ancestor, that *promeneur solitaire,* as he began to construct personal identity.

In its simplest form the self suggests the body, as is implied in the following sentence addressed to a member of the opposite sex: "I would like to practice birth control with you." The same sense appears in the cry of the man about to be executed: "I don't want to die!" Here the relation is that between prey and predator. The situation ceases to be clear, however, if the cry "I don't want to die" comes from someone dying of metastasized cancer. Since the body is hell-bent to die, the "I" cannot be the body; it is the self that wants to live. For a person on a suicide mission, the roles are reversed: the body is ready to live, but the self wishes to die.

In its most sophisticated, highly evolved form, the self is felt to be independent of the body and holds an ambiguous position in a person's reality because, as just sketched, it belongs both to the external world of space and to the internal world of feelings and time. Since having a distinct self makes sense only in respect to other selves that are in some ways similar to and in other ways different from one's own, selfhood and human society had to be born together. In a process of mutual definition, society grants personhood and the person grants legitimacy to society. Another name for self-awareness is "conscious experience." It emerges when a creature realizes that it serves two masters: a tangible biological one and an intangible mental one.

Let me recall von Neumann's claim that a system must reach a certain threshold of complexity before it can produce others of its own kind that possess equal or increased complexity and higher potentialities. Earlier I applied this notion to the issue of reproduction versus replication. It may now be applied again, this time to the human brain and nervous system. Only after the human brain crossed a certain threshold of complexity did it become possible for a human mind to create other minds of equal or higher potentialities by means of communication through symbols.

This idea may now be placed in a historical frame. The taxonomical family that would lead to humans diverged from the apes between 9 and 5 million years ago. Over 4 million years ago australopithecenes (literally, "southern apes") walked on their hind legs but had relatively small brains. The genus *Homo* diverged from the australopithecenes perhaps 3 million years ago. It is conjectured that members of that genus made stone tools over 2 million years ago. Molecular genetics traces the origins of modern humans in Africa to about 200,000 years ago.[9] Close relatives of modern humans, known as Neanderthals, thrived between 130,000 and 35,000 years ago along a broad belt that spread from Western Europe to the eastern Mediterranean and China. (All these numbers are subject to revision.)

Since the size of the human brain has not changed substantially for perhaps 100,000 years,[10] any subsequent mental improvement must have come through our learning how to use and educate it. It was not until perhaps 50,000 years ago that our ancestors began to display symbolic behavior and invented increasingly efficient ways of murder-at-a-distance. They crossed a threshold in development where the rate of cultural change, driven by individually learned behavior, began to outrun the rate at which behavior could be changed through organic evolution, which targets the species. Whatever the dates, the future-related, instinctive behavior of our forebears was modified by the addition of flexible methods of planning arrived at by reasoning from individual experience. The new capacity provided means for transmitting acquired knowledge through language, art, and artifact. The necessity of signs and signals in communicating feelings and thoughts, as well as in describing worlds possible and impossible, established the metaphorical nature of human discourse.

Of the symbols that entered such discourse, the self—the permanent companion—came to serve as the organizing principle of knowledge: it tied memory-guided conduct to collectively shared behavior. What emerged was the "person," who began to play the role of a younger but better informed brother joined to the older, biological individual, who—or perhaps that— was concerned only with maintaining biological continuity.

Animals organize their lives around their inherited rhythms. They prepare for the future when their instincts so direct them and have no alternative *not* to prepare. Humans gained their freedom from the predicament of not having a choice when their expanding temporal horizons granted them stores of thinkable future possibilities. I imagine that this expansion of skills and perceptions included refinements in the cognitive functions of individuals, the recognition of a highly differentiated environment, increasing division of labor in society, and the development of increasingly better articulated methods of communication. The changes helped to enlarge a store of signals that were biological correlates of immediate conditions (a grunt for hunger) by adding a store of other signals that stood for events and things not present (the rattling of a stick while preparing for the hunt). These changes would have reinforced one another in a way that resembles positive feedback in that each mutually amplified the others' effects.

How is this evolutionary expansion of temporal horizons manifest in the development of the individual?

During birth the fetus experiences a change in the nature of his world. He leaves an environment where his needs were immediately satisfied and enters one where instant gratification is replaced by periods of time that separate the sensing of the need from its satisfaction. He learns that to get his needs satisfied, he now has to act and wait. Hunger makes him cry, and crying brings food. If it does not, there will be no infant to grow to personhood. Slowly, but quite perceptibly, the young child learns the rhythm of life outside the womb; with each sunrise and sunset he adapts himself more intimately to the enduring and changing aspects of his environment. An "ask and you shall be given" theory of causation becomes established in his mind and remains there throughout his life as a sense or feeling of magic causation. The early forms of magic causation then become enlarged and acquire a structure: the child learns that certain actions usually but not always bring certain responses after a certain delay. The experience of delay leads to an existential grasp of time's passage, to the notion of cause and effect, and later, to the idea of time itself.

If the period of waiting for need satisfaction is too long, the infant becomes frustrated and experiences an intensifying inner tension. By and by he learns to lessen that tension by substituting for the gratification of his instinctual needs such other rewards as happen to be available.[11] As the child learns to accept extended delays in need satisfaction, he also learns to recognize stable objects and processes in a world that earlier comprised chaotic change. Into his universe of surprises and ceaseless novelties, examples of permanence are introduced: the world becomes populated by objects that retain their identities. Later he learns that such identities, including objects known as other people, often come to an end. That glimmer of mortality helps to propel the growing youngster into personhood. Intentionality, which the infant first learned from his efforts directed toward satisfying his needs, becomes assigned to some of the lasting objects: "My dead bird wants to fly"; "My bear wants to play." Spoken words become endowed with the power that were earlier attributed to wishing and imagination as language comes to define, maintain, and refine his ideas of reality.

Spoken languages are not simply enlargements of the store of signs and signals of animal communication. Human languages employ traits that either do not exist in animals or exist only in very primitive forms. What does the infant bring to this enterprise?

He cannot possess an inborn vocabulary.[12] What he does possess is an ability to separate the permanent and predictable from the impermanent and unpredictable, both in his environment and among his feelings. He also has the ability to associate whatever appears permanent with the visible and audible signs and signals appropriate to the social and natural environments into which he was born.

An object, process, or relation that is a ball at one instant, then the voice of the mother, and then the smell of whisky, after which it changes into a bellyache, cannot be given a single name either by gesture or by sound. Words, the smallest units of spoken languages, stand for objects, processes, feelings, or relationships that retain their identities through a noticeable stretch of time. If words are assembled by more or less stable rules, they can suggest conditions, memories, and intents. Through these categories, languages carry meaning for a temporal world.

It is here that the distinction between animal and human language may be well illustrated. Whereas animal communications pertain entirely to the present or to the immediate future or past, human languages, with their symbolic representations of experience, permit the shifting of attention to nonpresent categories of the world: to the future, to the past, and to locations elsewhere. There are many ways I can tell my dog "I am about to feed you" and expect a response that suggests that I was understood, but there is no way I can communicate to it or to any other animal the idea "I have fed you this morning" or "I will feed you tomorrow" and have any indication that I was understood.

In Greek mythology concerns with future and past were the attributes of two Titans. One was Prometheus, the creator of humankind; his name means "the one who foresees." He had the skills of attaining the ends he foresaw. The name of his brother, Epimetheus, means "the one who reflects after the fact." I propose to identify the emergence of humankind from its humanoid ancestors with the capacities of forethought and afterthought. The joining of the two Titans makes possible an imaginative enlargement of the biological individual into a symbol called the self, living in a world of open-ended futures and debatable pasts.

1.2   The Need for Human Values

The symbol we call the self may be imagined as functioning in the future, in the past, in the present right here, at some unreachable region of the universe, or in a world that could not exist. This remarkable feat of imagination is an accomplishment of the human brain. For reasons that have to do with the historical search for features that distinguish humans from other animals, the processes responsible for that imagination are reified as those of the human mind. This subsection relates human values to the necessary control of the human mind.

About Brains

What features of the human brain may account for its capacity to see the world in terms of time and the self as a symbol that is more or less permanent in that changing world?

Hummingbird brains weigh 0.2 grams; the brains of contemporary humans average 1,370 grams; those of the dolphin, 1,600 grams; an elephant's brain weighs 6,000 grams; and that of a blue whale, 7,000 grams. Heavier brains do not guarantee smarter conduct.

Is it, perhaps, the volume of the brain that matters? The three-to-one ratio between human and gorilla brain volumes is not persuasive enough to suggest it as a measure of the difference between gorilla and human cultures. Among human adults brain volumes differ slightly, but the differences bear no known relation to intelligence. Some people of extraordinary intelligence have very small brains, and autistic people tend to have larger than average brains. Microcephalic dwarves—humans with skeletal proportions of normal adults but seldom taller than three feet—have brain volumes of about one-half or less than that of the normal adult, placing them close to the gorilla brain volume, yet they can acquire language and master verbal skills on the level of a normal five year old.[13]

There have been attempts to use the ratio of brain weight to body weight as a possible index of intelligence. That ratio varies: birds do better than reptiles, primates better than birds, and porpoises better than humans.[14] The brain–body weight ratio is no more convincing a measure of human intelligence than is brain volume or weight.

Let us try a more subtle approach. The behavior of species with increasingly more complex nervous systems becomes increasingly more flexible. A minimal set of essential responses to token stimuli found in the primitive instinct-reflex mechanisms of sponges and coelenterates represents the action of thousands of neurons. An organism with a fully elaborated central nervous system of 10^5–10^6 neurons can learn to handle particularities of its environment, such as recognizing places (as do lobsters, honeybee workers, and birds). Organisms with 10^9–10^{10} neurons have the capacity to generalize and juxtapose patterns; their behavior is not totally programmed, and their socialization is prolonged.[15] This class includes humans, chimpanzees, and baboons.

Something is still missing. Hans Christian Andersen's ugly duckling knew what it is. It does not matter, said the duckling (which was really a swan), where you were born as long as you came out of the right egg. Within broad margins the brain's weight, volume, ratio to body weight, or number of neurons is irrelevant as long as the brain is human.

I propose that what allows the human brain to serve in a manner we associate with the functions of the mind is the degree of connectedness among its neurons, measurable by a variable I will call complexity.

The concept of complexity will be introduced gradually. In the subsection "From Having a Brain to Having a Mind," I will relate it to nature at large. Later I will discuss complexity in the context of the axioms of the hierarchical theory of time. There the reader will be referred to appendix B, "Complexity and Its Measure." Here I note only that whereas the human brain, through its minding functions, can behold the physical universe, there is nothing among the functions of the physical universe that seems to be able to interpret the workings of the human mind, even though nature at large gave rise to it.

Brains and Biological Values

In human embryos, four weeks after conception, a flat plate of cells that will become the nervous system seals itself off from other embryonic cells. Each of the cells begins to produce daughter cells at an average rate of 250,000 new cells each minute. The tube swells and bends, and in a week it becomes a two-lobed brain. Eighteen weeks after conception the embryonic brain has all the nerve cells it will ever have, but they are not yet connected into the dense network that they will later constitute. Cells formed during this period of development contact special tissues that guide them to what will become the cortex. There they homestead, as it were, sending out fibers that encounter fibers from other neurons and beginning to form junctions—called synapses—with them.

This developmental sequence holds for vertebrates in general. What distinguishes people from other vertebrates is a cerebral cortex of some 10^{10} neurons so densely networked that the estimate of $10^{10,000}$ possible brain states is not unreasonable (again, this will be discussed later).

There is another question that should be asked first. Why should the degree of connectedness in the human brain be higher than it is in animals with comparable brain sizes, brain weights, or number of neurons? The theory of neural Darwinism, formulated and worked out in impressive detail by Gerald Edelman and his colleagues, suggests an answer.[16] Its basic claim is that the human brain's immense neural population is subject to principles of population dynamics known from demography and from the behavior of gene pools. It envisages a process of editing and stabilization among populations of neurons carried out by natural selection. The selection forces are those of the internal milieu of the brain, itself subject to selection that targets the body at large.

The neurons of the brain reach their highest degree of interconnectedness around the age of six years. Thereafter the network of the cortex is shaped not by any increase in the number of synapses but by the elimination of those that are not used. In the editing process, which is carried out through competition among synaptic populations, the groups of neurons that are useful to the challenges of the specific environment survive; those that are inappropriate atrophy. The result is "the most complicated object in the universe."[17] It is capable of performing what Edelman sees as the central task of the mind: the perceptual categorization of stimuli.

He maintains that conceptual models or maps of the world or of the self are not fixed traces of any kind. Rather, they are connected neuronal groups that respond selectively to combinations of elemental categories of sense impressions, such as colors, shapes, and sounds. If this is indeed the case, it follows that the manner in which events and objects are defined by partitioning the world into its phenomenal details is relative to the nervous system of whoever is doing the partitioning. This, says Edelman, is the only way one can explain "how perceptual categorization could occur, without assuming that the world is prearranged in an informational fashion or that the brain contains a homunculus."[18] The world is an unlabeled one "in which the macroscopic order and arrangement of objects and events (and even their definition or discrimination) cannot be prefigured for an organism, despite the fact that such objects and events obey the laws of physics."[19]

Objects do not carry signs saying, "I am a spoon," "I am a bill," or "I am a spoonbill." There is no such a thing as immaculate perception; the perception of objects depends on the active participation of the perceiver through the synchronization of scattered mappings in his or her brain. That synchronization suggests the creation and maintenance of the mental present, an idea that I will introduce and examine in sec. 2.2.

The categorization of stimuli is carried out with the help of certain inborn biases Edelman describes as values and defines as "evolutionarily or teleonomically derived constraints favoring behavior that fulfills homeostatic requirements or increases fitness in an individual species."[20] Here *teleonomy*, a word coined by Colin Pittendrigh from *telos* (end) and *nomos* (law), means the property, common to all living systems, of being organized toward the attainment of ends.[21] *Homeostasis* refers to an organism's tendency toward stability through the regulation of its internal environment. If the system is a species, homeostasis is secured through coadaptive changes; if it is the web of life, it works through group selection. Common to these diverse controls is the favoring of permanence or stability.

Values as defined by Edelman are akin to homeostatic controls. Expressed in the selection policies of neural Darwinism, they favor propensities for invariance. They select for such connectedness among neuron groups as promotes collective (neuronal) behavior that helps to maintain permanence and continuity. In his formulation, the "value of a global pattern of neuronal responses to a particular environmental situation (stimulus) is reflected in the capacity of that response pattern to increase the likelihood that it will recur in the same context." Biological value, then,

> is not an invariant that can be used to label a known world. . . . Inasmuch as the environment is unpredictable and open-ended and no two individuals are the same, the value of an event cannot in general be specified precisely a priori. This limits the usefulness of value descriptors that ignore either the history of the individual or the context in which they are exercised. On the other hand, this very limitation makes apparent the advantage in evolutionary terms of having value systems which are themselves adaptive.[22]

These values are controlled by the global patterns of neuronal responses established by Darwinian selection in the developing brain of the individual; they are preferences for those organic processes that help to secure stability and have the propensity of perpetuating themselves. I will class all such conservative trends as *biological values*.

From Having a Brain to Having a Mind

How does one go from having a brain and biological values to having a mind and human values? First I will consider the step to having a mind. I start from what may initially appear to be far afield from the issue at hand.

There are several well-known boundaries to the physical world. Nothing may be larger than the universe, for instance, and nothing can be older. Nothing may be colder than absolute zero and or hotter than about $10^{12\circ}$ K. It is meaningless to assign physical significance to intervals shorter than about 10^{-43} sec., and nothing can be faster than light.

All these boundaries of nature may be approached through continuous changes from conditions whose dimensions are appropriate to humans. To reach the limiting speed, all one has to do is to go faster and faster (or imagine doing so). For limiting temperatures one makes a body colder and colder or hotter and hotter. To approach the lower limit of time you make the temporal separation between two events shorter and shorter (or imagine doing so). The behavior of nature at these boundary conditions, however, is unpredictable from human-dimensioned experience. Had it not been for the genius of a few gifted people, we could not have predicted the curious character of the world at limiting speeds, sizes, times, or temperatures.

To these variables of the physical world, each of which reaches a well-known boundary condition, I would like to add a new one. It is that of complexity. Our bodily facilities do not place us at the boundaries of the very large, small, cold, or fast, but possessing a human brain places us at the boundaries of biological complexity (complexity will be discussed in detail in sec. 2.2). I assume that its immense complexity is what allows the human brain to accommodate a dynamical model of the world of which the body is a part, a model of the body of which the brain is a part, of things and events not present, and of things and events that could not even exist. Our brains can dream of possible and impossible worlds. To paraphrase William Blake, the human brain can see the world in a grain of sand, heaven in a wild flower, or hold infinity within its insignificant volume and eternity within its fleeting life.

In the physical world, as I reasoned, the behavior of nature at its boundary conditions is unpredictable from knowing only physical behavior far from the boundaries. Likewise, in the organic world, the behavior of living matter close to the boundary conditions of complexity is unpredictable from knowing only organic functions far from those boundaries.

From thinking about the human brain let me turn to thinking about the human mind. *Mind* is a noun that suggests an object in space. But do not ask what mind *is;* ask what it *does.* It would be better to speak only about minding, using a gerund, instead of speaking about the mind.[23] The word *minding,* traceable to the tenth century, pertains to such actions as remembering, thinking, attending, intending, or having a purpose. One must have a human brain to be minding something, but it is no more necessary to have a body part called "mind" for remembering, thinking, attending, or intending than it is necessary to have a body part called "quilt" for quilting or one called "wink" for winking.

Given the immense complexity of the human brain as a single functional system, it can be described best or perhaps only by what it does and not by what it is. What we are dealing with here is a distinction between state and process descriptions of a dynamic system.[24]

A state description is a tabulation of data that defines the state of a system at an instant; a process description is an ongoing report about the functioning of a system. A vertical section of an orchestra score, identifying the sound that each instrument plays at a moment, is a state description. The complete score is a tabulation of state descriptions. The music actually played is a process description of the score. A state description is spatial; a process description is temporal. When it comes to specifying the functions of the human brain, process descriptions are the only possible ones. As Heinz Pagels describes it, the brain possesses an "unsimulatable complexity." By "unsimulatable" he meant that there is "a 'complexity barrier' between our instantaneous knowledge of the state of the neuronal network and our knowledge of its future development."[25] I am unable to produce a single state description of the trillion neurons in my brain at this moment, but I can give a process description of what they are doing at this moment by writing down these words. I could also give a process description of their activities by dancing, sculpting, riding, quilting, or winking. Language may well be the most versatile of all process descriptions of the mind: it permits the creation and manipulation of an infinite variety of imagined worlds, each furnished with possible and impossible things and events and each moved freely into the future or the past. My mind consists of the process descriptions of my brain.

Reaching for the Permanent

I reasoned that biological values for living organisms were preferences for processes that help to secure stability and have the propensity of perpetuating themselves. Human values are analogous preferences in the domains of human beliefs, conduct, and feeling. As a family of judgments, they tend to be associated with words that suggest opposition to time and change, such as eternity, timelessness, or immortality. When our distant ancestors began to bury jewelry, weapons, and food with their dead, they attested to their belief that death is not final.

The last time I visited the National Archaeological Museum in Athens, I saw displayed a gold-foil baby bootie made in the city of Mycenae around 1500 B.C. What purpose did it—perhaps with a lost mate—serve? Perhaps the booties were signs of rank, worn to remind one and all of the great and lasting might of their wearer. Perhaps they were made to protect a young life from visible or supernatural harm. Whether the child died or grew to healthy maturity, the booties could have served only as reminders of things past. The bootie survived the artisan who made it, the powerful people who ordered it made, the child who wore it, and even the civilization that provided for its fashioning. Through thirty-five centuries its untold handlers left it in its original form. Its gold was not reused but left to carry a family of meanings embodied in its shape.

The Mycenean bootie, all objects of art, all stories passed on from generation to generation, all equations of physics, all monuments, and the very languages we speak are witnesses to the human desire to reach for immortality.

The universe of the newborn, as I already mentioned, is mostly that of ceaseless novelty out of which permanent shapes and repeating processes emerge. Throughout childhood and mature life there remains in every person a desire to identify permanent structures and processes and with them to experience the certainties that were (normally) first conveyed by the parents. Much deeper, there are the inborn "biases" present in the selection policies of neural Darwinism, as postulated by Edelman, favoring conservative trends. As a consequence, we find a special appeal in the permanence expressed in objects, processes, and ideas that appear to be unaltered by time.

Plato generalized this yearning for permanence, projected it onto the heavens, and built his philosophy on the praise of permanence and mistrust of change. For him, as for millennia of Platonists and Neoplatonists, for mathematicians of all ages, and for physicists of our own days, the world remains divided into what is intelligible by reason, what "is always in the same state," and what "is conceived by opinion with the help of sensation and without reason [and] is always in a process of becoming and perishing and never really is."[26] In other words, the world is made up of things permanent and things changing, of events predictable and events unpredictable.

But even gold and bronze change with time, though they do so much more slowly than do humans.

O flowers they fade because they are moving swiftly. . . .
they are all time travelling
like comets, and they come into our ken
for a day, for two days. . . .
But a gem is different. It lasts so much longer than we do
so much much much longer
that it seems to last forever.
Yet we know it is flowing away
as flowers are, only slower.
The wonderful slow flowing of the sapphire![27]

It is for this reason that in Platonic thought the only eternal objects are ideas; everything else is merely a mutable embodiment of a corresponding idea. The absence of concrete, tangible examples of permanence—as an object that never changes would be—did not stop people from looking for stability in things, for the opposite, the inevitability of passage, is deeply disturbing. It is not death itself that is feared but oblivion, the vanishing of the self, the not belonging anywhere, the not belonging to anyone, that strikes fear into the heart. To lessen the tension between their knowledge of time and desire for permanence, people created a variety of opiates— objects, patterns of conduct, ideas—that could make passage itself appear insignificant or even unreal.

Although all animals die, and many can display mortal terror, only in humans has the knowledge of death become a generalized malaise, an ever-present tension that makes us seek permanence in the hope of decreasing that tension. It is the human need to search for deathlessness that helps to erect the edifices of religions and philosophies, the arts, the letters, and the sciences and to formulate the laws of nature, man, and God.

This remarkable achievement of the strange walker is made possible by the infinite store of the brain's process descriptions, usually spoken of as the powers of imagination. Human values are controls on those imaginative powers. They are selective forces that work through symbols. They take the form of collectively approved guidelines for beliefs expressed in terms of truths and untruths, rules for conduct stated in terms of good and evil, and suggestions for the management of emotions offered in terms of judgments on what is beautiful and what is ugly.

There are many ways in which issues of human values may be and have been discussed and understood. Here I will explore their nature and boundaries of effectiveness with the help of the hierarchical theory of time.

CHAPTER TWO

Perspectives on Time and Conflict

This chapter outlines the natural philosophy of time in terms of which I carry out the inquiries in the balance of this book. That natural philosophy was proposed, developed, and critically examined in prior publications.[1] In its structural features it is a framework for the interdisciplinary study of time; in its dynamic features it is a general theory of conflicts. Accordingly, it bears two names: the hierarchical theory of time and the theory of time as conflict.

Sec. 2.1 recognizes the evolutionary character of the relation between the knower and the known and offers a definition of reality consistent with this recognition. Sec. 2.2 sketches the nested hierarchical nature of causation, time, and modes of conflict in the dynamics of matter, life, the human mind, and society.

2.1 Reality and Its Moving Boundaries

With his usual pragmatism, Samuel Johnson explained that the "use of traveling was to regulate the imagination by reality, and instead of thinking how things may be, see them as they are."[2] But can one speak about things the way they really are without taking into account the ways of learning and the nature of the learner? Is there a final reality whose furnishings may be discovered, certified to be independent of the knower, and employed in specifying whatever is to be regarded as true, good, and beautiful?

For Plato the answer was yes. He saw absolute truth, beauty, and goodness as unchanging aspects of reality, directly apprehensible by the soul and existing independently of the senses.[3] Not so for Thomas Aquinas (1225–74), who maintained that whatever is known is known through the senses and interpreted by the intellect.[4] The satirist Cyrano de Bergerac (1619–55) sent a seventeenth-century version of an astronaut to the kingdom of the moon and recorded his discussion with a friendly lunar demon. The earthling wanted to know about the demon's life and mode of death. The demon replied that he could offer no meaningful answer: "If there is something you men cannot understand, you either imagine it is spiritual or that it does not exist. But both conclusions are quite false. . . . If I sought to explain to you what I perceive with the senses which you do not possess, you would picture it to yourself as something which can be heard, seen, touched, smelt or tasted, and it is, in fact, none of these things."[5]

For Immanuel Kant (1724–1804) the "true correlates of sensibility, the things-in-themselves," existed independently and apart from any human knowledge thereof, but they could not be known.[6] Read in context, this seems to have meant that appearances never disclosed the totality of the real, where *real,* in an eighteenth-century fashion, meant a stable world unchanging in its god-created nature. The philosopher Arthur Schopenhauer (1788–1860) believed that every man takes the limits of his own fields of vision for the limits of the world. Thomas Hardy (1840–1928), reflecting on the boundaries of the senses, remarked that those boundaries were not noticeable by the person possessing them. The "limitations of the capacity is never recognized as a loss by the loser thereof: in this attribute moral and aesthetic poverty contrasts plausibly with material, since those who suffer do not mind it, while those who mind it soon cease to suffer."[7]

For the poet Wallace Stevens (1879–1955) reality was malleable, a creation of the mystical musician in all of us.

> They said: "You have a blue guitar
> You do not play things as they are."
> The man replied, "Things as they are
> Are changed upon the blue guitar."[8]

You make the music yourself, says Stevens. Listen to it without worrying about what the tune "really" is. For Wittgenstein (1889–1951) reality was what our language said was real, and hence the boundaries of a person's language were the boundaries of his or her world.[9]

A scientific version of Stevens's blue-guitar model, combined with Wittgenstein's language model (where "language" is any mode of communication), may be found in the work of the German theoretical biologist Jakob von Uexküll. Early in the twentieth century he drew attention to the fact that for each animal the world as perceived and acted on is determined by the animal's receptors and effectors. Its receptors determine all possible stimuli it may experience; he called this universe the animal's *Merkwelt* (perceptual universe). The totality of responses of which the animal is capable is its *Wirkwelt* (universe of actions). These two universes form a functional loop that carries information. External signals become internal signals, which are processed, evaluated, and then passed on as commands for action that has the external world as its target. Through that action the external signals become modified and reenter the loop. The dynamic content of this loop forms the *Umwelt* of the species.[10]

The word *Umwelt* became naturalized into English. Fortunately so, because its translations—"species-specific reality," "self-world," "phenomenal world," "perceptive universe," "world horizons"—are all awkward. *Umwelt* is now defined as "the circumscribed portion of the environment which is meaningful and effective for a given species."[11] Since the information-retaining, -processing, and -transmitting capacities of the perceptive-cognitive and motor loop of any species is bounded, it follows that for each of its members, the umwelt of a species appears as a complete world that contains everything there is or can be known.

Note that the environment of which an animal's umwelt is a "circumscribed portion" is our human umwelt. It is our human reality.

The umwelts of animals change as their biological capacities evolve—that is, slowly. In contrast, enlarging the horizons of human reality does not have to await biological changes; the human skills of reasoning and sharing observations through language can accomplish that extension mentally.

With advances in technology and science it became possible to transpose the details of certain animal umwelts not naturally available to humans into forms of stimuli appropriate for people and thus to incorporate their umwelts into ours. For instance, patterns on the wings of certain butterflies show up only in ultraviolet light. They are visible to other butterflies but not to humans because vertebrate eyes are not sensitive to ultraviolet. Those patterns were not part of our reality until after we learned to photograph them in ultraviolet wavelengths and display them in the visible spectrum. "Visible" means visible to humans.

The boundaries of human reality explorable through the unaided and aided senses may be further expanded with the help of the abstract statements known as mathematical formulas. Through them we can learn about the strange world of black holes, traveling photons, and objects that are both particles and waves. But even these expanded horizons do not constitute the boundaries of human reality, for our umwelt also includes anticipations prompted by present needs, guided by memories, modulated by conscious and unconscious fantasies, and modified by sense impressions.[12] All this knowledge is modified by personal idiosyncrasies and by what society suggests and allows as acceptable reality. The poltergeists of past ages are the creaking steps of today. Although this reasoning implies that everyone is a distinct and different agent in the creation of his or her umwelt, there are large regions of interpersonal agreement on what is to be judged real because human perceptive and cognitive faculties are nearly identical among all people.

Human reality, so constructed, is something that the mind contributes to the body's efforts to survive in its specific environment. It is an enterprise characterized by drives toward bringing about changes that favor the needs of an organism. It consists of the sounds of Stevens's "blue guitar," together with imagined sounds and sights, placed into imagined possible and impossible futures with imagined possible and impossible pasts. All this wealth of internal-external mutuality is formally recognized by von Uexküll's umwelt principle.

The idea of umwelts may be easily formulated for the different sensory systems: one may think of visual, auditory, tactile, and olfactory worlds. For organisms all such umwelts coexist and influence each other yet may remain recognizably distinct. It is therefore only a step to go from special sensory systems to exosomatic extensions of our sensory systems known as scientific instruments. For instance, the umwelt of a radio telescope is electromagnetic radiation, often limited to the 21-cm line of hydrogen gas; the telescope is blind to the light of the moon and deaf to the sound of barking dogs.

We can put questions to nature directly through the senses and indirectly through instruments. We can also do so by experimenting with butterflies, dogs, and earthworms. We can go even further, much further. We can use mathematics and theories to explore aspects of the universe that are not otherwise accessible to any living creature, such as the world of a traveling photon, the motion of distant galaxies, the implosion of a star, or the explosion of the Big Bang.

Such umwelts often fail to display features of time or space that we normally take for granted. In addition, they may display features of time and space we already know but display them in unexpected forms. There are, for instance, processes that do not respond to the direction of time, and there are aggregates of objects that cannot behave any other way but probabilistically. If extended tests demonstrate such features of an umwelt as consistent and reproducible, then we must accept them as aspects of those umwelts, complete in themselves, even if they appear strange or incomplete from the point of view of daily human experience.

The extension of von Uexküll's umwelt principle to worlds we know only through instruments or formulas is the *extended umwelt principle*. Of course, the umwelts of molecules, galaxies, birds and bees, and baboons and babies, as they are revealed to us, are all part and parcel of our own, the *noetic umwelt*, or noetic reality.[13] Philosophers have long sought normative criteria for a categorical definition of reality. For our purpose all that is necessary and sufficient is to have established a working concept of reality—the extended umwelt principle—and to note that as our knowledge of the world expands, so does our reality. This amounts to equating epistemology with ontology: the world is the way we find it to be through the many forms of human knowledge, even if some of its features appear to be counterintuitive.

The generalized umwelt principle resembles but is not identical to realism, because it does not maintain that our senses and thoughts present us with details of a world whose furnishings are independent of the knower. Water is for fishes something quite different from what it is for cats. The generalized umwelt principle also resembles but is not identical to idealism, for it rejects the notion that ultimate reality resides in a transcendental realm. Rather, it is a form of descriptive naturalism that maintains that knowledge, the mind, and spiritual values must be explicable in terms of natural processes. In this it evokes the pragmatism of William James. It also resembles Kantian thought in its insistence that the intellect does not derive its laws from nature but prescribes them to nature. Nonetheless, it sees reality as evolutionarily open-ended in a way that Kant would have had to reject because such an open-endedness cannot admit the existence of things-in-themselves. It sees knowledge as valid only until we learn differently. It is close to philosophical anthropology and has affinities to the sociology of knowledge. It resembles Edelman's "qualified realism"[14] but differs from it because it is built on a hierarchical epistemology where the biological—fundamental in Edelman's view of the world—is seen as only one of the organizational levels of nature, and not even the most advanced one.

Is there a world beyond the boundaries of human reality current at any epoch and place and valid for any person? The language of this question is deceptive because it uses spatial metaphors to describe knowledge. It asks whether there is anything external to our sphere of knowledge. But knowledge is not a structure in space that has insides and outsides; it is a process of continuous, active recategorization of what is already known with what is being learned. The question, therefore, is this: is there anything that I do not now know but may yet learn at a future date by means yet unborn? Tennyson answers yes in the following terms.

> I am a part of all that I have met;
> Yet all experience is an arch wherethrough
> Gleams that untravelled world, whose margin fades
> For ever and for ever as I move.

These ideas about reality and its moving boundaries make possible the formulation of the hierarchical theory of time, in terms of which I propose to explore the nature of human values.

2.2   A Nested Hierarchy of Causations, Languages, Temporalities, and Conflicts

The hierarchical theory of time is built on a number of propositions. A proposition is a statement of belief that is not deduced from prior beliefs but arrived at through inductive reasoning, which appeals to aesthetic and affective elements. If inferences drawn from a proposition withstand sustained criticism, confidence in its validity increases. It may then be raised to the level of an axiom, its claim maintained as true until it is shown to be otherwise. Newton had this to say about propositions: "In experimental philosophy we are to look upon propositions inferred by general induction from phenomena as accurately or very nearly true, notwithstanding any contrary hypotheses that may be imagined, till such time as other phenomena occur, by which they may either be made more accurate, or liable to exception."[15]

The propositions of the theory of time as conflict, "inferred by general induction from phenomena" and in need of explication and critical employment, are as follows:

1. Nature comprises a number of integrative levels
2. which form a hierarchically nested and evolutionarily open system
3. along a scale of increasing complexity.
4. Processes characteristic of each of these levels
5. function with different types of causation
6. and must be described in different languages.
7. Each level determines a qualitatively different temporality, and
8. each adds new, unresolvable conflicts to those of the level or levels beneath it.

These eight axioms will now be considered, one by one.

1. Nature comprises a number of integrative levels. Fifteen billion years ago, take or leave a few million, the universe was less than 10^{-50} cm across. Then as now, there was nothing outside it.[16] That primeval world comprised the "first signals," the earliest as well as the fastest ones.[17] The umwelt of these signals, one of pure chaos or pure becoming, formed the foundation of the world and constituted nature's first stable integrative level, as it still does.[18]

Out of the primeval chaos arose objects that had nonzero rest mass and traveled at speeds less than that of light. The new world of particle-waves formed the second stable integrative level of nature, as it still does.

A billion years later—more or less—massive matter began to freeze out and protogalaxies began to form, collecting eventually into the 10^{10} galaxies of the universe. These float in an immensity of almost complete emptiness. The massive matter of the galaxies—chemical elements and compounds of different abundance—constitutes the third stable integrative level of nature.

On a small object in one of those galaxies, life arose. It has been said that life is fleeting, ephemeral, easily snuffed out by sword or ill wind. This is true for individual lives and, on a different time scale, for species. But life as a process is 3.5 to 4 billion years old. This is a reputable age even in cosmic terms: life is robust and lasting. This permits us to regard the totality of the organic world as the fourth stable organizational level of nature.

Our species, with its capacity for minding, emerged a mere 100,000 years ago—or earlier or later, depending on what recognizable features are taken to make us what we are. The world created by the human mind, using its skills for the symbolic transformation of experience and its capacity to appreciate nonpresent objects and events, is taken to be the next higher organizational level of nature. Despite our species' youth, this view is justified, for the genius and audacity of the strange walkers challenge the logic of matter and life, from which they arose. Thomas Mann speaks of human history as informed by a "riddling essence of which our own normally unsatisfied and quite abnormally wretched existence forms a part; whose mystery, of course, includes our own and is the alpha and omega of all our questions, lending burning immediacy to all we say, and significance to all our striving."[19]

The major fields of human knowledge—results of that striving—display a division of concerns that corresponds to the integrative levels of nature. Learning about the "riddling essence" of mankind by means of the scientific method is among the tasks of psychology and the social sciences. The study of the life processes is the task of biology. The science that deals with the astronomical universe is general relativity, that of particle-waves is quantum theory, and the science of light in ceaseless motion is the domain of special relativity theory. Pioneering, embracing, taming, protecting, nurturing, and tending to the concerns of all forms of knowledge, including the sciences, are the arts, the letters, and the other humanities. As a living, thinking, and social being made of matter, each person shares some of the potentialities and all of the restraints of these organizational levels.

2. *These integrative levels form a hierarchically nested and evolutionarily open system.* The term *hierarchy* usually signifies a system of successive positions used in classification. An example is the eighteenth-century taxonomy established by Linnaeus, dividing the organic world into kingdoms, phyla, classes, orders, genera, and species. Here a member of a level comprises members of the lower levels: a class comprises orders, and each order comprises genera. This is a hierarchically nested system. A hierarchy may also involve ranks that are not nested: a lieutenant colonel does not comprise her majors.

The idea of hierarchical organizations is ancient; the ranking of animals by their size or speed of motion, for example, is a part of many traditions. The notion that the universe itself is hierarchically ordered according to first principles may be found in both Plato and Aristotle and has been echoing down the path of cultural history to our own days. The philosopher Philo, a contemporary of St. Paul, maintained that the world consists of a great chain of hierarchically ordered beings, from the basest creatures to God. Pseudo-Dionysius, a Christian Platonist of the fifth century, wrote about celestial and ecclesiastical hierarchies, both ruled by God. In the medieval view of the world, the universe consists of a graded chain of beings that stretch from the deity down to the least perfect being on earth; the organization of the Church of Rome was seen as an image of that ordering. At the turn of the eighteenth-century Hegel saw the world as stratified along a hierarchy of stages according to a progression of the dialectic of *Geist*, spirit, immanent in the world. Marx and Engels removed the notion of spirit from Hegel's world but retained its dialectical dynamics. Official Marxist philosophy maintained that hierarchically organized forms exist in all spheres of objective reality: the inorganic, the organic, and the social. It also claimed that within Marxist philosophy, "the idea of hierarchy of qualitatively irreducible structural levels has been developed."[20] The principle of hierarchical organization entered higher mathematics through the classification of mathematical objects[21] and the theory of types, where it pertains to elements of logic. Some maintain that the concept of hierarchy is a reflection of a Western obsession with order,[22] whereas others reject it as a projection of social stratification. A review of the idea of hierarchies may be found in Joseph Needham's 1937 Herbert Spencer lecture, "Integrative Levels: Revaluation of the Idea of Progress."[23]

Nested hierarchical organization helps to secure stability by limiting the effects of perturbations to bounded regions; it has been suggested that it is this feature that makes hierarchical organization the policy of naturally occurring complex systems.[24] The largest but not the most complex organizational unit to which such a policy applies is the universe itself, having evolved from radiative energy to matter, life, and the capacities of the human mind. In this, the grandest of all enterprises, the advantages of hierarchical organization are clear: if all humans were killed, this would not mean the end of life; if all life on earth were exterminated, this would not mean the end of massive matter scattered across the universe; if all massive matter were to collapse into radiation, we would still have a radiative universe. Proceeding in the opposite, the evolutionary, direction, we see that as each higher level emerged from a lower one, it retained among its new structures and processes some of the structures and processes of its ancestral strata.

3. The hierarchically nested and evolutionarily open system of nature operates along a scale of increasing complexity. When comparing specific objects or systems, the meaning of different complexities may seem obvious: an ant is more complex than a sheet of polystyrene; the industrial society of twenty-first-century America is more complex than the agricultural society of ancient Assyria. Yet a polymer chemist familiar with giant molecular structures, an entomologist who knows social insects, or an anthropologist who worked in northern Iraq might well question whether it is possible to define a non-trivial variable that can be equally valid for polymers, ants, and industrialized societies—and even if it were convincingly formulated, whether it could lead to valid quantification. The chemist and the entomologist may also wonder what could be meant by the complexity of an integrative level, such as that of all living organisms or all elementary particle-waves.

In attempting to define and construct a measure of complexity, it will be useful to turn to Plato. He reports that Socrates asked Meno what virtue is. Meno answered that there are many different virtues and listed them. "Suppose I had asked you," said Socrates, "what a bee is, what is its essential nature, and you replied that bees were of many different kinds." That would not have answered the question, whose meaning was, what is "that character in respect to which bees do not differ from one another at all but are all the same?"[25] What is the character in respect to which the members of an integrative level do not differ among themselves but do differ in respect to the same character when compared with other levels? That character is complexity.

Appendix B, "Complexity and Its Measure," suggests a definition of the complexity of an integrative level using as the measure of that complexity the minimal number of different building blocks from which all members of that level are found to have been constructed by nature. It concludes that the complexities of the different integrative levels of nature, so measured, are sufficiently different to justify having distinguished them in the first place.

4. Each of nature's integrative levels is characterized by level-specific processes. * A process is any chain of events that may be judged connectable by a stable rule. A structure, then, is also a process. It differs from what is ordinarily called a process only by its rate of change. The rock of Gibraltar is a combination of atomic processes that, considered individually, are too rapid to be recognized without scientific instruments and abstract formulas but, with their help, are seen as ceaselessly under way. Their aggregate, which to our senses is the rock of Gibraltar, will also be recognized as changing if we use such instruments as old drawings and diaries. The names we give to processes—the Himalayan Mountains, a kurrajong tree, a ladybug—stand for families of parameters stable for shorter or longer periods of time.

5. The level-specific processes function by different modes of causation. A cause is anything that may be interpreted as being responsible for change (its effect). The relationship between causes and their effects is called causation. Whenever the form of connection between causes and their effects appears stable, the relationship is said to be lawful. Because of the different complexities of the organizational levels, there are different forms of causation and lawfulness.

The level-specific causation of the noetic umwelt is *long-term intentionality* in the service of distant, often symbolic goals. Examples are building a pyramid, constructing a space station, or planning to secure the equality or inequality of people before the law.

The level-specific causation of the organic umwelt is *short-term intentionality* in the service of organic needs. For those who must breath, it is that of obtaining air; for everyone, food; for many, mates.

Causation specific to the world of massive matter is *deterministic:* an unsupported apple always falls; a planet in a central gravitational field always moves along a conic section.

Causation specific to the world of particle-waves is statistical; the level-specific laws are *probabilistic.* The half-life of cobalt 60 is 5.3 years; that of rubidium 87 is 6×10^{10} years. These numbers are statistically reliable: after 5.3 years close to one half of an initial amount of cobalt 60 will have decayed. But it is impossible to tell exactly when the next decay particle will

---

*At this and at each of the following numbered axioms of the hierarchical theory of time, the reader may wish to look back to p. 26 and refresh his or her memory concerning the way the axioms of the theory, when taken together, form a seamless whole.

appear or which particle of the aggregate it will be. This quality is not a sign of our ignorance but a fact of nature, a hallmark of the integrative level of particle-waves.

In the umwelt of an object traveling at the speed of light, everything happens at once. An umwelt in which everything happens at once can be described only as one of *absolute chaos,* of pure Heraclitean becoming. Here no meaning may be assigned to the idea of lawfulness or stability.

These are the *canonical forms of causation.* Each form of causation communicates itself upward: chaos, probability, determinism remain types of causation on the organic, mental, and social levels, but they take different forms.[26] Let me list them again, this time in the sequence they appeared in the course of inorganic and organic evolution. The first was absolute chaos or pure becoming, for which causation has no meaning; probabilistic causation or lawfulness came next; to these were added deterministic causation, organic intentionality, noetic intentionality, and finally, so far unmentioned, social intentionality, or *historical causation.*

Because of the nested hierarchical organization of nature, the different types of causations can never be found in pure forms; all processes are amalgams of qualitatively different causal links organized in a nested hierarchical fashion.

— There can be no probabilistic processes without chaotic elements.
— There can be no deterministic processes without probabilistic and chaotic elements.
— Organic behavior always and necessarily includes deterministic and probabilistic causation as well as totally unpredictable, chaotic elements.
— Human conduct in the service of abstract or symbolic goals always includes biological (short-term) intentionality as well as deterministic, probabilistic, and chaotic elements.
— The processes of human history, while displaying collective intent, necessarily include noetic and biological intentionalities as well as deterministic, probabilistic, and chaotic elements.

The contributions from chaos (absolute unpredictability) take different forms at the different integrative levels: the laws of nature serve as filters. For instance, chaotic events in quantum physics, unpredictable from the probabilistic laws of the quantum world, differ in kind from chaotic, unpredictable events in mutations in mice, unpredictable behavior of a person, or unpredictable events in history.[27]

Any interpretation of the workings of human values, if it is to be appropriate for our current understanding of nature and humanity, must take into account the many-tiered membership of every person in his or her environment and of his or her share of some of the potentialities and all of the constraints of the canonical forms of causation. The simultaneous presence of qualitatively different causations in nature will be especially important when we consider the nature of both truth and ethics.

6. *The level-specific processes must be described in different languages.* The evolutionary continuity of nature demands that structures and processes that would fall in the regions between the distinct domains of complexities either still exist or existed at one time. But they are short-lived and hence statistically rare. They have been called transitional phases, transcendences, interfaces, or mesoforms. What are some of these mesoforms?

A species between animals and people would be one whose members are neither apes nor humans. Though at one time they had to exist, such creatures have become extinct. The types of behavior that one may speculatively associate with them survive in the skills and limitations of the archaic portions of the human brain. These are not copies of those earlier brains but evolved and integrated descendants of the ancestral centers of different drives.

A mesoform between the inanimate and living world would be a molecular clockshop in the process of changing from nonliving to living, a process known historically as spontaneous generation and more recently as biogenesis (see appendix A, "Time and the Origin of Life"). There is no spontaneous generation going on today, and none has been demonstrated in the laboratory. The biogenetic process is believed to have taken place rapidly, perhaps in as little as 100,000 years, which is a mere 3/100,000th of the 3.5 billion years that life has existed on earth. The environment then began to change, until spontaneous generation of life became impossible.

Mesoforms between the quantum world and that of massive matter would be objects varying in size between molecules and minigalaxies that—one might fancy—would fill intergalactic space. But that is not the way the universe is constituted. The astronomical world consists of massive galaxies within a certain size range, separated by distances that are immense compared to the sizes of the galaxies. The intergalactic space is filled with gas and dust. Galaxies, the islands of solid matter—no more than dots compared to the universe—float in a sea of practically nothing.

Mesoforms are metastable, and through their metastability they assist in maintaining the stability of the levels they separate.[28] They are, of course, not surfaces in space but intermediary states between different degrees of freedom. Let me explain.

When a society collapses, the freedom that was available to it through collective action is lost. When a person loses his mind, his human freedom of action is lost. When a living organism dies, the freedom of doing all things life can do is lost. When a solid body changes into the gases of its molecules, the possibility of taking the myriad lasting shapes solid matter can take and retain is lost. Along this devolutionary path, degrees of freedoms are lost. Obviously these are forms of freedoms that had to have been gained as levels of increased complexities emerged: radiation had to acquire the freedom of solid matter; matter had to acquire those of life; life, the potentialities of the human mind. The freedoms themselves form a nested hierarchy with human freedom subsuming all of them.

The increased complexities and potentialities have their corollary expression in their increasingly richer logics and languages. Here *language* stands for all rules or laws in terms of which the processes of an integrative level may become intelligible (to us). As we rise along the scale of complexities, the level-specific languages become richer in their structure and broader in their scope. In each case lower-order languages are inadequate for describing the events, processes, and governing principles of a higher integrative level. For instance, Maxwell's equations, although they govern the behavior of all electromagnetic fields at the foundations of the universe, are inadequate for the formulation of the laws of genetics; the laws of genetics are inadequate for the formulation of the general principles that guide statesmanship. The relative poverty of each level-specific language leaves certain areas of the next-higher organizational level unrecognized and hence undetermined. It is from these undetermined regions that the laws of the next-higher integrative level may be seen to emerge. The laws of the physical world, for instance, permit but do not demand the existence of self-perpetuating, thermodynamically open systems. The language of the life process permits, but does not demand, a capacity for the symbolic transformations of experience.[29]

The logics and languages of human values—guidelines for telling true from false, right from wrong, and beautiful from ugly—must work with the freedoms and restraints of nature. In the vernacular, they must acknowledge the facts of society, mind, life, and matter.

7. *Each integrative level determines a qualitatively different temporality.* W. H. Auden's poem "Progress?" expresses both doubt and awe about man seen in an evolutionary perspective.

> Sessile, unseeing
> The Plant is wholly content
> With the Adjacent.
>
> Mobilised, sighted,
> The Beast can tell Here from There
> And Now from Not-Yet.

Talkative, anxious,
Man can picture the Absent
And Non-Existent.[30]

The theory of time as a nested hierarchy of unresolvable, creative conflicts expands the horizons of Auden's poem. Through a number of small steps, this subsection introduces the idea of qualitatively different temporalities appropriate to the different integrative levels of nature. Noetic time is the nested hierarchy of all these temporalities. I will now explore the details.

For an organism to remain alive, it is necessary that the multitudes of its inner clocks be kept cycling according to their intricate demands of mutual dependence. Biochemical events that should happen simultaneously must do so, and those that should not ought not to do so, or else the integrity of the life process will be lost. The instant-by-instant synchronization in cooperative functioning, governed by stable principles, ensures collective viability. That viability is manifest as the *organic present* of a living system. It is with respect to the organic present that goals may acquire meaning in terms of present needs and behavior may be organized in their service.

For the personal identity of a man or woman to remain continuous, it is necessary that the trillions of neurons in his or her brain maintain their cooperative functioning according to stable principles. These principles are inadequately understood.[31] Whatever their mechanism, if the integration process fails, the mental life of that person comes to harm. The instant-by-instant integration of the immense neural population of the cortex is manifest as the *mental present* of a person. It is with respect to the mental present that ideas about future and past may acquire meaning and conduct organized in the service of distant, often abstract goals. And it is in the mental present that the ceaseless reclassification of events into future, past, and present creates the experience described by the metaphor of the flow of time.

To become and remain a tribe, a society, or a civilization, it is necessary for individuals to behave so that whatever ought to happen simultaneously if the group is to remain coherent does happen and that whatever ought not does not. Just as individual organisms define their living present through inner coordination, and as neuronal coordination defines the mental present, so groups of living organisms—molds, mice, and men— exchange signals and through that exchange create their communal present. These demands define the *social present* of societies. It is with respect to the social present that collective plans and memories are organized. The width of the social present in clock time is the amount of time needed for coordinating collective action. If messages travel by camel or boat, the

34

respective social presents are wider than would have been the case if they had traveled by sound or radio.

It is not possible to maintain a social present without the mental presents of the people involved or to maintain mental presents without functional organic presents. These presents are therefore necessarily simultaneous. Together, they form a *nested hierarchy of presents* in which each present serves as the anchor or reference for its respective future and past.

In stark contrast to living beings, inanimate objects have no needs to be satisfied in the future and do not display purposeful behavior. The future and past I imagine for a pebble are the future and past of *my* umwelt, *not* that of the pebble. This lack of a future and past is reflected in the form of physical laws: they have no features to which the idea of a present could correspond. The physical universe is not timeless; it is only nowless. Furthermore, since future and past can have meaning only with respect to a now, the flow-of-time metaphor does not apply to the time of the physical world. By the extended umwelt principle, the temporal umwelts of the physical world, though without a now or directed time, must be regarded as complete in themselves, even if from the point of view of our daily experience of time they appear incomplete and terribly odd. The experience and idea of time's passage must be brought to physics; they cannot be derived from it.[32] Even the much discussed entropic arrow of time is but arbitrarily assigned to the thermodynamics of closed systems and hence useless for defining a direction of time (see appendix C, "Entropy: Its Uses and Abuses"). The physical universe permits temporalities appropriate to living and thinking organisms to arise, but it does not itself demand an interpretation in terms of such higher temporalities.

The absence of directed time from all formal statements of physical change has sometimes been taken as evidence that the foundations of the universe are timeless. This presumed timelessness, contrasted with the human certainty of passage, favors the idea of a Platonic division of the world into whatever is eternal or unchanging and whatever is temporal or passing. But such a division is too coarse to accommodate the different types of causations and qualitatively different types of temporal processes revealed by contemporary science. A much richer epistemic framework is needed, one that admits and correlates qualitatively different causations and times across the organizational levels of nature. The hierarchical theory of time offers such a framework by revealing the structure of what has been designated with the single word *time*.

When the time-related teachings of the different sciences are combined with what we know of the human experience of time and the findings are sorted out, six distinct temporalities may be identified, corresponding to the six organizational levels of nature. The following description of those temporalities proceeds from the most familiar one, that of the human mind, to the most primitive and least familiar one, that of the electromagnetic world. I then backtrack to the temporality of society.

Nootemporality is the temporal umwelt of the mature human mind in its waking state. It may be represented by the line "You'll come to me, out of the long ago," from the motion picture *Doctor Zhivago*. The hallmarks of nootemporality are open temporal horizons and the necessary reference to a "you" and "me" and to a mental present with its continuously changing temporal boundaries and cognitive content. The characteristic connectivity among events of the nootemporal world (as discussed earlier) is that of intentionality directed toward concrete or symbolic goals and serving the continued integrity of the self. Nootemporality may be pictured as a long straight arrow: shaft, head, and tail.

Biotemporality is the temporal umwelt of living organisms, including humans as far as their biological functions go. Its hallmarks are a distinction among future, past, and present; limited temporal horizons; and the organic present, whose temporal boundaries are species specific. The mental present and the organic present are simultaneities of necessity (e.g., the necessity—or needfulness—involved in maintaining mental and biological identities). The characteristic connectivity among events of the biotemporal world (as also discussed earlier) is organic intentionality directed toward concrete goals and serving the continuity of the organism's life. Biotemporality may be pictured as a short arrow.

Eotemporality is the time of the physicist's "t"—that is, of the astronomical universe of solid objects gathered into galaxies. The prefix *eo-* has been used by scientists to identify the oldest of developing forms, as in *Eohippus*, the earliest ancestor of the horse, or *Eolithic*, the oldest period of the Stone Age. Eotemporality is the oldest form of continuous time, one without a present because the physical world has only simultaneities of chance. Only life, the mind, and a society can have needs. Eotemporal events are countable and orderable, as are the natural numbers, and as do those numbers, they form a pure succession without a preferred direction. The characteristic connectivity of eotemporality is deterministic causation. Eotemporality may be pictured as the shaft of an arrow.

The idea of a temporality without a now is a rather unorthodox one, in spite of the fact that physicists have been living with it for a century and even though nowless time is well known from daily experience, where it is mistakenly described as timelessness (see sec. 5.3, "Roving the Depths of the Mind"). To help elucidate what is meant by a nowless temporality, let me offer a visual metaphor.

San Francisco's cable cars move by attaching themselves to an underground cable. The cable, which is hidden from sight, is moved by distant machinery invisible to the riders. It would be tempting to claim that meta-phorically speaking, we attach ourselves to the present instant of a moving cosmic time much as the cable cars attach themselves to a segment of the moving cable. That metaphor would be misleading, however, for physics disclaims the existence of a moving present both locally and globally, as was explained in connection with the nested hierarchy of presents. All this is sufficiently counterintuitive to warrant a restatement in the language of natural philosophy.[33]

Life creates those conditions and operational properties of matter that give rise to the organic present and biotemporality; the human brain cre-ates those conditions and operational properties of living matter that give rise to the mental present and noetic time; and societies create those con-ditions and operational properties of living, thinking humans that give rise to the social present and sociotemporality. In the physical integrative lev-els—sans life, sans minds, sans societies—there is nothing that could define a present and serve as a reference for futurity and pastness.

Prototemporality is the time of the particle-waves of the atomic and nuclear zoo. The prefix *proto-* has been used by scientists to signify "first formed" or "parent substance," as in *protoplanet, protoplasm,* or *protozoa.* It is the most prim-itive form of time, that of the universe out of the cauldron of the Big Bang. In a prototemporal umwelt instants may be specified only statistically. The characteristic connectivity of prototemporal umwelts is probabilistic causa-tion. Its appropriate visual metaphor is the fragmented shaft of an arrow.

Finally, even the picture of the fragments may vanish, leaving us with a blank sheet of paper, a symbol for the *atemporal* world of electromagnetic radiation. Atemporality stands not for nonexistence but for a world of ab-solute chaos, a total absence of causation, such as is believed to have exist-ed in the primeval universe at the instant of the Big Bang or to exist in a black hole.[34]

From the most primitive temporality let me pass back up to the poten-tially most complex one: *sociotemporality.* In the hierarchical theory of time this is the postulated level-specific temporality of a society. Although its lit-erature is extensive,[35] distinguishing it from noetic time is difficult because of the absence of a yet higher organizational level in whose language the hallmarks of social time could be recognized. Such a language would have to have its vocabulary, syntax, and semantics derive entirely from collective experience, independent of, and with no recourse to, individual experience.

In spite of these difficulties, Anne S. Lévy has made a remarkably suc-cessful effort to come to grips with the nature of sociotemporality. "In its most basic sense," she writes, sociotemporality "means the way a culture represents time." It is a social consensus necessary for the survival of a soci-ety, a definition of that society's way of being. It is a collective evaluation of time, the ethical rules guiding society in view of its history and future goals. Both, of course, feed into each other, affecting both the social present and the more encompassing sense of direction.

On the one hand [sociotemporality] creates a sense of significant order in the present (which can be either liberating or constraining). On the other hand, it provides protection from oblivion by building historical constructs and chases away the finality of death by conjuring ladders to eternity.[36]

The temporalities I described are the *canonical forms of time.*

Having identified six different concepts of time and equated each with the reality of time appropriate for the respective integrative level, the hierarchical theory of time makes one of those leaps of imagination that are not arbitrary yet may be shown as having been justified only ex post facto, because it is not possible to arrive at them though deductions from previously established propositions. That leap of imagination is the postulate that the canonical forms of time are not different aspects of time that become increasingly significant as the particular object or system studied becomes more complex.[37] Rather, they are steps along the open-ended evolutionary development of time itself in what I have described as *time's rites of passage.*[38]

Received views tend to regard time as a background to reality, equate it with the human experience of passage, or define it through its distinctness from the timeless. At variance with these views, the hierarchical theory of time regards time as constitutive of reality, as a symptom of or corollary to the complexity of the processes of integrative levels. The proposition is that time had its genesis at the birth of the universe, has been evolving along a scale of qualitative changes appropriate to the complexity of the distinct integrative levels of natural processes, and remains evolutionarily open-ended.[39] Earlier temporalities are not replaced but subsumed by later ones.

Speaking about the evolution of time seems to be a contradiction in terms, yet consider the expanding universe. It does not expand into a pre-existing empty space. It is space itself, with nothing external to it, that expands. The hierarchical theory of time maintains that time does not evolve within a preexisting expanse of time. Rather, it is created as an aspect of the complexification that characterizes evolution. In contrast to the evolution of cosmic space, which is one of quantitative increase in scale, the evolution of time involves qualitative changes such as increasing degrees of freedom or unpredictability, issues to which I will repeatedly return.[40]

Because of nature's nested hierarchical organization, the canonical forms of time never appear in pure forms; all processes take place in amalgams of qualitatively different temporalities. This view distinguishes the hierarchical theory of time from the Platonic dichotomy between time and the timeless and from its elaboration by Christianity. That elaboration made the Renaissance birth of science and the subsequent rise of the scientific-industrial civilization possible. The very sciences born of the Platonic and Christian views of time and the timeless, however, made the dichotomy unacceptable for a post-Darwinian, post-Freudian, and post-Einsteinian world.[41] The hierarchical theory of time allows for a synthesis of the different temporalities into the totality of what is ordinarily called time, provided one gives up the belief that the experiential time of humans is appropriate for all the lower levels of complexity that inorganic and organic evolution have created.

   8. In time's rites of passage from the atemporal to the proto-, eo-, bio-, noo- and sociotemporal, each new integrative level adds new, unresolvable, creative conflicts to those of the level or levels beneath it. By *conflict* is meant the coexistence of two opposing trends, regularities, or groups of laws in terms of which the dynamics of an integrative level may be interpreted. On each organizational level those opposing trends define each other: all balance is but unperceived conflict. *Unresolvable* signifies that by means indigenous to an integrative level, the conflicts may (1) be maintained, thereby ensuring the continued integrity of the level; (2) give rise to a new, distinct integrative level with its own unresolvable conflicts; or (3) be eliminated (the level thus collapsing into the one from which it arose).

   Let me trace the nested hierarchy of the unresolvable conflicts, beginning on the top, with society.

   Society is said to be an organized group of people working for a common purpose. But this is only half the story. The complete story is that of a permanent conflict between conduct that supports the common good and conduct that supports the personal good. "The body politic" wrote Rousseau, "like the human body, begins to die from its birth and bears in itself the causes of its destruction."[42] A permanent reconciliation between collective and individual interests is impossible because of the mind's unbounded imaginative power and its subsequent ever-new demands on the community, as well as the community's ever-new demands on the individual. People may still exist if the conflicts cease, but their society will have collapsed. For this reason, the conflicts themselves, working in the social present, may be seen as constitutive of society. A society is a group of people with a family of conflicts that defines them and distinguishes them from other societies.

   A person is a member of our species who possesses a stable identity. The process that creates and maintains that identity involves a continuous reintegration of the neural population of the cortex, perhaps in some such manner as was discussed. But again, this is only half the story. The whole story is that of a ceaseless conflict between the processes that create that identity and the social, biological, and physical perturbations that oppose it. The opposing trends are coordinated in the mental present.

What conflicts are peculiar to personhood? First, there are those between the desired and the possible. "This is the monstruosity in love, lady, that the will is infinite, and the execution confined; that the desire is boundless, and the act slave to limit."[43] Second, there are those between the simultaneous awarenesses of living and dying. "Time held me green and dying / Though I sang in my chains like the sea."[44]

Freud perceived in such conflicts of identity the sources of an irreducible existential tension in humans. "No substitutive or reactive formation and no sublimation will suffice to remove the repressed instinct's persisting tension; and it is the difference in amount between the pleasure of satisfaction which is *demanded* and that which is actually *achieved* that will permit of no halting at any position attained, but in the poet's words, 'ungebändigt immer vorwärts dringt' [untamed, forever forward presses]."[45] The quotation is from Goethe's *Faust,* a drama of a paradigmatic human character: instinctual drives fire the search for intellectual knowledge but cannot be satisfied by it. Angelus Silesius, a seventeenth-century Polish-German poet, would have agreed with Goethe and Freud: you create time yourself, he wrote, and the senses are the clockworks; if their restlessness is inhibited, time vanishes.[46]

St. Augustine anticipated both Freud and Silesius with his often quoted remark, "What then, is time? If no one asks me, I know it. If I wish to explain it to someone who asks, I know it not."[47] His dilemma derives from the conflicts between time felt and time understood. Time felt is the temporal reality of the world interpreted by the older regions of the mind; time understood is articulated by the newer levels of the brain.

If the conflict ceases, a living body may remain, but not a person. For this reason, the conflicts themselves may be seen as constitutive of personhood: an individual is a human being with a family of conflicts that distinguishes him or her from other individuals.

Life is usually thought of as a process of growth through self-organization. Once again, this is only half the story. The whole story is that of a conflict between growth and decay coordinated in the organic present. "And so from hour to hour we ripe and ripe, / And from hour to hour we rot and rot; / And thereby hangs the tale."[48] The ripening and rotting, coordinated in the organic present, are going on simultaneously. If the conflicts between them cease, only dead matter remains. For this reason, the conflict may be thought of as constitutive of the life process.

Conflict is also constitutive of *inanimate matter.* Across the vast universe the behavior of matter is under the control of two sets of opposing principles: one set helps to increase organization (i.e., decreases entropy), and the other set decreases organization (i.e., increases entropy). The conflict is between these two opposing trends, which define each other. On balance, the entropy of the universe is taken to remain constant (see appendix C). If not only the conflicts that define social, mental, and organic processes but also those between the decreasing and increasing entropic processes of matter and energy were to cease, the world would be back where it began: in the primeval absolute chaos.

All cosmogonies, whether narrative or scientific, see the origin of the world in the emergence of a superior kind of order from an inferior one. But if our understanding of cosmic creation is to be appropriate to what we know of the dynamics of conflicts that define the integrative levels, then cosmogony must be reconceptualized. Creation must be understood not as the emergence of order from chaos but as the coming about of conflicts between different forms of ordering and disordering.[49] The story of the universe has been one of complexifying modes of conflicts that accumulate and form an open-ended system of nested hierarchy: all conflicts at each level subsume the conflicts beneath them.

As was already mentioned, the level-specific, unresolvable conflicts lead to complexification and, under some conditions, to the emergence of new integrative levels. For this reason, they may be regarded as creative. Here is a sketch of some specifics.

The material world has brought forth, through chance combinations, increasingly more complex physical and chemical systems. When these reached what seem to be the limits of ordering by chance (see appendix A), life emerged, a phenomenon able to increase the degree of ordering by inventing, as it were, future purpose. In due course this evolutionary path led to the most complex known object, one of possibly limiting complexity, that of the human brain (see sec. 1.2 and appendix B). The limitations to complexity represented by the human brain was overcome by the minding functions of the brain, that is, by its capacity to act out strategies of behavior without the need for changes in somatic structure (except for neural connections). Although the imaginative powers of the mind are unbounded, the learning capacity of any individual mind is bounded because of the limited potentialities of the body it serves. This limitation is overcome by combining individual creativeness in the collectives of many minds.

I proposed earlier that time should not be regarded as a background to reality or be equated entirely with the human experience of passage; rather, it should be understood as constitutive of reality, as a symptom of the complexity of the processes at the different integrative levels. In the immediately foregoing I suggested that certain families of unresolvable conflicts be identified with matter, life, the human mind, and society. Combining these two trains of thought, one arrives at the theory of time as a nested hierarchy of unresolvable conflicts.

There are only two known forms that concise accounts of vast and complex phenomena may take: mathematical physics and mysticism. The mathematical theory of relativity provides formulas from which one can in principle derive all statements one can make about the motion of massive matter. Of course, it takes years to learn how this is done. In Hinduism, OM is a sacred syllable said to contain the essence of the universe. Of course, it takes many years to learn why this is so.

The theory of time as conflict cannot claim the totality of mysticism or the pithy cogency of mathematical physics, though it has something to say about both. It is only an attempt to measure the limits of man against the order of things by methods that satisfy disciplined speculative curiosity. I believe it to be a novel system of natural philosophy, but it is not without its relatives and ancestors.

It echoes Bergson's emphasis on tension but differs from his philosophy in that it cannot accommodate an idea of vital impetus and in that it rejects a dichotomy between the time of natural sciences and that of experience. The principle of unresolvable conflicts evokes Hegel's dialectic of the spirit and Marx's dialectic of matter. Indeed, the theory maintains that contradiction (in many forms) is the motive force of the universe, an idea that may be traced back to Heraclitus and Empedocles. But it differs from Hegel's thought because in the hierarchical theory, the Hegelian *Geist* remains a feature of the noetic world, one to which nothing in the lower levels can correspond. It differs from the work of Marx and Engels in that it rejects the positivist thesis that valid knowledge may be obtained only through science, logic, and the philosophy of science.

The notion of atemporal beginning resembles Hawking's idea of having no zero point in time but differs from it in the following way. In Hawking's interpretation of cosmogenesis, nootemporality—called simply "time"—is seen as having emerged directly from the atemporal matrix. In the hierarchical theory, what first appears is a discontinuous and undirected time (prototemporality), and only with the complexification of nature do higher temporalities emerge, displaying continuity, direction, and later, expanding horizons.

The theory of time as a nested hierarchy of unresolvable conflicts is something of a Hegelian as well as a Marxian dialectic, arising from a Darwinian background and developed with the help of contemporary mathematics and natural science.

The punctuated continuity of evolution, with the emergence of increasingly richer capacities, degrees of freedom, and temporalities, may be represented by a poem from the Persian Sufi poet Jalal al-Din al-Rumi (1207–73).

> I died from mineral and plant became,
> Died from the plant, and took a sentient frame;
> Died from the beast, and donned a human dress;
> When by my dying did I e'er grow less?[50]

In an essay on faith and reason, Michael Polanyi remarked that

> as the rising levels of existence were created by successive stages of evolution, each new level achieved higher powers entrammelled by new possibilities of corruption. The primeval matrix of life was inanimate and deathless—subject to neither failure nor suffering. From it have emerged levels of biotic existence liable to malformation and disease and, at higher stages, prone also to illusion, to error, to neurotic affliction—finally producing in man, in addition to all these liabilities, an ingrained propensity to do evil. Such is the necessary condition of a morally responsible being, grafted on a bestiality through which alone it can exercise its own powers.[51]

Moral responsibility, grafted on bestiality, added Polanyi, is what Christian theology sees as man's fallen nature, whose converse is the process of redemption. Continuous fall and redemption are theological mappings of conflicts unique to humans. They are level-specific examples of the universal unresolvable, creative conflicts found in nature at large. Whereas theological reasoning sees the falling-redemptive struggle as directed toward the final victory of the divine, this account of nature sees the cosmic dynamics of unresolvable, creative conflicts as open-ended and, in the words of Lucretius, "uncontrolled by proud masters."

Human values, I hope to show, are instructions whose purpose has been, and remains, that of keeping alive the unresolvable, creative conflicts of the strange walker.

CHAPTER THREE

The Many Kinds of Truths: Guidelines for Beliefs

T he rules of number reveal the eternal logic at the foundations of the universe. Do they?

Planetary orbits are always conic sections. Are they?

"Who killed Cock Robin? 'I did,' said the sparrow, 'with my little bow and arrow.'" Did he?

God is just; God is merciful. Is she?

Deciding what to believe by distinguishing truth from falsehood has been a daily necessity for survival for people of all ages. Finding general rules whereby truths and untruths may be differentiated has been of concern to religions, philosophies, courts of law, and more recently, the sciences. Throughout the history of this ancient exercise, the passage of time has served as an unanalyzed, unquestioned background against which the last-ingness of claims of truth could be measured. This chapter suggests that time is not a background to, but an essential constituent of, all forms of truths, and with the help of the hierarchical theory of time, it constructs an epistemology on that basis. Such an epistemology should be "able to account for the qualitative differences between truth claims in the arts and humanities, the social science, and the natural sciences by arguing that the very notion of truth must be applied in a level-specific manner."[1]

It is rather well known that claims of truths differ qualitatively depending on the field of knowledge to which they apply. What is significant in the reasoning that follows is that these differences are shown to derive from first principles—namely, from the qualitatively different temporalities of the integrative levels in which truths are sought or asserted and from the nested hierarchical organization of the canonical forms of time.

3.1   A Working Definition of Truth

Specialized studies about truth in the sciences, in religion, in philosophy, and in human law abound; there is no need to review them here. Instead of compiling a list of who said what and then picking and choosing this man's art and that man's scope, I propose a semantic sketch of the equivalents of the English word *truth* in four major families of languages and use the findings to help formulate a working definition of truth.

"I am not so lost in lexicography," wrote Samuel Johnson in the preface to his *Dictionary* of 1755, "as to forget that words are the daughters of the earth, and that things are the sons of heaven. Language is only the instrument of science and words are but the signs of ideas."[2] What do these daughters of the earth, these signs of ideas and instruments of science, say about truth and time?

A word is a record of a captured idea or feeling; it is an audible signal that carries a message. It is vague. But as John Stuart Mill remarked a century and a half ago, if one were to attempt to give fixed, narrowly defined meanings to vague terms, one would endanger language's "inherent and most valuable properties, that of being the conservator of the thoughts of former ages which may be alien to the tendencies of passing time. . . . Language is the depository of the accumulated body of experience to which all former ages have contributed their part and which is the inheritance of all yet to come."[3] Individual words narrate stories through feelings and engender associations and anticipations through the memories to which they appeal. All words have long histories, even recently coined ones, because they either derive from earlier words or resemble them by combining familiar phonemes. Words carry shades of meaning that may or may not be consciously recognized by their users, yet mature speakers will respond to the many meanings of words used in different syntax. It is because they are depositories of a spectrum of meanings and emotions, as well as of the changing evaluations of reality, that words can acquire semantic depths.[4]

What kind of accumulated body of experiences and beliefs does the word *truth* conserve in English? The word suggests disposition to faithfulness, fidelity, loyalty, constancy, and steadfast allegiance. It may signify solemn engagement or promise or a covenant. It may refer to a moral stance that is judged consistent with divine or social standards and steadiness. It may also mean agreement with reality, a conformity with fact. Here *fact* stands for whatever quality of an event, object, or condition one believes to be unchanging with time—at least for a while.

Sanskrit, the scholarly language of contemporary India, is an Indo-European tongue dating to 1,500 B.C. and possibly earlier. In the Sanskrit of the Hindu tradition, arising from Vedic roots, the equivalent of *truth* is *satya,* a word derived from the present participle of the verb *to be,* to which the suffix *-ya* is added. The combination may be translated as "isness," meaning that which really exists.[5] In a philosophical-religious context, *satya* signifies an act of truth, a calling on facts to witness that a person has enacted his dharma, that is, remained true (steady) to duty and divine law, which are assumed to be permanent.[6]

Hebrew belongs in the family of Hamito-Semitic languages, which are presumed to have been spoken as far back as the seventh or eighth millennium B.C. The Hebrew word *emeth* is translated as "truth," "certainty," "honesty," or "faithfulness." Among Jewish philosophers the word was accepted to mean correspondence with reality, with the way things are. In common use it signifies permanence, lastingness, or absence of change.[7] In Judaism truth is primarily an ethical notion associated with the nature of God.[8]

Japanese and Chinese employ the same two ideograms to signify truth as a principle or concept: shinri 真理. In Chinese it is called *zhen shi;* in Japanese, *shinri. Shin* (on the left) is said to have its pictorial origin in the representation of a man who died while being hanged upside down, because such a man was believed to have entered the world of eternal truth.[9] Its ancient conflation included that of the sun, because the sun, unlike the inconstant moon, is steady. *Ri* (the ideogram on the right) signifies, in current Japanese use, the polishing of a gem so as to make its true figure emerge.[10]

These linguistic traces of thought offer no guidance as to what kind of philosophical, political, religious, scientific, or legal meanings the idea of truth ought to have, but they do make obvious what the hundreds of millions of contemporary and past speakers of these languages associate with the nature of truth. They believe that truth is a claim of correspondence to reality and that it relates to permanence, though not necessarily to eternity. Let me take advantage of these beliefs and propose a working definition of truth by concisely restating what has been said.

Let truth as a human value be defined as the recognition of permanence in reality.

By *reality* I mean the nested hierarchy of umwelts appropriate to the events or processes considered. The difficult term in the definition is *permanence.* Dictionaries define permanence as a condition or quality of continued existence without change; it is everlastingness. But to what in the phenomenal world may this definition correspond? I begin by exploring the nature of truth as permanence in mathematics and then turn to questions of truth in the worlds of matter, life, and society.

3.2   A Message from Mathematics

The identification of number and the rules of number with eternal, unchanging rules has long been a part of Western intellectual tradition. Mathematics, the science of numbers, has been held to reveal the permanent order that lies at the timeless foundations of nature. Does mathematics do so?

The Western Love Affair with Number

During the sixth century B.C. the doctrine that all things and forms are number and that *harmonia*—balance and order according to number—is the supreme law of the universe was central to the teachings of the Pythagoreans. Having found in the rules of number the key to eternal cosmic verities, the Pythagorean brotherhood appealed to those rules for the salvation of their souls, that is, for securing for their souls the blessings of everlasting lives. In Pythagorean doctrine numbers perform a divine dance and through it exhibit the ultimate, unchanging principles of the universe. The philosopher's task is to discover the rules of number. So began the West's long love affair with the magic of numbers.

The teachings of the Pythagoreans came to maturity in Plato's theory of knowledge. He saw number and geometry as aspects of reality vested in Logos, the timeless divine intelligence that grants order, reason, and spiritual light to the world. In the *Meno* Socrates set out to demonstrate that this intelligence is eternal, unchanging, and resident, among other of its manifestations, in geometry. He called a slave boy and asked him questions about squares, triangles, and diagonals, which he drew in the sand at his feet. Although the boy had no schooling, he gave the right answers. Afterward the boy was perplexed because, says Socrates—sounding like a good Freudian—before he actually gave those answers, he did not know he knew them.

The boy's knowledge, Socrates explained, came not from having been taught but from having been questioned. The right answers were in his soul from the time he "was not in human shape." Socrates was surely thinking not of anthropoid apes but of memories that were recorded in the soul before the boy became its incarnation in a body. This is the theory of anamnesis, or recollection, the belief that the human soul is privy to the unchanging truths of the universe, such as the laws of number. The soul contains them and may reveal them on the right kind of questioning. This doctrine has resurfaced in many different forms throughout the history of thought in connection with the continued attempts to explain why the rules of number appear to be eternal verities.

The *Book of Wisdom,* an apocryphal work of the Old Testament written in Alexandria around 50 B.C., maintains that God created the world out of formless matter and then ordered all things according to measure, number, and weight. Since the book describes Jewish doctrine in terms of Hellenistic philosophy, one may assume that its author was familiar with Pythagorean ideas. The Pythagorean-Platonic idea of number and geometry was later combined with biblical tradition and became a part of the spiritual synthesis worked out by the church fathers and the Scholastics as they tried to reconcile the timeless laws of God with the temporal and unpredictable fate of man. Around the end of the fourth century St. Augustine took it for granted that the truths of number are universal and eternal. In *On Free Will* he remarked that although wisdom may or may not be the same as number, it is clear that both are true and immutably true.[11] He added that wisdom shows itself to the seeker in the guise of numbers embodied in all things of the world.[12]

Twelve centuries after St. Augustine, in the preface to *Mysterium Cosmographicum,* Johannes Kepler echoed Plato's anamnesis. "Nay, the idea of quantities has been in God from eternity. Quantities are identical with God; therefore they are present in all minds created in the image of God."[13] In his *Harmonices Mundi* he declared that Christians knew that "the mathematical principles according to which the corporeal world was to be created are co-eternal with God."[14] In yet another 350 years, Einstein wrote in his autobiography, "In a man of my type . . . the major interest disengages from the momentary and merely personal and turns toward the striving of the mental grasp of things."[15] That mental grasp of things was the Pythagorean geometrization of the world, melding time and space into space-time, governed by the rules of number and measure. It is only a few steps from here to the view that "the whole world or any part of it . . . can now be treated as a unified system composed of nothing but dynamically curved space-time or 'superspace' or as nothing but gauge fields, or Salam's elementary particles."[16]

The adoration of numerical, quantitative truths led to the scientific revolution, which, in the words of Nathan Sivin, "was a transformation of our knowledge of the external world. . . . It established for the first time the dominion of number and measure over every physical phenomenon."[17] But it also pushed physics to a degree of abstraction (as represented by the quotation about gauge fields) that removed it from any obvious contact with existential concerns about time and space.

Enthusiasm for the power of number has not been limited to people in the exact sciences. The usefulness of number was well known to those latter-day Pythagoreans, the mercantile capitalists of Europe. The skillful use of number brought them increased prosperity while also supporting their conviction that their faith in the immutable laws of a Christian God was correct. For the merchants, no less than for Plato, God had to be a mathematician. Max Weber observed that "the favorite science of all Puritan, Baptist and Pietist Christianity was . . . physics, and next to it all those natural sciences that use similar methods, especially mathematics. . . . The [mathematical] empiricism of the seventeenth century was the means for asceticism to seek God in nature. It seemed to lead to God, philosophical speculation away from him."[18]

The power of number and geometry and their appropriateness to the world of experience are impressive. Let me illustrate that appropriateness by the history of conic sections.

Menaechmus and Aristaios, two Greek mathematicians who lived around 350 B.C., discovered that one can generate certain curves by cutting right circular cones with a plane. A century after them, in a treatise called *Conics,* Apollonius of Perga systematized the geometry of conic sections, naming them ellipses, hyperbolas, and parabolas. Nineteen centuries after him Kepler showed that the orbits of the planets are ellipses. Some 120 years later Jean Bernoulli identified the reasons for the shapes of these orbits in Newton's law of gravitation. Yet after another two and a half centuries Einstein concluded that planetary orbits are not ellipses after all but nonreentrant curves generated by a point that moves on an ellipse that itself rotates about a perpendicular to one of its focal points.

The equation of an ellipse in analytical geometry, stated in contemporary notation, is $x^2/a^2 + y^2/b^2 = 1$, where x and y are the coordinate variables of its points, with a and b as the semimajor and semiminor axes. How did the curves of Menaechmus, Aristaios, and Apollonius know that they were supposed to abide by this equation? How did planetary orbits learn about it? How did our minds extract these regularities from experience? Are we all Meno's slave boys and girls recalling, if correctly questioned, what we have known all along about the eternal truths of mathematics? Or is there another explanation for this universal knowledge?

Imagine Socrates drawing lines in the sand while explaining what he is doing. "Here is a straight line, here is a perpendicular to it, and here a perpendicular to that. I call the first and third lines parallels. If I extend them, do you think they will ever meet?" The answer would have surely been, no, and Socrates would have accepted it as a demonstration of anamnesis and of the fact that the answer must necessarily be no. But the (currently) right answer is that they may meet. It depends on the kind of space in which the construction is carried out.

Euclidean geometries, represented by the parallels-never-meet answer, were accepted through the millennia as obviously, absolutely, and, eternally true, even though Euclid himself had some misgivings about it. Around the turn of the nineteenth century, however, mathematicians began to construct alternative, non-Euclidean geometries. Gauss described one such system as an "astral geometry," meaning that the difference between Euclidean and non-Euclidean geometries becomes significant only at the immense distances of the cosmos.[19] Astral geometry, though not under that name, proved to be the geometry appropriate for contemporary physical cosmology. Would Socrates have given the answer "Yes, they may," if he had been questioned by someone who knew non-Euclidean geometries? I believe so. From where would his questioner have learned the right answer? From the unbounded imaginative powers of his mind. Therefore, let me turn to the issue of how number and its uses are born in the mind.

Number Born from the Search for Invariance

This subsection suggests that the human capacity to create and handle numbers evolved from the skill of subitization helped by the desire to identify permanence, as discussed in sec. 1.2 ("The Need for Human Values"). That skill was favored by selection because of the advantages that reside in the recognition of stable continuities.

In chapter 1 I showed the emergence of selfhood as an unchanging continuity in a person's life. Here I assume that the paradigm of numbers, beginning with "one," is that of the self. But the roots of counting are older than personhood. They may be found in the skill of subitization (from the Latin *subito*, "immediately"), which is the ability to apprehend at a glance the number of objects in a small set. Examples are a passing look at an upturned die ("five") or into a room ("three people"). This is a prelinguistic, nameless counting of small numbers, generally no higher than six or seven. What the literature describes as counting by animals are probably examples of subitization. Recent work suggests that infants as young as five months can subitize.[20] Our animal ancestors subitized their offspring; our human ancestors counted them.

Konrad Lorenz once remarked that the Kantian a priori is an expression of a hereditary differentiation of the central nervous system, one that has become characteristic of the species, producing dispositions to think in certain forms.[21] Something similar may be said about numbers and counting. Logic itself is a set of rules known to snails, horses, and humans in ways appropriate to their umwelts and stable on the scales of life for the respective species.

Counting involves the ability to assign different names to different sets. According to developmental psychologists, we first learn to group objects by their lasting identities (all smooth pebbles) and then recognize that spatial rearrangement of a set does not alter certain types of signs attached to it.[22] Numbers belong in such a family of signs. The competence to handle numbers is built on an innate ability: children process numerical information with great skill before they learn to speak. They learn number skills in identifiable steps such as the ability to disentangle numerosity from other factors, the ability for numerical reasoning, and the recognition of the cardinality of a set, that is, the equating of the set with the name of the highest number of its members.

As I theorized earlier, selfhood is the source and paradigm of oneness and continuity: the "I" serves as the single and continuous vantage point for a definition the world. The self is the only object besides God (in monotheistic religions) and the universe whose one-and-onliness is ensured by definition. Although I see myself as always changing, the observer who notices this remains unchanged. "The self and the others" and "one and the many" describe the same relationships in different contexts.

Out of one comes two. For the Pythagoreans and through the sixteenth century, "one" was seen as the root of every number but not itself a number.[23] For Shakespeare one "may stand in number, though in reck'ning none," because reckoning started with two. In its turn, the association of two with creativity, as represented by the mother who is originally one and then two, is present in psychology, custom, and languages.[24] Only a creature with selfhood can develop mathematics built on perceived elements of identities, recognize them through their invariance, and carry them beyond subitization.

Using oneness and knowing addition make possible the construction of numbers, provided one does not lose count. The Red Queen in *Alice in Wonderland* knew this:

> "What's one and one and one and one and one and one and one and one and one and one?"
> "I don't know," said Alice. "I lost count."
> "She can't do addition," said the Red Queen.

The steps from subitization to counting, from counting to numbers, and from there to the rules of numbers are evolutionary and developmental tools that help to promote conditions favorable for humans. Knowing numbers is a recall of sort—not of a preexistent, eternal message but of capacities acquired through organic evolution and personal and cultural development. Numbers grow out of an anamnesis in a Darwinian sense, that is, from the propensity for permanence and stability, favored by evolutionary selection.

As I reasoned at length in sec. 1.2, we continually seek proofs of the insignificance of death and of the passing that gets us there. "It is of the nature of reason to perceive things in the light of eternity," wrote Spinoza, with the corollary claim that "it is not in the nature of reason to consider things as contingent but as necessary."[25] It is only "love toward a thing eternal and infinite [that] feeds the mind wholly with joy, and is itself unmingled with any sadness."[26] The same search for permanence informs Kant's definition of time as a necessary subjective condition owing to the nature of the human mind, which seeks "the coordination of all sensibles according to a fixed law."[27] Helmholtz once remarked that the ultimate goal of theoretical physics is to find the final, unchanging causes of the processes of nature.

Nevertheless, although the usefulness and ubiquity of number suggest an underlying, absolute, and permanent structuring to the world, including, presumably, the possibility of predicting the future if we but knew all the rules, the universe is not without its peculiar freedoms.

Freedoms of Incompleteness and Inconsistency

Those who seek in geometry a haven against the fell hand of passage may take heart in the apparent permanence of mathematical truths in nature, from the mud cones of Aristaios to Kepler and beyond. Such historical continuities notwithstanding, the story of the sciences since Cusanus looks like a series of coups against certainty and timeless perfection.

Copernicus removed the earth from the center of the universe. Kepler condemned the heavens to imperfection and perhaps even temporality. He challenged the Greek ideal that the orbits of the planets must be circles because circles are seamless and uniform and thus allow motion on them to go on forever.[28] Darwin removed humans from the pinnacle of creation by revealing how they emerged from lowly creatures through an undirected process of which they need not be the final product. Einstein's general theory of relativity, in its super-Copernican manifesto, declared not only that we are not in the center of the world but that there can be no central location anywhere in the universe, and then Freud removed us from the company of angels. To add insult to injury, logic and mathematics were then removed from the company of Logos, the divine reason immanent in the ordering of the universe by eternally stable and inviolable rules, and placed into the intellectual tool kit of humans.

Since the time of Archimedes and Euclid, the variety of objects of interest to mathematics has increased tremendously, but the mathematical method has remained the same. It comprises the observation of mathematical objects, the identification in the behavior of these objects such properties as appear to be unchanging, and the formulation of axioms based on these observations. Then well-defined rules of logic are applied to the axioms so as to lead to theorems. The rules of logic, no less than the formulation of axioms, are intuitive creations: they are historical sediments of apparent causal relationships that became programmed into behavior.

The idea that logic is a universal science that embraces the principles underlying all other sciences was formulated around the end of the seventeenth century by Leibniz. In the nineteenth century the mathematicians George Boole, Gotlob Frege, and others attempted to derive mathematics from logic. During the twentieth century Bertrand Russell and A. N. Whitehead set out to show in their *Principia Mathematica* that all of pure mathematics can be stated in terms of logic, using no undefined terms other than those required for logic in general. Mathematics and logic, wrote Russell, are one. "They differ as boy and man: logic is the youth of mathematics and mathematics is the manhood of logic. . . . there is no point at which a sharp line can be drawn, with logic to the left and mathematics to the right."[29] The doctrine that all the laws of mathematics are derivable from and reducible to the rules of logic is known as the logistic thesis. In this frame of thought the science of mathematics has been held to be a consistent and completable edifice of the human intellect. To call mathematics *complete* is to claim that all theorems in a given branch of mathematics are provable using the language (mode of reasoning and appropriate signs) of that branch. To call it (logically) *consistent* is to claim that no subdivision of mathematics contains axioms from which logically contradictory statements may be drawn.

I now briefly detour to paradoxes.

A few years before Russell and Whitehead began their work on the *Principia* (1910–13), Russell came on certain logical paradoxes. A logical paradox is a statement from which contradictory conclusions may be drawn using reasoning that in other contexts creates no difficulties. He considered them to be semantic models of problems in mathematical logic and perceived in them a hierarchical structuring that, if recognized, could remove the contradiction. Russell saw the levels of semantic hierarchy as orders of propositions or logical types and generalized his findings by saying that no totality—such as a mathematical set—can contain members defined in a way that refers to the totality itself. If it does, paradox results. Such a paradox may be sometimes removed, however, by stating the problem in a language of an order higher than the one in which it first appears. His logical types are languages of different complexities.[30] I now leave the detour to paradoxes but retain the conclusion that a paradox in a particular language may sometimes be removed in the richer language of higher complexity.

In his work on automata, John von Neumann reflected on Russell's theory of logical types. "In the complicated parts of formal logic it is always one order of magnitude harder to tell what an object can do than to produce that object. The domain of validity of a question is of a higher type than the question itself. . . . The feature is just this, that you can perform within the logical type that is involved everything that is feasible, but the question whether something is feasible in a type belongs to a higher logical type."[31]

What in Russell's theory of types is a proposal about modes of reasoning was identified in mathematics by Kurt Gödel. He inquired into the nature of the axiomatic-deductive method, which is the thought process on which mathematical reasoning is based. Using a method he invented for this purpose,[32] he demonstrated that in any logical system rich enough to accommodate ordinary arithmetic, it is possible to formulate valid propositions that belong in the system but are neither provable nor disprovable within it. An unprovable proposition may yet be shown to be correct, however, and a paradox may yet be removed, in a language whose complexity is greater than the one in which the proposition was made and the paradox identified. Since the language of such a higher-order system cannot be obtained from the language of the lower-order system by deductive inference, the higher-order language must be created through inductive inference, such as the formulation of unpredictably new axioms. In mathematics, no less than in all other human endeavors, the capacities of the mind for creating unpredictably new notions are essential. In other words, mathematics is open-ended toward ever more complex systems, each with its own incompleteness and inconsistency.

Any mathematical-logical system that is rich enough to support the system of natural numbers can be consistent (contain no paradoxical axioms) only if it is incomplete (has theories that belong there but are unprovable in it). It can be complete (with all its theorems provable in it) only if it is inconsistent (contains axioms that lead to paradoxes). In the early part of the century, when Russell began his work on the principles of mathematics, he believed that the axioms of logic were truths. He abandoned this view in 1937. He was no longer convinced that the principles of logic are a priori truths and hence that those of mathematics are as well, since these latter derive from logic.[33]

Revolt against a logic that does not allow for the freedom of unpredictability has long been in the brewing. An exchange between the two protagonists of John Fowles's *Mantissa*—the Model and the Sculptor—sums up the situation. The Model is holding forth. "Has it never occurred to your poor little male brain that logic, as you call it, is the mental equivalent of the chastity belt? Where do you think the world would have been if we'd all worn nothing but logic since the beginning? We'd still be creeping around in that sickeningly dull garden."[34] The rules of number do not reveal an eternal logic at the foundations of the universe, but there is a structural isomorphism between our knowledge of mathematics and our knowledge of nature.

The Structure of Mathematics and That of Nature

What in mathematics and its logic is called incompleteness is isomorphic with natural phenomena's inexplicability in the language of the integrative level where they occur, although they may be explicable in the language of a higher level. This is the nested hierarchy of languages (lawfulness) explained in sec. 2.2 (pp. 32–33). Since the same condition of incompleteness holds for the higher-order language (lawfulness), it follows that both mathematics and nature are incompletable. They are evolutionarily open-ended and hence allow for the coming about of the unpredictably new. They partake in time's rites of passage.

What in mathematics and in its logic is called inconsistency is isomorphic with the unresolvable conflicts that define each organizational level.

What in the Russell-Gödel interpretation of the axiomatic-deductive method is the recognition of formal structures connectable only through inductive inference is isomorphic with the creative emergence of unpredictably new processes and functions. These sometimes constitute a new integrative level with its own incompleteness and inconsistencies.[35]

The isomorphisms between the structure of mathematical reasoning and that of the world are unlikely to be chance coincidences. Einstein remarked once that "as far as the laws of mathematics refer to reality they are not certain and as far as they are certain, they do not refer to reality."[36] What I am suggesting is that "the laws of mathematics" and "reality" are two families of ideas, two process descriptions of the brain that continuously define and refine each other. They are jointly created by the environment and the human mind. I assume that biologically speaking, mathematics is a product of Edelman's neural Darwinism as it selects for the propensity of invariance.

Numbers, being multiples of the oneness of selfhood, are the simplest icons of invariance. Subitizing represents number skills that are of biological value (as defined earlier). Its extension to the world of symbolic representations is the art of doing whatever one may do with number. The rules of these icons help to label macroscopic spatiotemporal order in processes of perceptual categorization, discussed in sec. 2.2. They help to identify truth as a human value.[37]

Morris Kline, distinguished historian of mathematics, commenting in his *Mathematics: The Loss of Certainty,* had this to say.

> The developments in this century bearing on the foundations of mathematics are best summarized in a story. On the banks of the

Rhine, a beautiful castle has been standing for centuries. In the cellar of the castle, an intricate network of webbing had been constructed by industrious spiders who lived there. One day a strong wind sprang up and destroyed the web. Frantically, the spiders worked to repair the damage. They thought it was their webbing that was holding up the castle.[38]

Concerned spiders need not worry about the castle of mathematics. Instead of speaking about a loss of certainty, it is more appropriate to recognize a gain of freedom, a formal acknowledgment of the necessary presence of becoming in mathematical reasoning. Since inductive thinking must have been present all along, mathematics cannot be regarded as composed of preexistent eternal verities. Nature permits the emergence of mathematical knowledge but does not prescribe its path any more than it prescribes the path of evolution. Mathematics remains the noble organon, the tool of learning that it has been all along, but it is not a source of timeless verities.

In 1958 Russell wrote that at the time he was working on the *Principia,* he wanted certainty in the kind of way in which people want religious faith. He thought that mathematics would be the most likely place to find it. Later he declared that this is not the case. He might have come to agree with Sigmund Freud: "Mediocre spirits demand of science a kind of certainty which it cannot give, a sort of religious satisfaction. Only the real, rare, true scientific mind can endure doubt, which is attached to all our knowledge."[39]

Science does not supply absolute certainty; that can come only from unquestioned dogma. What good science does is this: it raises the incomprehensible to the level of the obvious, and then it shows that the new obvious is incomprehensible. I should add immediately that good art is always both obvious and incomprehensible, and therefore paradoxical.

Four decades ago J. R. Lucas of Oxford University reflected on the functions of an idealized computing device known as the Turing machine and applied to it Gödel's incompleteness theorem.[40] He concluded that above a certain level of complexity, all computers become increasingly unpredictable. I argue similarly that the mathematics necessary for understanding the behavior of increasingly more complex systems must allow for increasing degrees of unpredictability. My speculative comment is that as mathematics keeps on developing, it will provide formal relationships among variables that recognize those degrees of freedom that biologists, psychologists, and historians already consider necessary for dealing with their subject matters.

If mathematics does indeed reflect the Logos of nature and if it is incompletable as well as inconsistent (in the manner defined), then, I conjecture, so must nature be. The three sections that follow confirm and give shape and content to this conjecture; the closing section draws some conclusions.

3.3   The Qualities of Truth in the Physical World

In sec. 3.1 I defined truth as the recognition of permanence in reality. To demonstrate the qualities of truth (so defined) in the physical universe, this section explores the natural history of permanence in the world of nonliving matter, using the hierarchical theory of time, outlined in chapter 2, as its guide.

The Eotemporal World: Deterministic Truth

The Western idea that nature obeys permanent laws arose from the Renaissance confluence of two belief systems. One, originating in Judaism and elaborated in Christianity, was the notion of a single, legislative God. The other was the Western love affair with number. The two beliefs merged with the concerns of early experimental science in the work of Galileo and then became codified in the thought of Newton. Sir Isaac envisaged a universe whose features are governed by eternal, deterministic laws stated in the language of mathematics. The mathematician Edmond Halley, a contemporary of Newton, said that much in his ode dedicated to Newton and "prefixed" to the *Principia.*

> Lo, for your gaze, the patterns of the skies!
> What balance of the mass, what reckonings
> Divine! Here ponder too the Laws which God,
> Framing the universe, set not aside
> But made the fixed foundations of his work.[41]

The law of gravitation formulated by Newton was assumed to have been eternally true: it held at the time of Creation and was imagined to remain valid until the day of the Last Judgment. When, a few decades after Newton's death, Linnaeus began to classify all plants and animals, he believed that he was classifying life forms the way they were made by God on the day of Creation. A hymn from around 1796 said so succinctly.

> Praise the Lord for He hath spoken,
>   World his mighty force obeyed,
> Laws which never shall be broken
>   For their guidance he hath made.[42]

One of the oldest notions of Western civilization, wrote Joseph Needham, is that just as earthly imperial lawgivers enact codes of law to be obeyed by humans, so also the celestial and supreme rational creator deity laid down a series of laws that must be obeyed by minerals, crystals, plants, animals, and the stars in their courses. The same belief gave rise to the idea of natural law, a juristic concept according to which human laws must be consistent with man's never-changing nature.

The notion of God-given, eternal laws of nature is culture bound, as may be seen if one considers the very different beliefs of Chinese civilization regarding the origin of order in the universe. "The Chinese world-view depended upon a totally different line of thought. The harmonious cooperation of all beings arose, not from the orders of a superior authority external to themselves, but from the fact that they were all parts in a hierarchy of wholes forming a cosmic pattern, and what they obeyed were the internal dictates of their own natures."[43]

The Chinese commanded great algebraic skills and possessed observational material similar to that on which early Western science was based, yet they never invented mathematized science. That, and its offspring, industrial civilization, had to be imported from the West. One reason for the absence of indigenous mathematized science might have been that they did not have the equivalent of Platonic philosophy, with its sharp separation of time from the timeless, its distrust of the temporal, and its praise of the search for the timeless as the noblest task of the mind.[44] In the West precise and deterministic predictability based on number remained the major test for scientific truth until the birth of quantum physics. The laws of the macroscopic physical world, both in Newtonian and Einsteinian physics, are deterministic and hence predictive and retrodictive. They are appropriate for the eotemporal integrative level.*

If truth is indeed the recognition of permanence in reality, and if permanence means everlastingness—the continuity of a condition or process without change—then the paradigm of truth is the behavior of massive matter as it is idealized in classical physics. I say "idealized" because deterministic behavior cannot exist without probabilistic and chaotic contributions. For this reason the proposition that planetary orbits are conic sections (with general relativistic corrections) is correct only to a first approximation. All actual orbits also display statistical as well as unpredictable, chaotic variations.

The Prototemporal World: Probabilistic Truth

That lawfulness need not be deterministic, that it may be probabilistic, was recognized in the seventeenth century, although it acquired its position

*It is suggested that readers with no prior familiarity with the hierarchical theory of time review the ideas of the nested hierarchy of causations, languages, temporalities, and conflicts, discussed on pp. 26–43.

among the fundamental qualities of nature only with the rise of quantum theory, to which I now turn.

The theoretical foundations of scientific atomism were laid in the eighteenth and nineteenth centuries by Lavoisier and Dalton, although the atomic nature of matter was suspected, on logical grounds, by Leucippus and Democritus in the fifth century B.C. In cosmic history as it is seen today, atoms are the firstborns of chaos; they are object-processes that jell from radiative energy. The doctrine that atoms are immutable has been long abandoned: they, and their constituent elements, are intricate creatures with nothing in their behavior that could be familiar to humans through direct experience.[45] If our senses could directly penetrate the quantum world, then probability would have been embedded among the attributes of divinity. Einstein could not have asserted that God does not play dice because everyone would have known that he does. It is as if Jehovah's commandments, written for the human-sized children of Israel, had been revised. "On the average, you shall not commit adultery. Generally, you should not kill. Do not covet your neighbor's oxen more than approximately 32 percent of the possibilities offered."

Once upon a time, on a Scottish heath, two generals dared three witches to tell their futures from a bushel of identical grain. Grain is a superb metaphor for indistinguishability.

> *Banquo:* If you can look into the seeds of time
>   And say which grain will grow and which will not,
>   Speak then to me. . . .
> *First witch:* Hail!
> *Second witch:* Hail!
> *Third witch:* Hail! . . .
> *Macbeth:* Stay, you imperfect speakers, tell me more.[46]

Macbeth assumed that the witches knew more than they said. Maybe they did. Einstein believed that the nondeterministic (statistical) laws of particle behavior are not statements about the world but witnesses to our ignorance; once the true laws become known, they will permit precise deterministic predictions in particle behavior.

But the probabilistic laws of nature do not know more than they say, because the furnishings of the world they govern do not possess more precision. Such laws do not report about a superior universe whose hidden rules, if discovered, may yet reveal the deterministic truths of the Almighty. Rather, the prototemporal is the most primitive organizational level of the physical world above chaos; it is not sufficiently evolved to be deterministic. From the point of view of higher umwelts, the prototemporal world is an "imperfect speaker." In its own terms, however, by the generalized umwelt principle, it is not imperfect. An infant does not babble to hide his thoughts and mislead or mystify mom and dad; he does not yet have well-defined thoughts to hide.

Probabilistic laws that govern the behavior of aggregates of objects assumed to be indistinguishable occupy an intermediate position between the absolute unpredictability of chaos (to be discussed in the next subsection) and the predictability and retrodictability of deterministic processes. One may object that although the umwelt of particle-waves is governed by probabilistic laws, the fact that they are probabilistic is itself permanent, unchanging. Such a comment leads us back to the nested hierarchy of languages; namely, the claim that the laws themselves are permanent (that the world of particle-waves is one of iron-fisted, unchanging, probability) can be made only in the language of a higher integrative level in whose umwelt permanence has meaning. It cannot be made within the prototemporal umwelt.

Because of these reasons, the working definition of truth must be adjusted to include, under "permanence," the recognition of probabilistic conditions or behavior. Although probabilistic truths first appear in the physical world, they remain constituent components of all higher-order truths. They take on different forms according to the complexities of the different integrative levels. Thus, macroscopic physical systems from pebbles to galaxies also follow probabilistic laws, as do biological species and as does human conduct both individually and collectively.

The Atemporal World: Pure Becoming

Having identified the forms of truth appropriate for the eotemporal and prototemporal worlds, I now turn to the nature of truth in the atemporal world. I enter through the idea of chaos.

The pre-Socratic notion of chaos, from the Greek word that meant "abyss," signifies the primeval emptiness of the universe or the dark gorge of Tartarus, the underworld. In Ovid it is the disordered mass out of which the creator of the world made the ordered universe. In terms of current ideas, it is necessary to distinguish between formal and absolute chaos. *Formal chaos* is found in the behavior of certain nonlinear dynamic systems and is due to their extreme sensitivity to initial conditions in combination with the physical limitations of computer precision.[47] Future states of a formally chaotic system are computable in principle, but never without error; nor are they precisely predictable from inspection, because they never retrace their pasts exactly. In contrast, *absolute chaos* is a state of pure becoming, a behavior totally unpredictable not only in practice but also in principle. It is a state of matter and energy to which none of our ideas of time or causation apply; hence, it is identically equivalent to the atemporal integrative level of the world. By an older name, it is a world of pure becoming.

Atemporal chaos—pure becoming—lurks beneath all natural phenomena. It is the primeval pool of potentialities out of which different forms of becoming may arise and into which all processes may collapse at any time. The first evolutionary product of absolute chaos is the formal chaos identified in chaos theory, displaying an infinite depth of self-similarity. That self-similarity is the most primitive form of being, the ancestor of all later forms of permanence.

Chaos contributes to, and is an uneliminable part of, the processes at all higher integrative levels. It takes different forms on each level because the governing principles of higher integrative levels restrict the regions of unpredictability to the uncontrolled niches in the lattices of their rules. There is evidence of chaotic events in quantum physics, unpredictable from the probabilistic laws indigenous to the prototemporal world. There is also chaos in deterministic processes, where its presence is confirmed by what has been called deterministic chaos.[48] By another name, absolute chaos is the primeval form of creativity in nature. By "creativity" I mean the coming about of unpredictable events, conditions, or structures, regardless of whether they would be judged constructive or destructive from the point of view of humans.

From Becoming to Being

Considering what we have learned about probability and determinism, and the claim that these forms of lawfulness emerged in that sequence from the primeval chaos of pure becoming, the idea comes to mind that what we call "permanence" is an evolutionary quality of nature.

My reasoning in support of this suggestion begins with the clever arguments given twenty-five centuries ago by Zeno of Elea. They were constructed to convince his fellow philosophers that motion and change are virtual and that reality is timeless, that it is pure being. Imagine a flying arrow, he proposed. At every instant it occupies a region of space equivalent to itself, but never longer than that. It has no room to move; it cannot move; it does not move.[49]

This strange conclusion, drawn from sound premises by reasonable arguments, raises two questions. (1) If the logic is correct, why do we perceive motion? (2) If the senses are correct, what is wrong with the logic? All solutions of which I am aware take the side of the senses and seek fault in the reasoning. They also assume that rest is a more fundamental state of nature than is motion, that permanence is ontologically and epistemologically prior to change. Therefore, the basic question is whether it is possible to compound motion from elements of rest, and if not, why not?[50]

Motion, as perceived by the eye and interpreted by the nervous system, has always meant motion with respect to something. That something used to be the earth, resting stably in the center of the universe. Copernicus altered the reference: henceforth motion was referred to the stable sun. By letting the earth loose among the planets, he created a higher-order unity; after him motion meant displacement with respect to the starry heaven, itself in eternal rest. This comfortable model of absolute motion with respect to absolute rest remained current until the rise of modern physics. It was demolished when Einstein gave motion a reference of a higher class of absolute.

Einstein began by stressing the need for invariance (permanence), placing the following demand at the foundation of relativity theory. "The laws of physics" he wrote, "must be of such nature that they apply to systems of reference in any kind of motion."[51] He complied with this demand by changing the framework with respect to which bodies should be judged to be in motion. The idea that motion takes place with respect to absolute rest (to which, as it turned out, nothing in nature corresponds) was replaced by the idea that motion takes place with respect to absolute motion (to which there is something in nature that does correspond: the propagation of light). Motion thereby acquired a new, absolute reference. Do not ask how quickly Robin Hood's arrow flies with respect to the Nottingham woods or the background of the stars. Ask instead how slowly it flies with respect to the universal, ever-present motion of light, which speeds always, and for all observers, at the same velocity.[52] Special relativity theory revealed a universe of ceaseless motion within which conditions of relative rest can be only local.

Quantum theory added that even such relative rests are only apparent: all rest is unperceived motion. It did so by changing our understanding of matter from that of a collection of well-defined atomic objects to that of seas of vibrating, probabilistic clouds or foam. Here is an illustration.

An archer's arrow contains about 10^{24} molecules. Each molecule has a number of atoms, each atom being made up of a number of particle-waves, which may be leptons or other objects. Those other objects are made of quarks. In turn, quarks come in six flavors: up, down, strange, charm, beauty, and truth (the latter two are also called "bottom" and "top," respectively). Each flavor comes in three colors: red, blue, and green. None of these names has any literal meaning.[53] With equal abandon, let me call all these objects "thingies" and add that thingies are also changelings. Writing about elementary particles, Paul Davies remarked that all particles are apt to flip their identities from time to time, a photon becoming an electron-positron pair, a pion a proton-antiproton pair. . . . [We are forced to admit] that every particle has mixed into it somewhere something of every other type of particle, however dilute. [It seems] conceivable that there are actually no such things as "elementary particles" at all. No particle is more fundamental than any other. Every particle is made up of every other.[54]

Nothing in the material of Robin Hood's arrow has lasting identity; nothing is ever at rest; nothing is or can be at a well-defined point in space; nothing can happen at a well-defined instant in time. There is nothing in nature to which Zeno's premise ("in any instant the arrow occupies a region of space equivalent to its length, but never longer") could correspond. Well-defined instants and portions of space are artifices of the senses and the mind; they are useful for humans as categories of perception.

The usual perspective on Zeno's remarks is thus backward. Motion is ontologically and therefore epistemologically prior to rest; becoming is prior to being. Evolution has been a journey from pure becoming to increasingly more complex forms of beings or lastingness, that is, slow change.

The question is not how one may compound motion and change from elements of rest and permanence but how one may construct rest and permanence from elements of motion and change. The answer is simple. We may do so by constructing ideas of rest and permanence, using our crude sensory data, inadequate to detect atomic vibrations or to recognize light as the never-resting reference of motion. We may also do so by appealing to our desire to identify, name, and live with ideas of rest, continuity, permanence, and identity.

One may counter that the paradox of the flying arrow is an issue in logic and must be resolved with reference to rules of thinking, without an appeal to what we know of the arrow's material. But a logic formulated for an arrow that may sometime be at rest in the ordinary sense of rest would be the logic of a nonexistent world. It would have no more legitimate standing in phenomenal reality than an analysis of the DNA of a unicorn.

Zeno's or Robin Hood's arrow, whether flying or quivering in its case, is an archaeological sample of the universe, a record of cosmic history. Its processes are chaotic, statistical, and deterministic. So are those of the stone walls of Connecticut and the moons of Jupiter. From among these processes only the deterministic aspects of the arrow's behavior resemble the idea of permanence as continuity without change—resemble but do not correspond, because no deterministic process can exist without having statistical and chaotic components. Obviously the evolution of the physical world has been a journey from complete chaos to different forms of being, as I suggested earlier.

What qualities must a claim in the physical world possess before it may be admitted to be true? It must allow for probabilistic and chaotic or for deterministic, probabilistic, and chaotic elements. This reasoning authorizes us to look for evolutionary forms of permanence beyond and more sophisticated than the forms of permanence that first appear in the physical world.

3.4 The Qualities of Truth in the Organic World

The life process gives rise to a type of continuity or permanence that is qualitatively different from what one finds in the physical world. It is called intentionality (see pp. 30–32), and it enables the emergence of truths that hold only from this day forward and possibly only until another day. All along, it must continuously refer to a present. Intentionality does not replace deterministic, probabilistic, and chaotic connections but adds to them a new kind of connection, one that combines with the older forms of connectedness in infinitely many ways.

Need and Intent

There are a number of ways in which the behavior of living matter may be distinguished from that of nonliving matter. One such set of distinctions appeals to metabolism, another to self-reproduction, and yet others to the mutability of structures and functions without losses of the identity of the whole. Still another set of distinctions is offered by thermodynamicists. They think of living organisms as systems that absorb matter, energy, and information at a high degree of organization; eliminate matter, energy, and information at a lower degree of organization; and assimilate the difference to preserve the continuity of their lives.

The hierarchical theory of time sees the essential difference between living and inorganic matter in the ability of living systems to create and maintain an organic present. Recall from sec. 2.2 (on the nested hierarchy of temporalities) that physics disclaims the existence of a moving present both locally and globally. Life, therefore, cannot be imagined as attaching itself to a moving cosmic present. Rather (as was said in that section), life creates those conditions and operational properties of matter that give rise to the organic present and biotemporality. The human brain in turn creates those conditions that give rise to the mental present and to the experiences of noetic time. Likewise, society creates and maintains its social present.

The creation and maintenance of the organic present is a necessary and sufficient condition of life. There is an immense variety of life forms built on carbon chemistry, and other life chemistries can certainly be imagined, such as one based on silicon instead of carbon.[55] But no life process can be imagined without a capacity of defining an organic present.

As organisms use up their store of matter, energy, and information, they become ready to absorb replacement matter, energy, and information from their environment to help them maintain their dynamic equilibria. This readiness, this chronic incompleteness of life, is the primeval form of *need*. In sec. 1.2 ("The Need for Human Values"), following Gerald Edelman, I introduced the notion of biological value, defined as a family of conservative trends that help to secure stability in the life of an organism and have the propensity of perpetuating themselves. From a different perspective, biological values are judgments that prompt *intentional behavior*, which is directed toward need satisfaction. Only living organisms can have needs and hence display intent. A sodium ion can retain its identity for an indefinite length of time without acquiring an electron; it does not need to become an electrically neutral atom. My car never needs new tires; I need new tires for my car so that I may drive safely.

In sec. 1.2 I quoted Edelman as saying that the brain categorizes impressions with the help of certain inborn biases that he described as teleonomically derived constraints on behavior. Teleonomic behavior arose through selection that favored stable, self-perpetuating traits. A different way of saying the same thing is that useful, repeated behavior resulted in the evolution of organic memory systems as parts of the genetic heritage. It is through such memory systems that the life process added to the forms of truths appropriate to the physical levels a new quality or form of truth appropriate and unique to life. The newcomer was *organic* or *organismic truth*. It arose from need as a quality of life and began to generate intent in the service of self-directed purpose. "I am hungry, therefore I shall capture and eat you," expressed in a myriad ways through the behavior of living organisms, is an example of organismic truth. Necessarily, organismic truth is never without deterministic, probabilistic, and chaotic components.

Intentionality and the Experienced Direction of Time

That intentionality and purpose were evident in the physical world, that their presence demonstrated the intent of a divine designer, was the belief of many a great intellect, from Robert Boyle to Samuel Clarke, Leibniz, and Newton. The origins of this belief go back at least to Plato, who argued that since matter cannot move itself, motion is an evidence of the presence of mind in nature. In the history of ideas these beliefs are classed under "physicotheology."

According to currently valid common sense, however, there is nothing in a pot of water that insists on its becoming frozen or in a stone that insists on its rolling. Changes in the states of matter are acquired passively, through chance coincidences. This is consistent with the absence of a now in the physical world: purpose must have a referent now.

In contrast to nonliving matter, living organisms are characterized by the existence of mechanisms that demand and make possible goal-directed, purposeful behavior. To distinguish the goal directedness of living organisms from whatever might appear as goal directedness in the physical world, Colin Pittendrigh coined the word *teleonomy*, as explained earlier. His idea was elaborated by Ernst Mayr: "A teleonomic process or behavior is one which owes its goal-directedness to the operation of a program. . . . All teleonomic behavior is characterized by two components. It is guided by a 'program' and it depends on the existence of some endpoint, goal, or terminus which is foreseen in the program that regulates the behavior."[56]

It is in the service of need satisfactions that purposeful behavior evolved and began to provide distinctions between two types of nonpresent conditions, events, and things. One such a set is called the future. It is into the future that living organisms place their hopes related to the fulfillment of their needs. In Mayr's words just quoted, the desired future is foreseen in the program that regulates their behavior. The other nonpresent category of time is the past. In animals and in humans, as far as their biological functions go, the past is the source of the inherited or learned traits that direct teleonomic behavior. What we describe as the experiential directionality of time in the biotemporal umwelt is rooted in the teleonomic division of the phenomenal world into the two nonpresent categories of time as referred to present conditions.

The claim that the directional qualities of experienced time derive from need and intentionality may appear unwarranted, but not unintelligible, to psychologists and to philosophers with training in classical and premodern thought. For those who, because of metaphysical convictions, insist that the experience of time's passage must necessarily derive from a directionality already present in the physical world, the argument will seem wrongheaded. Admittedly, there are two serious problems with the proposal that the direction of time has, in its simplest form, a biological origin.

Problem 1: If every creature defines—creates and maintains—its own organic present with respect to which future and past may acquire meaning, then how does one explain the fact that the "now" is the same for all organisms on the globe and, certainly, for all living things in a room?

Comments on problem 1: Local swallows do eat local insects by being at the same place at the same time; they share a common present wide enough in clock time to perform the deadly act. Living organisms in a room share a broader present, one whose width is determined by the speed of diffusing scent or sound or the speed of a bullet. But all animals on earth do not share a common present with respect to which they could take concerted action. And the nature of the largest possible room, the universe, categorically prohibits the establishment of a cosmic present.

Answer to problem 1: The now is not shared across the universe, across the earth, or even across a room. It appears to be shared for limited regions of space where the absence of precise simultaneity is masked by the crudeness of the way we test for it.

Problem 2: If every living organism divides the nonpresent categories of time into futurity and pastness, if not mentally then at least biologically, then how do we explain the fact that time's flow is the selfsame passage, from instant to instant, for all fleas on a dog, dogs on the block, and creatures on earth?

Comments on problem 2: As is the case with the definition of a collective present, collective futures and pasts are established through communication and shared purpose toward which the members of a group direct their behavior. Collective pasts demand shared traits and, in humans, shared memories vested in tradition and artifact.

Answer to problem 2: Time is not a shared passage unless it is made to be so through acts of synchronization, to the extent such acts are permitted by physical and biological constraints.

Life broke the eotemporal symmetry of physical time through the creation and maintenance of organic present.[57] The inorganic world permits but does not demand directedness for an explanation of physical processes. The eotemporality of the physical world is directable, but it is not directed (see appendix C, "Entropy: Its Uses and Abuses").

The coming about of life broke not only the symmetry of time in the physical world but also its logic. It created a new type of logic, that of organic intentionality, one that is goal rather than rule directed and that therefore depends on the direction of time. T. S. Eliot gave the reasons:

> . . . only in time can the moment in the rose-garden,
> The moment in the arbour where the rain beat,
> The moment in the draughty church at smokefall
> Be remembered.[58]

And, I might add, only in time can it be anticipated.[59]

Summing up this section: Truth, as it applies to the organic world, possesses qualities to which nothing in the physical world corresponds. They relate to the creation and maintenance of the organic present, to the emergence of need, to behavior directed to need satisfaction, to biological values defined in terms of needs, and to futurity and pastness defined with respect to the organic present.

"Who killed Cock Robin?" I do not know the answer for certain; maybe it was the Sparrow. But I do know that for an answer to be believable, it must allow for evidence of short-term intentionality as well as for evidence of determinism, probabilistic behavior, and instants of unpredictable chaos, manifest as becoming or creativity.

3.5 The Qualities of Truth in the Historical Process

The temporal horizons of intentionality in the service of organic needs came to be vastly expanded when members of early human groups began to be concerned with futures beyond their deaths and to draw lessons from pasts before their births. To the concrete goals of satisfying hunger for food and for mates there came to be added intentionality directed toward symbolic causes, such as the benefits of postmortem wellbeing. The story of collective intents, of their implementations, their successes and failures, and all in-betweens, is that of the historical process.

The universal cosmologies of humankind were early thoughts about the historical process. By "universal" I mean that their concerns included the world with all its furnishings. They offered explanations about the behavior of people, animals, and stars; acknowledged the memories, hopes, and fears of their audience; and through all these helped to expand the temporal horizons of those who followed the stories. These cosmologies included both cosmogonies (ideas about the beginning of the world) and eschatologies (ideas about its ending) or else, if they held the universe to be eternal, ideas about provisional beginnings and endings.

The endings and beginnings had to be the projections of human and animal births, lives, and deaths in the world at large, because no humans witnessed the coming about or the ending of the world, nor could anyone claim to have observed that it has existed from all eternity and will exist forever.[60] Also, within the compass of the life of a person, a tribe, or even a civilization, nature remains, on the average, unchanging. Day and night follow day and night, seasons follow seasons, calamities are followed by recoveries, and recoveries by calamities.

It is not surprising that universal cosmologies are all set in the countrysides where they were invented; they report conflicts among people, between people and their gods, and among gods. They record social conditions and natural events in which men and women serve as observers as well as participants. The stories speak of good and evil, rewards and punishments, rights and wrongs. Whatever else they say, they offer guidelines for beliefs and conduct. Primarily, they are documents of ethical and aesthetic principles, judgments on a cosmos with its island of human life.

During the centuries just before and just after the birth of Christ, the cosmological speculations of the pre-Socratics were complemented by the mathematical and astronomical studies of Alexandrian and Christian scientists. After the Renaissance, as the sciences began to claim authority over all truths about nature, universal cosmologies separated into two lines of inquiries. One was the history of humankind, with the universe taken for granted as a background. The other was the history of the universe from the point of view of the natural sciences, with the presence of humankind taken as mostly irrelevant.

Scientific cosmologies became the showpieces of the Western love affair with number and examples of the power and limitations of mathematical modeling of the world. The theoretical framework of physical cosmology since the early twentieth century has been a particular geometry that is regarded not as a description of the universe but, in the Pythagorean tradition, as actually constituting the world.[61] Physical cosmology reports about a world in which predictions and retrodictions are of equal validity and in which, as was already discussed, a present cannot be defined. Appendix D ("A World without History: The Astral Geometry of Gauss") concludes that this cosmology's truths are of the types we find in the physical world: deterministic, probabilistic, and chaotic, with time undirected. Therefore, I leave the question of truth in physical cosmology to its limited devices and ask about the quality of truth in the history of humankind. That is, I leave the astral geometry of Gauss for Robert Burns's daily life, where

> The best laid schemes o' mice and men
>   Gang aft a-glay;
> An' lea'e us nought but grief and pain,
>   For promised joy.

In ancient Greece and Rome, writing about the past was considered to be a branch of literature and judged as much on its literary merits as on its presumed faithfulness. The Scholastics maintained that human nature had been set once and for all at the time of Creation, and henceforth the history of humankind was the working out of its given potentialities through free choices between good and evil. Writers of medieval Europe, when reporting on the past, sought to identify the workings of salvation history; the Renaissance was fascinated by pre-Christian antiquity.

For Giambattista Vico (1668–1744), a philosopher of cultural history, history consisted of the working out of the plan of Providence; for Kant, in the late eighteenth century, it was a plan of nature. He saw the laws of history as being probabilistic: what appears unpredictable for "a single individual may be seen from the standpoint of the human race as a whole to be a study of progressive though slow evolution of its original endowment." It is the task of the philosopher "to try to see if he can discover a natural purpose in this idiotic course of things human."[62]

Early in the nineteenth century Hegel identified history with what man makes of death and suggested that it is the dialectic of the spirit, which is manifest in the cunning (strategy) of reason. It is a dialogue between concepts and their opposites, with each such dialogue leading to a higher unity, ready for a dialectic on the next level.[63] This view of history, but with the dialectic of the spirit replaced by the dialectic of matter, inspired the philosophies of history of both communism and nazism. The past and its presumed facts are always seen—can only be seen—from a particular social and mental present interpreted in terms of an available store of knowledge and judged in terms of criteria and values convincing for the inquirer. Past facts (from the Latin *facta*, "things that have been made") and data (the Latin plural of *datum*, "something given") are identified and shaped by active agents: by historians as professionals and by the historian in everyone. Since facts usually become legitimate only as parts of hypotheses, whenever hypotheses about past processes, conditions, or events change, so do assumed facts.[64] Since this reasoning holds equally for all past evaluations of the (then) past, historical sources themselves must be approached with a critical mind. But the critical mind works by whatever guidelines are current. Hence historiography, the practice of writing history based on the critical examination of the sources, is an ever-changing evaluation of the past.

Here are some of the concepts that have been employed in the twentieth century in pursuit of truths in the historical process. I am following Leonard Krieger in his comparative survey of philosophies of history, old and new.[65]

Historicity may refer to an assertion that a past event has been a fact. It may also mean an insistence on finding the organizing principles of historical data within those data rather than in fields outside the study of history, such as in anthropology or social psychology. *The philosophy of history* seeks to understand the nature of historical change by examining—from a distance, as it were—the story of humanity and the means by which that story is told. *Historicism* is the belief that an adequate judgment about the significance of an event can and must be built on an understanding of the role that the event has played in the process of historical development.

An early meaning of historicism was the view that all forms of truths and values are relative and are historically determined. It is this idea that Ortega y Gasset endorsed when he remarked that man has no nature but only a history that shapes him. The concept of historicism, introduced into England and the United States during the early decades of the twentieth century, underwent many twists and turns in its early meaning. In its most rigorous form it came to stand for a belief that history is governed by laws in the way that physical and organic processes are and that knowing them could make the course of history predictable. This form of physics envy has few believers. Working historians are more likely to seek principles that can serve as protocols of reasoning. Such (hypothetical) protocols have a name: they are called the covering laws of historical explanation. Antigone sided with historicism and proposed the tragic as the covering law. "Near time, far future, and the past / One law controls them all: / Any greatness in human life brings doom."[66]

The nineteenth century, writes Krieger, witnessed the triumph of history and has probably been the most historically minded of Western eras.[67] This "passionately intellectual" phase in the study of history was followed by the gradual "dissolution of the absolute, any absolute, as an external source for intellectual and scientific definition of coherence" in the past of humankind.[68]

The ancient Greek word *historia* means "inquiry" or "study." The adjective *polyhistor* describes the kind of persons Heraclitus must have had in mind when he remarked that men who love wisdom and seek truth must be inquirers into many things. Those requirements still hold. Anyone seeking truth resident in history must be a *polyhistor* because any such search involves the whole nested hierarchy of qualitatively different truths discussed so far, each in its level-specific language, each with its peculiar degrees of constraints and freedoms.

Once again: "Who killed Cock Robin?" According to some scholars, Cock Robin of the Mother Goose rhyme refers to Robert Walpole (1676–1745), regarded as the first British prime minister. The rhyme is an allegorical description of the intrigues that attended the downfall of the Walpole ministry, popularly known as Robinocracy. As is the case with my knowledge of the bird's killer, I do not know what led to Robert Walpole's resignation in 1742, but I do know that the jury of historians considering the truth implied in his "fall" must recognize a nested hierarchy of qualitatively different truths that make for the historical processes and allow for a tracing of histories along many different yet often simultaneously valid paths.

History is moved by our biological needs to survive and noetic needs to reach for the deathless. It is driven less by reason than by passion, and when it comes to passion, Carmen in Bizet's opera has it right. We may consider love the archetype of all other passions, including those that drive history. "L'amour est l'enfant de bohème, / Il n'a jamais, jamais connu de lois." Love is the child of wild abandon; it never ever knew of law. Whether history knows any laws is difficult to decide because we do not have a language appropriate for the integrative level above the sociotemporal in whose terms such laws could be expressed.

Mark Twain once remarked that history does not repeat itself, but it does rhyme. The nonrhyming part is the component of pure becoming. The rhyming components are the probabilistic and deterministic relations together with organic and mental intentions. This complex machinery of different causations hardly corresponds to the idea of eternal verities. The only types of truth in history that can claim eternal verity are those interpretations that a person or a group decided to maintain, come what may, such as "God is just, God is merciful." But even these kinds of truths last only as long as their proponents do. Sic transit gloria mundi.

3.6   The Office of Truth as a Human Value

The search for truth, so I reasoned, is prompted by the mind's propensity for whatever is enduring, whatever seems to defy death. This hypothesis is supported by the witness of large language groups, those whose members are spoken by a few hundred million people. In these languages the most frequent equivalents of the word *truth* are words that signify permanence and correspondence to reality (assumed to be final and stable). The hypothesis, taken together with this observation, suggested the working definition of truth as the recognition of permanence in reality.

The definition was tested against truth in mathematics and against what we know about the behavior of inorganic matter, living matter, and people in society, that is, in the historical process. The conclusion we must reach, based on these explorations, is that there is nothing in nature to which the idea of truth as eternal verity can correspond. The search for truth as permanence appears to be a wild-goose chase, as indeed it is. There are no fixtures in nature, wrote Emerson. "In nature every moment is new . . . the coming only is sacred. . . . No love can be bound by oath or covenant to secure it against a higher love. No truth so sublime but it may not be trivial tomorrow in the light of new thought. People wish to be settled; only as far as they are unsettled is there any hope for them."[69]

If there is no permanence, then we cannot expect to find examples of truth as permanence. But humans most definitely have a basic need to seek truth as permanence, even if it is never found. This helps to answer a question raised by the philosopher Huw Price: of what use is the concept of truth to creatures like us?[70]

Since here we come to this problem from the natural philosophy of time, the question should be rephrased: "What is the evolutionary office of truth as a human value?" It has at least two important offices in this respect.

The first is an obvious one: knowing what appears to be permanent helps in the struggle for survival. Knowing the habitual hideout of the wolf, even approximately, makes the life of Little Red Riding Hood safer and, as evolutionary biologists would say, increases her chances of reproductive success. Knowing the laws of nature, even if they are only ever-changing educated guesses, helps in the making of better mousetraps, better medicine, and better atomic bombs. And as Saint Paul knew well, believing that one is privy to eternal verities can help men and women to face suffering and death. "O death, where is thy sting? O grave, where is thy victory?" Such capacities extend immensely the domains of thought and reasoned conduct available to humans.

The other office of truth, its prime task as a human value, is a subtle one. It relates to the dynamics of civilizations and of the identities of persons. This role becomes evident if, instead of asking what truth is or what is true, we ask what the search for truth does to the searchers.

There is a universal conviction that knowing what is true helps to secure balance in the affairs of society and, generally, a peace of mind for the knower. It is better to light a candle than to curse the darkness; the truth shall make you free. In the short run, these beliefs may often be correct. Historically, however, personal and collective beliefs in possessing the truth, whether those of facts presumed, ideas held, or feelings voiced, have had the opposite effect. Seeing the light of truth imparts restlessness on the knower because all truths are incomplete and incompletable and hence carry the threat of impermanence. Knowledge generates a desire to share, to convince, and even to force, as well as to sacrifice one's own life or the lives of others to the cause of spreading the truth. We inherited this trait from our prehuman ancestors, who could survive only through socializing all or most of their knowledge.

Knowing what is believed to be true has been a perennial source of unresolvable conflicts. Attempts to resolve them lead to new conflicts and to cultural change paid for by social upheavals and bloody wars. Untold millions have suffered either because they did not agree with some asserted truth or because they did. Instead of securing balance, searching for truth has tended to create conflicts and imbalance in the individual affairs of men and women and in the collective conduct of societies. Expressed in myriad ways in artifacts, in the arts and letters, in the sciences, in politics, in religion, and in the cruel conflicts of civilizations, searching for truth has served as an elemental force in the creation of changes in beliefs.

The conclusion follows. Although searching for truth is driven by the desire for permanence and stability, its historical function has been the creation of conflicts and, through them, social, cultural, and personal change.

CHAPTER FOUR

Good and Evil:
Guidelines for Conduct

During the summer of 1963, with almost a million Algerian refugees flooding France, a beggar knelt next to the Notre Dame gate of the Palace of the Popes in the medieval fortress of Avignon. He was already there early in the morning and was still there as sunset approached. He was on his knees, his trunk upright and rigid, his body motionless, his arms extended straight ahead, hands cupped. He wore the remnants of an army uniform and, hanging on a chain around his neck, a silver model of a Roman instrument of execution. His eyes were closed. Maybe he was listening to the man on that machine of torture: "Come to me all ye that labor and are burdened and I will give you rest."

How did the strange walker of Sophocles, that hyperactive creature who faced no future helpless, change into the catatonic penitent of a soldier in Avignon?

There is no need to think of him as having changed. He remained the same ethical animal, possessing an unlimited variety of alter egos that differed mainly by their convictions about what is right and what is wrong in conduct and thought. This chapter examines a number of those convictions (sec. 4.1), places them in the perspective of the natural philosophy of time (sec. 4.2), and asks how effective they have been in reaching the goals they have set for themselves (secs. 4.3 and 4.4).

4.1 Visions, Instructions, and Promises

Relating the idea of truth to time—doing so, for example, through beliefs expressed in families of languages—was a relatively simple task. Relating ideas of right and wrong to time is not that simple. A working definition of the good in relation to time requires a survey of many and varied opinions. This section is such a survey.

Distant Stones and Distant Peoples

Our Stone Age ancestors were observant and sensitive enough to create mobiliary and cave wall art, clever enough to make tools, and mean enough to torture and kill their fellows and then rationalize their acts in terms of what later ages would classify as rites of religion or state. They must have held collectively approved rules of behavior, but since they left no written records, it is difficult to know what those rules were. Whatever they were, the rules served humans stably for a hundred thousand years or more. Or did they? It might be more accurate to guess that their rules of behavior did change, but only at the slow pace of organic evolution.

Somewhere along the path of prehistory, before there were societies that needed an awareness of past and future to regard themselves as societies,[1] the temporal horizons of the protohumans must have begun to open up. Images of nonpresent conditions and events joined impressions of the present, giving rise to the perception of new challenges. In addition to dos and don'ts in conduct, there were dos and don'ts in imagining. The world became an interesting but dangerous place where one could be threatened by more than whatever could be touched or seen. For guidelines on dealing with this larger world of challenges, they had to depend on the same gifts of imagination that were responsible for the new, expanded world in the first place. The mind had to learn how to control itself. This, the dawning of noetic time, was surely a collective act, for as the philosopher Feuerbach explained, the "single man for himself possesses the essence of man neither in himself as a moral being nor in himself as a thinking being. The essence of man is contained only in the community and unity of man with man."[2]

In sec. 1.1, "Life, Time, and Mortality," I quoted current estimates of the age of modern humans. When trying to guess how long abstract notions such as right and wrong have been around, it is more practical to listen to the nonnumerical comments of Thomas Mann, a literary archaeologist of the distant, elusive past.

Very deep is the well of the past. Should we not call it bottomless?

Bottomless indeed, if—and perhaps only if—the past we mean is the past merely of the life of mankind. . . . For the deeper we sound, the further down into the lower world of the past we probe and press, the more do we find that the earliest foundations of humanity, its history and culture, reveal themselves unfathomable. No matter to what hazardous lengths we let our line they still withdraw again, and further, into the depth . . . for the unresearchable plays a kind of mocking game with our researching ardours.[3]

Let us settle, therefore, for an origin of the moral sense *in illo tempore*, "at that time." This Latin phrase from the New Testament was effectively employed by Mircea Eliade in alluding to events in an uncertain past, events that are re-created by repetition in rituals of an eternal return.[4] Such rituals involve narratives that praise preferred standards of conduct and implant ideas of rights and wrongs in the minds of the celebrants. Funerals are examples of such rituals: they return almost as frequently as do births. They remind us of the origins of our concerns with good and evil, way back, *in illo tempore.*

My distant ancestors must have felt that each time a person died, the world of those around the deceased had changed in some fundamental manner, but they did not accept the finality of death itself. Although burying the dead might have arisen from instinctive action, its social significance was more than sensitivity to the stench of rotting bodies. Ritual burial is about 100,000 years old. Paleolithic burial practices at both ends of the Eurasian continent (in western Europe and eastern Asia) attest to the belief that the dead continue to have needs that require attendance by the living: burying weapons and food with the dead, and sometimes servants specially murdered for the occasion, is an ancient custom.

A 60,000-year-old Iraqi grave is witness to the placement of flowers around the dead: yarrow, ragwort, grape hyacinth, and hollyhock, preserved as clusters of pollen. A circle of goat horns found surrounding a boy's grave in Uzbekistan suggests ceremony and hence the presence of articulated feelings. To assure the survivors about the postmortem life of the deceased and about their own lives after death, imagination created a world of elsewheres. The need to be protected from the forces of those elsewheres, no less than from the invisible forces of the here and now, is likely the origin of the main vehicles of ethical teachings: magic and religion. "The communication of the dead," wrote T. S. Eliot, "is tongued with fire beyond the language of the living."[5]

Bronislav Malinowski, the founder of social anthropology, remarked in "Magic, Science, and Religion" that there are no people without some form of magic and religion. Although in many of their forms the two practices are indistinguishable, they do differ in important ways. Magic, he suggested, attests to the belief that the future may be controlled if one knows the rules that govern the world or has the right connection to those who do, whereas religions tend to confess to human impotence in certain matters.[6] To these distinctions we may add differences in temporal horizons. Magic tends to promise results in the near future; religions, while also seeking immediate reliefs, tend to cater to the extended temporal horizons of their clientele. The steps from early magic and religion to the abstract ideas of good and evil is witness to a shift from tangible goals here and now to intangible ones in an imagined elsewhere; delivery from the waters of Babylon demanded the temporal horizons of salvation history.

Rudolf Otto, seminal thinker on issues concerning the sources of religious feelings, posited the existence of a sense of the sacred or numinous in the human mind, an awe for and appreciation of some ultimate power beneath phenomenal reality. The holy, he maintained, is an a priori category of perception, with religions being attempts to satisfy the need for the holy through whatever forms of holiness—I add—happened to be acceptable at a place and age.[7] S. G. F. Brandon, a scholar of comparative religion, was more specific. In *History, Time, and Deity* and other writings he suggested that religions originated from the sense of insecurity that stems from the human awareness of passage and of the inevitable end of life.[8] In his *Man and His Destiny in the Great Religions,* after outlining what the major religions and religious philosophies say about time and man, he concludes that all

cultural activities of which we have evidence are seen to involve a prophylactic element, in that they represent attempts to preserve him against future contingencies which might in some manner threaten the security of his existence. . . .

Thus most social and political institutions are inspired by a spirit of conservatism, being designed to secure the community from changes which might disturb the prevailing social or economic equilibrium; even in modern states where the ideal of progress has become accepted, planning is undertaken in order to ensure that the life of the community and of the individual will be even more secure against harmful contingencies which time might bring. If the civilizations of mankind thus represent the effort made for social and economic security, its religions signify an agelong quest for spiritual security. . . .

Man's awareness of time renders him incapable of complete immersion in present experience; it causes him ever to be looking ahead beyond the immediate moment, and from that disposition stems his abiding sense of personal insecurity, which in turn inspires him to seek such a form of refuge as represents his ideal of safety from all that he fears and the conservation of all that he desires.[9]

When a possum's life is threatened, it plays dead. If a grizzly accosts you, we are told, you should pretend to be dead. The begging soldier in Avignon became cataleptic as the best available defense from all he feared in his life as a homeless refugee. The inventiveness of Sophocles' strange walker covers a broad spectrum of conduct.

The Eastern Mediterranean

Judgments about human conduct without reference to the world are unthinkable if humans are regarded as part and parcel of the great everything. Early ideas about the good and the right had to be intimately tied to notions of the universe and society. From such ancient conditions, through steps that took millennia, was born the Greek genius.

In Hesiod's *Theogony* (ca. 800 B.C.) out of the Void came Earth and Eros, as well as Darkness and black Night; out of Night came Light and Day, her children conceived after her union in love with Darkness. Earth produced the sky and the mountains; then came Law and Memory and a family of gods, and with them came the creation and destruction carried out by man. In his *Works and Days* Hesiod tells us that man may choose among goddesses of virtue, such as the Horae (the hours), Dike (justice), Eirene (peace), or Eunomia (order), or select hybris (recklessness).[10]

Ideas about right and wrong that began as occasional remarks by the pre-Socratics came to full maturity in the systematic and extensive ethical deliberations of Socrates and Plato. These great statesmen of the spirit sought to identify the rules that govern the world and proposed to deduce from them those guidelines for conduct and thought that all men and women should judge to be right. So Timaeus, Plato's spokesman for cosmology, remarked that "the world is the fairest of creations and [the maker of the world] is the best of causes."[11] To achieve his goal, the creator looked to "that which is eternal," that which is timeless, and used it as a model on which to fashion the universe. "God desired that all things should be good and nothing bad," said Timaeus, adding with the pragmatism of a good merchant, "so far as this was attainable."[12] Accordingly, people can do no better than to pattern their conduct so as to help their social world resemble the timeless order of the universe (as far as attainable). It is this theme that ties Plato's idea of the good to the eternity of the cosmos.[13]

What specific things are good and what are evil? There are many answers to this question in the Platonic writings; the following may represent them.

"That which destroys and corrupts in every case is evil; that which preserves and benefits is the good."[14] Discontinuity is bad; permanence and continuity are good. The political morality in the Greek city-states reflected a desire to maintain permanence, stability, and order; *ethikos* means "custom." But the foremost good is the possession of eternal wisdom.[15] Aristotle's *Nichomachean Ethics* is concerned with the human good within the science of politics: good is what good does. Ethics in Stoicism stressed the need to make the personal and collective lives of people as orderly as is the universe: the goal was that of spiritual peace, tranquility, and a sense of moral worth.

While the intelligent and quarrelsome Greek world lived its centuries of wars and ambitions, searched for rational order, and formulated rules of rights and wrongs, ethics of a different texture emerged along the eastern Mediterranean. Its standards were based on the story of a certain Eve who ate a fruit from the tree of knowledge and gave some to her man. With that deed their "eyes were opened and they knew that they were naked." God then said, "Behold, the man has become like one of us, knowing good and evil," and forthwith, not wishing to lose his monopoly on such knowledge, he banished them from the land of eternal bliss.

In Catholic theology these events assume the dimensions of the dogma of original sin. Pope Pius XII, in his encyclical *Humani Generis* (1950), maintained that "original sin is the result of a sin committed, in actual historical fact, by an individual man named Adam, and it is a quality native to all of us, only because it has been handed down by descent from him."[16] It is a moral defect. In contemporary terms, the dogma of original sin is a way of perceiving a fall from ignorance into knowing: Adam and Eve learned their identities, recognized their erotic drives, and began their history as humans.

Through the alchemy of ideas, the Platonic, Aristotelian, and Stoic concerns with the good and the eternal became wedded to the concerns of the God of the Old Testament. Ideas about salvation history and beliefs about the destiny of individuals and humankind were then gradually added to this union. The historical assembly of ethical principles into a system of beliefs reached its fullness in the medieval synthesis of human values, divine purposes, and cosmic time. According to that theological-ethical tour de force, all the world is a stage and all the men and women are merely players in a divine comedy. The plot involves the struggle of all people against the sinful drives with which they are born. The momentum so gained was then enlisted in support of a particular family of beliefs pertaining to time and salvation history.

Central to the drama of mankind is the self-sacrifice to which Jesus of Nazareth drove himself. It was a cosmic denouement offered in redemption from the original sin, an act of love for humankind.[17] To lessen the inherited burden of the primeval guilt, compounded by the murder of the Son of God, people were to follow the words and imitate the life of Christ, summed up in the many meanings of love.

The resurrection of Christ, according to Saint Paul, reconciled eternal life with the human experience of time. To get around logical difficulties and the paucity of dead people we observe living in their eternal bodies, Christian theology generalized the mystery of the resurrection. It extended its promise to all the followers of Christ, conferring on them the potentialities of a new and permanent postmortem life elsewhere. This theology posed certain difficulties to the secular understanding of the world. Let D. H. Lawrence sum them up. He used as the vehicle for his ideas the daily lives of three generations of an English family in Derbyshire, nineteen centuries after St. Paul's spiritual and intellectual mission.

> So the children lived the year of Christianity, the epic of the soul of mankind. [Their] hearts were born and came to fullness, suffered on the cross, gave up the ghost, and rose again to unnumbered days, untired, having at least this rhythm of eternity in a ragged, inconsequential life. . . .
>
> What was the hope and the fulfillment? . . . [Was it] all only a useless after-death, a wan, bodiless after-death? . . . For from the grave the body rose torn and chill and colourless. . . . Alas, for the Ascension into heaven, which is a shadow within death, a complete passing away. . . . Alas, that the memory of the passion of Sorrow and Death and the Grave holds triumph over the pale fact of Resurrection!
>
> But why? Why shall I not rise with my body whole and perfect, shining with strong life? . . . The Resurrection is to life, not to death. Shall I not see those who have risen again walk here among men . . . whole and glad in the flesh, living in the flesh, loving in the flesh, begetting children in the flesh, arrived at last to wholeness . . . ?
>
> Is the flesh which was crucified become as poison to the crowds in the street, or is it as a strong gladness and hope to them, as the first flower blossoming out of the earth's humus?[18]

Humankind's dream in overcoming death is the desire to regain life lost in death, but without its problems. True resurrection would be one into a world of passing but untroubled life. The heritage of the West from the much-troubled lands of the eastern Mediterranean is the idea of resurrection from organic, noetic, and social temporalities into a world of eternal death. The hallmark of this heritage is the other-worldliness of human values broadly maintained until the Reformation and the Renaissance.

Westward Ho!

In an imaginary Danish castle, a young prince of a secular land, just back from studying philosophy in Wittenberg, was unhappy. "Denmark is a prison," he said. "We think not so," responded a courtier. "Why, then, 'tis none to you; for there is nothing either good or bad but thinking makes it so; to me it is a prison." Though the story of Hamlet comes from tenth-century Iceland, the opinion of Shakespeare's prince is more like that of Shakespeare's contemporary, the philosopher Thomas Hobbes (1588–1679). Hobbes saw life as a manifestation of matter in motion that follows the laws of nature. The first such law is that every man strives for peace; if peace cannot be had, he may then resort to war. Hobbes maintained that there is no "natural law," no uniform and shared ability of all humans to recognize a distinction between good and evil. Nature is oblivious to human needs; rules of preferred conduct are derived by human reasoning and serve the purposes of human life.

For Spinoza, born sixteen years after Shakespeare's death, good and evil referred to pleasure and pain. He maintained that these ideas arise from and are defined by psychological needs, especially our needs to secure continuity of personal identity. He introduced the idea of conatus, meaning by it a drive toward self-preservation, a type of inertia; good and evil may then be distinguished by being helpful for, or opposing, the needs of conatus.

Immanuel Kant (1724–1804) saw moral laws as categorical imperatives: unconditional, absolute for one and all, and independent of personal motives. But he identified only one such law: "Act only according to that maxim by which you can at the same time will that it should become a universal law."[19] Whereas Spinoza began with the needs of the individual, which he saw multiplied in society, Kant made society the prime arbiter of what is to be morally right.

Jeremy Bentham, twenty-five years younger than Kant, saw good in whatever gives the greatest happiness to the greatest number of people and began his treatise on morals and legislation (1823) as follows: "Nature has placed mankind under the governance of two sovereign masters, pain and pleasure. It is for them alone to point out what we ought to do, as well as to determine what we shall do. On the one hand the standard of right and wrong, on the other hand the chain of causes and effects, are fastened to their throne."[20] Stressing kinship among pleasure, happiness, and the common good is a hallmark of Enlightenment beliefs, such as was expressed by Jefferson in the Declaration of Independence: "We hold these truths to be self-evident that all men are created equal, that they are endowed by their creator with certain unalienable rights, that among them are life, liberty, and the pursuit of Happiness."

Bentham's intellectual heir, John Stuart Mill (1806–73), refined the unstructured category of pleasure in what he described as a utilitarian calculus and suggested that good and evil are measures of pleasure and pain. The next step along this path, as seen ex post facto, was the ethics of deism, which was embraced by leading intellects of the time: in early America, by Washington, Jefferson, and Thomas Paine; on the European continent, by Voltaire, Rousseau, and Kant. Their particular form of deism involved the assertion that the individual has the right to think for himself on all subjects, including good and evil. These ideas are parts of a natural religion that rejects revealed truths or at least does not uncritically accept them. They became hallmarks of the American intellect and remained recognizable until the fragmentation of human values on the time-compact globe.

The Good as Seen by Our Neighbors

During the long prehistory of China—from half a million years ago to the second millennium B.C.—people there did what their European counterparts did: they denied the finality of death. There is much resemblance between extant objects from Stone Age China and those of Europe. During the transition from the Shang dynasty (the most ancient house) and the Chou dynasty, the East Asian lands changed from a tribal to a feudal society, from the Bronze Age to the Iron Age, with its new tools, art, and values. It was at this formative age, between the early eighteenth and late twelfth centuries B.C., that the Chinese preference for humanism over metaphysical speculation seems to have been born.

Between the sixth and third centuries B.C., around the time of the Greek city-states, an epoch in Chinese history known as the age of the Hundred Schools, arose the two great philosophical-religious systems that came to constitute the foundations of Chinese national character: Confucianism and Taoism. Confucianism has been described as the doctrine of worldly social-mindedness; Taoism, as the spiritual search for order in nature. Confucianism is concerned with society and social responsibility; Taoism, with what is inborn, natural to man.

Tao means "the way" in the same sense in which Jesus used the latter term when talking to his disciples: "I am the way, the truth, and the life." Following the Christian way, the cultural and ethnic ambience of the Mediterranean and European world began to build a tightly organized, rigid body of tradition of the good and the right. In contrast, the people on the vast lands of East Asia formulated the Tao as admitting a wealth of human experiences and an ability to change with the ages. Joseph Needham remarked that the "Europeans suffered from a schizophrenia of the soul, oscillating forever unhappily between the heavenly host on the one side and the 'atoms and the void' on the other; while the Chinese, wise before their time, worked out an organic theory of the universe which included nature and man, church and state, and all things past, present, and to come."[21]

Taoism seeks to identify a code of conduct that unites nature and humankind in harmony. The universe is seen as a hierarchically organized system in which every part reproduces the whole, resembling Leibniz's monads and the self-similarity at infinite depths of the fractals of chaos theory. Since man is assumed to be a microcosmos, the human body is seen as reproducing the plan of the universe. Tao, as a force, is seen as continuously shaping the universe from primordial chaos, employing the dynamics of yin and yang, the feminine and masculine principles. These are seen as complementary forms of energies that hold the world together in an unchanging unity, the permanent Tao. It is this structural-dynamic understanding that makes Taoist ritual not an oblation but a systematic, classificatory study of the world in a manner that Sinologists sometimes describe as a science.[22] The Taoist attitude toward life is that of accepting and yielding, of being carefree and joyful; the Tao recognizes a kinship between water and the feminine and advocates a conduct that corresponds to this association: "The highest good is that of water. The goodness of water is that it benefits the ten thousand [i.e., a very large number] creatures, yet itself does not wrangle, but is content with the places that all men disdain. It is this that makes water so near the Tao." Being adaptable is not to be mistaken for being powerless, because "what is of all things most yielding / Can overwhelm that which is most hard."[23] The summum bonum, the highest good from which all other values derive, is a long life during which a careful conformation to the Tao as a way of life succeeds in promoting what is universal in Tao: the eternal dialectic of yin and yang.

For Confucius (551–479 B.C.) ideal virtues were those of the Perfect Sage: benevolence, righteousness, propriety, and filial piety.[24] His ethical theories, set forth by his disciples in the *Analects*, maintain that morality has no supernatural sanction: virtuous conduct constitutes its own reward. Unlike Taoism, with its commitment to the feminine, Confucian morality teaches that women's place is an inferior one. Women must serve their husbands' parents and their husbands. Confucianism has been synonymous with learning (by males): its tenets have been followed for two millennia; its key concept of *jen* has been alternately translated as "human-heartedness" or "love." The ideal for the individual is *chün-tzu*, "superior man," reminding one of Nietzsche's *Übermensch*, one who succeeds in subordinating his passions to his higher goals and, through that act, becomes an extraordinarily creative member of society. Compared with Taoist morality, Confucian teachings on right and wrong are aristocratic.

The foundations of Hinduism were laid in northern India during 800–300 B.C. They comprise a variety of beliefs and practices followed by the peoples of India, parts of Pakistan, Sri Lanka, and Bangladesh. Hinduism does not demand exclusive allegiance, but there are three beliefs that all the 700 million Hindus tend to share. One is that of inborn duty, virtue, or destiny, called dharma. Another one is that of karma, a cosmic law of credits and debits for good and evil acts that add up, at the end of a life, to a net worth that determines the destiny of the soul in its next incarnation. The third is a belief in moksha, a release from the cyclic reincarnation of the soul through yielding one's individuality to Brahman, the cosmic self. Time, while real enough for daily chores, is unimportant in the Hindu economy of the universe.[25]

The quintessence of Hindu doctrines is an insistence that all the pain and suffering of life derives from beliefs in the reality of the self and of the world. Furthermore, since the self is reincarnated after death, this miserable, dreary process, unless broken, will go on and on.[26] There is thus a need to negate selfhood, to get out of this prison by a radical break in the transmigration of souls, an escape from the impermanence of life into eternal principles of Brahma. To reach that salvation and its eternal peace, man must detach himself from worldly objects and vanish into the oblivion of an ecstatic union with the divine lord.

Buddhism is a pan-Asian religion and philosophy and, again, a way of life. It arose in northern India during the sixth century B.C. in response to many elements within Hinduism. Siddhartha Gautama, the Buddha, the Enlightened, taught that the characteristic condition of humanity is that of suffering, unease, and illness, caused by the basic evil of desire. Suffering can be lessened only by forsaking desires, by following the Noble Eightfold Path—precepts of conduct—that, after many transmigrations of the soul, may lead it to the timeless state of nirvana.

4.2   A Working Definition of the Good

What, if anything, is common to the many ideas encountered in the preceding section? Since a consensus is not offered, it is necessary to construct one. The following working definition is not inconsistent with most of the visions, instructions, and promises surveyed.

Good as a human value is an assertion that a certain conduct, intent, or character trait will promote stable balance and harmony in the mind and affairs of a person and in the dynamics of society here on earth or elsewhere in a postmortem world.

I now turn to survey human conduct to which those instructions have been addressed.

4.3   A Natural History of Morals

This section starts by identifying the evolutionary position of human freedom with respect to the qualitatively different, limited freedoms available
to other forms of life. It then asks how people have conducted themselves
in matters that require moral judgments. This exercise prepares a test for
the validity of the proposed definition of the good.

Cellular Slime Molds and the Nuclear Family

By the logic of evolutionary continuity, the rules of behavior favored in early
human groups had to be continuations of behavioral patterns that had been
selected for earlier. Out of those patterns arose the organizing principles
of moral conduct. Their stability was maintained through rituals and whatever other means were available to help conserve tradition and continuity
in families, tribes, and alliances. But collective action among living organisms is rather older than are human groups. How far back should one look?

I choose to go back 1.6 billion years because it was then that cellular slime
molds, those curious social creatures, first appeared. Their life cycle divides
into a free-living and a colonial stage. In the free-living stage, members of
this species are amoebas that feed on bacteria and reproduce by dividing.
At a point in their life cycle, however, they begin to congregate, climb on
each other, and form a mound; they integrate themselves into a living unit
and move as a unit. In the next phase some of the cells form a stalk and
die. Other amoebas climb up along the stalk consisting of their dead fellows and become spores. They grow into new amoebas, and the life cycle
starts again. The swarming of the free-living cells is initiated by any chance
aggregate of individuals that crosses a certain threshold of population density; the group then begins to serve as the kernel for the colonial, or social,
stage. The kernel produces a chemotactic substance that diffuses across the
region of still free-floating amoebas and induces them to follow the chemical concentration gradient upward to its source.

Temples and cities have been playing analogous roles in the movement of
people. Writing about the symbolism of the center as a cosmic archetype, Eliade noted that every temple or palace, every sacred city or royal residence,
has been thought of as a sacred mountain. Serving as an axis of the world, it
was regarded as the spiritual navel of the universe, the earthly terminal of the
umbilical chord that joins heaven and earth.[27] It was to such a center that "Joseph also went up from Galilee . . . to the city of David, which is called Bethle-
hem, because he was of the house and lineage of David, to be enrolled [count-
ed for a census] with Mary, his betrothed, who was with child" (Luke 2:4–5).

It is not accidental that, on the level of observable behavior, identical figures of speech may be used to describe the community's power over the individual: "following the chemical gradient up to its source" and "following the government's order to go up to the mount." The actions are isomorphic. What for the mold is chemotaxis (control by chemical means) is moral conduct for humans. The qualitative difference between the motion of responding amoebas and responding people resides in their immensely different degrees of freedom. (Compare the measures of their complexities represented by the numerals 10^{40}–10^{50} and $10^{10,000}$ in the calculus of appendix B, "Complexity and Its Measure). The cells have no alternative behavior available to them: they must and do respond to the stimuli. Joseph and Mary could have refused to go to Jerusalem, but they did not; they went because they judged it to have been the right thing to do.

Darwinism, Neo-Darwinism, and Beyond

The possibility that the moral sense of right and wrong is the product of natural selection was discussed extensively by Darwin in *The Descent of Man* (1871),[28] where he wrote that any animal endowed with social instinct—the skill and need to act together with others—would inevitably acquire "a moral sense of conscience" as its intellectual powers approached those of humans. He suggested four necessary developmental steps to the possession of a moral sense. First, the social instinct leads the animal to taking pleasure in the company of its fellows. Second, time enters, for

> as soon as the mental faculties had become highly developed, images of all past actions and motives would be incessantly passing through the brain of each individual: and that feeling of dissatisfaction, or even misery, which invariably results . . . from any unsatisfied instinct, would arise, as often as it was perceived that the enduring and always present social instinct had yielded to some other instinct, at the time stronger, but neither enduring in its nature, nor leaving behind it a very vivid impression.

Darwin did not quote Shakespeare's sonnet 129, but he could have.

> The expense of spirit in a waste of shame
> Is lust in action. . . .
> Enjoy'd no sooner but despised straight;
> Past reason hunted; and no sooner had,
> Past reason hated as a swallowed bait. . . .

Third, Darwin continued, after the species acquired language, these feelings could be shared. And last, through habit and sharing, they could become the wishes and judgments of the community. Conscience, so acquired, looks backward in time and serves as a guide to the future.[29]

"There can be hardly any doubt," Darwin remarked, that if humans were raised as hive bees, "our unmarried females, like worker bees, [would] think it their sacred duty to kill their brothers, and mothers would strive to kill their fertile daughters; and no one would think of interfering."[30] Although man is not a hive bee, his actions are still judged right and wrong as they affect the welfare of the community.[31] Darwin summed up his views by remarking that man's moral constitution, with the aid of active intellectual powers, leads to the golden rule: "As ye would that men should do to you, do ye to them likewise."[32] His biblical-Confucian-Kantian conclusion, reached through an unbiblical appeal to our nonhuman ancestry, entered the great nineteenth-century debates about the origin of morality.

For Darwin time did not merit special attention in the structure of consciousness. In contrast, Thomas Henry Huxley, a younger contemporary of Darwin, expanded the Darwinian view of morality into a philosophy of morals in which time is central. Ethics, he maintained, can be defined only in reference and in opposition to the restlessness of the cosmos, which he saw, in a Heraclitian way, as a process unfolding in time. At each instant, he wrote in *Evolution and Ethics* (1894), the state of the cosmos is the "expression of transitory adjustment of contending forces; a scene of strife, in which all the combatants fall in turn."[33] Rest is only unperceived activity; the seeming peace of rest is but silent and strenuous battle. The most obvious attribute of the cosmos is its impermanence. Life itself "is far from possessing the attribute of permanence. Rather its very essence is impermanence. . . . That which endures is not one or another association of living forms, but the process of which the cosmos is the product. . . . [In] the living world, one of the most characteristic features of this cosmic process is the struggle for existence."[34] He saw this struggle as being between the cultural and what he called the cosmic processes. Ethics comprises the rules of human conduct in the service of the cultural process and in conflict with the cosmic process. The result is pain and suffering, manifest in their highest forms not in man as a savage or half-savage "but only in man, the member of an organized polity."[35] Morality consists neither in imitating the cosmic process nor in running away from it but in combating it through the creation of permanence and continuity, in opposing the organically evolved conflict through the order of the humanly created artificial. For thousands of years, Huxley continued, people have asked whether there is "a sanction for morality in the ways of the cosmos."[36] To answer this question, he wrote, people have to appeal to their knowledge of "the old and new worlds of the past and the future, wherein men dwell the more the higher the culture."[37] Brought "before the tribunal of ethics" the cosmos stands condemned; man revolts against "the moral indifference of nature, and the microscopic atom [humans] finds the illimitable macrocosm guilty."[38] In the opinion of this brilliant and dedicated Darwinian, morality, from the point of view of Darwinism, is a permanent conflict.

The principle of natural selection as formulated by Darwin identifies the method whereby nature provides for the coming about of unpredictably new forms and functions of life. But Darwin did not—for he could not at that time—identify the sources of variations among individuals on which natural selection could work. That had to await advances in the science of genetics. Darwinism extended to embrace genetics is called neo-Darwinism.

In Darwinism fitness is an index of the success of adaptation, gauged by the number of offspring contributed to the next generation compared to the number of offspring required to maintain a particular population constant in size. In neo-Darwinism fitness remains an index of the success of adaptation, but its measure becomes refined: it is the increase of those genotypes that enhance the chances of survival compared to corresponding increases among competing genotypes. This reasoning will remind the reader of the idea of biological values considered in sec. 1.2. The recognition of the genetic complement of animals as the true target of natural selection confirmed what Darwin already suspected, namely, that natural selection operates on the level of populations, although he had no way of knowing how this is accomplished.

A current view would appeal to inclusive or kin selection, thus incorporating collectively controlled behavioral rules. It would note that genetic predisposition for behavior is shared by the individual with its kith and kin according to degrees of relationships: the genes of an individual occur in its offspring as well as in its siblings and, with decreasing frequency, in offspring of siblings, cousins, and offspring of cousins. Appropriately, the neo-Darwinian mechanism of organic evolution is described as that of inclusive or kin selection. Self-interest, in the biological domain, may thus be seen to be extended to the interest of all genetically related individuals, weighted according to their genetic market shares. In its broadest term, kin selection favors the life process itself, never mind whose life.

The science that most fully studied the natural history of morality as emerging from biology is sociobiology. Although the term was coined in the nineteenth century, Edward O. Wilson was the first to create a unified discipline bearing that name, which he outlined in his *Sociobiology: The New Synthesis*.[39] His work integrated population biology (the quantitative handling of qualitative features of social organizations), ethology (the study of animal behavior in natural environments), and genetics into a biological study of social behavior. If carried out with safeguards against losing sight of the nested hierarchical organization of persons, such a program has the potential to identify the biological roots of human behavior.[40]

Evolutionary biology's efforts to trace the origins and evolution of ethics begins with a model of ideal societies defined as those that lack conflict and possess the highest degree of altruism and coordination.[41] *Altruism* refers to those actions of an organism that help another to survive but have no obvious benefit to the actor; on the contrary, it might involve danger and lead to its death.[42] In its most refined version, called reciprocal altruism, defined as the trading of altruistic acts by individuals at different times, it demands the presences of individual expectations and memories. In this view of things colonial invertebrates are the most perfect societies because the behavior of their individual members, called zooids, is completely subordinated to the common good. Next on the scale of perfection are insect societies: they function with "impersonal intimacy." Members recognize castes but not different individuals within castes; unavoidably, the relative independence of the castes brings about a degree of discord, not present in colonial invertebrates. Aggressiveness and discord are carried much further in vertebrate societies, where group membership is advantageous but not mandatory and altruism is infrequent. When altruism does occur in such societies, it is usually directed to kin, especially to offspring. Finally, humans break "the old vertebrate restraints not by reducing selfishness, but rather by acquiring the intelligence to consult the past and plan for the future."[43] In this view the evolution of social development is one of degeneration: the harmony of colonial invertebrate societies is shattered by increasingly intense conflicts.

Wilson maintained that human societies approach insect societies in cooperativeness and exceed them in their power of communication. This reverses the "downward trend . . . that prevailed over one billion years"—namely, the competition among members of a society arising from the division of labor. To establish on the human level an ideal society—which Wilson identifies with the society of colonial invertebrates—will be possible only if and when "absolute genetic identity makes possible the evolution of altruism."[44]

Reading this assertion, one may share the consternation of Niki Jumpei, Kobo Abe's protagonist in *The Woman in the Dunes*. A woman lures a young entomologist into a house at the bottom of a sand trap, where she keeps him to help her supply sand for a village industry and to impregnate her. The plot, the characters, and the horrors of the setting are real as well as allegorical. At one point the entomologist wonders, "Was it permissible to snare, exactly like a mouse or an insect, a man who had his certificate of medical insurance, someone who has paid taxes, who was employed and whose family records were in order?"[45]

Let us reflect on the evolutionary path of altruism without an entomological bias. The postulate that absolute genetic identity makes possible the evolution of ideal altruism reminds one of a hallmark of prototemporal umwelts: the indistinguishability of its constituent members. For instance, all electrons are absolutely identical, and for that reason, any one of them rather than another may be "sacrificed" when the atom changes into an ion. They would be the most altruistic creatures if they had selves to give up. But they have no selves, and neither do the zooids of colonial invertebrate societies: their identities are definable only in terms of their positions in the colony. As with the cellular slime mold in its colonial stage, the right conduct consists in doing whatever their society needs, and they always do it because they have no choice.

Since such dutiful behavior in animals often has definite collective value for the species, one might maintain that altruistic behavior in animals (and in our own animal ancestors) is the evolutionary ancestor of the moral stance in man. Its ancestor, yes; the source of moral values, no. To identify those sources one must go beyond the organic and enter the noetic and social worlds.

From Altruism to Compassion

The term altruism, from the Latin *alter,* "other," was coined by August Comte, the nineteenth-century founder of positivism, to stand for the opposite of self-centeredness. If altruism is understood as it is in sociobiology, then the most altruistic creatures, as already mentioned, are colonial invertebrates. But their genetic identity makes it impossible for zooids to have selves to be sacrificed, in the sense in which "sacrifice" is used in ethics. Cellular slime molds in their amoebic form do not commit suicide when they change into a cell in a stalk. The cells in the tail of a tadpole, when it changes to a toad, kill themselves but do not commit self-slaughter; they have no selves to be slaughtered. For many mammalian cells, survival depends on the receipt of continuous signals from their environment amounting to the instruction "do not kill yourself."[46] A dog may fight to its death to protect its master, but only the human mind can create and maintain the symbolic construct called identity; only humans can walk up to the guillotine and say, or think that they should say, "It is a far, far better thing that I do, than I have ever done." Although it is the inclusive fitness altruism of our prehuman ancestors from which moral judgment emerged, and although moral conduct may involve acts of life protecting life, morality in its peculiar manifestations pertains to symbolic existents and causes. Biologically based arguments about the origins of ethics may well give good partial answers to the question of why a man protects his children or his wife, but they can give no credible answer to why someone should and would try to spread the teachings of an ideology by killing those who think differently about the size of the universe, or why people build homes for invisible, intangible, inaudible beings.

To accommodate the powerful yet incomplete idea of altruism as used in population biology, I propose to distinguish between altruism and compassion. Altruism pertains to the life process of a species, whether that of man or beast. Compassion pertains to human life in its spiritual, mental, and cultural dimensions.

The Compassionate Pilgrim: A Brief Practicum

This subsection samples areas of moral issues in the life of the altruistic *and* compassionate pilgrim, alias the strange walker. They arise in connection with the pilgrim's desire to perpetuate his or her biological and symbolic identities, in both their individual and their collective dimensions. The issues are anything but simple.

Hunger and Thirst Hunger and thirst are fundamental needs; the desires to satisfy them are fundamental drives. They are also the most universal metaphors for desire: one hungers for food and for love, and one thirsts for bliss and for knowledge. Hunger, thirst, and their gratification are the first experiences of the infant at its mother's breast and the first forms of its communication with the rest of the world. Activities necessary to obtain food and drink are communal; hunting and gathering no less than eating and drinking are ritualized in many species, and much of the evolution of human anatomy, physiology, and behavior has been shaped by the need to procure and process food.

Bread, the oldest man-made staple, first appeared in Neolithic times, perhaps 12,000 years ago. Here are some contemporary words about it, heard in Scotland.

> Be gentle when you touch bread
> Let it not lie uncared for, unwanted—
> Too often it is taken for granted.
> There is much beauty in bread.

Chickadees prefer fermented berries, which make them slightly tipsy. Among humans, wine making is 7,000 years old; the Code of Hammurabi, circa 1770 B.C., already contains regulations on drinking houses. Wine is the drink of gods, the blood of God, a detestable cause of evil behavior, and the firewater of political chicanery. Dietary laws and food customs contain behavioral elements not found in other species because their purposes include securing benefits for the distant future, reminding people of the distant past, and nurturing symbolic continuities. Although no dietary customs or instructions for conduct are universal, there is no human group, literate or preliterate, where the taking of bread and wine is not governed by prescriptions and proscriptions.

Customs and instructions about food also help to distinguish a social group from the rest of its cohort and strengthen its shared moral judgments, because they order people's perception of reality by separating the timeless and sacred from the temporal and profane. Specifications concerning the preparation of food and the timing and conditions of related rituals vary greatly. A substantial portion of the world's 700 million Hindus, 560 million Muslims, and 17 million Jews follow dietary laws. Others follow other rules either by tradition, by necessity, or by scientific or pseudoscientific reasoning.

In addition to bonding community members, food and drink often serve to join the group to the gods on whom its well-being is believed to depend. Accordingly, bread, water, and wine have been elements of ritual sacrifices offered to secure the favor of divinities or minimize their hostility. Libation of water or wine and the offering of meals play a prominent role in religious rituals, although the most important sacrifice has been that of the blood of animals or people. In the words of Leviticus, an instruction book on priestly duties, "the life of every creature is in the blood of it."[47] In the Zoroastrian rites of ancient Persia, haoma, an equivalent to the Hindu soma, was a sacred drink believed to bestow health, fertility, and eternal life. It was the name of a plant that had to be pounded and squeezed to extract its potent juice. Haoma, inter alia, was also personified in the son of Ahura Mazda (Wise Lord and Creator), incarnate in the sacred plant. There are obvious similarities between the haoma ritual and the Christian communion. Both use a drink as a sacrament. One is the juice of a plant that is also a god and that must be destroyed to yield its life-giving liquid; the other is the blood of a god who must be killed so that the drinking of his blood may help people to eternal life. Combining food and drink, flesh and blood, the divine and the human, time and eternity, the sacrament of bread and wine remained the central, stable element of Christian liturgy as the Eucharist, the Lord's Supper, or Holy Communion.

While communion unites Christian churches, the forms of taking communion separate the Orthodox, Protestant, and Catholic churches. Part of the theological struggle during the Reformation focused on the issue of transubstantiation, the doctrine that the substance of the bread and wine is changed into the body and blood of Christ during the consecration part of the Mass. In the mid-twentieth century there have been sustained efforts by theologians to restate the dogma of transubstantiation and see in the consecration a change in meaning, a transsignification.

Food-related rituals are conservative forces, seldom questioned; to those in any particular culture they tend to appear as unproblematic practices. The Roman conquerors of ancient Britain ate dormice fattened in an earthenware vessel called a *glirarium*. It was named after *glis*, the Latin name of the creature. Once cooked, the rodents were dipped in honey.[48] Innuit women have eaten duck wings to help their children become good runners, whereas the busy men and women at the end of the millennium select their food by their presumed usefulness in maintaining health, beauty, agility, sound sleep, or sexual prowess. To know where to stop disagreeing about dietary rules is not easy, as was learned the hard way in the terrible war between Lilliput and Blefuscu over whether the egg ought to be broken on its larger or smaller end.

In humans hunger and thirst do start with the craving for food and drink, but once satisfied, they go much beyond it: attitudes toward food tend to shape attitudes toward all forms of wealth and the sharing of it. Mosleh Oddin Sa'di, a thirteenth-century Persian poet, summed it up well.

If of thy mortal goods thou art bereft
And from thy slender store two loaves alone to thee are left,
Sell one, and with the dole
Buy hyacinths to feed the soul.[49]

Reproduction Having taken milk from *alma mater*, the nourishing mother, and having consumed bread and wine during adolescence, people become ready to beget their own children. The mode of their involvement with members of the opposite sex and the handling of their related emotions is the subject of moral teachings about sexual conduct. As we learned in sec. 1.1, death by aging and sexual reproduction emerged together: the gametes took over the task of carrying the know-how about maintaining the organic present, and the collection of somatic cells took over the husbanding of the gametes. A consequence of this evolutionary rite of passage was the privilege of being able to have children who, in substantial ways, are different from all other children. The bill paid for this privilege is rendered by the mind's knowledge of time: an awareness of death by aging and of the social consequences of mating choice.

Emotional maturity in humans includes the realization that every person begins his death sentence in the moment he starts his life sentence. Those interested in altruism and compassion will note that sex plays a double role in this drama. It is the savior that secures continuity, while as a biological agency, its existence is a corollary of death by aging.

I already quoted Plato on the origin of sexual reproduction: the slicing of the original four-legged creature into two halves and, thereafter, the ceaseless search of those halves for each other. Beneath these goings on, he continued, all souls

> are longing for a something else—a something to which they can neither of them put a name, and which they can only give an inkling of in cryptic sayings and prophetic riddles. . . . And so all this to-do is a relic of that original state of ours, when we were whole, and now, when we are longing for and following after that primeval wholeness, we say we are in love. For there was a time . . . when we were one, but now, for our sins, God has scattered us abroad. . . . Moreover. . . there is every reason to fear that, if we neglect the worship of the gods, they will split us up again, and then we shall have to go about with our noses sawed asunder, part and counterpart like the basso-relievos on the tombstones. And therefore it is our duty one and all to inspire our friends with reverence . . . so we may ensure our safety and attain that blessed union by enlisting in the army of Love and marching beneath his banners.[50]

The topology of the slicing operation has its problems, but the contents of the message is profound and beautiful. I also mentioned Saint Paul's severe version of life, sex, death, and time.

Neo-Darwinian teachings about sexual mores appeal to the notion of reproductive success. A woman's genes are represented only, but surely, in all offspring she herself produces, whereas those of the males reappear in the progeny of each female they inseminate, though always with a degree of uncertainty.[51] In the human female pregnancy requires a biological and social investment of some length; in the human male the biological investment is a fleeting instant, and the social investment is much more variable than in the female. "Sigh no more ladies, sigh no more, / Men were deceivers ever; / One foot in sea, and one on shore, / To one thing constant never." To promote their genes, females do well by attending to their young; males, by attending to their females. This recognition of the crude facts of sexual reproduction is in agreement with received stereotypes: women, looking for men, seek permanence and the whole; men, looking for women, easily settle for the transient and the part. Moral judgments include intricate elaborations of these stereotypes: no one fits either of them exactly, and everybody fits both of them somewhat.

Understandably there is a temptation to reduce the torrent of dos and don'ts and maybes to simple instructions. But how is that to be done in an ever-complexifying society? One way is to reduce morality and equate it with its biological roots. Reflecting on the relationship between the biological roots of behavior and society, Wilson remarked that "to the extent that the specific details of culture are nongenetic, they can be arrayed beside it [beside the genetic components] as an auxiliary system."[52] As a consequence, "Scientists and humanists should consider together the possibility that the time has come for ethics to be removed temporarily from the hands of philosophers and biologicized."[53] This assertion was somewhat softened in the author's later writings, but it never lost its aspects of an invitation to one's own beheading. It is epistemologically equivalent to a proposal that biology should be temporarily removed from the hands of biologists and physicalized. Because of the nested hierarchical organization of nature and its languages, both propositions must be rejected: psychology cannot be biologized any more than biology can be physicalized. There is no escape into simplification. Moral tenets remain specific to the noetic and sociotemporal worlds, although not independent of the lower integrative levels.

Instead of trying to understand human sexual conduct by referring it totally or almost totally to biology, I prefer to turn to gifted observers of humans as whole beings. Concise observations come from literature, such as from this early twentieth-century naturalistic view by D. H. Lawrence expressed in the poem "Tortoise Shout."

> I thought he was dumb,
> I said he was dumb,
> Yet I've heard him cry . . .
> Tortoise in extremis.
>
> Why were we crucified into sex?
> Why were we not left rounded off, and finished in ourselves,
> As we began,
> As he certainly began, so perfectly alone?
>
> The cross,
> The wheel on which our silence first is broken,
> Sex, which breaks up our integrity, our single inviolability,
> our deep silence,
> Tearing a cry from us.[54]

The shout Lawrence heard has given no indication of subsiding.

Here is an earlier, nineteenth-century report about five women and a man from Goethe's dramatic poem *Faust*. The name of the first woman is Gretchen. She killed her illegitimate infant and was condemned to death by a court (of males). The second woman is Mary of Egypt, an Alexandrian prostitute who, after seventeen years in that occupation, left Alexandria on a pilgrimage to Jerusalem. In the desert she wore no clothing; she was covered only by her long hair. The third is a Samarian woman, a sinner of sensuality. The fourth woman had five husbands, but the man she was last living with was not one of them. The magistral last scene of the drama is set in heaven. The three women welcome Gretchen to the presence of a fifth woman who, while she was on earth, became pregnant before she was wedded. The reason for the welcome is given earlier in the drama: if you strive relentlessly for the good, you may be saved from the decay of death.

The male hero, who sold his soul to the devil for the privilege of Gretchen's love, pursued his own path to salvation: he carried out a vast engineering project. After he dies and his immortal part is carried to heaven, Mephistopheles is left alone, complaining about a violation of his rights and looking for a lawyer.[55]

The women met their challenges not through abstract purity but through their involvement, each in her own way, with the conflicts of human sexual reproduction. All this leaves Gretchen and the other women, rather than Faust, as the true protagonists of the drama. Appropriately, the poem ends with the line "The eternal feminine raises us forever upward."

The angelic choirs of Faust would have agreed with the Chinese *Tao-te Ching*, "Classic of the Way and Its Virtue," written between the eighth and third centuries B.C.

> The Valley Spirit never dies,
> It is named the Mysterious Feminine.
> And the doorway to the Mysterious Feminine
> Is the root (from which) Heaven and Earth (sprang).
> It is the thread for ever woven,
> And those who use it can accomplish all things.[56]

Poets often sum up for learned heads and for each other. Yeats did it for Plato, Saint Paul, Goethe, and Freud.

> A woman can be proud and stiff
> When on love intent;
> But Love has pitched its mansion in
> The place of excrement;
> For nothing can be sole or whole
> That has not been rent.[57]

This is a beautiful endorsement of the theory of time as conflict.

The Visiting Waif If food has been regularly taken and sexual acts performed, children are often born. This subsection is a thumbnail sketch of the human care of human children.

Not all species care for their young, but all give them a head start. Turtles lay their eggs in the sand and let the sun do the hatching, after which the hatchlings scurry to the water. Mother cats nurse and care for their kittens, but they also recognize the sickly and the runt, which they separate from their litter and stop feeding. They act like the Spartans, who had all infants judged defective thrown from a cliff of Mount Taygetus, to die on the jagged rocks below.

In advanced animal societies individuals other than the parents routinely assist in the care of offspring; the practice, called alloparenting, promotes the socialization of the young. It is an expression of inclusive fitness altruism: an individual helps to promote its own genetic endowment by helping certain others. In humans alloparenting is carried out with the imaginative powers and needs of the mind and the complex demands of civilizations added. Mother love, originally a gender-related emotion and conduct, also expands to a broadly based fondness and caring for children.

Demographic data on the nurture and social status of children in prehistoric times is limited to scattered evidence of buried Upper Paleolithic children, a practice that suggests parental affection or else the social importance of those children.[58] The first creation account of the Book of Genesis, written during the tenth century B.C., defines the destiny of humankind as that of multiplying and filling the earth; childlessness was seen as a curse—although, we are told, one should not rejoice in unworthy children.[59] Plato maintained that a man should marry before he is thirty-five years old or else be penalized, because begetting children is "partaking in immortality through procreation," making the human race "time's equal twin and companion."[60]

Until the rise of industrial civilizations, even prosperous years were only precarious balances between elementary needs on the one hand and uncertain food supplies and natural disasters on the other. The reasons for having or not having children have themselves been precarious. The Petri papyrus of ancient Egypt (written around 1850 B.C.) and the Ebers papyrus (ca. 1550 B.C.) describe means to avert pregnancy and bring about abortion, though widespread availability of contraception did not begin until the twentieth century.[61] The sin of Onan, for which he was slain by Yahweh, was not what since the eighteenth century has been called "onanism" (masturbation) but the act of spilling his seed on the ground instead of using it to impregnate his brother's widow and thus beget a son to carry on his name.

Begetting more offspring than can survive has been a policy of organic evolution by natural selection; humans, left to their biological devices, are no exceptions. The elemental power of sexual desire, rooted in the life process and in selfhood, has been continuously producing more children than societies were ready and able to feed, house, educate, and employ. The question arose in all ages: what is to be done with unwanted children?

Induced abortions, as just said, were known to the ancient Egyptians and have been practiced ever since. Infanticide is at least that old and is still being practiced.[62] And there is abandonment, a custom faithfully reported about a certain baby Moses, who was set afloat on the Nile in a reed basket daubed with pitch when he was three months old. The medieval ages, writes Barbara Tuchman, had very little interest in children. Emotion in relation to them seldom appears in that time's art or literature or in documentary evidence. Women appear as "flirts, bawds and deceiving wives in popular tales, saints and martyrs in the drama, unattainable objects of passionate and illicit love in the romance," but very seldom as mothers.[63] Medieval illustrations show people in almost every human activity, but rarely with children. "Owing to the high infant mortality of the times, estimated at one or two in three, the investment of love in a young child may have been so unrewarding that by some ruse of nature, as when overcrowded rodents in captivity will not breed, it was suppressed. Perhaps also the frequent childbearing put less value on the product. A child was born and died and another took its place." As a consequence, "On the whole, babies and young children appear to have been left to survive or die without great concern in the first five or six years. What psychological effect this may have had on character, and possibly on history, can only be conjectured. Possibly the relative emotional blankness of a medieval infancy may account for the casual attitude toward life and suffering of the medieval man."[64]

By the Middle Ages abandonment had become a social custom involving a large number of children; it was a ritual that transferred ownership and responsibility. The Latin phrase *aliena misericordia* is a legal term that describes the presumed motivation of persons who rescued abandoned children. John Boswell translates it as the title of his sobering work *The Kindness of Strangers*.[65]

Reasons for abandonment were many: poverty, disaster, unwanted gender (i.e., a daughter), an already large family, or the child's being the result of rape or an incestuous or illegitimate relationship. Abandonment was a widespread and familiar part of domestic life, a custom accepted and regulated by ecclesiastical and civil authorities. The Greek name for the practice was *ekteris,* a cognate of the Latin *expositio* (exposure) but without the connotation of necessary death. It meant the placing of the infant at a public place where it would be noticed. The word survives in the common

Italian surname Esposito. In classical Greece a name frequently given to foundlings was Eutyche, "happily found."[66]

Though Christian moralists held irresponsible sexuality to be reprehensible, the act of exposure was not in itself condemned. The theologian Clement of Alexandria, writing at the end of the second century, asked, "How many fathers, forgetting the children they abandoned, unknowingly have sexual relations with a son who is a prostitute or a daughter become a harlot?"[67] It was the danger of incest to which Clement objected, not abandonment. Children could be legally sold or rented; females were often sold into prostitution; and in ancient Rome they could become slaves or servants, although if freeborn they were not without certain rights. Oblation, an act of the same kind as offering bread and wine, was another form of abandonment. It consisted of exposing the child at the door of the church as a gift, an offering, to a monastery. Similar practices were known in Ming and early Ch'ing China, where children aged seven or eight were deposited in monasteries.[68]

Around the beginning of the thirteenth century, through a confluence of cultural and political changes, the medieval universe began to open up. From a closed and finite Aristotelian world it changed to an open and possibly infinite one. Europeans became interested in earthly goods and wanted to pass them on to their offspring; children came to be tokens of better things to come. "Primarily in times of growth and optimism, the ways of succession seem especially valuable. [Children] are what one works for, and they seem to be worth the effort," wrote Ricardo J. Quinones in his spirited work *The Renaissance Discovery of Time.*[69] The Renaissance was an age of intellectual rebirth and spectacular growth, of Dante, Petrarch, and Boccaccio, but also of plague, famine, and urban violence. As Renaissance art, unlike medieval art, became populated with happy little humans, unwanted children began to be hidden in institutions. With the social change, "the intricate, gentle complexities of the system of transfer developed in ancient and medieval Europe were transformed into a simple technique of disposal—in a hauntingly literal sense."[70] That it was intricate for its age seems certain, but I am not convinced that it was in general gentle. In any case, by the end of the fourteenth century all major European cities had foundling and foster homes. A feature of these homes or hospices was

a revolving door in a niche in the wall which allowed a parent or servant to deposit a child safely without being observed. In France it was called the *tour,* in Italy, the *ruota.* . . . In Renaissance cities the infants disappeared quietly and efficiently through [these] revolving doors of state-run foundling homes, out of sight and mind, into social oblivion or more likely, death by disease. Abandonment now became hidden from the public behind institutional walls. . . . The strangers no longer had to be kind to pick up the children: now they were paid to rescue them. But because it was their job, they remained strangers.[71]

Of the 15,000 infants accepted at the London Foundling Hospital in the first four years after its founding in 1741, fewer than 5,000 lived to reach adolescence. Of the 500,000 foundlings admitted to parish workhouses in England between 1728 and 1757, 60 percent died by the age of two.[72]

The word *waif,* from Old Norse, originally meant "something washed up by the sea but unclaimed, abandoned"; later it came to mean "a homeless child." The words of the Psalmist and the last words of Christ, according to the New Testament, were "My God, my God, why hast thou forsaken me?" The power of this cry is in its appropriateness to all people all the time. The child is the oldest and most stable part of the person, the first to be born and usually the last to perish, and it is always a waif. That these words survived and echoed in numberless complaints about the injustices of the world—Huxley's cosmos standing condemned because of its moral indifference—attests to the perpetuity of the human conditions that they represent.

Childhood is not so much a biological phase of development as it is a socially defined state of being and process; child raising has always been a preparation for abandonment to the kindness, indifference, and hostility of strangers, friends, family, and the self. Childhood's end is a readiness to recognize that the awesome freedom that does or should emerge from that abandonment and the conflicts it engenders are irreducible elements of the unresolvable conflicts of being human.

Justice and Law The idea of "justice done" stands for the end product of a process in which the powers that be—human, natural, or supernatural—have repaired the results of a disturbing deed and thus established or, presumably, reestablished lasting harmony in human affairs. Opinions about what constitutes a disturbing deed and the desired harmony differ by epoch, society, and person. These differences are so great that what a person or group judges as justice done is often held by another person or group to be a heinous crime. The idea of justice may be defined only because all people share a sense of justice, even though they fight bloody wars about what specifically constitutes it.

Laws are institutionalized regulations of conduct appropriate to different ideas of justice. Anthropologists know of no society that does not have some kind of codification of preferred behavior in matters that are essential for maintaining its identity and continuity, such as in sexual behavior and marriage, the taking of life, and the regulation of property. The earliest written legislation is that by Ur-Nammu, founder of a Sumerian dynasty; it dates to about 2100 B.C. and deals with issues of witchcraft, the flight of slaves, and responsibilities for bodily injuries. Later laws of the people of Mesopotamia (Sumer, Babylon, and Assyria), such as the Code of Hammurabi early in the second millennium B.C., concern economic matters (prices, tariffs, trade and commerce), family law (marriage and divorce), and criminal and civil law (slavery and debt). Its penal code was the law of retaliation—an eye for an eye—a principle as close to animal behavior as one can get: if you bite me, I bite you, and just to make certain that you won't bite me again, I growl.

The authors of the book of Genesis must have realized that a legal system that demands an eye for an eye and tooth for a tooth is likely to leave the land full of blind and toothless people; accordingly, they appealed to feelings of awe and compassion rather than to retribution. They formulated their laws in the context of a covenant with God and with the assumption that man is free to select between the good and the wicked. God is a lawgiver, they held, and the Ten Commandments specify the rights and wrongs.

According to the doctrine of natural law, ideas of what is right and what is wrong are universal and naturally shared by all people.[73] The idea was first formulated in the Greek city-states. The ethical principles that follow from it came to constitute a persistent legal doctrine concerning the moral basis of human law and became, in our epoch, the foundations of both humanism and Marxism. In a simultaneous historical development, roughly between the third and seventeenth centuries, the concepts of natural law common to all people and of a body of laws of nature common to all non-human things separated.[74] It was the idea of the laws of nature that made possible the formulation of modern science.

The common origins of natural law and the laws of nature are explicit in the U.S. Declaration of Independence, which speaks of "the Laws of Nature and of Nature's God" as entitling a nation to assume among the powers of the earth a separate and equal status. The Declaration also asserts that certain claims, such as that "all Men are created equal, that they are endowed by their Creator with certain unalienable Rights," are self-evident truths. The reason for claiming such self-evidence was the conviction that they represent universal, permanent, natural beliefs.

But the relationships among the laws of nature, the laws of human societies, and the laws of God—all of which are formulated by people—and their relation to the sense of justice have never been simple. Let me represent the relentless storm that has been raging on the sea of justice by two examples from literary fiction.

In the first example the sense of justice is expressed through a collectively endorsed ideology. In Arthur Koestler's *Darkness at Noon*, Rubashov, an old Bolshevik, confesses to treason he did not commit. The party wants him to so confess so that his example may be used to show what happens to traitors. In my earlier terms, he is called on to be compassionate even against the desire of his body to do its altruistic best by remaining alive. Having been sentenced to death, he is returned to his cell. "Rubashov stood by the window and tapped on the empty wall with his pince-nez. As a boy he had really meant to study astronomy, and now for forty years he had been doing something else. Why had not the Public Prosecutor asked him: 'Defendant Rubashov, what about the infinite?' He would not have been able to answer—and there, there lay the real source of his guilt. . . . Could there be a greater?"[75] He did not remember Giordano Bruno, who was burned at the stake because, among his other heresies, he maintained that the world is infinitely large whereas his judges were certain that it is not.

In the second example the collective sense of justice finds expression in the views of a jury and the proceedings of a court of law. Enid Bagnold's play *The Chalk Garden* concerns the life of a woman named Madrigal who was sentenced to death for having killed her half-sister. The sentence was changed to fifteen years in prison, however, because "there were doubts." Madrigal is now working as a nanny and a companion. She and Maitland, the butler, are polishing glasses while discussing the case of a man accused of murder. Maitland is unaware of Madrigal's past.

Maitland: —this murderer, that's lying in his cell—
Madrigal: No man is a murderer until he is tried!
Maitland: . . . when he first *sees* the Judge—
Madrigal: Why do you think only of the Judge? It's the jury they work on.
Maitland: But it seems when you read about such trials, that it must the Judge.
Madrigal (*fiercely*): Read more and you will see it's neither. (*To herself*) But fate.
Maitland: But they work, don't they, to get at the truth?
Madrigal: Truth doesn't ring true in a Court of Law.
Maitland: What rings true then?
Madrigal (*To herself, trancelike*): The likelihood. The probability. They work to make things hang together. What the prisoner listens to there is not his life. It is the shape and shadow of it. With the accidents of truth taken out of it.[76]

In an attempt to disentangle the epistemic issues implicit in these two paradigmatic narratives, I turn to a poem of Jorge Luis Borges commenting on the chain of command in the world. It is called "Chess." Each figure on a chess board, he says, acts consistently with its character by following stable rules. But the figures do not know that their "adamantine fate," their destiny, is controlled by the player who lays the battle plan. And that player, too, "is captive of caprice." "God moves the player, he in turn the piece / But what god beyond God begins the round / Of dust and time and sleep and agonies?"[77]

The poem traces an ascent toward higher organizational levels: from the inanimate chessboard to the living mover, to the mind of the mover, and to God and beyond. The ascent involves increasing degrees freedom. Whose freedom of choice prevails at the end?

Let the stories of Rubashov and Madrigal stand for the uncountably many acts of law-based justice. The only possible conclusion, then, is that jurisprudence is irreducibly an experimental art of trials and errors, that there is no final rule for justice. Following collectively maintained and always transient tenets of justice often helps to soothe social turmoil and personal passions and satisfies needs according to judgments acceptable by many. In the long run, however, the sense of justice continuously outruns the laws or even finds itself in direct opposition to them. The tension between the sense of justice and the substance and functions of laws is permanent; the intensity of that tension is a measure of the viability of a society. No society may remain viable without laws, nor may any remain viable without conflicts between peoples' sense of justice and the laws. Contrary to the notion of natural law, doing the right things by shared judgments does not come "naturally." It is the desire to revolt for the purpose of righting the wrong that does.

War as a Way of Life Next to concern with bread and wine, reproduction, aging and death, and approximate justice on earth—and intimately related to all of them—cruel conflicts have been humanity's most faithful companions. Early tribal hostilities were surely the continuations of animal competitions and combat, demanding brawn and fortitude, to which the leaven of human imagination, skills, and restlessness were added. Warfare was the next step in the historical development of organized conflict. It differed from tribal hostilities in its magnitude, duration, and unpredictability. Somewhere along this historical trajectory, the human capacities for long-term memory and planning extended the skill of tactics to the art of strategy.

Carl von Clausewitz, a Prussian general and military strategist of the early nineteenth century whose ideas on war have remained influential to our own days, had this to say: "[War] is not merely an act of policy but a true political instrument, a continuation of political intercourse, carried on with other means. . . . The political object is the goal, war is the means of reaching it, and means can never be considered in isolation from their purpose."[78] Those purposes change, but wars as the means remain. A survey of the history of warfare shows that there has never been a period of any appreciable length without cruel conflicts. The leading reference work on the world's wars, *Brassey's Battles*, lists over 7,000 battles during 3,500 years, and it does not include invasions, skirmishes, local wars, and the uncountable number of massacres.[79]

An examination of over 2,000 of the battles listed in *Brassey's Battles* reveals a yearly cycle in the onset of hostilities. The number of new wars peaks during the months of long days and ebbs during the months of short days, both for northern and southern latitudes.[80] The cyclicity is a reminder of people's dependence on their environment: to commit low-tech murder, it helps to be able to see the victims. The turmoil of spring months, such as the ides of March revolutions, have been amply discussed. Statistical and demographic analyses of wars are numerous, as are studies attempting to relate wars to everything from sunspots to the earth's magnetic fields. Advances in science and technology have removed many environmental constraints on warfare; the dependence of cruel conflicts on the imaginative powers and unresolvable conflicts of the mind remain.[81]

In *The March of Folly* Barbara Tuchman sampled four of the thousands of wars. She regarded those four as representative examples. She then asked whether any country can be shielded from "protective stupidity," that is, from policies that would be seen as against self-interest were they examined with cool reason. She concluded that because we neglect moral and social virtues in favor of money and ruthless ambition, we can only muddle on as we have done during the last three or four thousand years, "through patches of brilliance and decline, great endeavor and shadow."[82]

Her reasoning is built on two assumptions. One is that there exists a faculty of cool reason that can examine the world unemotionally; the other is that what constitutes self-interest either is clear or can be made so. But cool, detached reasoning is impossible because of the evolutionary structuring of the human nervous system: we can feel without thinking but cannot think without feeling. As to self-interest, that depends on value judgments as well as on the political, geographical, ethnic, historical, linguistic, and temporal horizons of what is to be meant by the self. Who is the self whose interest is to be served? Is it a person, a family, a tribe, an institution, a nation, a civilization, or humankind? These interests seldom coincide. Millions have died and countrysides were laid to ruin in the process of deciding which of these selves is to be the reigning one. The legal systems of all civilizations have had, as one of their important tasks, the adjudication of goods, services, and rights among the different selves. Wars have been fought for all conceivable real and imaginary causes and have been so ubiquitous and perennial that one must ask whether there are some deeper reasons the compassionate species is so bent on destruction. An entry to a discussion of this question may be found in an exchange of letters between Albert Einstein and Sigmund Freud concerning war.

In 1932 Einstein wrote to Freud asking whether there was "any way of delivering mankind from the menace of war?"[83] This has often been attempted, he said, but never successfully. "As for me," he continued, "the normal objective of my thought [the behavior of inanimate matter expressed in equations] affords no insight into the dark places of human will and feeling." Being "immune from national bias," he was puzzled by the fact that a small group "can bend the will of the majority, who stand to lose and suffer by the state of war." Had Freud made any "recent discoveries," he asked, to "blaze the trail for new and fruitful modes of action?"

One must wonder about Einstein's immense epistemic naïveté. What kind of response did he expect? Perhaps he anticipated concise statements of precise and inviolable laws that control human behavior as the laws of physics control that of matter.

"It is a general principle," answered Freud, "that conflicts of interest among men are settled by the use of violence." After tracing the history of the use of force from muscles to weapons, he remarked that the final purpose remained the same: each side wants to gain its objective. And the safest victory has always been the one in which the opponent is killed. He could have quoted Clausewitz. "War is . . . an act of force to compel our enemy to do our will. . . . Force, to counter opposing force, equips itself with the inventions of art and science. Attached to force are certain self-imposed, imperceptible limitations, hardly worth mentioning, known as international law and custom, but they scarcely weaken it."[84] In the course of the development of civilizations—here I move back to Freud—the community took over the guarding of the peace by directing violence against those persons who challenged its power and the violence of the community at large against other communities. "Here, I believe, we already have all the essentials: violence overcome by the transference of power to a larger unity, which is held together by emotional ties between its members."[85]

The reason a minority can sway a majority to favor war may be found in the nature of human instincts, Freud continued. Popular understanding sees love and hatred as polar opposites, yet "neither of these instincts is any less essential than the other; the phenomena of life arise from the concurrent and mutually opposing actions of both."[86] The instinct of love also calls on a desire to master a person and, with it, an element of hatred. It follows that "there is no use in trying to get rid of man's aggressive inclinations."[87]

Recently a biologist joined himself to the views shared by the Prussian general and the Viennese professor. E. O. Wilson, assessing human aggression as seen from the perspective of population biology, asks, "Is aggression in man adaptive? From the biologist's point of view it certainly seems to be. It is hard to believe that any characteristic so widespread and easily invoked in a species as aggressive behavior is in man could be neutral or negative in its effects on individual survival and reproduction."[88] But how does this trait, assumed to be useful and even necessary for adaptation, relate to moral tenets?

> The lesson for man is that personal happiness has very little to do with [the innate aggressiveness of all living species, helping them along in the process of adaptation]. It is possible to be unhappy and very adaptive. If we wish to reduce our own aggressive behavior, and lower our catecholamine and corticosteroid titers [the adrenaline hormones] to levels that make us happier, we should design our population densities and social systems in such a way as to make aggression inappropriate in most conceivable daily circumstances and, hence, less adaptive.[89]

From philosophers, psychologists, and biologists, let me turn to the words of a sensitive Englishwoman, a convinced pacifist and feminist. In *Testament of Youth* Vera Brittain recalled her stay on Malta as a nurse with the British Army during World War I.

> I may see the rocks again, and smell the flowers, and watch the dawn sunshine chase the shadows from the old sulphur-colored walls, but the light that sprang from the heightened consciousness of wartime, the glory seen by the enraptured ingenious eyes of twenty-two, will be upon them no more. [The] world, for all its excitement of chosen work and individual play, has grown tame in comparison with Malta during those years of anguish.
>
> It is, I think, this glamour, this magic, this incomparable keying up of the spirit in a time of mortal conflict, which constitutes the pacifist's real problem. . . . The causes of wars are always falsely represented . . . but the challenge to spiritual endurance, the immense sharpening of all senses, the vitalizing consciousness of common peril for a common end, remain to allure those . . . who have just reached the age when love and friendship and adventure call more persistently than at any later time. The glamour may be the mere delirium of fever . . . but while it lasts no emotion known to man seems as yet to have quite the same compelling power and enlarged vitality.
>
> I do not believe that . . . any Disarmament Conference will ever

rescue our . . . civilisation from the threatening forces of destruction, until we can somehow impart to the rational process of constructive thought . . . that element of sanctified loveliness which, like sunshine breaking through thunderclouds, from time to time, glorifies war.[90]

The longer a war lasts, the more those who are not in privileged position will see the quality of their lives deteriorate, until it becomes a dog-eat-dog misery. The poor, who are also the many, caught in the whirlwind, do not sense a romance as did the young Englishwoman. Paradoxically, however, the very same poor-and-many can and do experience the ecstasy of chase and sex wrapped up in the spirit that presages war.

Only someone who experienced this as a young man or woman can appreciate the power of its mind-boggling ambivalence. From my witness of the coming about and resolution of World War II, the steps appear disturbingly clear. First, the emotional load stored in the power of spoken, printed, and acted-out words was released through the ritualized dances of the crowds.[91] Then followed an outburst of ecstasy for the right cause, because all causes may be judged right from one or another point of view. Next came the mutual onslaught of the armed hordes of Nazi Germany and the USSR. With the inevitability of classic tragedies, enthusiasm turned into a relentless horror of carnage and suffering. In that theater of the absurd, what looked like the "sunshine breaking through thunderclouds, from time to time," was the spiritual greatness and mammalian warmth of nameless men and women. The simultaneous presence of joy and horror and the magnified impressions of good and evil in the folly of war are unintelligible in terms of the liberal view of man as being essentially good. The Sophoclean model of the strange walker is closer to being right.

Surveying World War II with the wisdom of an eighteen year old, and interpreting what I saw with the help of a good humanistic education, I made a mental note: to account for the frenzy of the human animal, we must invoke not the absence of moral judgment but rather its presence. The deeper the moral indignation about real or imagined harm, the more the collective desire to right some wrong, the more cruel the conflict, the more need for redress. During the six decades since the end of World War II, high-tech magic introduced impersonality into manslaughter. The unresolvable conflicts of the mind, its resentment against the difference between imagined satisfaction and reality, a condition that earlier had found outlets in large-scale violence, was shifted into the conflicts of Tribal Interest Cells (TICs), to be dealt with in sec. 6.2, "Conduct à la Mode."

Let me describe the human capacity for supporting collective actions— including wars, whether for food, power, an idea, or all of these mixed—as the enthusiasm of the tribe. In ancient Greek *entheos* means "having the god within." A possible English rendering would be "passion." The stirring up of enthusiasm in the collective will has been the role of charismatic leaders, who carry out their task through persuasion, terror, greed, intelligence, shrewdness, and conviction and often by sensing what people want to hear and do. Whatever the dimensions and modes of cruel conflicts, the warring factions become involved in them through the primeval enthusiasm of the tribe.

When it comes to people sacrificing for a cause, is there anything beyond the skills of leaders that helps to bring about organized cruelty? Yes: the ever-present ambivalence of love and hatred, clamoring for action, ready to swing to compassion or cruelty, expressed through giving and taking life. The driving power of wars, with their mixture of hatred and magnanimity, is human compassion riding on animal altruism.

Altruism, it will be recalled, is life protecting life, a body promoting the survival of another body. The inventiveness of altruism is the creativity of organic evolution. Whereas altruistic behavior is mostly programmed, the conduct of the compassionate pilgrim is creative, that is, unpredictable in its form and detail. It is for this reason that moral fervor, let lose in wars, is so much more impressive and human destructiveness so much more horrifying than is the altruism or fight of animals. Nature, red in tooth and claw, is pale compared with the atomic fire of humans armed to their teeth with truth and justice.

Human Freedom

Morality would be meaningless without assuming the possibility of choice among alternative courses of conduct: bread to be shared or not shared, mating held or delayed, child attended to or abandoned, enemy killed or lived with. The possibility of such choices have traditionally been discussed under the heading of free will. This is an idea with a long, interesting, and emotionally and intellectually loaded history that carries heavy metaphysical baggage. To divest my reasoning of some of that baggage, I will instead consider human freedom understood as follows.

In the service of a goal, the mind can usually imagine more alternative paths of conduct than are practical or even possible. These, our imaginable possibilities—more numerous than those permitted by physical, organic, and social constraints—give rise to a feeling of having a choice. "I could, but I do not." That awareness is the source of the idea of human freedom. A necessary corollary of human freedom is unpredictability in conduct, which comprises a nested hierarchy of unpredictabilities.

Organic or biological freedom is the lowest level of unpredictable choices. It comprises, as we saw, the possibilities available to living organisms in selecting paths of behavior. Ants have less such freedom, and apes have more. The next level of freedom is the capacity of men and women to make unpredictable choices in the service of goals peculiar to the noetic umwelt. This freedom is made possible by the availability to human conduct of the nested hierarchy of chaotic, probabilistic, deterministic, and goal-directed organic processes. From among them the mind selects such combinations of plans as seem best for reaching a goal. The broadest, most encompassing freedom is that of society: collectives have the power to restrain, incarcerate, and kill people and in general to perform acts that individuals are seldom authorized to perform based solely on their personal judgments. Sorting out what kind and degree of freedom belongs to the community and what to the person has been the staple of legal explorations since human law itself was invented.

Human freedom is the means whereby men and women may alter the conservative sweep of the cultural process. By "cultural process" I mean the totality of the preferred ways of daily life: all the knowledge, beliefs, art, morals, laws, customs, and any other capabilities and habits acquired by people as members of a society, including the peculiarly human ways of loving and hating, living and dying.[92] The conservative power of this accumulated knowledge, deposited in language and in other signs and symbols of the cultural process, is immense. Elsewhere I have described this power or resistance to change as "linguistic inertia."[93] Where ceaseless change is ensconced as the preferred way of life—where change has become a tradition—linguistic inertia will resist any alteration in that very commitment. Could anyone convince U.S. manufacturers *not* to continuously redesign, repackage, rename, and redefine their products and not to regard newness as the highest recommendation for their wares?

In a treatise on authority, time, and value, the legal scholar Joseph Vining had this to say:

[We] are helpless before our language, which comes to us together with its structure, organizing concepts, and categories, in organized form; and organization is necessary to change and replace it. . . .

The innate conservatism of legislatures with ostensible sovereignty and freedom is far more striking than their capacity to break the bonds of the past, and this should not be surprising, since legislators speak the same language and think in the same terms as lawyers, judges, and citizens.[94]

But we are not really helpless before the conservative nature of the cultural process: if we were, language would have never come about from grunts, nor atomic bombs from flint arrowheads. And although moral traditions have their own great inertia, we are not helpless before them either. In fact, the very signs and symbols that help to make societies conservative— the flag, the cross, the jingle—are at the same time the most efficient means through which the direction of cultural motion may be and has been changed. Patterns of conduct may be altered much more quickly by changing peoples' beliefs, expressed in their languages, arts, artifacts, and sciences, than by changing their genetic traits through natural selection.

What methods are available for changing received traditions by changing beliefs? Earlier in this section I introduced Darwin's comments about the feeling of regret as a necessary step for the development of moral sense, followed by Shakespeare's sonnet 129, about that predicament. What both Shakespeare and Darwin saw in the power of regret became central in Freud's psychology under the name of the sense of guilt. It was his intention, he wrote "to represent the sense of guilt as the most important problem in the development of civilization and to show that the price we pay for our advance in civilization is a loss of happiness through the heightened sense of guilt."[95]

The sense of guilt is the knowledge or belief that one has violated some moral or ethical principle, causing harm either to others or to one's own life or self-esteem. Punishment then appears appropriate according to the ever-present sense of justice. The people who gave their lives in supporting or opposing different values, perceiving guilt in themselves and others, constitute a substantial segment of humanity.

By committing a punishable act and through it inducing guilt feelings in others, a person can appeal to those feelings in furthering his own goals. Socrates decided to violate the laws of Athens and then drink the deadly hemlock to make a lasting point about the freedom of speech. Jesus of Nazareth drove himself to crucifixion to be able to replace the well-established, thundering Jehovah with the Son of Man. Sir Thomas More chose to be beheaded rather than to agree to the supremacy of the king of England over the Church of Rome. Giordano Bruno knew that he would be burned as a heretic if he kept on insisting that the world is infinitely large, but he maintained his views just the same; in our own age Ernesto ("Che") Guevara was a martyr by his own choice for the communist cause.

I believe that any change in prevailing ideas of right and wrong demands sacrifice, and although it does not always need to be that of life and limb, it is the risking and giving of life that moves historical changes in matters of public judgments of morals. Tertullian, a second-century theologian, remarked that the blood of Christian martyrs is the seed of the Church.[96] In Shakespeare's *Julius Caesar,* Cassius, a conspirator against Caesar's life, wonders aloud, "How many ages hence / Shall this our lofty scene be acted o'er, / In states unborn and accents yet unknown!" In a country that was yet unborn in Cassius's time, Thomas Jefferson remarked that "the tree of liberty must be refreshed from time to time with the blood of patriots and tyrants. It is its natural manure." Why so?

The sacrifice of life brings forth responses through sympathetic induction, known in all advanced forms of life; in humans it does so with exceptional power when it involves the lives of other humans. Assassinations, bloody terror, public executions, and self-immolation are long remembered after sermons are forgotten; cries of pain are very effective in unseating established mores.[97] It has been one of the tasks of civilizations to replace blood sacrifice by debates and by sacrifices of a less radical kind. Judging from the turmoil on the time-compact globe, this task has not been accomplished with any great success. Sacrificing human life is still the leading method for efficiently revising public opinion and moral principles. Referring to the layout of newspapers' front pages, journalists say that "if it bleeds, it leads." Human freedom rides on the back of bloody, primeval drives. Does that lessen the power of the good as a human value? Not at all. On the contrary, perfectibility is proportional to corruptibility, with the two measuring each other. Only a creature that sees the depth of its corruptibility with horror can decide to use its freedom to strive for ideals of the good, forever out of reach.

4.4   The Office of the Good as a Human Value

The beggar-soldier kneeling in front of the Palace of the Popes in Avignon, his arms rigidly extended ahead, his eyes closed, was bargaining with his fate. He was using whatever relevant skills he possessed. Shamans and chieftains, kings and politicians, poets and prophets, no less than judges and jailers, have been promising peace here on earth or in some postmortem elsewhere provided people conduct themselves according to their visions of the good and the right. I cannot speak for postmortem conditions, but on earth, in sharp contrast to the green pastures and quiet waters of the elsewheres and elsewhens, the perennial present has been closer to Yeats's "Into the Twilight."

> God stands winding His lonely horn,
> And time and the world are ever in flight;
> And love is less kind than the grey twilight,
> And hope is less dear than the dew of the morn.[98]

Animals struggle for food, mates, territory, and conditions favorable to their young. They communicate by chemical exchanges, by dance and song, by bites, snarls, and nudges. Using such signals they urge action, deprive another of satisfaction, or grant the same. Punishing strategies that establish and maintain dominance, discourage cheats, and discipline offspring or prospective sexual partners have been identified for animal societies.[99] Examples of delicate social balancing operations in which competition among lower-level units is policed and suppressed in favor of the integrity of higher evolutionary units have been identified in systems as fundamental as meiosis.[100]

The bites, snarls, and rewards that help to uphold the rules of behavior in the animal world have expanded in humans to degrees of compassion and cruelty unknown among nonhuman species. The viciousness of people in meting out punishment to those who break collectively endorsed principles, and the suffering that men and women are ready to endure to do just that, are little short of incredible. But neither courage in the defense of conduct or intent judged right nor beastliness of attacks on conduct or intent judged wrong has ever secured more than transient stability in human affairs. Whether in the face of unfavorable conditions or else with the help of favorable ones, human life has remained one of armed and unarmed conflicts. Considering the very moderate success of moral teachings embedded in the great religions and philosophies and in the words of charismatic leaders, the question of the evolutionary usefulness of ethics naturally arises.

History, including social and cultural changes often subsumed under the idea of progress, has been not a glorious ascent hindered only by occasional troubles from the bad guys but a ceaseless turmoil of conflicts with only an occasional decrease in their intensities. One may object that this is too pessimistic a view, that it sees the glass half-empty when it should be seen as half-full. My reply is that perceiving humans as creatures in continuous conflict about their conduct helps to make sense of history, whereas an image of men and women as naturally peaceful and balanced does not.

Is it, perhaps, that moral instructions of all kinds have failed to provide a steady balance among the passions and needs of humans because they were poorly informed or their enforcement was incompetent? Is it the case that, given time, money, and more research, we should be able to identify the kind of moral tenets and modes of enforcement that would finally secure permanent social balance? Or is it that the role of ethics and morality in the development of civilizations has been consistently misinterpreted? The case, I believe, is the last alternative: a misjudgment of what ethical rules do in fact accomplish.

James Russell Lowell, a nineteenth-century New England poet, sensed the drama and dimensions of the strife of his country long before the hostilities of the Civil War began. A dedicated abolitionist, he beheld the history of his days in cosmic terms and expressed his puritanical convictions in no uncertain thunder. These lines are from his poem "The Present Crisis."

> Once to every man and nation comes the moment to decide,
> In the strife of Truth with Falsehood, for the good or evil side;
> Some great cause, God's new Messiah, offering each the bloom
>   or blight,
> Parts the goats upon the left hand, and the sheep upon the right,
> And the choice goes by forever 'twixt that darkness and the light.[101]

In the first line, instead of writing "once" I would opt for "continuously." This would confuse the meter but correct the perspective. And I would retitle the poem "The Permanent Crisis."

Organic evolution by natural selection never led to a lasting balance, nor is it expected to lead to one. There are evolutionarily stable strategies, but there is no such thing as a forever stable strategy, no more than there is a perfect, final shape for a sheep. Every sheep, every frog, and every human body is only another experiment in the collective process of life. Likewise, there is no such a thing as a final set of rules for right conduct. In the history of ethics each repair, intended to create stable harmony among human needs and passions by way of redressing some wrong of the past, has produced only partial repairs and generated new wrongs in need of new repairs, thus giving rise to new conflicts.

Beneath these comments is the distinction between Plato and Darwin. Plato directed attention to the perfect and saw humanity as irresistibly drawn to a store of ultimate, preexisting values.[102] Darwin directed attention to the imperfect and saw evolution—in biology as well as in behavior—as a ceaseless repair job. "There is no infinite plan," wrote the novelist Isabel Allende, "just the strife of the living."[103] Our ethical journey is the blazing of new trails of conduct; it is a form of creativity.

The conclusion follows. The role of ethics, under many and different names, has been grossly misjudged. The genie of compassion, once out of the bottle, has been doing the opposite of what the inspired and inspiring spiritual leaders of humankind imagined it would do. They failed to stress that moral judgments, driven by compassion, cannot lead to more than stopgap measures, to damage controls with promises.

The desire for permanence, balance, and harmony, expressed in the support of what is judged right and opposition to what is judged wrong, has been responsible—among other causes—for the historical imbalance of persons and societies. Si vis pacem, para bellum: if you wish peace, be prepared for war, said the Romans; si vis vita, para mortem: if you wish life, be ready to die, added others. We may continue: if you wish changes in ideas of right and wrong, strive for permanence in ethics. Since our awareness of passing and consequent insecurity leaves little room for doing anything else but reaching for the permanent, a ceaseless change in matters ethical is guaranteed.

If moral judgments and ethically proper conduct bring that much headache and suffering, would it not be better to embrace anarchy, a belief that ethical rules are harmful? The answer, consistent with the theory of time as conflict, is a definite no. Such a path would parallel the suggestion that the suffering of cancer be eliminated by murdering everyone. If moral conflicts were to cease, so would the identity of persons and of humankind.

Moral beliefs, serving as comfort and certainty to persons, are needed and are precious. But they are not precious because they are eternal. On the contrary, they are dearly held because they are temporal, because we know that moral judgments are subject to changes that make what is judged good today evil tomorrow and what is judged evil today good tomorrow.

The working definition of the good, formulated in sec. 4.2, is sometimes valid for the short term. But the long-term office of the good has been the opposite. Moral judgments have been creating and maintaining conflicts concerning behavior, and through them, they have been keeping alive a steady revolt against whatever principles happen to be guiding people's conduct.

CHAPTER FIVE

The Beautiful and the Ugly: Guidelines for the Management of Emotions

I n the woods around Lake Desert, Quebec, the wolves bay at the full moon. The poet Yeats observed related behavior in cats.

> The cat went here and there
> And the moon spun around like a top,
> And the nearest kin of the moon,
> The creeping cat looked up.
> Black Minnaloush stared at the moon,
> For wander and wail as he would,
> The pure cold light in the sky
> Troubled his animal blood.[1]

Humans also go here and there; they also wail at objects inanimate and alive, real or imagined. They can also be troubled by the cold light of the universe, enlivened by mammalian warmth, disturbed by hatred, fired by love, inspired by thought, or haunted by emptiness.

People have learned to manage their plethora of emotions by expressing them in sound, shape, color, and movement (sec. 5.1). These expressions make emotions communicable, shareable with others, and open up the possibility for the collective formulation of guidelines. The skills necessary to accomplish this feat are built on the aesthetic sensitivities of the species (sec. 5.3).

With the help of the natural philosophy of time, this chapter examines the origins and workings of aesthetic sensitivities. It identifies the way in which they are integrated into the family of human values and help to maintain the continuity of human life and of personal and collective identities (secs. 5.4 and 5.5).

5.1 From Imitation to Creation

It is reasonable to assume that art emerged from a pragmatic combination of necessary daily activities with both play and experimentation and that it became established because it offered a means of sharing information for which speech was inadequate. Neanderthaler settlements dated between 85,000 and 35,000 years ago included pieces of black manganese dioxide and red ochre in the form of rounded and pointed pencils. They were used, it is believed, for body painting, a practice that harks back a million and a half years. Red seems to have been the favorite color of apes and early humans.

By the time apes were able to have favorite colors, life was 3.5 billion years old, the nervous control of behavior was 750 million years old, and nervous systems that could be credited with generating the feelings necessary for aesthetic judgments were perhaps 100 million years old. The capacity to appreciate beauty has a long ancestry.

A 200,000-year-old decorated ax handle attests to the skills and needs of its maker; 100,000 years ago a Neanderthaler fashioned an amulet from a mammoth's tooth. It is believed that music and oral literature existed by the time of the Upper Paleolithic in Europe, 45,000 years ago. Objects of that age, unmistakably those of art, show the sophistication and skill unique to humans. Whatever purposes art might have had, such as healing or sympathetic magic, extant material attests to its makers' appreciation of orderability in shapes, colors, and spatial proportions. Appreciation of temporal orderability is also evinced: symbols that may represent the phases of the moon in relation to natural cycles were engraved on bones and stone plaques 35,000 years ago.

Europe's Upper Paleolithic, or later Stone Age, consisted of several civilizations of increasing sophistication. Each had its characteristic tools used for the daily necessities of survival and for satisfying the need for communicating in shapes and visual rhythms. The tools included stone knives with one or two sharp edges, woodworking tools, needles, spears, fishing equipment, and sharp devices used to make engravings and drawings on bones. When combined with colors, the same tools were used to paint pictures on cave walls.

The oldest known painting, on the wall of a cave in the Ardèche region of southeastern France, is estimated to have been made more than 30,300 years ago. It shows over 300 animal images and a series of red handprints. Around 30,000 years ago low-relief sculptures and larger sculptures of animal figures appeared. What many of the hundreds of extant objects represented for their makers and admirers must remain conjectural, but some conjectures are convincing. For instance, on the walls of a cave named Les Trois Frères, also in the south of France, there are some 280 figures of bison, stags, reindeer, horses, and ibex. Scattered among them are human figures, some of them dressed in animal furs and believed to represent magicians doing their ritual dances. Towering over this swirling animal and human world, some thirteen feet above the cave floor, is a composite figure painting with engraved outlines. It has a stag's head with antlers, an owl's face, a bear's paws, human legs and feet, a large human penis, and a horse's tail. The prevailing opinion is that it represents a shaman in animal disguise performing hunting magic.

Beyond the question of what the figure represents is a more intriguing one: why was it depicted? The conjecture of the English scholar of comparative religion S. G. F. Brandon is that the painting was intended to secure for the members of the tribe the benefits of the dance in perpetuity (whatever those benefits might have been).[2] In our epoch we have the wedding photograph on the piano, a magic device intended to secure for the couple the perpetuation of their early love.

Cave paintings could not have been easy to make. The artists had to carry their tools and their smoky lights; they risked losing their way in the unfriendly depths and had to work under conditions that must have been uncomfortable, even to them. Animals lay low in darkness unless they are nocturnal and tolerate discomfort only if they must. What drove the artists to do their work? Was it only the desire to ensure lasting benefits to the tribe, as Brandon conjectured, or was it a need to satisfy a kind of hunger that arose from within—or both? The great wealth of Paleolithic art shows an appreciation of certain images and patterns of behavior. These suggest a desire of the artist and the tribe to organize their knowledge of the world and, through such an organization, manage their feelings and control their fates.

Around 25,000 years ago female figurines called Venuses, strikingly uniform in their size and shape, began to appear across the region between northern Spain and Russia. They emphasize their large buttocks and breasts so much that these two features, most obviously involved in reproduction, are virtually the only ones depicted. I imagine that for the Paleolithic Pygmalions who made these portable women, the figurines were images of the living sources of milk and honey; they helped to focus their sexual fantasies.

By twisting fate's arm through the shaman's dance, by sympathetic magic for the success of the hunt, and by their carved Venuses to help promote success in creating offspring, the Paleolithic celebrants joined modern humanity. Their artists left no written record of their motivations, but they did leave their art to speak about them. We can imagine those motivations because we know the life of one of their latter-day colleagues who worked under conditions resembling those of the cave painters.

Between 1508 and 1512 Michelangelo Buonarotti painted the ceiling of the Sistine Chapel, most of the time lying flat on his back, on a high movable bridge that could be reached only by a series of ladders. There he ate his soup and bread, which were carried up to him by a servant, the only person beside the pope who was permitted to enter the chapel. When he left his Renaissance "cave" after four years, he could not walk but only wobble; his head was bent back, so that he could look only up. Twenty-three years later he returned to paint his monumental *Last Judgment* over the main altar of the chapel. In both tasks he was driven by the fear that he might die at any moment, and not having finished his work, he would not be worthy of resurrection. His design of the *Last Judgment* was inspired by the medieval hymn Dies Irae—"Day of wrath and repentance"—which speaks of the devastation and terror at the end of time. I am not about to attribute to our hairy ancestors the fear of a Christian Last Judgment or a concern with resurrection, even though they believed in postmortem life and provided the dead with practical necessities for their journey into another world. What I do submit is that the cave artists, no less than Michelangelo, were concerned about their long-term futures and that those concerns drove them to create art to influence those futures. In the process they learned to manage their feelings—more or less.

From prehistory, let me take a giant step to the days of the Trojan War and contemplate a remarkable object of art that tradition associates with it: the shield of Achilles. It was made by the lame god Hephaestus using twenty bellows and his cunning skill. The design on it was an encyclopedic record of the days of Odysseus. It showed a field with many plowmen, harvest hands whetting their scythes, a happy king surveying it all, and the king's servants preparing a banquet. There was a vineyard with boys and girls, some of whom broke into a song. An artisan fashioned longhorns from gold and tin. There were dogs and a bull caught by a pair of lions. There were huts and sheds and a dancing floor with young men and the most desirable maidens of the price of many cattle dancing on it, touching each other's wrists. The girls were in linen, in soft gowns, the men in tunics glistening with oil. And running around the shield was a picture of the ocean.[3]

Achilles' shield is not in any of the museums in Athens, for it existed in the shape described only in the mind of blind Homer. But that it could be thought of and described in such fine detail is witness to the immensity of the cultural journey that began with the Stone Age.

The idea of beauty appropriate to post-Homeric Greece was given commanding form and substance in the thought of Plato. When I explored the relationship between time and truth (sec. 3.2, "A Message from Mathematics"), I discussed a Socratic view: the belief that geometrical knowledge once possessed by the soul in an earlier body and then forgotten could be recovered under the enlightened questioning of one such as Socrates. A parallel doctrine holds for the Platonic idea of the beautiful.

In seeking and finding the beautiful, says Socrates, guidance comes through diligent work. He quotes Diotima, "a Mantinean woman . . . who was deeply versed in this and many other fields of knowledge [and] who taught me the philosophy of Love."[4] Whoever wants to behold beauty, she said, must work toward that knowledge along a series of partial and dimmer beauties. Erotic love leads the way, such as that fired by the charm of comely boys just ripening to manhood. Out of such love the seeker of beauty will learn

> how nearly related the beauty of any one body is to the beauty of any other. . . . Having reached this point, he must set himself to be the lover of every lovely body. . . . Next he must grasp that the beauties of the body are nothing to the beauties of the soul. . . . [He will learn] to contemplate the beauty of laws and institutions. . . . [And] from institutions [he must move] to the sciences, so that he may know the beauty of every kind of knowledge.
>
> And so. . . . starting from individual beauties, the quest for the universal beauty must find him ever mounting the heavenly ladder. . . . [from] institutions to learning, and from learning in general to the special lore that pertains to nothing but the beautiful itself.[5]

Plato would surely say that the Socratic reasoning held for the Paleolithic artist no less than for the artists of his and of our epochs.

Whereas Plato's concern was that of beauty in a cosmic context, Aristotle wanted to know of the effects of the beautiful on the beholder and how these effects are achieved. He concluded that all art consists of skilled imitations of reality and that beauty resides in the pleasure derived from beholding that skill.

> Imitation is natural to man from childhood, one of his advantages over the lower animals being this, that he is the most imitative creature in the world, and learns at first by imitation. And it is also natural for all to delight in works of imitation. . . . though the objects themselves may

be painful to see, we delight to view the most realistic representations of them in art. . . . [To] be learning something is the greatest of pleasures not only to the philosopher but also to the rest of mankind, however small their capacity for it. . . . Imitation, then, being natural to us . . . it was through their original aptitude, and by a series of improvements . . . that they [the poets] created poetry out of their improvisations.[6]

The argument of mimesis as the source of the beautiful shares with modern science the metaphysical belief in a reality independent of the beholder. It adumbrates the notion of art as an adaptive or a learning process. The pro-Aristotelian wag would say that beauty is what beauty does, although there are some rules.

To be beautiful, a living creature . . . must not only present a certain order in its arrangement of the parts, but also be of a certain definite magnitude. Beauty is a matter of size and order, and therefore impossible either (1) in a very minute creature, since our perception becomes indistinct as it approaches instantaneity; or (2) in a creature of vast size—one, say, 1,000 miles long—as in that case, instead of the object being seen at once, the unity and wholeness of it is lost to the beholder.[7]

An analogous argument holds for the beauty of a plot in regard to the narrative time of its events. It must allow for the hero to pass through a series of probable or necessary stages from misfortune to happiness or from happiness to misfortune. For something to be beautiful, its character and measure must be appropriate for the human umwelt. With that reasoning, beauty left its heavenly abode and became tied to the nature of the beholder of beauty.

Seven centuries after Plato and Aristotle, Plotinus (A.D. 205–70), a Hellenized Egyptian, combined the Socratic notions of beauty with mysticism and placed it all in a pantheistic framework. Sensations, he maintained, provide a direct perception of the material world, but since impressions ceaselessly change, they are not useful in themselves. They must be coordinated by the *nous*, the intellect, which together with *psyche*, the soul, is an emanation from the One. Oneness he in turn identified with God. Happiness, then, is the recognition that one's soul is a part of the oneness of the World Soul. The beautiful is the splendor that shines forth from that oneness.

Beauty addresses itself chiefly to sight, but there is beauty for the hearing too, as in certain combinations of words and in all kinds of music . . . and [those] minds that lift themselves above the realm of sense to a higher order are aware of beauty in the conduct of life, in actions, in character, in the pursuits of the intellect; and there is the beauty of the virtues. . . . What, then, is it that gives comeliness to material forms and draws the ear to the sweetness of perceived sounds . . . ?

[Let us inquire about] the Principle that bestows beauty on material things. . . . It is something that is perceived at the first glance, something which the soul names as from an ancient knowledge and recognizing, welcomes it, enters unto union with it. But let the soul fall in with the Ugly and at once it shrinks within itself. . . .

[If we wish to reach the beautiful] what must we do? How lies the path? . . . This is not a journey for the feet . . . you must close the eyes and call, instead upon another vision which is to be waked within you, a vision, the birth-right of all, which few turn to use.[8]

At the end of that journey, in a manner that would have made Plato proud and budding Christian theologians annoyed, the soul will find the Principle of Primal Beauty, which is the ultimate home of us all.

A century and a half after Plotinus, St. Augustine (355–403) allowed for conditions other than harmony to enter the nature of beauty. He acknowledged that "the beauty of the universe . . . becomes, by God's ordinance, more brilliant by the opposition of contraries."[9] The world is one of antitheses: man knows honor and dishonor, sorrow and joy. Oppositions lend beauty to the course of the world arranged by conflicts through the "eloquence . . . of things." The oppositions are played out by the furnishings of the world, which are themselves governed by number. "Examine the beauty of bodily form, and you will find that everything is in place by number."[10]

From Roman antiquity to the mid-thirteenth century, the sweep of Western reasoning about the beautiful was overwhelmingly theological. With the evaluation of life on earth as a transient and unsatisfactory state, that reasoning saw beauty as a metaphor for and servant to the good, with good itself defined in terms of the tenets of Rome. In their turn, these centuries of theology bequeathed their intellectual power to a new age—named the Renaissance ex post facto—that gave birth to an esteem of the world and of man himself.[11] The immeasurability of God's providence gave way to an increasingly immeasurable cosmos, the joys of the Christ child and pains of martyrdom to the joys and pains of people, and the beauty of faith to the comeliness of body.

Petrarch (1304–74) called for a revival and reinterpretation of classical learning with the help of the new freedoms of the human condition. Leonardo da Vinci, artist and inventor (1452–1519), maintained as self-evident that art is not imitation but imaginative creation.[12] From the early seventeenth century on, British empiricists began to elaborate the importance of imagination, memory, and reason in the experience of the beautiful. In *Leviathan* Thomas Hobbes spoke of mental processes that rearrange parts of what has been received and known and thereby create images that never existed before, as "when from the sight of a man at one time, and of a horse at another, we construct in our head a Centaure [*sic*]."[13]

The term *aesthetics,* from the Greek *aisthetikos* ("things perceptible by the senses"), was coined by the German philosopher Alexander Baumgarten in the mid-eighteenth century to mean a scientific and philosophical criticism of taste. He saw art not as an imitation of nature but as a representation of nature enriched, and hence altered, by the artist's reasoning and feelings.

Late in the eighteenth century Immanuel Kant paid considerable attention to the sublime, which he saw as an aspect of experience generated by contemplating certain objects. Sublimity, he maintained, does not adhere to objects but is instead our reaction to them.[14] The poet Friedrich Schiller (1759–1805) saw in art and beauty the medium that renders man human and determines the character of his societies. It is through art that the person and humanity advance by a dialectic of the spirit, proceeding from the sensuous to the rational level of being.[15] The sensuous, he suggested, spiritualized through art, leads to the highest forms of expression of the *Geist* (the moral and spiritual essence of man and the world).

The nineteenth century witnessed a shift from regarding beauty as an attribute or property to regarding it as a process. Leo Tolstoy (1828–1910) remarked that "art is a human activity consisting of this, that one man consciously by means of certain external signs, hands on to others feelings he has lived through, and that others are infected by these feelings and also experience them. . . . The stronger the infection the better is the art, as art, speaking of it now apart from its subject-matter—that is, not considering the value of feelings it transmits."[16]

In *The Sense of Beauty* (1896) and *Reason in Art* (1905) George Santayana (1863–1952), the Spanish-born American intellectual and man of letters, developed his ideas about aesthetics based on a scientific understanding of human nature. All preferences, he suggested, including aesthetic ones, are expressions of vital needs. Beauty is an emotional element, a pleasure of ours, which we nevertheless regard as a quality of things. It is a process in the moral economy of reason; it is "pleasure objectified" on a subjective manner.[17] His contemporary John Dewey (1859–1952) maintained in *Art as Experience* that knowledge is never the report of an uninvolved spectator, that it always demands active participation, and that this includes aesthetic knowledge.[18] Benedetto Croce (1866–1952) described art as a cognitive awareness informed of feelings, a form of knowledge that shares with all other forms of knowledge the possibility of epistemic interpretation.[19] Susanne Langer (1895–1985) suggested that "art is the creation of forms of symbolic human feelings."[20]

At the other edge of the Indo-European world, in India, aesthetics was developed in the theory of *rasa*, first proclaimed around A.D. 500 and elaborated in the eleventh century; thereafter it was broadened and became a general theory of art. The Sanskrit word means "sap," "juice," or "essence"; it is usually translated as "emotional flavor."

> By *rasa* we mean a transcendent mode of emotional awareness by which all aspects of a performance are integrated, an awareness that rises above the circumstances which awakened it . . . and generalizes the individual emotional states of the spectators into a single emotional "field." The idea has often been compared to Aristotle's conception of catharsis . . . but the differences are more important.[21]

> Beauty [is] an epiphany, a manifestation of the light of creation to the senses, bringing the taste of delight and a glimpse of the ultimate in sensible, graspable form.[22]

The *rasa* theory acknowledges and allows for eight different *rasas:* the erotic, the comic, the compassionate, the furious, the heroic, the terrible, the odious, and the wondrous. Indian philosophers have tried to systematize the spectrum of human emotions in these categories. In the *rasa* theory aesthetic experience consists of "tasting" works of art according to a person's emotive and intellectual preparedness. The linguistic hint of sap, juice, or flavor reveals certain features in the nature of knowledge: we learn and know through the mouth ("she has good taste in shoes"), through the genitals (as in "carnal knowledge"), and through the eyes ("I see what you mean").[23] Sanskrit words important in aesthetics reflect a tacit awareness of these features of aesthetic knowledge.

> *Kanti* is perhaps the most popular word for beauty, with the following semantic range: beauty in general, especially female beauty; desire; decoration; loveliness; splendor; light. . . . It derives from the second verbal root *kam* (to love, have sexual intercourse with, desire, long for), and thence from the adjective *kanta* (that which is pleasing, lovely). [This concept of beauty] is deeply rooted in typical feminine qualities. . . .
>
> Also contributing to the general notion of beauty are a large number of other Sanskrit verbal roots [such as] to shine, be pleased. . . .

Taken together they suggest an idea that Plato would have endorsed—
that beauty is an epiphany, a manifestation of the light of creation . . .
bringing the taste of delight and a glimpse of the ultimate in sensible, graspable form.[24]

In his massive comparative study *The Ways of Thinking of Eastern People,*
Hajime Nakamura identifies the hallmarks of Indian thought with introspec-
tion, preference for metaphysics over the observation of nature, and a "sub-
servience" to universals. In contrast, the Japanese way of thinking empha-
sizes sensible, concrete events intuitively comprehended. It welcomes the
fluidity of the phenomenal world and equates the impermanence of that
world with the absolute and real. The thirteenth-century sage Master Dogan
maintained that "impermanence is the Buddhahood. . . . The impermanence of grass, trees, and forests is verily the Buddhahood. The impermanence of a person's body and mind is verily the Buddhahood. The impermanence of the land and scenery is verily the Buddhahood."[25] Japanese art
and reflections on aesthetics, represented by the quotation from Master
Dogan, and in contrast to those of India, are always close to nature.

Whereas in the West aesthetic desires are expressed in making only some
things beautiful, in Japan beauty is regarded as an integral part of civilized
existence, appropriate and necessary for all occasions. In his seminal paper
on Japanese aesthetics, Donald Keene describes four of its traditional hallmarks.[26] The first one is that beauty should be hinted at rather than told. This
tradition is consistent with the structure of the Japanese language, which
commonly omits the subject of sentences, leaving it to the listener to decide
what that subject is. Beauty is not a brilliant revelation, as Plato would have
it, but an aspect of creativity, a feminine quality, whose workings are hidden.

The second hallmark of Japanese aesthetic practice is the avoidance of
symmetry and regularity. Simplicity is its third hallmark. An object of beauty
should have unobtrusive elegance and provide a rest for the senses. Beauty lies not in instant impression but in accumulated experience that exudes
the power of quiet permanence. As Lewis Rowell remarks in his paper on
Ma—the phenomenon of pregnant in-betweenness—the intent of art in
Japan is not to elicit "a vision of the divine, a change of heart or behavior,
or any of the other aims of religion" but "to evoke aesthetic savor."[27] In such
terms the Sistine Chapel would be found to be too busy, too explicit, too
obvious, and hence not beautiful.

Finally and significantly, Japanese aesthetics appreciates perishability.
Whereas Western aesthetic ideals relate to the desire to conquer passage,
Japanese ideas of beauty praise the passing, the impermanent. Beauty is the
grief over the all too fast passage of the desired, a feeling not at all alien to
the West, as Shakespeare's sonnet 64 illustrates.

Ruin hath taught me thus to ruminate
That Time will come and take my love away.
This thought is as a death which cannot choose
But weep to have that which it fears to lose.

Whereas the most accomplished examples of Western art are monuments erected to conquer passage, Japanese aesthetics assimilates it. In both cases time and timelessness—two experiences or feelings that define each other—are at the roots of aesthetic judgments.

With these perspectives on the many different shields of Achilles, all of them designed to protect people from emotions as enemies and to help them with emotions as friends, I am now ready to formulate a working definition of the beautiful.

5.2   A Working Definition of the Beautiful

The varied tapestry of ideas about the nature of beauty and the myriad different objects, conditions, actions, and thoughts that have been judged beautiful suggest that anything and everything that may be sensed, done, or conceived may become aesthetically relevant. The specific objects, acts, or thoughts judged beautiful vary from time to time, culture to culture, and person to person, but the need for beauty transcends any of its specific examples. In an attempt to place order into this embarrassment of riches, I propose to seek the sources of aesthetic experience neither in the stars of the sky above, nor in the dance of dragonflies below, nor in the expressive works of people called artists—all of which are external to the beholder. Rather, I seek the sources of beauty within the beholder, in certain time-related functions of the human mind and body. This idea draws on many sources: the thoughts of Augustine, da Vinci, Hobbes, Croce, and Susanne Langer; the Hindu theory of *rasa;* and the Japanese appreciation of perishability.

Instead of asking what is the light that shines from certain events and objects, illuminating the lives, loves, and sufferings of men and women, I prefer to ask this: what is the light that shines from the feelings and thoughts of men and women, illuminating the impersonal, ruthless, and uncaring universe by sometimes making some of its features appear beautiful? In other words, I submit that aesthetic judgments derive from the quality of feelings mobilized by external or internal events, conditions, or processes, both real and imaginary.

If the quality of feelings is such as to make one desire its perpetuation, then whatever is believed to be responsible for it is said to be beautiful. If the quality of the feel-

ings is such as to make one desire it to be absent, then whatever is believed to be responsible for it is said to be ugly.

What kinds of feelings would I want to perpetuate? Those—so I will reason—that suggest timelessness in time.

The suggested working definition of the beautiful allows beauty to take as many different forms as there are persons and lets those judgments vary with time and place. It allows them to be attached to manmade or naturally occurring objects, events, or processes. This understanding answers Santayana's complaint that aesthetics has suffered much from the prejudice against the subjective. It assumes that all men and women, at all times, experience feelings they would wish to perpetuate, to make last, and even to judge timeless and other feelings they would prefer to deny or even make vanish. It does not assume that anything held by a person to be beautiful or ugly generates the same feelings, thoughts, and aesthetic judgments in others. Yet it also allows for broad and steady aesthetic agreements across civilizations and historical epochs consequent on shared biological, psychological, and social characteristics among people. It also recognizes that the terms *beautiful* and *ugly* designate idealized boundaries of a spectrum of emotions along which the objects and events held responsible for those feelings may occupy varying and ambiguous positions.

5.3 Roving the Depths of the Mind

King Lear, as he approached the end of his tragic life, wished for a world where he could pray and sing, tell old stories, and laugh at gilded butterflies. Do butterflies have emotions that help them to appreciate the pretty patterns on other butterflies? The complexity of the lepidopteran nervous system does not entitle them to have feelings of the King Lear kind; the designs on their wings are strictly for the birds. Butterflies developed poisonous and distasteful substances to repel predators while simultaneously developing loud color patterns to provide warning about their unpalatable bodies. One can almost hear a bird promise itself never again to touch such ugly objects.[28]

Aesthetic judgments in humans have similar roles: they help us to evaluate the desirability or otherwise of food, friend, and foe. They guide the management of human conduct through classifying the world of the senses in terms of the categories "I like it" and "I like it not." Whatever I do not like should be, as far as I am concerned, transient, passing. Whatever I like should last, be permanent. Should I not dream about them as being timeless?

This section explores the nature of experiences usually, but erroneously, described as those of timelessness.

The Usefulness of Feelings

Early in Western intellectual history, Plato displayed strong feelings in his disapproval of the emotions that he saw as spawning poetry and the mimetic arts: "And so in regard to emotions of sex and anger, and all those appetites and pains and pleasures of the soul which we say accompany all our actions, the effect of poetic imitation is the same. For it waters and fosters these feelings when what we ought to do is to dry them up, and it establishes them as our rulers when they ought to be ruled, to the end that we may be better and happier men instead of worse and more miserable."[29]

Twenty-three centuries after Plato, a fellow nobleman of the soul but not of society, Jean-Jacques Rousseau, recognized emotions and passions not as impediments to human knowledge but as the sources and conditions of it. In the beginning of the *Confessions* he remarked that we suffer before we think and that this is the common lot of humanity.[30] Be it pain or pleasure, we certainly feel before we think: expressions of emotions in the infant are evident from the instant she or he is born.

In *The Descent of Man* (1873) Charles Darwin argued at length that the evolutionary development of mental powers, among which he included feelings, is continuous between animals and man. He remarked that "the fact that the lower animals are excited by the same emotions as ourselves is so well established that it will not be necessary to weary the readers by the many details."[31] His interest, however, was not in emotions, which he could not directly explore, but in the expressions of those emotions, which he could. He maintained that expressions of emotions are remnants of previously useful adaptive behavior.[32]

From the point of view of a person, feelings are modes of reconnaissance. In military use the term *reconnaissance* means "an exploration," "a gathering of information about friend, foe, and terrain," all of which are external to and independent of the scout doing the survey. The information gained is then used in making decisions about the conduct of a campaign. Likewise, feelings gather information about the many benefits and dangers to the self posed by events, things, and conditions external to the body as well as events and conditions internal to it. This reconnaissance is much more intricate than its military kin because here the friend, the foe, and the terrain are the scout itself.

Feelings are wordless evaluations of the totality of a person's state of life at a moment and of his position in the world. The psychological term that designates the undifferentiated aggregate of all organic sensations about which feelings report is *coenesthesia*, from the Greek *koinos* (common) and *aisthesis* (sensation). It signifies the instantaneous record of all sensations en masse, a collective overview, as it were, an executive summary of the inner world combined with an assessment of the external one. By their reconnaissance, feelings help us to make judgments about future rewards and dangers. My feelings inform me of the threat posed by a still distant terrorist or rewards by a still distant lover. They do so much more quickly than reasoning and calculation can: feelings are the first signals we have about the future. This suggests that the evolutionary explanation for the blossoming of human emotions is to be sought in the advantages they offer in preparing one's self for the future.

Although judgments based on emotions are more deeply seated in the mind than are those of reasoning, the two are not independent. But neither are they on equal footing. They are hierarchically related. It is possible to have emotions without reasoning, but it is not possible to reason without emotions.

Forms of Timelessness in Time

Unlike the body, the human brain evolved by growing new structures around the old ones, with the result that it includes modified versions of its own evolutionary ancestors.[33] The surviving ancestors, different in their structuring and in an evolutionary sense eons apart from the most evolved parts of the brain, retained their functional kinship to the brains of reptiles, early mammals, and late mammals. Together they form what the neurologist Paul MacLean called the triune brain—the brain stem, the limbic system, and the cortex—a single coordinated unit where each layer carries on in ways related to its archaic responsibilities while remaining in communication with its skullmates.[34] A consequence is that our ancestral ways of perceiving the world, including the nature of time, survive in the human brain.

The functions of the reptilian brain are those of signaling hunger, pursuing a foe, and possessing a mate. Its temporal horizons are limited; its demands must be met immediately or else they are judged unmet. Its umwelt is biotemporal: in its world distant futures and pasts do not exist. The paleomammalian brain is also concerned with the preservation of the body and continuity of the species, but it has greater flexibility of response than does its neighbor and ancestor. The neomammalian brain is responsible for hearing, seeing, smelling, and controlling the muscles. The nerve tissues of its most recently evolved part, the neocortex, are responsible for language, long-term anticipation, and memory.[35]

Working as the executive organ of the nervous system, how does the triune brain determine the rate at which time is experienced as passing? Answers such as "it has a clock" or "it is a clock" are unacceptable because of a basic principle of measurement theory. Namely, all measurements, including the measurement of time, consist of comparisons. Any assertion that time passes slowly, rapidly, or at just the right speed can result only from comparisons among two or more clocklike processes. No clock in itself may be fast, slow, or right. One must have at least two clocks as well as a stable relationship of some kind—an identifiable process or an abstract theory—that makes a comparison between them meaningful. Then, and only then, may one of the clocks be said to be fast, slow, or right with respect to the other clock.[36]

What mental processes allow a person to announce that time, as he experienced it, has passed rapidly or slowly? I imagine that those processes consist of comparisons made among different "clock readings," or rather, among different reality assessments by the archaic and more recently evolved layers of the brain. Each such assessment involves needs and potentialities evaluated in terms of its level-specific significance and meaning. The same external or internal conditions are read by the reptilian brain in terms of their significance for hunger, foe, and possession of mate; by the paleomammalian brain in similar terms but with greater flexibility; by the basic neomammalian brain in terms of hearing, seeing, and smelling; and by the neocortex in terms of language, long-term anticipation, memory, and, perhaps, geometry or symphonic music. (For ideas about the brain's self-scanning activities, see appendix E).

Consider next that from the perspective of nootemporality, all lower temporalities appear to have a deficit. To identify what these may be, recall the hallmarks of the canonical forms of time. Atemporal umwelts are characterized by total chaos; the hallmark of prototemporality is statistical (probabilistic) connectedness; and that of eotemporality is deterministic relationships. The hallmark of biotemporality is goal-directedness referred to a present, with narrow temporal horizons; that of nootemporality is directedness toward symbolic goals with open temporal horizons.

The hallmarks of these different temporalities, if thought of as features of umwelts in which we are required to live, bring forth different feelings. These, the affective dimensions of different temporalities, are the different *moods* of time.

The atemporal mood is the suffering of the schizophrenic who feels the pull of chaos and panics at the danger of losing his nootemporal reality. The prototemporal mood is the feeling engendered by any probabilistic world, whether that of indistinguishable people, an aleatory painting swirling with incoherent islands of local coherence, or the babble of an autistic child.

The eotemporal mood is an oceanic feeling, a sense of continuous but directionless time. The biotemporal mood is the fright or happiness of an hour that has no distant futures or pasts. The nootemporal mood is the affective dimension of the reasoned and examined life, with its open temporal horizons and broad potentialities for suffering and joy. Because of the nested hierarchical organization of nature, the nootemporal mood subsumes all the lower temporal moods.

Whenever the higher brain functions are short-circuited, such as in sleep or states of ecstasies, our minds invest their psychic energies now in this and now in that temporal assessment of reality. A noetic evaluation of time will then suggest that what is being experienced is not time as usual but a different temporal umwelt, one that may miss a present, or continuity, or futurity and pastness. In the absence of more precise, generally available terms, such experiences are usually described as those of timelessness.[37]

Experiences described as those of timelessness appear throughout recorded history. They have often been regarded as privileged states of the mind and body, perhaps direct links to a divinity or to some evil agency. The ancient Greek word for such moods is *ekstasis,* which means "to cause to stand outside one's self," to behold the world from a point of view superior to the ordinary perspective. What I suggest is that feelings said to be those of eternity, absolute rest, or infinite peace are descriptions of moods in which one or another lower temporality has become dominant.

Do such experiences make us stand outside ourselves, having ascended into a world that is in some way superior to that of the mature waking mind? Not at all. On the contrary, they take us to the archaic umwelts of the brain, which are less evolved than the noetic. Such umwelts may be experienced as beautiful or terrifying, depending on whether they are perceived as aids or threats to the continuity of the self. The elation that may accompany the descent may be that of a person who has jettisoned the burden of individuation, including responsibilities for the future and regrets about the past; it may be the joy of someone who returned to an earlier, less complex, and less burdensome reality but then climbed back into the noetic world or at least feels that he could do so. But the experience may also be horrifying: the intense present-orientedness of love may be heavenly, but the intense present-orientedness of pain is hellish.

Whenever I make a judgment about the experienced rate of time's passage in terms of "I like it" or "I don't like it," I have made an aesthetic judgment. It is here that the aesthetic sensibilities and the human sense of time merge. But this neatly analytic claim is only a cover, as it were, over an unceasing turmoil of feelings and thoughts.

Hence beware of dreams of eternal beauty. At the beginning of Goethe's *Faust* the hero misses the body and soul of a female and is bored to death by his book learning. He strikes a bargain with the devil: should ever there be an instant when he wants time to abide because the moment is beautiful, he offers, then the devil can take his soul. As M. P. Soulsby reminds us, should the conflicts of individuation vanish, so would the freedom of growth. Replacing the tensions of existence by "rest in timeless serenity and peace, *that* already spells death and damnation."[38] Experiences of timelessness under noetic control may be inspiring, but only if they are not carried out by giving up one's identity and with it the privileges and pains of being human.

Galatea and the Wife of Lot

This subsection sketches a literary model, an allegory of the scanning process that mediates aesthetic judgment by way of a balancing act between time felt and time understood. The allegory involves the figures of two women of Western mythology.

One of these women is known only by her husband's name: she is Lot's wife. She and her family were spirited out of Sodom by two divine messengers so that they could escape the brimstone and fire that were about to be visited on that city. The family was instructed not to look back or else they would also be consumed. But Lot's wife did look back, as did Orpheus in another story. She was punished by being changed into a pillar of salt. We may imagine her, a woman of mind, life, and limb, changing to a mindless living body, a dead body, and then an amorphous rock. Whatever the broadly shared fantasy that underlies the myth, we may take it to represent a journey of collapse from the nootemporal umwelt through the bio- and eotemporal worlds to the prototemporal; a return to dust.

The story of the other woman begins with Pygmalion, king of Cyprus or else a sculptor—depending on whether one reads Greek mythology or the Roman poet Ovid—who ordered made (or himself fashioned) a milk-white statue of a maiden and then promptly fell in love with her. The goddess Aphrodite was so moved that she brought the statue to life as Galatea, who, we are told, bore a son and a daughter to Pygmalion (and to herself). Galatea's journey was that of emergence along the evolutionary umwelts from dust to life and mind. We may imagine the cosmic story of solidifying dust, of matter assuming form, form acquiring life, and finally life acquiring mind and with it the capacity to fear, hope, remember, anticipate, hate, and love.

The sciences follow Lot's wife: they reduce. The "theory of everything," widely discussed during the last decade of the twentieth century, has as its purpose the identification of an equation from which one should be able to derive the phylogeny of ostriches, the conduct of Teddy Roosevelt, and the poetry of Azerbeijan. Alas, the inductively coupled organization of nature's integrative levels makes the execution of such a plan not simply difficult but impossible.

In contrast to the sciences, the humanities travel with Galatea: they ascend; they create the unpredictably new. Galatea—or in Shakespeare's *Winter's Tale,* Hermione—changes from herself as a statue into herself as a living woman. Art may praise both women, but I greatly prefer the woman named Galatea to the salt pillar named Lot's wife because only Galatea can report on her journey and examine its details with the help of her critical intellect. Beneath all this remain the unresolvable conflicts between growth and decay. That is why Alexander Argyros concludes his poem "Lot's Wife and Galatea" with these lines about Galatea.

> Yet, I imagine that at times she softly cries
> while in her lover's arms, before she sleeps,
> because alive and free she still feels
> the need for the old congeries
> of stone and walling air. This, she keeps
> quite to herself, wild dreams of descent and reel
> back into braids of salt.[39]

If humans did not continuously feel the pull of primeval dust, there would be little merit in being and remaining sane. There would be no peculiarly human unresolvable conflicts, nor, consequently, could there be anything called human creativity.

5.4   The Travelers' Reports

Let the figures of Lot's wife and Galatea represent our round-trips into the depths, the continuous journeying of the self into and out of the archaic levels of the mind followed by the compilation of "travel reports" by the organizing and critical capacities of the intellect. That reporting starts early.

Healthy infants laugh at an object they like and keep looking at it; they frown on whatever they do not like and turn their heads away. They vote by the lengths of their gaze, by a pattern of behavior that has been used in the developmental psychology of infants as a measure of the intensity of interest. With the passing years the lengths of preferential gaze and listening expand from seconds to hours, years, and, collectively, centuries. Infantile likes and dislikes mature into cultural prowess in the form of aesthetic judgments. The infant devours the breast by his look and with his lips, and if his name is Ben Jonson, he will later write, "Drink to me only with thine eyes / And I will pledge with mine." Others, generations after him, will know what he meant.

There are innumerably many different inner worlds of which a person can give what I called executive summaries, but the need to share them with others has jelled these reports into traditional forms. They are known as the arts and letters. Refracting through them is a desire to reach for permanence, for timelessness, in the sense explained earlier.

"Dance, then, wherever you may be . . ."

One evening, many years ago, in the Cantabrian Mountains of northern Spain, I watched spellbound the undulating lacework at the hem of the skirt worn by a woman dancing the flamenco. It was a flamenco *jondo,* or profound flamenco: intense, brooding, metaphysical, celebratory. The dance is of Andalusian origins; the word *flamenco* is believed to derive from the Arabic *felag mangu,* "fugitive peasant," having been a dance of runaway serfs. The white lace rose and sank, folded and unfolded; set against the warm brown color of her shapely legs and the deep yellow of her dress, it was temptation at its best. Her male partner stood like a soldier erect, arms folded over his chest as if protecting his teased ego; then he began his steps with toe and heel clicking and started to move around like an exclamation mark rolling on its point.

At its ancient roots this strongly carnal dance was surely a celebration of the sexual union to come. Not so were the steps of the Shakers, who danced to bring about and celebrate a life free from the passions of the body.

> Come life, Shaker life,
> Come life eternal;
> Shake, shake out of me
> All that is carnal.

The Shakers, the whirling dervishes of Sufism, and many other groups held that in dance the sense of time's passage may lessen or even disappear. Dancing to a regular beat focuses the dancer's feelings on the beat: a steady bump-bump-bump has no preferred direction in time, just as the ticks of a clock do not; the umwelt of such beats is eotemporal. It is the absence of temporal direction that the dancer notices while, in his mind, there remains an awareness of noetic time. Ordinarily we live in a continuous tension between our knowledge of passing and a latent image of eternity. During spirited dancing that tension lessens; the dancer's identity loses its sharp definition as he or she comes to feel a unity with another person or even with the world of the stars and planets. The experience is a return to childhood, when time seemed infinite and only the present existed. This mental condition is a form of ecstasy, the "standing outside one's self" mentioned earlier. Let us call it the *ecstasy of the dance*. A man and a woman, if they dance the flamenco *jondo* as an expression of their love, dissolve their identities into the communality of rhythmic motion in the ecstasy of the dance. That state of mind may then continue in the *ecstasy of the bower*, where conflicts vanish and time stands still in postcoital peace.

It was dance that made Zorba the Greek, in Kazantzakis's novel by that title, lose his self to a devil within.

> Whenever I feel I'm choking with some emotion, he says: "Dance!" and I dance. And I feel better! Once, when my little Dimitraki died, in Chalcidice, I got up . . . and I danced. The relations and friends who saw me dancing in front of the body rushed up to stop me. "Zorba has gone mad" they cried. . . . But if at that moment I had not danced, I should really have gone mad—from grief. Because it was my first son and he was three years old and I could not bear to lose him.[40]

Salome danced as she offered the severed head of John the Baptist; during the French Revolution Parisians danced the carmagnole around the guillotine, a machine designed to increase the efficiency of severing heads. The French dancers were kin of the Hindu Shiva in his form as Nataraja, the cosmic dancer. Shiva was said to have reconciled in his nature the opposition between perpetual motion and eternal stasis, creation and destruction, change and permanence. The center of the universe, where his dance takes place, is said to be the human heart; his perfect rhythm is an expression of triumphal joy, a sign that in the heart of the disciple everything disappears except the god himself.

In the *ecstasy of the forest* the feeling of directionless continuity comes about by focusing not on ceaseless rhythmic change but on what appears to be absolute rest. This is the mood of the lonely eminence of the northern Cascades, a continuous now, where future and past are rolled together into an eternal present. The tension of selfhood lessens as the wayfarer feels himself integrated with the eternity of the forest. At the celebration of Max Planck's sixtieth birthday, Albert Einstein described it this way:

> I believe . . . that one of the strongest motives that lead men to art and science is escape from everyday life with its painful crudity and hopeless dreariness, from the fetters of one's ever shifting desires. A finely tempered nature longs to escape from personal life into the world of objective perception and thought; this desire may be compared with the townsman's irresistible longing to escape from his noisy, cramped surroundings into the high mountains, where the eye ranges freely

through the still, pure air and fondly traces out the restful contours which look as if they are built for eternity.[41]

The language and setting of these remarks are those of German romanticism, much of which was swept away by World War II, the cold war, and the post–cold war ailments and crazes. Be that as it may, the contemplation of unchanging vistas relieves the mind of individuation and replaces the noetic mood by an eotemporal one.

Before World War II and during its early years, I witnessed the *ecstasy of the crowd* brought about by, as well as expressed in, choreographed dances. These dances consisted of the tramping of massed uniformed men to the tune of military music and the rhythmic waving of banners and the singing of victory songs by hundreds of thousands of people. They were collective descents into the experience of timelessness. In a biography entitled *Hitler*, Joachim Fest describes such an event. Hitler, he writes, "delivered one of his passionate speeches that whipped the audience into a kind of collective orgy, all waiting tensely for the moment of release, the orgasm that manifested itself in a wild outcry. The parallel is too patent to be passed over, it lets us see Hitler's oratorical triumphs as surrogate actions of churning sexuality unable to find its object."[42] The crowds were willingly seduced to become his lovers in the collective ecstasy of a political bower. The rhythmic chants of "Sieg Heil!" made people shake in the presence of their Führer as Shakers shook in the presence of the Lord.

The Marseillaise is an earlier example of the ecstasy of the crowd. In stirring words and music, each line pushes the marcher toward losing more of his identity; psychiatrists call this phenomenon "depersonalization."

> Allons enfants de la patrie!
> Le jour de gloire est arrivé!
> Contre nous de la tyrannie
> L'étendard sanglant est levé. . . .

Line by line: We are all children without personal identities. Our interest is only in the immediate; the day of glory is at hand. We are united in a single purpose, to kill the unnamed tyrant in the name of us all. Death guarantees our brotherhood, represented by a flag dripping blood.

In the words of an old Cornish carol that became a favorite song in the United States of the 1960s, all dancers are kin of Christ, the Lord of the Dance. Sung to the music of Aaron Copland's "Simple Gifts," a Shaker tune, the narrative tells of the crucified Christ descending from the Cross and leading not only the people of the earth but the whole world in a cosmic dance, in a "life that will never, never die." His instructions are for celebration: "'Dance, then, wherever you may be / I am the Lord of the Dance' said he." The words would equally befit Shiva.

The evolutionary origins of dance vanish in the courting behavior of birds, the wiggling of fish, and the oscillations of microorganisms. Early archaeological records suggest that rhythmic motion was regarded already by Paleolithic people as a privileged activity. Dividing time by beats, however, and structuring the beats according the force needed to lift and lower the foot in dance and according to the lengths of times involved had to await the genius of early Greece. In dance a foot may, for example, be lifted slowly and lowered rapidly or lifted rapidly and lowered slowly. *Arsis* (the lifting of the foot) and *thesis* (the lowering of the foot) are combined in the fundamental elements of "feet," the units of prosodic analysis of rhythm in music, dance, and poetry. Classical meter recognizes such phonological features as stress, pitch, and length and organizes them into binary opposites: stress versus unstress, long versus short, and deflected versus level (in pitch). From such foundations of stresses and durations evolved the system of classical feet. From the Renaissance on the classical rules remained very much alive, but new organizational forms of longer durations were invented and added to the aesthetic structuring of dance, music, and poetry.

I will regard dance as the oldest and most general form of artistic beauty, the mother lode of the arts and letters. In what follows I will think of music as the audible dimension of dance; poetry as dance mapped into words; prose as poetry changed to shuffle, walk, or run; painting, sculpture, and architecture as snapshots of dance steadied by meaning; and film as dance, music, literature, and painting in virtual reality.

Music

Western efforts to understand the power and beauty of music grew from Pythagorean roots. Ask what delights you in dancing and number will reply, here I am, wrote Saint Augustine around the end of the fourth century.[43] It was harmony by number that made music the *ars bene modulandi*, the art (skill, science, know-how) of measuring (playing) well.[44] Thirteen centuries later Leibniz asserted that music is the pleasure the human soul experiences from counting without being aware that it is counting. Music appreciation surely includes subitization, but its aesthetic appeal derives from something much more sophisticated.

Once, listening to Bach's Toccata and Fugue in D Minor, I was hypnotized by the running and rushing of its musical emotions, its cosmology of ambivalent and paradoxical feelings. It spoke of the logic and structure of timelessness, of the freedom of passion, of the pain of passing. The notes were gone before I had time to grasp whatever went by. I was pummeled by the onslaught of ever new emotions, by the climbing of one breath on another in a ceaseless descent into chaos and ascent out of chaos into a world of time deeply felt but only vaguely understood. The stirring of emotions through music is a universal human experience; it cuts across cultures, epochs, and individual temperaments. What kinds of skills create the universality and power of music, and what kinds of reports about the moods of temporalities explain those properties?

Chimpanzee groups sometimes go on carnivals: they shout loudly and drum on tree trunks, apparently to keep the dispersed animals together. Gorillas beat their chests and thump, often in predictable sequence and rhythms, either to threaten or to play. Individual whales have their own variations of species-specific songs used for mutual recognition as they migrate. Many birds sing. Their purposes range from announcing danger to marking territory and seeking mates. Some bird species improvise in ways analogous to musical composition by humans: the skeletons of their songs are innate, but a population-specific overlay is acquired by learning and then modulated by individually invented variations. Cranes, sea eagles, quail, and grebes often sing in duet. In spite of the importance and broad range of animal sounds and related inventiveness, however, the separation of music-like and speechlike sounds in animals is either impossible or at best marginal. I believe that music in humans evolved from a combination of rhythmic motion and articulate cries as the physiology of hearing became refined. Speech and music became separated when the minding functions of the brain learned to distinguish between predominantly emotive and predominantly cognitive utterances.

The spectrum of cycles audible to humans is between 21,000 and 15 Hz, which makes it about ten octaves wide, although the effective spectrum of music is much broader, for it extends into very low frequencies. Musical rhythms are measured in seconds, melodic sentences in minutes, compositions in hours, and musical traditions in years and centuries. The ten octaves of audible sounds are included in the lower frequencies in the spectrum of the cyclic order of life, which extends seventy-eight octaves (see appendix A, "Time and the Origin of Life"). In the intuitive wisdom of language, music is said to speak to people. It does. It enters the audio loop that helps to define the cognitive self through language; it also enters the kinesthetic range of motional rhythm and beyond it, the range of culturally determined rhythms.[45]

In sec. 2.2, on temporalities, the organic, mental, and social presents were interpreted as the phenomenal manifestations of simultaneities maintained from instant to instant among biological, neurological, and social events. The maintenance of these presents was seen as defining and guaranteeing the integrity of the life process, the self, and the collective self.

Likewise, the *musical present* is created by the simultaneities of sounds related to one another by whatever rules composers, performers, and listeners find desirable. The composer, performer, and listener may of course be the selfsame person, for example, someone who whistles while he works. The musical present defined through sound is necessarily synchronous with the organic and mental presents. Once established and maintained, the combination of pitches, rhythms, melodies, stases, and variations in timber and texture may then create musical memories and anticipations and, with them, the musical experience of time's passage. This process in the affective domain is analogous, in the organic, cognitive, and social domains, to the ceaseless reclassification of expectations and memories into the categories of future and past with respect to the organic, noetic, and social presents. Music making and music hearing continuously classify and reclassify musical expectations and memories with respect to the musical present. What emerges into awareness is the musical forms of the passage of time felt.

The moods of time in musical experience may vary from instant to instant and are specific to the individual. Permanent configurations of feelings then combine into the individual's signature of his or her emotive self. In the words of David Epstein,

> time on all musical levels exists in a continual state of coordination and/or conflict, found in the relations of the metric to the rhythmic, with their attendant properties. Beat and pulse, the minimal units of time, often deviate slightly from each other. . . . On larger levels, metric and rhythmic quanta are also dissynchronous at times, the pull and conflict between the two domains creating a continual balance of tensions until the ultimate resolution of final closure.[46]

By mobilizing a person's aesthetic sensibilities, music appeals to memories and expectations, and through them, by association, it appeals to intellectual judgments and puzzlements. It does so without the need of being specific. By assisting in the definition of the emotional self, it helps to order feelings into those one would like to perpetuate and those one would like to banish.

Music enters the process of self-definition through a continuous analysis of what is being heard into elements of recognizable permanence and unpredictable change. This is analogous to what happens in the visual domain, where motion is separated into apparently stable continuities and unpredictable changes. The separation of change from permanence in the cognitive domain helps to define the cognitive self; similar separation in the musical domain helps to define the emotive self. In the words of the music theorist J. D. Kramer, the moods of temporalities give "artistic voice to the archaic umwelts from which we, as individuals, as members of human society, and even as physical entities, evolved."[47]

We "regard music or any artistic process as seemly when it invites and rewards our instinctive efforts to identify with its persona and respond with affect to the vital rhythm within which it moves and the symbolic transformations it undergoes," wrote Lewis Rowell.[48] The identification with the persona of music is not carried out on an intellectual level. I do not feel like molding myself into a particular sonic universe because I know that the music is written in B-flat but because it addresses my emotive self and generates in me moods of temporalities whose combinations I would like to perpetuate.

On a Holy Thursday many years ago I heard the monks of the Benedictine abbey of St. Pierre de Solesme, in Cambray, France, sing the medieval hymn "Ubi Caritas et Amor, Deus Ibi Est" (where charity and love abide, God is also nigh). I felt at one with the God of Christ and understood the quiet ecstasies of monkish life, working toward the assumed ultimate reality of undirected time. A good name for this example of "timelessness" is the *ecstasy of the chalice*. Although the name implies the Catholic belief in the transubstantiated presence of Christ's body and blood in the sacramental bread and wine, the metaphor is well suited to many religious ecstasies.[49]

In this form of ecstasy—mood of temporality, type of timelessness—music served as an audible support for a religious cosmology. Let me suggest a secular version of musical cosmology using the English art of change ringing as a model of cosmic passage.

Change ringing consists in ringing a set of variously pitched bells following a stable rule of permutations. A set of rings is called a "change," and a set of changes, a peal. Three bells can ring a peal of 6 changes; five bells, 120 changes; twelve bells, a peal of 479,001,600 changes. This would take forty years of continuous ringing, with no change ever repeated. A peal teases the listeners, leaving them with a feeling of ceaseless change. The mind attaches itself now to this and now to that pattern of sound in search for a stable melody, but it finds none, even though there is an unchanging mathematical rule beneath the music. The continuity, the permanence sought in a peal of 479,001,600 changes, could be found only by a memory that would recognize the beginning of a new stable cycle after forty years of listening. Instead of the rules of permutation, we could select as the basis of change ringing the rule of the Maya calendar, which repeats itself every 260 years, or Plato's "perfect number," which is so many thousands of years between two consecutive conjunctions of all the planets. As the scope of change ringing (a model of time and music) expands, we leave the domain of sound and enter first the cyclic and then the aging orders of life, then the history of mankind, and finally that of the universe. The universe itself may be thought of as a process of change ringing by innumerable oscillators according to principles of organization that themselves evolve.

These changes ring a cosmic melody in the cyclic order of nature, having a frequency range that extends beyond the audible, beyond the lifetimes of persons, and even beyond that of life itself. People have sought metanarratives of stable patterns in these melodies beyond the ear, and it is in this sense that music is an audible cosmology. It generates moods that people often wish to perpetuate because they suggest the negation of passage.

The Literary Arts

How do the literary arts go about creating feelings among which reader-listeners may select some to perpetuate, others to reject?

They do so through (1) the skilled use of the musical dimensions of language, (2) narration that creates new processes for familiar and unfamiliar worlds, and (3) the creation and use of metaphors to furnish those worlds.

The Music of Language There are two loosely defined forms of the literary arts: verse and prose. *Verse* comes from the Latin *vertere* ("to turn"); *prose,* from the Latin *prosa oratio* ("straightforward talk"). I think of verse as dance mapped into words and prose as walking mapped into words. Verse, then, relates to prose as dance relates to walking. But there are people who walk their dance and others who dance their walk, and so it is in literature: literary forms embrace both verse and prose in an infinite number of combinations.

People can enjoy listening to poems in a language they do not understand and can enjoy nonsense verse. Children can sit spellbound listening to a poem long before they can understand its meaning. In all these cases people are listening to the music of the spoken word. The musical dimensions of language are deeper than its gnostic ones because emotions to which the music of language appeals are older than reasoning: a person will remember poems in his mother tongue long after he has lost his ability to speak it. It follows from the essential involvement of the music of language in the literary arts that, beneath whatever else a literary piece conveys to the reasoning self, it also addresses the affective identities of its listeners or readers. Through its musical dimensions language thus mobilizes the different moods of time, as does music. The discipline that deals with the musical dimensions of language in terms of its rhythm, meter, pace, sound, tone, accent, and rhyme, and with the cadences of its syntax and semantics, is called "verse theory" or "prosody."[50] The latter term comes from the ancient Greek *prosoidia,* which means a song with accompaniment and also the tone or accent on a syllable. Prosodic analysis of texts in terms of their metrical patterns—whose elements, the feet, we already encountered—is called "scansion." The process of analyzing meter is called "scanning."

Over eighty years ago, in an essay called "Poetry of the Present," D. H. Lawrence distinguished between poetry that deals with distant pasts and futures and poetry that deals with present instants. These different temporal locations, he suggested, are reflected in their meters. Poetry about the long ago and yet to come "must have that exquisite finality, perfection which belongs to all that is far off. [Such distances are conveyed by] the perfect symmetry, the rhythm that returns upon itself like a dance where the hands link and loosen and link for the supreme moment of the end. Perfected bygone moments, perfected moments in the glimmering futurity, these are the treasured, gem-like lyrics of Shelley and Keats."[51] This, he said, is metric poetry, by which he seems to have meant quantitative verse, that is, verse that uses classical Greek and Latin feet as its meter. This claim limits the validity of his assertion because although all poetry has meter, its elements differ. Stable, repetitive meter does indeed often suggest but does not demand feelings of stability and evenness, whether in the distant future, the past, or the present and whether consoling or disturbing.

But there is another kind of poetry, continued Lawrence, one that deals not with the long ago and the yet to come but with the immediate present. This recognizes that a

perfect rose is only a running flame, emerging and flowing off, and never in any sense at rest, static, finished. Herein lies its transient loveliness. [This is the] unrestful, ungraspable poetry of the sheer present, poetry whose very permanence lies in its wind-like transit. [It] sweeps past for ever like a wind that is forever in passage. . . . [It has] no rhythm which returns upon itself, no serpent of eternity with its tail in its own mouth. There is no static perfection, none of that finality which we find so satisfying because we are so frightened [of passage]. We do not speak of things crystallized and set apart. We speak of the instant, the immediate self, the very plasm of the self. We speak also of free verse.[52]

Free verse is distinguished from quantitative verse by the absence of structuring whose elements are to be counted in linguistic units, whatever those units may be. In free verse cycles and rhythms on the phonetic level are optional. What is not optional is a prosody on the syntactic and semantic levels, a flow of images, symbols, and meanings. Free verse mixes the predictable with the strikingly unpredictable; it creates a churning present of rapidly passing instants. But it is also right for conditions, feelings, and events of the long past and future *if* they were or will be those of restlessness. Free verse is popular in contemporary poetry around the world because it is appropriate for a globe that copies Walt Whitman's America. In that America, he wrote, contraltos, carpenters, duck shooters, deacons, spinning girls, freaks, half-breeds, squaws, patriarchs, peddlers, and opium eaters were kaleidoscopic forms of the selfsame identity, an unrestrained multiform unity. "Come Muse migrate from Greece and Ionia . . . For know a better, fresher, busier sphere, a wide, untried domain awaits, demands you."[53] Today the whole world is a stage for contraltos, carpenters, duck shooters, spinning girls, and freaks. Here is free verse by Whitman (1867).

> Out of the rolling ocean the crowd came a drop gently to me,
> Whispering *I love you, before long I die,*
> *I have travel'd a long way merely to look on you to touch you,*
> *For I could not die till I once look'd on you,*
> *For I fear'd I might afterward lose you.*
>
> Now we have met, we have look'd, we are safe,
> Return in peace to the ocean my love.[54]

"On the Pulse of the Morning" is by one of the contemporary masters of free verse, Maya Angelou (1991).

> A Rock, A River, A Tree
> Hosts of species long since departed,
> Marked the mastodon,
> The dinosaur, who left dried tokens
> Of their journey here.[55]

Let us look beyond our Western garden of verse. As already mentioned, the musical elements of literary language need not be feet. In Chinese each character has a monosyllabic pronunciation whose tonal variation indicates differences in meaning. The ideogram-syllables and their syllabic tones constitute the smallest prosodic units of Chinese just as feet are the smallest prosodic units of classical Greek and Latin poetic forms and their derivatives. The Chinese language forces prosody upward, from syllables to words and images. Classical Chinese poetry was successfully translated into English only after the translators set aside the rhymes and meters of English verse together with Western concepts of poetic diction and theme and began using a free form that permitted the power of the original to shine through.[56]

Chinese and Japanese poetry no less than free verse in Indo-European languages demonstrate how hazy are the boundaries between verse and prose. In Japanese and Chinese that haziness is native to the acoustic properties of the spoken language and the ideographic-syllabic character of the written tongue; in free verse it stems from a rejection of any prescribed micromanagement of form.

The examples offered could not have displayed their rhythms and cadences if language itself, any language, did not have a strong musical dimension. Like mathematics, present in everything but obvious only in the work of mathematicians, the music of language is inherent in language but obvious only in the works of its great practitioners. Charles Dickens was praised for his "secret prose," by which was meant the delicate musical sequences of Dickensian English.[57] Here is an example from *Bleak House.*

Fog everywhere. Fog up the river, where it flows among green aits [inlets] and meadows; fog down the river, where it rolls defined among the tiers of shipping, and the waterside pollutions of a great (and dirty) city. Fog on the Essex marshes, fog on the Kentish heights. Fog creeping into the cabooses of collier-brigs; fog lying out on the yards, and hovering in the riggings of great ships; fog dropping on the gunwales of barges and small boats. Fog in the eyes and throat of ancient Greenwich pensioners, wheezing by the firesides of their wards. . . . Chance people on the bridges peeping over the parapets into the nether sky of fog, with fog all around them, as if they were up in a balloon, and hanging in the misty clouds.[58]

Creation by Telling Animals narrate; they tell stories. Hens cluck to announce the successful delivery of an egg. A mountain goat's warning cry is a story told to bring forth appropriate actions by others, as is the dance of bees returning from a foray. The verb *narrate* has its distant roots in the Latin *gnarus,* "knowing." Narration is a way of communicating knowledge. In humans it is the telling of a story in such detail and manner as is appropriate for the narrator's language, values, and concerns.

Whether a narrative pertains to the lives of generations in an Irish village, to an instant on the Ohio River, or to the cry of a cyborg, all literary expressions are moved by narration. They may tell stories seen under a time microscope that reveals the delicate fabric of life, feeling, and thought. They may tell stories seen through a time telescope that shows the designs of a caring or uncaring providence. Finally, since literary devices may be combined according to any rhyme or reason, they may be the joint venture of time microscopes, time telescopes, and observations made by the naked eye or the naked body. Narration consists in arranging phonetic, syntactic, semantic, affective, and cognitive elements into texts that are sufficiently consistent with the canonical forms of temporalities and causations to enter the nested hierarchy of the reader-listener's noetic umwelt. Here the reader-listener may be the writer-talker himself.

Story telling has surely been around since human language emerged: there are no cultures without stories, and there is no indication that stories would cease to be important in cyberspace. What explains the vitality of narrative as a form of communication? The literary theorist Michael Holquist proposed that

> the journey from birth to death serves as a biographical rhythm that entrains information into narrative so that it may best be processed as meaning by men and women who are born to die. Transition . . . from one point to another is the essence of life as it is of narrative, and it is therefore not surprising that . . . such movement has so often been mapped as a journey. . . . When viewed in this light, narrative is the terminal level of a process beginning at much earlier and deeper levels; the ability to narrate is itself part of an immense journey.[59]

Biography, he suggests, is a "master narrative that imposes itself on any attempt to arrange chronologically instanced phenomena into a sequence that has meanings over and beyond the brute seriality of their appearance."[60] He calls this the biographical imperative. "Time, not language as such, is the fundamental category of narrative," working via biography.[61] That is, time in narration works through the family of meanings given to the temporal events that constitute a life from its beginning to its end.

Narration, biography, and the creation and furnishing of new realities taken together form a family of time-based capacities that help to organize feelings and knowledge by the fundamental aesthetic distinctions of "I like it" and "I like it not." Whether the narrative describes reality in the ordinary sense of the term (meaning our umwelt) is irrelevant to its task of conveying the conflicts of being human. Let me illustrate this irrelevance.

Marina Tsvetaeva (1892–1941) was one of the great twentieth-century poets in the Russian language. Her life, from Russian intellectual upper-middle-class origins, through a passionate and troubled love affair, to exile abroad, return home, exile at home, and suicide in an obscure Asian town, is what cheap journalism would call a real-life human interest story.[62] Her life is neither less nor more wrenching and inspiring than the life of Boris Pasternak's fictional Doctor Zhivago. Tsvetaeva gave up her infant daughter to a Russian orphanage where the infant starved to death. Sophie in William Styron's fictional *Sophie's Choice* gives up her son to a Nazi officer in a death camp where he dies in the gas chambers. There is no internal datum whereby Tsvetaeva's biography may be told apart from Zhivago's or Sophie's. In an earlier age we had Sidney Carton witnessing the French Revolution in *A Tale of Two Cities*. Would anyone be foolish enough to lay down his life insisting that Carton's story is fiction or nonfiction? Common to all these stories is that they are forms of narration.

Is the story of the Nativity real or is it fiction? Is it the kind of story that W. H. Auden described as feigned history? Is the story of Siddhartha Gautama real? Israel's captivity in Egypt? The Great March of Mao? The creation of the world in theology or physics? Is it perhaps the case that good narratives are feigned histories and good histories are feigned narratives that take on lives of their own? Life, says the Bard of Avon, is a tale told by an idiot, full of sound and fury, signifying nothing. We may play out his tune: narratives are tales told by idiots (all humans), full of sound and fury (if they are good storytellers) and signifying whatever the listeners or readers desire.

Alexander Argyros captures this prescription when he remarks that "not only is narrative a stubbornly universal manifestation of human culture, but . . . it constitutes one of the most remarkable and desirable inventions of biological evolution."[63] He adds that one of the tasks of the human brain has been the creation of internal maps whose organizing principles, employing the different levels of causation, are also the organizing principles of narration. It has often been stressed that narratives convey information. This is certainly true for the hen announcing the laying of her egg. It is also true for human narration, but there it is a fatally incomplete view. Narratives do not simply re-present objects, ideas, or cognitive structures. They are "isomorphic to the dynamics of nature—[to] the cruelty and beauty of the deep dialectical interpenetration between conservation and creation."[64]

"Literature can *do* to us what other forms of discourse talk *about*," remarked M. P. Soulsby in her paper "Order and Disorder: Creating Temporality in Literary Experience."[65] Much has been written *about* time within the domain of the literary arts. But if the literary arts could do no more than convey ideas about time as do books in philosophy, psychology, or biology, there could be no reason ever to reread a poem or a novel. Nor does the unique power of literature rest simply in conveying a story line. I already know what Quentin Compson thought of the South in Faulkner's *Absalom, Absalom!* and that Doctor Zhivago died of a heart attack. I revisit those narratives not to find out what happened but to reexperience the descents and ascents into the archaic depths of my own mind, to reassess the nested hierarchy of realities I encounter, and to reexamine them in terms of my own changing critical powers and thus discover infinitely many new aspects of the world suggested by the genius of the writer. Literature arrests the instant and rules it or else urges time on; through either magic it helps to make the writer, reader, and listener participate in the creation of reality. Common to all literary expressions is a search for order: "The light, the light, the seeking, the searching, in chaos, in chaos," in the words of a Maori creation myth.[66]

Metaphor Making A metaphor is an imaginative extension of the meaning of a word or phrase in a manner that grants new qualities to a known object, event, or process. Here is a poem from the twentieth dynasty of Egypt, ca. 1186–1069 B.C., a century or two after the fall of Troy and the Hebrew Exodus.

> I am thy first love, I am thy garden,
> Scented with spices, fragrant with flowers.
> Deep runs my channel, smoothed by thy tillage,
> Cooled by the North Wind, filled by the Nile.[67]

Of the eight half-lines of this quatrain, the first may mean what it says, though it might also refer to a senior concubine. How do I know that the rest of the poem is not a report on agricultural conditions? The answer is that the first half-line casts doubt on the literal meaning of the second half-line. If, following that doubt, I focus on the idea and experience of love suggested at the outset, the imagery of the poem becomes coherent. My mind changes the literal meanings to similes: she is as beautiful as a garden, as exciting as the scent of exotic spices, as soothing and fragrant as flowers. She is ready to receive her man deep in her body, which awaits the work of the plowman (an old figure of speech).[68] Finally, I remove the similes and find myself with a metaphorical garden in the shape of a loving woman.

Languages, one can assume, evolved from animal cries, which could not have had precise, literal meanings. Each new meaning given to an utterance had to be metaphorical first, then literal, and then literal as well as metaphorical. It must be the case, therefore, that all contemporary words were once metaphors. The result is a continuous tension among meanings. Paul Ricoeur observed that "a metaphor is alive [only] as long as we can perceive, through the new semantic pertinence—and so to speak, in its denseness— the resistance of the words in their ordinary use and therefore their incompatibility at the level of literal interpretation of the sentence."[69] Once the tension between the old and new meanings wears away, the metaphor acquires a literal meaning and is ready to serve as a metaphor once again, this time for new conditions or things.[70] I call the birdhouse on our shagbark hickory a honeybun because it houses a mellifluous bluebird. If people were to keep on using this metaphor and extend it to mean a lover, then I would expect Webster's Dictionary of 2020 to contain the following entry: "*Honeybun:* (i) sweetheart; (ii) birdhouse of a songbird."

Psychoanalytic theory adds some useful details to our understanding of metaphor. "Metaphor constitutes an outcropping into conscious expression of a fragment of an unconscious fantasy. The aesthetic effectiveness of metaphor in literature is derived, in large measure, from the ability of the metaphorical expression to stimulate the affects associated with widely entertained, communally shared unconscious fantasies."[71] The theory authorizes a technical rule in psychoanalysis, namely, that the words and adjectival phrases that the patient uses to describe a dream are to be considered part of the dream proper and may be used as a point of departure for eliciting associations. Of interest here are the imaginative powers of our minds, which can "dream up" new meanings for old words.

It is the mind's metaphor-making ability that the linguist Terence Hawkes was thinking of when he maintained that

> language is an organic, self-contained, autonomous system which divides and classifies experience in its own terms and along its own lines. In the course of the process, it imposes its own particular shape on the world of those who speak it. In effect, then, language and experience interact and prove fundamentally implicated with each other to the extent that makes it difficult to consider them as separate entities. A language creates reality in its own image. To use language thus essentially involves getting at one kind of reality through another.[72]

The process is one of comprehending the world in terms of metaphors. From this point of view all languages are fundamentally metaphorical. Metaphor, concludes Hawkes, is the way language works.

The power and beauty of skilled metaphor making reside in a conflict contained, to wit, the tension between the unpredictably new and the received meanings of words, phrases, and images directed to serve the purpose of a piece of writing. Each metaphor exemplifies the human capacity to make furnishings for new realities.

Reflections In the introduction to *The Bow and the Lyre,* the Mexican poet Octavio Paz described poetry and, by extension, the poetic in verse or prose—the totality of the literary arts—in a score of paired terms. Each pair comprises two logically contradictory and hence presumably mutually exclusive elements.

> Poetry is knowledge, salvation, power, abandonment. . . . Bread of the chosen; accursed food. It isolates; it unites. Invitation to the journey;

return to the homeland. Historic expression of races, nations, classes. It denies history: at its core all objective conflicts are resolved. . . . Art of speaking in a superior way; primitive language. . . . Madness, ecstasy, logos. Return to childhood, coitus, nostalgia for paradise, for hell, for limbo. . . . Voice of the people, language of the chosen, word of the solitary. Pure and impure, sacred and damned, popular and of the minority, collective and personal . . . spoken, painted, written.[73]

It seems impossible to specify a set of unambiguous criteria whereby a text could be tested and declared to be a literary creation. Yet most people can recognize such a text. The recognition has to do, I believe, with the very contradictions that make a definition impossible: we know poetry by the tension it creates and contains. This is what Wordsworth observed, writing in 1798. "In spite of differences of soil and climate, of language and manners, of laws and customs: in spite of things silently gone out of mind, and things violently destroyed; the Poet binds together by passion and knowledge the vast empire of human society, as it is spread over the whole earth, and over all time."[74]

I conclude that the power of the letters resides in the generation of feelings rich enough for reader-listeners to pick and choose among them— some to perpetuate, some to deny or even forget, and much in between to keep, arrange, and rearrange, all in the ceaseless process of constructing and maintaining personal and collective identities.

The Fine Arts

For my purposes, the fine arts comprise painting, sculpture, architecture, and film. How do these arts create feelings that their admirers and critics may choose to maintain, reject, or view with uncertainty?

I begin with painting. The amount of gray matter in the cerebrum devoted to a particular part of the body depends on the importance that part has come to have in the natural history of humans. The sensory areas of the cortex, for instance, are largely devoted to integrating sensations from the face, hands, and genitals; the larger parts of motor capabilities are devoted to controlling the face and thumb. The face has come to be of great importance because it is used for vital communication: it sends and receives signals on the states of mind and body and indicates intentions.

It was useful but not necessary to appeal to the relative amounts of gray matter in the human brain: painters have known the importance of the face all along. Among paintings, portraits are legion; hands are much less frequent but still significant. There are national portrait galleries, whereas there could be but there are no national hand galleries. And there are no national genital galleries. This restriction is culture dependent, however;

in Hindu art the lingam and the yoni, the male and female genitals, are frequent artistic representations of the creative principle of the universe.

The brain structure called the amygdala is a part of the limbic system. In nonhuman animals its stimulation produces rage, and its removal produces docility. In humans its destruction severely impairs the person's reactions to social signals: he will be unable to discern fear in facial expressions or identify direction of gaze.[75] These are fatal deficiencies because visual signs are the most facile means used by humans to foretell another's behavior. In the development of the infant, the first lines and shapes it contemplates are those of the mother's face: the child learns how to read her face as a guide to conduct. Portraits are landscapes of faces; landscapes are images of the faces of mother earth. These figures of speech are not accidental: a visual mapping of reality may always be described as a landscape. Therefore, let us consider landscape painting.

The origins of landscape painting are difficult to date because early in the history of our species sky, mountains, fish, beast, and humans were all integral parts of the great everything. Stone Age cave wall paintings, though not composite landscapes in the contemporary sense, contain enough horses, bulls, warriors, and ritual ceremonies to be considered records of the faces of the Paleolithic environment. Landscape representations were found in predynastic Egypt in the fourth millennium B.C. and in Mesopotamia during the third millennium B.C. Landscape painting proper appears in the frescoes of Roman villas and is traditional in China, where changes in the seasons have held a spiritual significance.

In an essay entitled "Church, Humboldt, and Darwin: The Tension and Harmony of Art and Science," Stephen Jay Gould sought the sources of the universal fascination with landscape painting. He suggested that "maximal diversity of life and landscape [is] the *summum bonum* of aesthetic joy and intellectual wonder."[76] Anyone familiar with Frederic Church's majestic canvasses can appreciate Gould's enthusiasm: they are visual treats and careful records of the lushness of nature. If realism means a representation of the way the world looks to us here and now, then his paintings are realistic. But there is no immaculate realism. The beauty of Church's images consists not in their vibrant wealth alone but in their ability to convey a dynamic order beneath the riches and confusion of motion and life, one steadied by meaning. In the words of the art critic Franklin Kelly, the "genius of his artistic invention was the catalyst that helped him transform what he learned from others into a vision of the world that is still original and powerfully expressive."[77]

Artistic vision is that extra something that completes an image by the emotive and cognitive identities of painter and viewer over and above optical specifications. J. M. W. Turner is reported to have said that he did not copy nature; he improved on it. Similar thoughts were expressed by the eminent French scholar Étienne Gilson. He remembered a definition of art by Francis Bacon as "man added to nature." Then, in a pantheistic framework that resembles the generalized umwelt principle and is quite at variance with Gilson's otherwise Thomistic philosophy, he argued as follows:

> Since man is part and parcel of nature, he cannot be added to it. Rather. . . art should be conceived as man adding to nature, or, better still, as nature enriching itself by all the additions that it received at the hands of man. . . . the painter is neither a philosopher nor a scientist in whose mind nature mirrors itself; but he is not, at the same time, one of those engineers whose cleverness harnesses the forces of nature . . . [;] he is one of the creative forces of nature, in this sense at least, that he gives existence to certain beings that, in nature, nothing else than himself could possibly have produced.[78]

Church's vision of the world, Turner's improving on nature, and Gilson's artist as a creative force of nature are different ways of identifying the process of steadying by meaning. This is the work of the imaginative powers of the mind crystallized into a waking dream. It is not by chance that those who can express in universally understandable terms whatever is in the depths of their minds are called visionaries or dreamers: their visions are kin to dreams. Let me elaborate this point by following a monograph on creativity by J. D. Ormeland, who used Michelangelo's Sistine ceiling as his example.

A dream, Ormeland wrote, "is best considered as a composite of condensed metaphorical visualized images representing the topical, the personal and the archetypal."[79] Michelangelo's Sistine ceiling, he suggests, is a dream expressed; it is "homologous with a dreamer's account of his perceptual [dream] experience."[80] Creative expressions are reports that show an appreciation of reality by our archaic selves, refined, organized, and critically assessed by the brain's more recent articulate faculties.[81] A powerful example of this process in the visual arts is the oft-reproduced *Creation of Adam,* from the second triptych of the Sistine ceiling. It shows a severe bearded Jehovah on a high, dark *Nebelheim.* With his left arm he embraces a young woman while his right arm reaches down toward a green earthly meadow or cloud, toward a beautiful young Adam appropriate to Michelangelo's belief that the divine may best be identified in the perfect young male body.[82] Jehovah points and by that gesture commands, "Let us make man in our image, after our likeness." Adam, totally relaxed, points toward Jehovah and by that gesture suggests, "Let us make God in our image, after our likeness."

The summum bonum of aesthetic joy in painting may be, but need not be, the maximum diversity of life, body, or country, as Gould proposed. A painting may show the emptiness of a desert or of the arctic or the structure of a salt crystal. The working essence of a painting or drawing is the dialogue that its landscape creates in the viewer's mind, with the painter serving as the first viewer.

A landscape, in the general sense I am using the term, may be three dimensional: it is then called a model or a sculpture. The oldest known statue is a 7.2-cm-tall figurine, a woman carved from dull green serpentine about 30,000 years ago and dubbed the Dancing Venus of Galgenberg, after the Austrian village where it was found in 1988.[83] (I already mentioned these Venuses and speculated about them in the introductory section of this chapter.) Its sophistication suggests that it was preceded by a long tradition of carving. The woman's right hand is on her hip, her upper body twisting so that her left breast is shown in profile. I imagine that my distant brother once watched a dancing woman with the same fascination I felt as I watched the Spanish dancer in the Cantabrian Mountains. The next day he carved a figurine because he wanted to be able to carry with him her portable image just as some people carry a copy of the *Portable Arabian Nights*. During the millennia that the statue lay underground or kept company to birds and bees above ground, it had no meaning. It became a record of feelings and thoughts only when a person, beholding it, once again integrated the mental image of the statue into his or her experiential flow of time. The statue was then reconstituted into an object of art, the way dehydrated chicken soup is reconstituted by adding water to powder. For the little dancing Venus the water of life and that of meaning are the bio-, noo-, and sociotemporal umwelts of her admirers.

There is a continuous path between the Galgenberg Venus and Michelangelo's Pietà in Rome's St. Peter's basilica. I do not mean that the Buonarottis of Caprese were descendants of the Stone Age artist; rather, both artists were humans and hence shared the same potentialities. Michelangelo carved that statue in 1498 when he was twenty-three years old. He was two years older than I was in 1946, when, in an empty St. Peter's, I stood spellbound in front of the Pietà. Just out of the havoc of World War II, I was ready to jettison all received teachings about the identities of the two people carved of marble. I failed to see the Virgin holding the body of Christ. What I did see was a young woman of exquisite beauty holding the body of her man, murdered by the powers of law and order. Her face has an expression of infinite sadness as the irreversibility of his death penetrates her unbelieving mind. Her beauty suggested to me that she was with child, for I believed that women were most beautiful when they were pregnant. In a melodrama the woman of the statue would faint. In the Roman Pietà she bears up because she carries the child of the man whose body she is holding.

Michelangelo carved other pietàs. His Florentine Pietà was completed when he was eighty years old. The central figure is not a young woman who lives for the future but a hoary old man who lives in the past. The old man's personal battle is almost over: his body has been making its fateful decisions; the number of its biological choices has narrowed; he is approaching death. With his looks and his gestures he embraces a woman who, once again, is holding the dead body of her man. There is also a smaller female figure, perhaps a daughter. It is a family held together by the tragedy of their common loss. The statue is rough and unfinished, as is all human life as it approaches its closure. Whereas the Roman Pietà is one of protest, the Florentine Pietà is an image of the words "it is accomplished."

Haleman Ferguson is a mathematician and sculptor who makes mathematical sculptures. Finished in different colors and textures, his pieces mobilize our aesthetic faculties through our appreciation of shapes and forms, which is both learned from nature and elaborated by fantasy. For a fly they are objects on which to crawl and perchance to find food; from human beholders they invite touch. The objects are three-dimensional loci of the solutions to equations that, in the Platonic view of the world, are more lasting than the material of the objects. What for the two pietàs were the official interpretations—this is Jesus Christ, this is the Virgin Mary, this is Joseph of Arimathaea, this is the narrative that holds their drama together—are for the mathematical sculpture the variables x, y, z and the equations that hold them together in a stable relationship.[84]

What is appealing in these mathematical objects has little to do with the mathematical origins of the work. They suggest motion, which cannot come from the static equations; it comes from us. The figures are doing a sacred dance of numbers that members of the ancient Pythagorean brotherhood perceived at the foundations of the universe. In case there is objection to talk about the dance of numbers, it is useful to remember that the Venus of Galgenberg is said to be dancing although it does not. Makers and viewers of sculptures alike sense the freedom of forms that space allows and feel the power of dancing without motion; they dance in their minds. If this dance induces feelings they would like to perpetuate, they will describe the presumed causes as beautiful.

A sculpture may be large enough to be visited within. Making such sculptures and offering them as protection from inclement weather or an enemy is the task of architects. Buildings create an inner space and separate it from the outer space; they are wombs that protect, embrace, and hold men and women in thrall or in straitjackets. As sculptures, buildings can declare beliefs and views of the world that those who know the codes read easily. They can serve as places of ritual for worship or legislation. Abodes of animals and humans also serve as symbols of collective and personal identities, of personal and collective memories and hopes, and as links to the space of the universe. They may serve as homes for the dying and the dead, for people long gone or not yet born, and for creatures only imagined. They express attitudes to time, display shapes of nature and imagination, locate themselves with respect to the stars and the planets, embody geometry and mathematics, and reflect the geologies, geographies, and cultures of their environment.

Architecture mobilizes our aesthetic faculties by making our minds narrate around forms; without that narration Salisbury Cathedral or the structures of Disneyland remain inert furnishings of an irrelevant world. One evening during the summer of 1963, I was sailing back to Athens from the island of Hydra. The Acropolis was already dark, but the Parthenon still reflected the setting sun, making it appear against the sky as an inviting, shiny goddess reigning over darkness and beckoning to sailors. Had I been Japanese, the object of my awe might have been the Himeji Castle of the White Heron instead of the Parthenon, but my relation to the art of architecture would have been the same: that of the creator scanning the play of his temporal moods, seeking protection in the created against the passage of time, seeking a haven from the metaphysical winds of the supreme architect of the universe.

Since the 1820s the visual arts have been joined by a new way of making images that are steadied by meaning. It is called photography. The behavior of light as it enters a dark room through a small aperture and projects an image of the external world on the back wall of the room was known to the Chinese in the eighth century A.D.. During the late Middle Ages such an arrangement, the camera obscura (dark chamber), was used to study solar eclipses and the movement of birds and clouds. The first photograph, made in 1826 with a camera obscura, was called a "heliograph": "written with light." The exposure time was eight hours. During the first decades of the nineteenth century, the phrase "snap shot" was a hunting term; it did not come to mean an instantaneous photograph until the 1880s. With the development of faster shutters and films with increasing sensitivities, exposure lengths kept on shortening; the current lower limit is around 10^{-9} seconds.

These technical developments brought with them questions about time and the nature of the art of photography. Over two hundred years ago the German dramatist Gotthold Ephraim Lessing wrote that since painting and sculpture, unlike poetry, can represent only a single moment of action, they must show a telling instant of time, a present pregnant with future and past. Can the remarkable technology of a billionth-second snapshot help in carrying out Lessing's program and catch, photographically, the most telling instant in the flight of a bird, a bullet, or a warrior?

An answer to that question may be developed by beginning with the essay "Moment and Movement in Art," by the art historian E. H. Gombrich. If a drama were filmed, he asked, which "of the frames would be suitable for publication as a still from the film? The answer is that none might do. The so called stills which we see displayed . . . are especially made and very often specially posed on the set, after the scene is taken."[85]

Gombrich's question involves Zeno's paradox of the moving arrow. How short do we have to make the exposure before the arrow may be seen as one at rest? The answer is that the arrow is never at rest. For a fast enough arrow, the image will always be a blurred one until the exposure time approaches the physical chronon (10^{-24} sec.), where it would dissolve into a probabilistic cloud, which is anything but a resting arrow. A still image, whether that of a resting arrow, sleeping babe, creator god, or derby hat, is a mental construct; nothing in nature corresponds to any of these ideas. Still images as forms of art are painted, drawn, or photographed forms of our idea of permanence applied to objects that change. They are always posed, whether in the form of a dancing Venus, a Michelangelo pietà, a mathematical sculpture, or a Church landscape. The camera eye that was invented to show nature as it "really" is renders only images appropriate to our ideas of rest. Realism, for which the camera and some paintings have been praised, does not show an ultimate and stable reality but only illustrates our species-, society-, and person-specific umwelts. The great paintings, drawings, and still photographs of the world are so selected as to allow the viewer to narrate his or her story and frame his or her feelings around ideas of permanence.

Paintings and still photographs seek instants that look as if posed for an identifiable meaning, as is illustrated by the art historian Van Deren Coke in *The Painter and the Photograph*.[86] The book is a collection of over 250 photographs that served as models for that many paintings; photographs and paintings are reproduced side by side. As one examines them, it becomes obvious that photography's remarkable capacity to provide optical details is not in itself sufficient to do what is central to the art of still images, which is to suggest meaning resident in change. Good photographers know this intuitively and have learned from painters the as-if-posed selection and editing process; painters learned from photographers the instrumental enlargement of our perceptive umwelt. The great photographs of the art world, such as those in Steichen's collection *The Family of Man*, may be termed realistic because they show our visual umwelt in a dreamlike, as-if-posed fashion appropriate to carrying meaning.[87]

Instead of matching mustache to mustache and breast to breast, as in *The Painter and the Photograph*, the exhibition "Two Lives: Georgia O'Keeffe and Alfred Stieglitz—a Conversation in Paintings and Photographs" spoke through a shared language of gestalts and feelings. The exhibit was a visual dialogue, such as between apples (painted) and apples and drops of rain (photographed).[88] The conversation was built on the mental cohabitation of two passionate image makers. O'Keeffe's famous flowers are, for many people, just blobs of paint; for others, they have the power of sexual arousal. Stieglitz's still lives are meaningless objects for some people; for others, they are loaded with feelings. The cross-fertilization entices viewers to quicken these images with rhythm, life, pulse, and through them, the passage of time. Whereas in literature the listener or reader seeks and adds permanence and continuity, in the visual arts the viewer seeks or adds time and change.

Adding time and change to what is seen painted or sculpted may be performed on behalf of the viewer—prefabricated, as it were—by the makers of motion pictures.

A good way to understand the relation of film to time is to note the works of the French physician Étienne-Jules Marey (1830–1904) and the American Eadweard James Muybridge (also 1830–1904). These two men, wanting to study the microstructure of motion, independently developed photographic methods for recording increasingly shorter, consecutive segments of animal and human locomotion.[89] Chronophotography, as it was called, came to mean the making of a closely timed series of brief exposures in an attempt to timesect motion. In collections of early chronophotographs we see men and women jump, run, carry different objects, ride, and fence. There are wiggling fish, falling cats, and embarrassed ladies disrobing while photographed from three directions. There are elephants and bearded men marked with white paint, their motions photographed in closely timed stills against dark backgrounds. Interesting as these pictures are, they are not motion pictures but geometrical exercises in the appreciation of the mechanics and physiology of the motion of animals and people.

From the confluence of the visual arts, narration, music, drama, and chronophotography was born the most popular and by far the most influential fine art: the motion picture. Ordinary motion-picture technology consists of making still photographs at rates between sixteen and twenty-four frames per second and then projecting those stills, as stills, at the rate at which they were taken. In film Zeno's flying arrow is artificially stopped, made to vanish, and then made to reappear in a slightly different position. The motion observed is a virtual one. It appears to be continuous because the eye and its associated nervous system perceive such series as continuous motion as long as the stationary images are presented at a rate faster than about eighteen per second.[90]

Watching a motion picture shares with dreaming a kinesthetic condition. Namely: during dreaming the motion of the body is minimal; the only detectable motion is the occasional rapid or slow motion of the eye. The activities in dream images, whether strange, frightening, or beautiful, are carried on silently in the brain while the dreamer's head remains still. Likewise, when someone watches a motion picture, the movement of the viewer's head is minimal. Since all activities on the screen have already been completed in the past, what one watches is the residue of recorded memories—strange, frightening, or beautiful—spanning months or years. Let me illustrate what I mean by the dreamlike kinesthesis of film.

— Camera movements correspond to possible, deadly, or impossible human movements. Film thus provides the viewer, motionless in a comfortable seat, with visual worlds divorced from the associated kinesthetic experience. It can even show worlds that no person could possibly enter. The space of motion pictures is virtual, ready to be furnished by imagination.

— The actual size of the projected image is seldom the same as the size of the object: it is usually much smaller or much larger. The head and body thus need not move as would be necessary to behold that image in experiential space. This aspect of the camera eye adds another dimension of unreality to motion-picture space.

— Zooming techniques record images and motions in which the viewer is faster than a bird on the wing, as fast as imagination. As the camera attacks and escapes from scenes, the rate of visual change has no correspondence to experiential reality. It is dreamlike.

— The amount of time a viewer is permitted to spend on each event and the tempo of action seen are subject to the director's judgment and manipulation.

— Montage, color, tempo, and special effects all combine to create a world that is as close to the way one remembers dreams as is known to the visual arts. Of all art forms, film is the most dreamlike, which I believe is why it captures audiences of all ages and across all cultural regions.

The film provides its creator, the filmwright, with a freedom unavailable in any other fine art. Because of the nature of motion-picture production, "the filmwright" includes the cinematographer, director, writer, scriptwriter, actors, editors, persons responsible for sound and color, and many others. Unlike *playwright, filmwright* is a collective noun.

The dreamlike quality of motion pictures is beautifully expressed in Ingmar Bergman's *Shame* in the words of its heroine, Eva. It is as if motion-picture art itself makes a cameo appearance in her words.

A new group of people are pushed into the room. The electric light is switched on. A guard says there will be food in an hour. Someone shouts out that the buckets ought to be emptied. . . . A child screams in a piercing voice, someone is talking on and on in agitated tones. Jan rests his head against the wall and closes his eyes. . . .

Eva: Sometimes everything seems like a long strange dream. It's not my dream, it's someone else's, that I am forced to take part in. Nothing is properly real. It's all made up. What do you think will happen when the person who has dreamed us wakes up and is ashamed of his dream?[91]

This is humankind dreaming and perpetuating itself through the fine arts.

The Tragic

This subsection suggests that the tragic is the most universal narrative that may be told of humans. Therefore, it informs the arts and letters, which record its presence in daily life and in the historical existence of humankind.

Goats, Gods, and People As a dramatic form peculiar to Western civilization, tragedy evolved from communal celebrations in Attica during the sixth century B.C. These included dances and chants through which the misfortunes of Homeric heroes were told. Later the chorus became the voice of the gods: it commented on the affairs of man as played on the stage, offered moral judgments, and guided the emotions and thoughts of the audience. The compound word *tragoeidia,* or "goat song" comes from *tragos* ("goat") and *aeidein* ("to sing"). The word *tragos* relates to *trogein,* "to gnaw." Plato spoke of a tragic life as a goatish life, perhaps as a reference to life gnawed by unkind fate. He might have meant goats themselves, always at hand in Greek life and always rambunctious, even in the sympathetic form of Pan.

A dog or a horse, if abused, will display obvious signs of misery and anger, but it will never behave so as to suggest that it believes some universal injustice has been done. Not so humans. If events are perceived as effronteries to a person's sense of justice, the anger can take the form of a feud between a person and his society or among a person, God, and Satan, as it does in the Book of Job. At about the time when that book was written by an unknown author at an unknown location, the Greek dramatists—well known by name and location—wrote their tragedies. These literary masterpieces pit human desires against ethical judgments, the needs of the instant against values held eternal, and the principled struggles of mortals against the whims of immortal gods.

Tragedy, wrote Aristotle, "is essentially an imitation not of persons but of action and life, of happiness and misery."[92] Its incidents bring about catharsis in the viewers, a purging of feelings that they do not wish to perpetuate. The events of tragic drama gain generality because they are not idiosyncrasies of a particular person but follow from what today we would describe as necessary biological and psychological elements of human thought and conduct.

Tragic drama demands a continuous comparison and steady contrast of present happenings with reflections about the future and the past. Jacqueline de Romilly, a scholar of the classics, remarked that the necessary awareness of time in tragedy may be "why we find in tragedy so many general remarks about time, and may also suggest that it is not by chance that tragedy was born at the same time as history."[93]

After the decline of Athens as a city-state, tragedy as a form of drama performed on the stage went into hibernation until it woke with great vigor in Elizabethan England and seventeenth-century France.[94] But the history of tragedy is not that discontinuous. A few centuries after the crucifixion of Jesus of Nazareth, his followers established a liturgy that amounted to the daily reenactment of a divine tragedy. The background to that tragedy is salvation history, a view of man's fate as a necessary conflict between his awareness of past misdeeds and present earthly desires on the one hand and, on the other hand, a much desired eternal life in timeless peace. The crucial events of salvation history are retold in the Mass, where God comments on the affairs of humankind and guides the emotions of the celebrants. The comments provide paradigms for right behavior that the faithful are expected to emulate so that, individually and communally, they may reach a cosmic denouement in the salvation of humankind. The tragedy resides in the Son of God's lonely fight against the many forms of evil on earth, leading to his torture and execution and, through that catharsis, the victory of God's light over the forces of darkness. Just as the Greek tragedies helped to form the cultural character of ancient Greece, so the tragedy reenacted in the Mass helped to develop the West's communal identity and collective attitude to time.

Early in the fourteenth century Dante called his epic narrative of salvation a divine comedy rather than a divine tragedy because comedies, he reasoned, begin in trouble and end in peace, whereas tragedies begin in calms and end foul and horrible.[95] Dante's guided tour is a report about the struggle of mankind that, against all odds, ends in the union of man with God; this is the feature of the story that permitted Dante to call it a comedy. By parallel reasoning, a belief in the success of Christ's mission, in the resurrection of the dead and in life everlasting, makes the celebration of the Mass the reenacting of a divine comedy. For those who do not believe in the resurrection of the dead and life everlasting, the mission of Jesus of Nazareth is a classic tragedy: although in the short run it ended in his unjust execution, in the long run it made those ideas of conduct for which he is said to have died survive him by far.

At the end of Dante's century, in "The Monk's Tale" of *The Canterbury Tales,* Chaucer offered this definition:

> *Tragedy* means a certain kind of story
> As old books tell us, of those who fell from glory,
> People that stood in great prosperity
> And were cast down out of their high degree
> Into calamity, and so they died.[96]

By the seventeenth century the Greek world of Aphrodite and Pan, of human heroes and immortal gods with their lovers aplenty, came to be told simultaneously with salvation history and retold in word, music, and picture in innumerable exegeses of hope and sorrow. It was into this cultural environment of Olympus and Calvary, modified to the temperament of "this blessed plot, this earth, this realm, this England," that Shakespeare was born, and it is from that wealth of tradition that he succeeded in culling the major representations of the tragicomedy of being human. This cultural cross-fertilization allowed Roger Cox to describe Shakespearean tragedy as Pauline or Christian-intellectual and Dostoyevski's tragic dramas as Johannine or Christian-prophetic and to remark, "Across the pages of *Hamlet* and *King Lear, Crime and Punishment* and *The Idiot,* the words of St. Paul and St. John are written in huge, calligraphic letters."[97]

Two centuries after Shakespeare the philosopher G. W. F. Hegel (1770–1831) saw tragedy in human fate as a correction to moral imbalance, a dialectic among alternate values of good and right, a mapping of the dialectic of history into everyday life. Arthur Schopenhauer (1788–1860) perceived the tragic dimensions of human life as an outcropping of something inherent in all Creation.[98]

Friedrich Nietzsche (1844–1900) suggested that tragedy arises from the conflicts between the Apollonian and Dyonisian natures of the world at large and hence is innate in history and people. Apollo was the god of order, measure, and restraint. Dionysus was the god of fruitfulness, wine, and collective ecstasy; he represented sap, juice, the lifeblood of nature. It was in *The Birth of Tragedy from the Spirit of Music* that Nietzsche first introduced the idea of Appollonian-Dyonisian conflict. Sixteen years later, rereading it, he felt he had made beauty a divinity, with "God as the supreme artist, amoral, recklessly creating and destroying, realizing himself indifferently in whatever he does or undoes, ridding himself by his acts of the embarrassment of his riches and strain of his internal contradictions. Thus the world was made to appear, at every instant, as a successful *solution* of God's own tensions, as an ever new vision projected by that grand sufferer for whom illusion is the only possible mode of redemption."[99] Music, he observed, expresses the Apollonian-Dionysian conflict in sound, and tragedy does so in literary form, hence the kinship between music and tragedy. Dionysus is said to have won converts among women, who followed him, formed holy bands, and danced in torchlight to the flute and kettledrum. If one is permitted to mix epochs and cultures but remain true to the evolutionary continuity and steadiness of human nature, then one may say that the Venus of Galgenberg could serve as the patron saint of the Dionysian bands.

The philosopher Susanne K. Langer wrote of "tragic rhythm," which she defined as "the pattern of life that grows, flourishes, and declines, is abstracted by being transferred from that natural activity to the sphere of characteristically human action, where it is exemplified in mental and emotional growth, maturation, and the final relinquishment of power. In that relinquishment lies the hero's true 'heroism'—the vision of life as accomplished, that is, life in its entirety, the sense of fulfillment that lifts him above his defeat."[100]

Langer remarked, generalizing more than one would dare to do half a century later, that

> In Asia the designation "Divine Comedy" would fit numberless plays; especially in India triumphant gods, divine lovers united after various trials . . . are the favorite themes of a theater that knows no "tragic rhythm." The classical Sanskrit drama was heroic comedy . . . a serious, religiously conceived drama, yet in the "comic" pattern, which is not a complete organic development reaching a foregone, inevitable conclusion, but is episodic, restoring a lost balance, and implying a new future. The reason for this consistently "comic" image of life is [a regard of life] as an episode in the much longer career of the soul which has to accomplish many incarnations before it reaches its goal, nirvana.[101]

But when it comes to time-knowing humans with a single life and death, the appropriate drama is not heroic comedy but tragedy, because it must involve the decisions a person must make in terms of his assets—life and limb, love and hatred, freedom and duty—and in full awareness of the finity of his life.

Decisions, Decisions Latent in the unfolding of tragedy is the assumption that people can make free choices. In sec. 4.3, on the natural history of morals, this was understood to mean that the number of imaginable paths of conduct for humans is larger than what may in fact be traveled.

But the capacity to make choices was not born with *Homo erectus*. Every living organism continuously makes decisions in its biological functions. For humans, this amounts to decisions such as the following: now breath this, now digest that, now increase your heart rate, now decrease your temperature. Because of these decisions the domain of biological alternatives available to the bodies of snails, eagles, and men and women keeps on narrowing in a process called aging, until there are no alternatives left and death becomes inevitable. The evolutionary usefulness of death by aging is that it allows newer generations to differ from their ancestors in a fashion that is advantageous for the continuity of life at large.

What death by aging is on the organic level, tragedy is on the noetic and social levels: both are unavoidable and necessary. The usefulness of the tragic process is to enable newer generations to differ from their ancestors in their values and conduct and to do so in a manner that is advantageous for the continuity of civilization. Obligations, memories, hopes, and fears are weighed in terms of prevailing value judgments: they then lead to decisions, made with the help of steady reflections on future and past. The value judgments themselves, modulated by the decisions taken, are frequently changed. The changes are then communicated to others in the ceaseless experimentation with values. Because of the decisions made and actions taken, the number of remaining alternatives narrows until there is no choice left but the denouement, the disentangling of the threads of the story. For the tragic hero of a drama, this may be the loss of sight in its many meanings, as in *Oedipus Rex;* the loss of life, as in the drama of Jesus of Nazareth; the loss of love's passion or of the possibility of providing continuity to human life through offspring, as in the story of Heloise and Abelard; or the death of the self, as in Tennessee Williams's play *A Streetcar Named Desire.*

What for the tragic hero are the challenges to his ideas are in the life of each and every person the consequences that follow from his or her awareness of time's passage. This knowledge demands deliberate choices. It is a selection pressure that works from within. It is more implacable than any external selection pressure and more tyrannical than any social convention or political tyranny. The knowledge of time thus generates a steady tension between the dream of permanence and the biological facts of passing, lending to human life its irreducible aspects of the tragic.

Why endorse tragedy as central to the human narrative? Why see the glass half-empty rather than half-full? The reason is one of epistemology. Tragedy has immense explanatory power; Donald Duck has none. The empty, unfilled half of the glass is the imaginative, creative power of the mind, capable of beholding the universe and enriching it in ways that only the mind can do.

Just as dance is the mother lode of all art, so the tragic is the mother lode of all narrative, for all stories deal with life, with death by aging, and with sex, a constellation of phenomena with common evolutionary origins.

There is another, important role that tragedy plays in the dynamics and economy of human values. In sec. 4.3 I remarked that any change in prevailing ideas of right and wrong demands sacrifice. Tragedy, because it involves life and death, appeals to the oldest assessments of reality, to those that pertain to survival in "nature red in tooth and claw," where "Time, a maniac, [is] scattering dust / And Life, a Fury, slinging flame."[102] Simultaneously, since the tragic involvement is usually made in the name of some human ideal, tragedy addresses the mind's highest noetic and social capacities. Between the ideals of love, the right, and the orderly on the one hand and the ruthlessness of instincts flinging flame to assist survival on the other, tragedy mobilizes the complete spectrum of temporal moods available to the mature mind.

Tragedy describes a world where conflict is endemic, resolvable only in transient fashion, and where men and women, to be able to live with their dreams of a better world, must make present sacrifices for very chancy future returns. The tragic is a form of unresolvable conflict in the nested hierarchy of such conflicts: it is native to the nootemporal and sociotemporal worlds. In this it joins the lower-order unresolvable creative conflicts: those of life (between growth and decay) and those of matter (between forms of permanence and the ever-present absolute chaos).

5.5   The Office of the Beautiful as a Human Value

In their oldest and simplest role, as observed in animals and people, emotions serve as first signals in evaluating food, friend, and foe. In their most highly evolved forms they are feelings experienced and recognized by the self. In humans issues of food, friend, and foe are so intricately intertwined, are so kaleidoscopic in terms of related affects and thoughts, that it has become necessary to draw up intricate guidelines for ordering them by personal and communal value judgments. This chapter suggested that the necessary ordering is carried out by relating aesthetic judgments to time: the beautiful was said to describe those objects, events, or conditions held responsible for feelings that a person would like to perpetuate and even declare timeless.

Whatever its biological and psychological origins, experiencing the beautiful has certainly given joy, granted strength, and offered inspiration to men and women through all ages by allowing them to feel victory over transience. But its long-term role is something quite different. With the help of an essay by the art historian Erwin Panofsky bearing the title "Et in Arcadia ego,"[103] I would like to suggest what that long-term role is.

According to the Roman historian Polybius, a native of Arcadia, his country was poor, bare, and rocky; it could scarcely supply the necessities of their goats and shepherds. Early Greek poets knew better than to select Arcadia as the scene of their pastorals.[104] But in later Greek and Roman bucolic poetry and in the literature of the Renaissance, Arcadia came to stand for a land of beauty, love, and inner peace, a setting of dreams incarnate. In the words of Panofsky, it became "the retrospective vision of unsurpassable happiness, enjoyed in the past, unattainable ever after, yet enduringly alive in memory."[105]

In his essay Panofsky discusses a score of paintings that bear the title *Et in Arcadia ego* or have a closely related theme. He places their iconographies into a literary background that stretches from Virgil to the nineteenth century. His purpose was to decipher the meaning of the Latin phrase with the help of the paintings because, taken verbatim, the phrase is incomplete: "And in Arcadia, I." Among the paintings Panofsky selected as the most helpful is one by Poussin. It shows a rough stone tomb with a half-effaced inscription, "Et in Arcadia ego." In front of the tomb are three young men and a young woman who seem to have come on it unexpectedly. One of the men is cleaning off the ancient dirt from the face of the tomb so as to read the inscription; another one is turned toward the woman, perhaps commenting on the words; the third shepherd seems lost in his thoughts. The woman has an expression of elegiac amusement as she contemplates fate and time. It is, writes Panofsky, as if the young people are pondering "the message of a former fellow being: 'I, too, lived in Arcadia where you now live; I too enjoyed the pleasures which you now enjoy; and yet I am dead and buried.' We instantly perceive a strange, ambiguous feeling which suggests both a mournful anticipation of man's inevitable destiny and an intense consciousness of the sweetness of life."[106]

The four figures might well stand for all men and women, disturbed as well as challenged by the conflicts between their dreams of eternity and their certainty of being mortals. In terms of this understanding, the appropriate free translation of the phrase would be "Even in Arcadia there is transience." The painting, as I interpret it, represents art in general. By *art* I mean the skill of mapping the unresolvable conflicts of the mind into a world of shapes, words, or sounds that share Wallace Stevens's "Sunday Morning" thoughts.

> "But in contentment I still feel
> The need of some imperishable bliss."
> Death is the mother of beauty; hence from her,
> Alone shall come fulfillment to our dreams
> And our desires.[107]

Indeed, the beautiful never opened vistas of eternal, unchanging forms that, once so recognized, could be noted and taught from age to age to age as examples of timelessness and eternity, assuring one and all of the existence of a haven against the ravages of time. Its role has never been, nor can it be, the generation of satisfaction stably fulfilled. Rather, the experience of the beautiful has been serving as a goad, a reminder of the irreducibly tragic dimension of human life in the sense explained. Beauty is precious not because it is timeless or eternal but because a whiff of the wind can collapse the delicate configuration of conditions—internal and external—by which those feelings have been generated. This formulation of the nature of aesthetic judgment helps to separate art from the beautiful. Art need not be beautiful. It need only set up sufficiently profound conflicts between feelings I would like to perpetuate and those I would like to banish and permit me to make a selection.

The conclusion suggests itself. The evolutionary office of the aesthetic faculties is to generate and maintain conflicts between the world as we find it to be and that other world of imagination to which art can give transient forms and changing names.

CHAPTER SIX

The Global Laboratory

T he first skirmishes of the American Revolution took place at Concord, Massachusetts, in April 1775. It was there and then that "the embattled farmers stood / And fired the shot heard around the world." The shot was not actually heard, of course, but echoed in peoples' minds. There, in the course of history, it acquired meanings that relate to such freedoms as are set forth in the U.S. Bill of Rights.

An echo is a delayed response made possible by distances and time. On the time-compact globe a shot fired anywhere is immediately heard everywhere; the privileges of delayed and reasoned actions in response to any shot are often denied to one and all. Under such conditions human values become the primary navigational guides. Those values, to continue the metaphor of navigation, are now called on to help us sail in uncharted waters. The earth has become a single laboratory in which humanity is experimenting with time compactness in the lives of persons, nations, and the world itself. This chapter surveys the ferment of judgments concerning the true, the good, and the beautiful evident around the globe and asks questions about their current role in controlling the unbounded imaginative powers of the mind.

6.1   The Brief Lives of Truths

"Although searching for truth is driven by the desire for permanence and stability, its historical function has been the creation of conflicts and,

through them, social, cultural, and personal change." How does this conclusion of sec. 3.6, on the office of truth as a human value, fare on the time-
compact globe?

I showed that the organic, mental, and social presents are created by
coordinating appropriate processes from instant to instant in the service
of a living organism, functioning mind, and viable social group. The *global
present*, a new member of this nested hierarchy, is now being constructed
through the coordination of social presents across national and ethnic
boundaries. Its construction is driven by the needs of economic and cultural survival and is made possible by advances in technology.

The width of any social present was defined in sec. 2.2 as the minimum
time needed for coordinating collective action. For instance, the social
present shared by the cities of St. Joseph, Missouri, and Sacramento, California, in 1860, communicating by the Pony Express, had a width of twenty days. This was the time that had to elapse before a man in Sacramento
who sent a message to his sweetheart in St. Joseph asking, "Will you marry
me?" could receive a definite "No!" and remain single or else a definite
"Maybe!" and begin to act according to a plan shared by two members of
an incipient family.[1] By the turn of the twenty-first century the Pony Express
has been replaced by billions of miles of worldwide wire and radio links that
define the width of the social present between any two points on earth.

Maintaining a global present through coordination does not mean that
everyone does or should retire and rise at the same time. It signifies instead
a communal reference instant or period with respect to which actions across
the surface of the earth may be and increasingly more often are taken. If
all electronic communication links were to become inoperative, there could
still be civilizations, nations, ethnic groups, and families, but the global
present would revert to the period of time needed for air and surface transportation. If those were to become unavailable, the global present would
have widths of months or years.

In the daily lives of people in the developed and, increasingly, the developing countries, the global present intrudes as images of instant every-
wheres. A good metaphor for such images is the "split-screen present," suggested by the split-screen images of Iraqi preparations for the bombing of
Jerusalem in 1991 on the left of the screen and preparations of the air-raid
shelters in Jerusalem on the right.[2] This God's-eye view is made possible by
a technology of an inert universe of signals called cyberspace.

The Contents and Discontents of Cyberspace

Space in the term *cyberspace* is borrowed from mathematics, where it means
an abstract container of any set of mathematical objects a mathematician

wishes it to contain. *Cyber-* comes from the Greek *kybernetes,* meaning "steersman." *Cyberspace* means the content of the global communication networks at any instant.[3] It consists of all the electronic signals that carry voices, images, and computer data; the signals of our garage-door opener; the signals of the library's book-thief detector; and all the other signals necessary to keep the exploding population of gadgets in operation.

Cyberspace is an advanced form of telephone space (which carried the voices of its time). Telephone space was an offspring of telegraph space (which carried Morse code). Telegraph space came from yodel space (which carried yodels in the Alps). Cyberspace is the high-tech version of Borges's Library of Babel. That library, wrote the poet, "is a sphere whose exact center is any one of its hexagons and whose circumference is inaccessible." Borges also wrote that at one time it was "hoped that a clarification of humanity's basic mysteries—the design of the Library and of time—might be found."[4] Borges's Library of Babel contains in printed form everything that could fill yodel space or any of its descendants.

The following description of cyberspace is from "Release 1.0" of the Progress of Freedom Foundation. It is entitled "A Magna Carta for the Knowledge Age."

> More ecosystem than machine, cyberspace is a bioelectronic environment. . . . This environment is inhabited by knowledge, including incorrect ideas, existing in electronic form. . . . Most of the knowledge in cyberspace lives the most temporary (or so we think) existence. . . . But people are increasingly building cyberspatial warehouses of data, knowledge, information and misinformation in digital form. . . . Cyberspace is the land of knowledge and the exploration of that land can be a civilization's truest, highest calling. . . . [Let] personal computing take over while mainframes rot.[5]

This Magna Carta assumes that people who use cyberspace will regulate their conduct by following some (so far unspecified) rules. The role of the government, says the charter, need not go beyond legislating such ownership and tax-accounting rules as will allow "the creation of a new civilization, founded in the eternal truths of the American Idea."

The philosopher Hegel saw the history of mankind as the dialectic of the spirit and perceived the apotheosis of this spiritual process in the way Protestantism had developed in the German-speaking countries. Half a century after Hegel, Marx and Engels preferred to see history as the working out of the potentialities of matter, of which human civilization, they said, is a special manifestation. If one replaces Hegel's "spirit" or Engels's "matter" with "information" and replaces German Protestantism (Hegel) or the collective power of the workers (Marx and Engels) with industry, and if one leaves the cunning of reason as Hegel had it, one arrives at the idea of salvation through cyberspace. The fervent advocates of personal computing and the commercial interests that profit from selling the devices that should make all the glory feasible are the spiritual heirs of Hegel, Marx, and Engels.

The technological preferences for speed and demands for prescribed formats of communication mold the quality of truth in cyberspace. I will now explore that quality under the headings images, rhythms, and numbers.

Images It is reasonable to assume that writing arose from earlier skills of drawing and painting. It was a step useful in the communication of articulate thoughts, inarticulate feelings, and prosaic demands. Pictures on cave, castle, and church walls were means of reaching those who could not read and complemented discursive texts for those who could. During the second half of the twentieth century pictures came into ascendancy over the written word as the favored method of mass communication because, as we learn from Shakespeare's early poem *The Rape of Lucrece,* "To see sad sights move more than hear them told / For then the eye interprets the ear." Images in cyberspace abound: from weather maps to photos taken from spy satellites, from baby pictures to mug shots, and from scientific graphs to nude women. Instead of appearing on cave, church, or castle walls, the pictures adorn the walls of board rooms, bedrooms, and classrooms. They appear in places of work and entertainment, in houses of healing and slaughter. Instead of being stationary, moreover, they continuously wiggle: dancing images on the screen have become domesticated animals, but they are not yet housebroken.

I remarked earlier that film is the art form closest to the experience of dreaming. Moving figures on the screens are the fantasies of the cavemen and -women in all of us; we like to imagine our paintings come alive. Screens cross cultural and political boundaries more easily than do printed words because they employ an older and hence more universal mode of communication: even birds can see and tell stories.

But conveying information by dancing petroglyphs has a number of side effects that are becoming some of their main effects. Most notable among these effects is that the proliferating use of images is pushing the great masses of their users toward preliterate forms of communication. In our televised world many millions are slaves in Plato's cave, where their attention is riveted to the walls on which they see the tendentious shadows of reality. These shadows report about a world that does not stand still long enough to suggest stability as an aspect of human life; it places premium on speed and stresses the primacy of the instant.

Rhythms Cyberspace also carries rhythms. These help synchronize schedules and promote uniformity of tempos in all parts of the world that are within their reach. Patriotic and religious rhythms and tempos, built into traditional calendars, are very much alive in some regions, but increasingly they are being replaced or ruled by those of commerce and industry. This shift signals a change in temporal perspectives: whereas national and religious holidays are reminders of eternal returns placed into their historical backgrounds, calendars constructed by commercial interests speak only about presents with immediate futures: "Buy your motor oil today!"

Sometime before the sixteenth century, calendar makers began to indicate ecclesiastical feasts by marking them with red numbers and letters; the color implied a holy day, an interruption in the labor of black-letter days. The red-letter days of the time-compact globe, mixed with the black ones, have turned into gray-letter days worldwide. The *World Holiday and Time Guide* of the J. P. Morgan Company lists holidays and workdays for over 200 countries.[6] A special section lists every day of the year with the names of countries where that date is a holiday. There is no single day that is not a holiday somewhere and a workday somewhere else.

We also witness a colonization of the night, to use the felicitous term coined by the sociologist Murray Melbin.[7] The point is not that humans are about to establish night as the exclusive domain of their lives but that they are assimilating night as a full-fledged equivalent of their daily existence.[8] In the United States many shops are open twenty-four hours a day, as are laundromats, gas stations, diners, and machine tellers. Most of the world's people do not care or even know about machine tellers, but the American way of life is being copied even where it is berated. Public service workers also labor through the night. Some such workers serve the homeless in their shelters and on the streets; they are joined by police and the military on alert, those who work in hospital emergency rooms, the patrols along the U.S.-Mexican border, and engineers who drive the mile-long freight trains across the heartland of the nation. There are night weddings and preparations for early morning executions.

During the night U.S. telephone operators encounter the intensity of the business and political day halfway around the world. They also hear the voices of loneliness, calls whose sole purpose is to lessen that loneliness by hearing a human voice—preferably that of a woman—even if it is an impersonal "AT&T, may I help you?" Such calls are cheaper than this country's "900" numbers, where the lonely may listen to sex by voice or talk to psychics twenty-four hours a day. A telephone call to an airline office in Chicago placed at 2 A.M. is likely to be answered by a wide-awake employee in London.

Well over a century ago Robert Louis Stevenson expressed in charming cadences the fascination of the night as seen from the safety of a Scottish home.

> Whenever the moon and stars are set,
> Whenever the wind is high,
> All night long in the dark and wet,
> A man goes riding by.
> Late in the night when the fires are out,
> Why does he gallop and gallop about?

The answer is now at hand. The riding man is the Paul Revere of the nonstop society: he carries news of the needs, horrors, and challenges of humanity's nonlocal half.

Changing the length of the circadian rhythms entrained in humans would require radical measures, but shifting their phases away from the rising and setting of the sun is fairly easily done. Just as the lunar cycle of the menses, once probably synchronous with new moon, came to be distributed across the lunar month as tribal life became independent of the moon, so the circadian rhythm of individuals is now shaking itself loose from sunrises and sunsets. Increasingly, industrial and commercial practices also come to favor independence from the master cycle of the sun, so as to satisfy the schedules of production and distribution as these schedules adapt to the time-compact globe.

Numbers In the industrially advanced lands and increasingly in the developing countries, many people spend their lives in the company of computers. Through them everyone else has computer connections: it is like living at the seashore, where everyone is either a sailor or related to one. Computer literacy has become as necessary for the conduct of daily life as is car literacy for most people and diesel engine literacy for persons so employed. Computers demand special ways of thinking. This communicates itself to peoples' assessments of the nature of reality and affects the collective scale of values.

For instance, problems of qualitative concerns that call for qualitative judgments are preferentially formulated in terms of mathematical relations because that is what computers demand.[9] Unlike the Grinch, however, who stole Christmas and then returned it, computers cannot return computerized societies to preferences for qualitative judgments because of a paradox rooted in the practices of popular democracies. The most efficient ways to provide the most people with the most goods and services must enlist the number-crunching services of computers. Efficient bureaucracies and computers have much in common: both must work reliably, without ambiguities, and according to stable laws. Because of these similarities, bureaucrats and computers can be easily combined. An ideal, computerized bureaucracy receives instructions (laws, or "software") and appropriate supplies (paper, data, weapons, medicine, prisoners, and canned sardines). It then processes the supplies according to the instructions and produces printed words, bills, checks, lottery tickets, mass-educated masses, meals on wheels, and objects of popular art. The resulting homogenization narrows the spectrum of ideas from which responses to new challenges may be selected; as a consequence, inference, analysis, interpretation, and creative thought are becoming the domains of specialized groups: governmental policy institutes, private foundations, think tanks, and institutes of advanced studies. We are witnessing the emergence of a new class of scribes in search for qualitative truths, while the population at large is being administered by the quantitative, numerical truths of cyberspace.

The Written Word

After a youth spent in the company of wine, women, and song, followed by a period of search for what he described as the changeless light, St. Augustine was in a Milan garden when he heard "from the neighboring house a voice, as of a boy or girl . . . chanting and oft repeating, 'Take up and read! Take up and read!'" Thinking that such words could not have come from a child, he concluded that they were the words of God himself. He picked up the Book and opened it randomly. What he read determined the direction of his life: "Not in rioting and drunkenness, not in chambering and wantonness. . . ."

Children's voices today speak of the same kinds of needs they spoke of sixteen centuries ago, but once fed, children in the industrialized lands are more likely to say, "Turn on and watch!" And thereby hang many tales, such as the ambiguous position of the book in postliterate societies. The situation, wrote George Steiner in 1985, "is almost classically that of a Marxist analysis: the concentration of the marketing and the dissemination of books not only in a very few hands, but in hands which are politically and sociologically scarcely distinguishable. Whatever the differences of style, of personality, of anecdote, they constitute as far as culture goes, an almost monolithic and monopolistic vision."[10]

In a 1984 report to Congress, Daniel Boorstin, then librarian of Congress, spoke about the "proverbial convenience, accessibility and individuality of the book," which is unrivaled by any new technology in sight. But to take advantage of these properties, he added, "we must face and defeat the twin menaces of illiteracy and aliteracy—the inability to read and lack of will to read—if our citizens are to remain free and qualified to govern themselves."[11]

In 1996 Americans spent $26 billion for books, or just below $100 per capita. The spending includes purchases of faddish best-sellers, how-to books, and pulp, so that reading the figure as an index of cultural life is difficult. It is, instead, an index of the success of merchandising.[12] At the 1997 Frankfurt Book Fair some 10,000 companies exhibited over 300,000 titles, of which 80,000 were new. These figures praise industrial productivity and reflect the advantages of the book as an easily handleable format of information. That 27 percent of the exhibited books were new titles suggests that the shelf life of the average title cannot be much over three years.

What do people read? More and more, they read what is on the screen. Whether one reads a sentence on a screen or on a page may be irrelevant, but the kinesthetics of books and computer screens are different. Computer displays favor quantity and a rapid finding of answers; printed pages, because of their unhurried permanence, are better suited to accommodate involvement in depth. The book format, however, tends to demand more time than people have in societies that prefer speed and concentrate on the present. Yet profound understanding of intricate subjects still demands sustained concentration. Moreover, since sustained attention is discouraged by postmodern media that must keep on rolling, the separation between people who know how to reflect and those who do not is becoming increasingly more pronounced.

At the same time as the computerized search for information is expanding without totally replacing books, television is replacing though not eliminating the printed word. Robert MacNeil, creator and former executive editor and coanchor of *NewsHour* on America's civilized Public Broadcasting System (PBS), believes that the television format encourages the habit of limited attention, discourages sustained concentration, and through these, contributes to the widespread aliteracy.[13] Attention Deficit Hyperactive Disorder (ADHD), an increasingly common ailment of uncertain causes, is manifest in its victims' inabilities to concentrate on anything for more than a few moments. It has been noted that in the food-scarce environment of our hunter-gatherer ancestors, a hyperactive, get-up-and-go behavior might have been useful. It is, so the speculation continues, this early behavior latent in modern humans that is awakened by contemporary life's tempo and narrow concentration on the present. Extensive childhood exposure to television and video games, which favor speedy action without allowing time for reasoning, combined with an information glut pressed into narrow, discontinuous instants, may have already begun to promote culturally conditioned ADHD.[14]

All past examples of great literary art display their authors' desires to record for posterity such feelings and thoughts as would guide peoples' value judgments for ages to come. It is difficult to imagine a literary work written today that could remain significant long enough to serve as a catalyst for a stable, collective view of man and the world.

Shards of Time, Shards of Truth

Early in the morning of April 15, 1865, Abraham Lincoln died silently on a bed that was too short for him. His secretary of state, Edwin M. Stanton, then uttered a phrase that has come to identify tragic greatness. "Now," he said, "he belongs to the ages." One hundred and twenty-four years later the *New York Times* carried a full-page advertisement: "Graffiti-covered subway trains are now history. We cleaned them up yesterday." The ages, which used to be thought of as stretching from Creation to the Last Judgment, have deteriorated into yesterday, today, and tomorrow.

The dynamics of headlines seen and heard does not permit the past to be comprehended as a connected set of events responsible for the present, because the media ceaselessly update the present in such a peremptory manner as to make what has gone by appear not only irrelevant but also somewhat uncouth. James Reston, keen observer of the American and international scene, remarked in a 1985 *New York Times* editorial that in spite of the immense storehouse of historical information available, history has no presence in the United States. The result is an "intellectual defenselessness, an inability to understand the workings of either our own or other societies."[15] Reston's comments are becoming valid for the world, well beyond the boundaries of the United States. The quality of the mass media brings to mind the words of William Blake; in preparing to build New Jerusalem, he wrote, there are some people he would prefer not to include, such as

> the idiot Questioner who is always questioning
> But never capable of answering, who sits with a sly grin
> Silent plotting when to question, like a thief in a cave,
> Who publishes doubt & calls it knowledge.[16]

Paul Alkon, a critique of postmodernism with special interest in the cultural position of history in relation to attitudes to time, remarked that the

> disappearance of the past is a peculiar feature of our century, although a tally of historical studies published since 1900 would suggest that we now live at the brightest moment in a golden age of historiography. Paradoxically, the very proliferation of histories undermines in-

dividual and collective ability to apprehend the past. . . . History is pushed to the periphery of school and even university curricula. . . . [Also,] postmodern theorists cast doubt that we can ever in any rigorous sense know the past, thus doing their bits to make it vanish from our horizon.[17]

This loss occurs in spite of the fact that, as David Lowenthal argued in *The Past Is a Foreign Country,* there exists a cult of preservation, a nostalgia to recover an imagined past.[18]

An observation on the detachment of the present from the past, no less than from a realistic future, was discussed in a *New York Times* op-ed contribution with reference to children's toys at the turn of the century. No historical battles will be refought by children; no more will Sir Lancelot of the Lake or American or world history inform their play. Instead, the "powerful Red Dragon Thunderzord will mix it up with Lord Zedd's Evil Space Aliens. Dr. Cyborn, the evil Cyber scientist of the Skeleton Warriors, . . . will aim his acid blaster at Wolverine of the X-Men, and Drago from the Superhuman Samurai Cyber-squad . . . will launch its shoulder-mounted Pyrotronic missiles at Kilokhan, overlord of the digital world."[19] The world of children's toys in the developed lands has become a nonhuman universe without a timeline.

The narrowing of the global present to seconds and the dancing dreams of immediacy on the walls of so many caves do not in themselves demand a narrowing of temporal horizons, either in personal lives or in public policies. But they do promote such a narrowing when combined with pressures for fast profits, immediate satisfaction of radically increased expectations, and the hysterical speed of news reporting. There is a demand not simply for social, economic, and cultural changes but for an increasing rate of such change. The speed of changes forces everyone to focus on the present and exclude not only history but also commitments to the future if they demand present sacrifice. It is as if our civilization, joined by cyberspace, has regressed, as far as attitudes to time go, from a nootemporal to a biotemporal umwelt.

This narrowing of the sociotemporal horizons to shards of time, however, does open the way for a reinterpretation of the past with such emphases and such selection of beliefs as will be appropriate for the identity of humankind on a time-compact globe.

The Nascent Identity of Humankind

Chapter 3, discussing guidelines to beliefs, distinguished among truths appropriate for the physical, organic, mental, and social worlds. It also noted that the paradigm of continuity above the biological level is that of identity: personal identity for noetic truths and collective identity in the development of history. This reasoning may now be extended: the quality of truth peculiar to processes and institutions of a time-compact globe is determined by the nature of the identity of humankind at large. But what is that identity?

Individual and collective identities are established by delineating boundaries and noting similarities to and differences from other members of the same class: persons, tribes, religions, nations, civilizations. A unique difficulty arises when one considers humankind, because there are no other humankinds with respect to which the identity of this one could be delineated; we have no cohort to wake us from our collective fantasies and keep our conduct within some kind of bounds.

Let me transfer the question of identity into the temporal domain. When does a group acquire identity? Consider the history of a married couple. Although each member has a past, as a married couple they can have a history only in respect to their communally maintained present; they can have no history stretching back to the years before they met. Likewise tribes, nations, and civilizations can have a history only forward from that epoch when they first established a collective present.

What is generally understood as the history of humankind is a collection of unrelated or loosely related stories of groups believed to have had common origins. It is only with the establishment of a global present that we can begin to think about collective planning for the future. Only after such planning and action has begun can there be a shared reevaluation of the past. And only then, with a viable global present, collectively planned future, and collectively interpreted past, can an identity of humankind be defined.

In 1992 much attention was paid to the idea of an "end of history," proposed and defended by Francis Fukuyama.[20] He maintained that insofar as there remain no viable alternatives to some form of market-oriented democracy, the experimentations of history have effectively come to an end. The foregoing reasoning about the identity of mankind suggests an opposite view. Namely, it is only with the establishment of a global present that one may begin talking about humanity as a single social entity, and only from the epoch when such a global present becomes established can mankind as a social unit begin its history.

This challenge is novel and brings a novel problem. Namely, although mankind is heterogeneous, the time-compact globe is entering the set of those systems of which there is only one of each, such as the universe, nature, or in monotheistic religions, God. The difficulties of delimiting the boundaries of effectiveness and defining the identities of these one-and-onlies are notorious. In the absence of another humanity, any economic, cultural, military, or commercial experimentation, if it involves a substantial part of mankind and if miscarried, can lead to socioeconomic or cultural oscillations that can go out of control.

Conditions of imbalance are certainly in the making. The electronic media carry powerful but kaleidoscopic images, words, and numbers about gore, money, and semen (to use an expression popular among journalists). Extremes that are judged newsworthy simply because they are extremes are indiscriminately dumped on the public. Infotainment—entertainment that is said to be information, which is said to be knowledge—is served up for the benefit of a mythical creature, the well-informed public. But an indiscriminate kaleidoscope of sound, image, and number bites amounts only to a bazaar of goods at best and an information cesspool at worst. The extent to which a walk in that bazaar or poking in that cesspool benefits body, mind, and society depends on the maturity, education, and intelligence that the walker-poker brings to it. If they are to profit from the flow of information on the split screen, men and women must become as intelligent and as enlightened in their value judgment as are the best of their fellow humans. Such challenges are as old as humanity, as are the disagreements about who those best fellow humans are and in what ways they should be imitated. What is unprecedented is the magnitude of the challenge: it now involves a feuding global family of man.

Writing by the Yalu River in 1895, the French poet and philosopher Paul Valéry recorded an imaginary dialogue with a Buddhist sage. The monk reflected on the Western ways of doing things. "You have neither the patience that weaves long lines nor feeling for the irregular. . . . You are in love with intelligence until it frightens you. . . . [You] rage with desire for what is immediate and destroy your fathers and sons together."[21] The sage failed to foresee that a century later his criticism would apply to all cultures of the time-compact globe.

"Learn from me," wrote Dr. Victor Frankenstein before his death, "if not by my precepts, at least by my example, how dangerous is the acquirement of knowledge and how much happier that man is who believes his native town to be the world, than he who aspires to become greater than his nature will allow."[22] Globalization has a related problem: how to make the world, connected into a global present through cyberspace, a shared native town of all people and endow all people with appropriate magnanimity.

On what shared truths or beliefs is the identity of mankind to be based?

In his 1967 presidential address to the British Association, Joseph Needham identified scientific knowledge as the necessary and sufficient foundation for a fraternal mankind. He compared historical developments in mathematics, astronomy, physics, chemistry, botany, and medicine in China and in Europe and considered the respective contributions of those cultures to what he called ecumenical science. By *ecumenical science* he meant those forms of the sciences that have been or may be expected to emerge from the confluence of Chinese and European knowledge. His survey suggested the existence of "fusion points," epochs when these sciences, although grown from separate historical roots, did or will merge into a single, universally acceptable body of scientific truths. He observed that the

> more "biological" the science, the more organic its subject matter, the longer the process seems to take; and in the most difficult field of all, the study of the human and animal body in health and disease, the process is yet far from accomplished. Needless to say, the standard here adopted assumes that in the investigation of natural phenomena all men are potentially equal, that the oecumenism of modern science embodies a universal language that they can all comprehensibly speak [and that] an oecumenical natural philosophy . . . will continue to grow among men, pari passu with the vast growth of organization and integration of human society, until the coming of the world co-operative commonwealth which will include all peoples as the waters cover the earth.[23]

Needham's remark about the extent to which a subject matter is organic recognizes the increasing degrees of freedom found at increasingly more complex integrative levels (see the discussion about level-specific causations and languages on pp. 30–33).

A "fusion point" in mathematics was reached long ago. In physics it may or may not be reached within the foreseeable future. Approaches to biology, especially to issues of organic evolution, depend greatly on the culture; in matters of psychology and sociology, the differences are profound and seem unreconcilable among civilizations; and in ethics, ideas and practices are in open wars.

S. P. Huntington defined civilization as the highest cultural grouping of people and the broadest level of cultural identity people have short of what distinguishes humans from other species.[24] While stressing that modernization does not demand Westernization, he perceives in our world a three-cornered cultural conflict involving the Christian West, Confucian/Communist China, and the Islamic world. The distinctness of these civilizations does not, of course, prohibit inner turmoil within each. His reasoning is convincing, though not without its critics.[25]

Whether or not one agrees with Huntington, the "world co-operative commonwealth" envisaged by Needham is unlikely to come about by discovering correct answers to scientific truths about nature and man, for the nested hierarchical character of causations and languages allows multiplicities and often contradictory yet equally valid answers to questions about what one ought to believe as true. If a worldwide agreement concerning the position of mankind in the universe does come about, it will more likely do so because some ideology will have succeeded in converting or else killing the adherents of other ideologies.

Consistent with this stark view I observe cultural conflicts of substantial dimensions in the making. They are helped by the development of science itself, which has played havoc with received teachings about the position of man in the world. The Copernican revolution removed the earth from the center of the world; Kepler's recognition that the planetary orbits are (roughly) elliptical broke the Aristotelian faith in the perfection of the heavens; Newton showed that it is possible to formulate mathematically couched physical laws, open to human understanding and criticism, that are valid everywhere and everywhen in the universe; Darwin removed humans from the guaranteed pinnacle of all species; and Freud removed men and women from the company of angels and devils and established them as nature's very unusual but not transcendental wonders. Einstein showed that the universe cannot have a center and bequeathed to mankind the finite but unbounded, inert, and inhospitable immensity of dumb matter.

This constellation of opinions is itself based on Western thought and values, as are the criteria for what may constitute universal truth and how to test for it. There is now a common cause between the idea of truth and the pronouncement of scientists. Yet simultaneously, the public understanding of science is rapidly sinking.[26] Also, although there is an extraordinarily popular respect for scientific authority as the final purveyor and absolute judge of truth, there is also a resentment of science as something unintelligible to common folks. Perhaps the resentment stems from the need for sustained mental effort to understand science, to which popular attitudes nurtured on market claims of all things easy and fast have become allergic.[27]

Our age, a transition between nation-states and an uneasy global community, is a metastable one. Beliefs that used to be held as eternal truths, from moral standards to mathematics, now change rapidly and tend to break into shards.

In one of the metaphysical poems of Pasternak, the poet is Hamlet himself as well as Hamlet the actor. This complex character reflects on the predicament of mankind. "I step forth on the boards," he says, and "strain the far-off echo yield / A cue to the events that may come in my day." On the time-compact globe the far-off echo is immediate and gives cues only to what may come during the next few seconds or hours at the most.

Section 3.6, on the evolutionary role of truth as a human value, concluded that the human desire to identify things and ideas that are permanent and to appeal to them as demonstrations of the unimportance of passage has as its primary consequence the generation and perpetuation of changes in what is believed to be true. The speedier are those changes, the more intense is the desire for continuity and permanence; the more intense the need and search for stability, the faster the changes. Our age displays this feedback process at an ever-increasing speed. The question of what people should believe as true—whether proposed by science, philosophy, religion, political ideology, the arts, or the letters—is being driven toward new crises of surely vast proportions but unknown resolution.

6.2 Conduct à la Mode

Summing up the evolutionary role of moral teachings in sec. 4.4, I quoted from James Russell Lowell's poem "The Present Crisis." I even proposed to retitle it "The Permanent Crisis." Here are two lines from the concluding stanza of the poem: "New occasions teach new duties, / Time makes ancient good uncouth." This section considers some of the new occasions and new duties of our epoch arranged under several headings that are mutually interdependent.

America

In an unpublished doctoral dissertation in the American History Department of Yale University, "America Discovered a Second Time: French Perceptions of American Notions of Time from Tocqueville to Laboulaye," Anne S. Lévy examined the "invisible but omnipresent issue of time manifested in Jacksonian America" as perceived by Alexis de Tocqueville (1805–1859) and three other French travelers during the early and mid-nineteenth century. The three others were Edouard Laboulaye, a historian (who proposed the Statue of Liberty); Gustave de Beaumont, a writer and friend of Tocqueville; and Michel Chevalier, an economist.[28]

"I am after Tocqueville and his contemporaries' articulation of an ideology of time," writes Lévy. These men were looking for historical motion beneath the storms, waves, and squalls of the day, and those patterns are fundamentally temporal. For many of our "contemporary social historians that steadily moving tide is the market revolution[;] for Tocqueville it is a mentality of time which shapes the external phenomenon in light of culture, identity and goals, a deep and powerful inner current which directs reaction to the outside forces assailing Americans."[29]

For five selected topics I will use Lévy's work as a guide to early and mid-nineteenth-century American attitudes to time. I will then trace each topic forward to the vibrating turmoil of contemporary America.

Patriotism and Religion The French travelers observed "a deep-running patriotism making itself felt in daily affairs and also carrying Americans along an ideal stream of blended morality and freedom into the future; a heartfelt conviction that the profound and practical presence of religion was obligatory in maintaining and directing that flow; and an overpowering current of egalitarian attitudes and values which focused generously and unremittingly on individual potential."[30] In 1881 Walt Whitman praised "Victory, union, faith, identity, time / The indissoluble compacts, riches, mystery / Eternal progress, the kosmos, and the modern reports." Riches, progress, and the modern reports are now thought of as achievements of industry; mystery and the cosmos are domains of science, religion, and Hollywood; victories are to be handled with care; and many-sidedness is preferred to union. Faith and identity are open, time is in short supply, indissoluble compacts are held impossible, and the bisexual lava that fired Whitman's patriotic spirit has been tamed to don't ask, don't tell.

James Russell Lowell, already cited, saw humanity sweep forward in spite of "Truth forever on the scaffold / Wrong forever on the throne." A century later his great-grandnephew Robert Lowell, also a poet, spent a year in jail for refusing to serve in the war against Hitler's wrong-on-the-throne. In the 1960s Peter, Paul, and Mary sang praises of the land and pride in its people. Others, forty years later, stress multiculturalism and hold patriotism to be an outdated sentiment, while yet others regard an application for driver's license as the curtailment of individual freedom, jury duty as bondage, and taxation as theft.

While patriotism in America is thus deconstructed so as to fit a yet unformed international order, religion is being reconstructed so as to be appropriate for a society that was once the New World now becoming an even newer one. This reconstruction follows the marketplace model: American religions reflect the same wealth of options as does the consumer society. "The Pledge of Allegiance to the Flag of the United States," written in 1892 and amended in 1954, contains the line "one nation under God." For the early twenty-first century it would be more correct to say, "one nation under many gods."

Americans belong to some 400,000 churches confessing 2,000 different faiths.[31] Although the multiplication of religious groups continues, half of all churchgoing Americans attend only 12 percent of the nation's churches; the trend is toward the creation of megachurches. These institutions, which are almost entirely Protestant, offer around-the-clock availability to their members and sometimes attract as many as 10,000 people to a service. They offer their members seamless, multimedia worship and a large community. Their congregations model themselves after commercial organizations and employ public relations methods.

The graying of the calendar has been forcing a rapprochement between ecclesiastical and civil rhythms that in turn helps to mix religious and secular obligations. Large budgets and large volunteer pools offer megachurches the capacity to diversify without limits and develop new "product lines" to meet the needs of their congregations. Harvey Cox, writing about the shaping of religions in the twenty-first century, remarked that the wealth, ostentatiousness, and efficiency of these churches explain why Mexicans complained that "their North American brothers and sisters had gotten so carried away by the health-and-wealth gospel and were so much under the sway of the right-wing group known as the Christian Coalition that they had forgotten their original mission to the downtrodden."[32] The thundering Jehovah, the loving Christ, the self-denying Buddha, and the noble Confucius now walk the earth together, inspiring a many-colored mixture of beliefs—a mixture, not a harmonious blend, because ancient and profound differences among different families of culturally based religions remain.

Much of the world, not only America, is afloat with religious ideologies claiming scientific support and scientific ideas claiming religious support. The degree of intellectual weight and spiritual substance carried by such claims depends on the level of critical knowledge they command. These range from crude and tendentious ignorance of science, religion, or both to serious preparedness.[33]

But there is little feeling abroad about beauty in daily life, for the articulation of the day from matins to compline, or for the cycling of the seasons, because much of the industrialized world lives with the grayed calendar just mentioned and with a colonized night. The paucity of ways in which contemporary life, including religious life, relates to history and to the cosmos leaves an emptiness that demands to be filled. That need, in turn leads to experimentation with new forms of spiritual commitments. Members of the Heaven's Gate cult in Southern California committed suicide so that they could be "beamed up" to a spacecraft they believed was hiding behind the Hale-Bopp comet in 1997. The rapidly growing focus on high-tech mysticism is accompanied by a shift of preference from the natural to the artificial, including the replacement of natural rhythms with artificial ones.

As if to compensate for the intrusion of the artificial, the forms of religious expressions are changing. There have been attempts, for instance, to enrich Christian liturgy by recognizing areas outside the Middle East, where the Old and New Testaments are set. This is the Introit of a Celtic mass: "East by North, / Send thine eyes forth / Over whales foaming"; its Kyrie follows: "God of elements, Have mercy on us."[34] The desire to expand the traditional boundaries of religions has also prompted attempts to reimagine God. Groups within that movement have challenged the bread-and-wine symbolism of Christian communion by using milk and honey instead and by invoking a female personification of God. At the conclusion of a service, participants prayed in a language that reaffirmed feminine sexuality and sensuality. "'Our maker Sophia, we are women in your image; with the hot blood of our wombs we give form to new life,' the group prayed. 'With nectar between our thighs we invite a lover,' they continued, and 'with our warm bloody fluids we remind the world of its pleasures and sensations.'"[35] Tocqueville would not have been too surprised.

Work and Urgency In 1836 Michel Chevalier observed that work lay at the heart of the meaning and experience of American life. The mission of work was "to conquer rapidly, to the profit of humankind, an immense country; to substitute in the briefest possible time, civilization for the silence of the primitive forests." The Americans whom Chevallier observed could endure a constant, unrelieved application to work. As a result, he said, "Everyone produces a great deal because the country consumes a great deal; everyone consumes a great deal because he earns a great deal, handles a great deal of business matters, has no worries about his future or his children's future, or does not worry about that future."[36]

The universal consumption that Chevalier remarked acquired the name "consumerism" and became institutionalized. In a 1997 issue of the quarterly of the Federal Reserve Bank of Boston, we read about the joy of consumption. "Living standards have risen enormously over the century, and Americans still feel pressed to consume more. . . . In a market economy we must buy the things we need to take our place in the community. [However] rising incomes don't relieve the pressure on the middle class to keep up, and may put extra burdens on the poor."[37] These lines assume the infinite expandability of consumer needs and the possibility of meeting them, whatever they are.

For advocates of mass consumption as a way to techno-utopia, writes Jeremy Rifkin, "converting Americans from a psychology of thrift to one of spendthrift proved a daunting task."[38] Daunting, perhaps, but considering the present-orientedness of Americans, not so difficult. Simultaneously people began to pine for a workless paradise as part of the American dream.

> There is a land that's fair and bright
> Where the hand-outs grow on bushes
> And you sleep out every night;
> Where the box cars all are empty,
> Where the sun shines every day
> On the birds and bees
> And lemonade springs . . .
> In the Big Rock Candy Mountains.[39]

The Puritanical model of hard work and the popular model of Big Rock Candy Mountain thus play hide and seek as economic and political conditions change.

Tocqueville remarked that "to clear, cultivate, and transform the huge, uninhabited continent which is their domain, the Americans need the everyday support of an energetic passion; that passion can only be the love of wealth."[40] The distribution of wealth in contemporary America is uneven. The difference in income between the best- and worst-paid 10 percent is greater in the United States than in any other industrial land. In the 1980s 40 percent of the nation's wealth was concentrated in 1 percent of American households. Between 1980 and 1995 the inflation-adjusted earnings of the highest bracket rose 10.7 percent, the median income fell 3.6 percent, and the lowest bracket fell 9.6 percent.[41] In 1993 the U.S. child poverty rate was 44 percent for African Americans, 37.9 percent for Latinos, and 16.2 for whites. Elsewhere the child poverty rate was much lower: 9.9 percent in the United Kingdom, 6.8 percent in Germany, and 2.7 percent in Sweden.[42]

That America and its political system still serve as an inspiration to the Old World, as well as to newer ones, despite the recognition that its distribution of wealth resembles the Marxist scenario, attests to the survival of the hope embodied in the robust convictions of the nation's founding fathers.

Now back to Chevalier. "The pure Yankee is not only a worker, but a traveling worker. . . . Whether it be the system of competition which has given him the habit, or he is unduly worried about the value of time, or that the mobility of everything surrounding him and of his own self keeps his nervous system in a perpetual state of disturbance, or that he was so created by the hands of nature, he is always busy, always in a hurry, in an excessive hurry."[43] The need for speed was originally prompted by the urgency of work. But speed was later removed from the company of work and acquired desirability in itself. It does not matter what one does; as long as it is done quickly, it is meritorious: I hurry, therefore I am. The British still stand for public office, while Americans run for it.

Hurrying has its corollary in the narrowing of temporal horizons, which is often observed in and sometimes noted by the business community. "A preoccupation with short-term results and instant economic gratification is undermining the long-term viability of American companies and in some cases, entire industries." American companies have to bring their product to market in four years to show profit, whereas foreign competitors may have twenty years to commercialize the same technology. The cause resides in the high price of capital, that is, in peoples' demands for immediate gains.[44]

Again, Chevalier remarked 170 years ago that for Americans, land was merely a quantifiable investment rather than a place that they might endow with meaning.[45] George Kennan, former ambassador to the USSR, wrote that in 1965, while traveling back to his native Wisconsin, he fell to wondering what home was for those such as himself. "From the time the family came to Wisconsin, in 1850, to the time when I myself left for good, in 1921, barely seventy years elapsed. Was this span of residence for a family enough to make a place 'home'?"[46] Considering the restless mobility of Americans, he felt as a stranger not in his land but in his time.

Work and urgency, houses and lands as investments in real estate rather than as homes—all these combine in the emergence of the "business homeless." They are members of "a new elite of glazed nomads with all their needs catered to—except those that really matter," to wit, steady belonging, a home, family, warmth.[47]

The French travelers also discovered that "due to the pressures of equality, the character of social time has been whittled down to and postulated in terms of the temporal scope of the individual's life." That tightly focused horizon, writes Lévy, leads to great enterprise, "but its very tightness suggests a willed deficiency in temporal assessment, the ethical repercussions of which are still with American culture today."[48] In the new land, ethics became narrowed to private, individual dimensions and to a belief that a future well-being will miraculously flow from gambling with the present.[49]

By the end of the twentieth century, urgency has come to inform all civilizations via the scientific-industrial way of life. The global market- and workplace, connected by dense communication networks, have helped to create an urgency in demands for social advances. The immediate causes of these demands are needs of many kinds, but their historical roots are as old as those of ecological problems. They may be found in the Christian evaluation of time as the medium of salvation, strongly evident in Puritan tradition. In the economic domain this urgency came to demand immediate gratification; in the cultural-intellectual domain, instant value judgments.

What was said about religion, patriotism, work, and urgency may be summed up in the Quaker motto: "Hands to work, hearts to God."

Violence, Spectacle, and Law Breaches of decorum or even occasional violations of the law were as often hailed as condemned by Jacksonians. "In the Jacksonian mind," we learn, "only liberation from the constraints of law could produce a truly health-giving natural order."[50] Our traveling Frenchman, Michel Chevalier, judged such conduct not as health giving and hopeful but rather as frightening. "When accosting someone in the morning, you ask for and give news. Here a black was hanged, elsewhere whites were thrashed; in Philadelphia ten houses were demolished. . . . Then you move on to the price of cotton and of coffee, to the arrival of flour, planks and tobacco. . . . Long live the interest of the moment, interpreted by who knows who, for the success of who knows what political or business intrigue!"[51] As violations of the law multiply in number, added Chevalier, they produce less and less sensation.[52]

The day after the assassination of John F. Kennedy, in 1962, James Reston remarked that "Kennedy [became] a victim of a violent streak he sought to curb in the nation. . . . The grief was general, for somehow the worst in the nation prevailed over the best. The indictment extended beyond the assassin, for something in the nation itself, some strain of madness and violence, had destroyed the highest symbol of law and order."[53] The media portray social upheavals and natural disasters, petty and heinous crimes, heroic selflessness, and vast and historical pageantry as only momentary spectacles. They are forgotten before they can settle in the long-term register of memory because other, equally transient impressions demand attention. Enough violent infotainment has been pumped into public consciousness to make its consumers increasingly insensitive, requiring increasing doses of mayhem for the same intensity of arousal. Violence has become a ritualized spectator sport.

In trying to control violence, the courts educate the public in matters of right and wrong. In the process the nation's lawyers have become businessmen and -women responding to the market. In thus shedding its image as a noble calling, the legal profession has not improved the public image of jurists.[54] The "criminal justice system is in crisis," concluded a report of the National Criminal Justices Commission. "The prison population has tripled since 1980 and the expenditures for law enforcement have quadrupled."[55] Curiously, the overall crime rate in America remained unchanged and is no higher than in comparable nations, but our sentences are longer for lesser crimes.[56] Fear is high, the report suggests, because the media are overhyped and overheated, crime dominates network news, and television drama is dominated by violence.[57]

To have the laws keep up with the problems of the day and do so in a fashion acceptable to the governed is essential to modern participatory democracies. In its attempts to do just that, the web of laws and regulations in the United States fills all available nooks and crannies, producing a crisis in legal ecology. For complex societies, wrote the economist Joseph Tainter, there comes a time when repairing existing legislation is less attractive than not making repairs.[58] New legislation, no matter how thoughtful, is likely to produce too many administrative burdens and too many unintended consequences. Judges and attorneys face an increasing inability to apply the law so as to achieve the desired results. This in turn is a consequence of everyone's increased critical involvement—locally and globally—in the legal process. The situation evokes a scene from John LeCarré's post-Soviet spy novel *Our Game*. In it, one of the characters accuses an Englishman named Larry of having violated the law by helping to run guns to the Chechens in their war against the Russians. A friend of Larry replies: "What *law* has Larry broken, please? . . . Whose *law* do you throw at me? British law? Russian law? American law? International law? United Nations law? The law of gravity? The law of the jungle? I don't understand whose law."[59]

Contemporary legal scholars tend to view laws as forms of community discourse subject to continuous revision. That discourse tends to seek the simplest format, as is exemplified by the use of impoverished scientific reductionism and psychopharmacology to explain and resolve issues of justice. But reductionist solutions are at best quick fixes to suffering and social disorder; ultimately they do not work. If legislation appropriate to the problems of the day proves to be too hard to enforce, if the public's love of violence remains or even increases, if poverty and ignorance remain broadly spread and keep on serving as hotbeds for crime, then the overwhelmed judiciary system will surely demand help and will lean toward modifying human conduct using whatever the tool kits of science can offer.

Privacy and Philosophy "On a land to be colonized," wrote Chevalier, "you can throw isolated Americans; they will form a multitude of little centers, which, as they each expand outward, will end up embracing a large circle."[60] History gave this prediction a twist: the "little centers" metamorphosed into what George Kennan saw as an exaggerated desire for privacy. It is a

> sad climax of individualism, the blind alley of a generation which had forgotten how to think or live collectively. . . . [Yet] I recalled the truly wonderful fashion in which . . . these same people would rise to the occasion and subordinate their personal interests to collective efforts in the event of a natural catastrophe such as a flood, a hurricane, or a war; and I could not help but feel that one ought to welcome almost any social cataclysm, however painful, however costly, that would carry away something of this stuffy individualism and force human beings to seek their happiness and their salvation in their relationship to society as a whole rather than in the interests of themselves.[61]

As to the usefulness of calamities, Machiavelli believed that political virtue is born of crises and can be renewed only in crises; Jefferson wrote that "the tree of liberty must be refreshed from time to time with the blood of patriots and tyrants. It is its natural manure." We have no shortage of calamities, but just what dimensions catastrophes must have to force Americans to "subordinate their personal interests to collective efforts" is uncertain. As to the extraordinary stress on the importance of privacy, that has met head on the rapid loss of privacy, as will be seen in the subsection "From the Comintern to the Internet."

How can we strike a balance among violence, spectacle, and law? Philosophical criticism, which could help to untangle the endlessly retangling social issues, is not a popular sport because most Americans side with Romeo:

> Hang up philosophy!
> Unless philosophy can make a Juliet,
> Displant a town, reverse a prince's doom,
> It helps not, it prevails not: talk no more.

If cellular phones had allowed Romeo and Juliet to survive adolescence, they might have learned that philosophical criticism *can* displant towns and reverse a prince's doom and that genetic engineering might even make a Juliet. But nothing can guarantee that the displants, reversals, or cloned Juliets would make for a better world. The lovers might still have had to say that "a greater power than we can contradict / Hath thwarted our intents." Yet even after having been banished to outer space, they could still be victorious by having made their point in an example of the role of the tragic. "See what scourge is laid upon your hate."

Excellence and Anxiety In a study entitled "Anxiety and the Formation of Early Modern Culture," William J. Bouwsma traced the cultural causes of the steady increase of anxiety that has characterized the West since about the thirteenth century.[62] In what he identified as anxiety we can recognize the existential tensions I have attributed to the unresolvable conflicts stemming from the human sense of time and simultaneous recognition of the finitude of the self. A sentence in a footnote to his paper is of interest. "The novel anxiety appearing among the populations of the new cities of the developing countries [in Africa] seems to be a result not so much of the new urban experience directly as of the loss of traditional culture."[63]

Of all areas of the globe, America is the land where the past is continuously rejected. The following comments, again by George Kennan, make the point: "The trouble with American cities is that they have grown and changed too fast. They have never had time to clean up after themselves. The new is there before the old is gone. What in one era is functional and elegant and fashionable survives into the following era as grotesque decay. These cities have never had the time to bury their dead; and they are strewn with indecent skeletons in the form of blighted areas."[64]

The condition is what Alvin Toffler called "future shock": America is in a perennial crisis of having lost its past. The overall anxiety follows. The revolution of the sixties was a youthful countermovement to that anxiety driven by so many Romeos and Juliets. Unlike the Shakespearean ones, these star-crossed youths turned to debates and discussions; they continued the American dream for their generation. In its early form the American dream was the Jeffersonian idea of happiness as satisfaction in the wake of difficult work well done. In 1778 the word *Excelsior* was adopted as the motto on the seal of the State of New York: it was interpreted to mean "for ever higher." In 1841 Longfellow used the word as the title and refrain of a poem about a youth who followed a voice calling him forever higher in the mountains. His pursuit led him to his death, but even in his frozen hands he held on to "that banner with the strange device, 'Excelsior.'" The poem became popular as a representation of the inventive, driving spirit of America.

Bill Cosby, a popular black actor of the 1990s, gave his five children first names that begin with the letter *E*—Erika, Erinn, Ennis, Ensa, and Evin—to remind them of the need to excel. In 1996 Ennis was murdered on a Los Angeles freeway while changing a tire. The assassin had his eyes on Ennis's car, which had a list price of $135,000, an amount he would have needed thirteen years to earn.

In 1849 Longfellow reflected on his America: "Humanity with all its fears, / With all the hopes of future years / Is hanging breathless on your fate." A century and a half later it has become impossible to say much about the world without acknowledging new occasions and new duties that first emerged in America, the products of the immense resourcefulness of its people. It is equally impossible to say much about America without acknowledging the rest of the world, to which the New World is now ecologically, economically, and culturally bound.

"Town born, turn out"

On a March evening in 1775, when English ships entered Boston harbor, the people were rallied by the cry "Town born, turn out!" Oppose foreign imposition, they were exhorted; help secure independence. The issues were clear cut. Before independence from the ecological problems of the earth may be achieved, it will be necessary to rally people with the cry "Earth born, turn out!" Defend yourself against your home-grown invaders.

But the ecological problems are not as simple as distinguishing between British redcoats and American farmers. The poor countries, which have the world's worst environmental problems, have neither the funds, the energy, nor—consequently—the popular will to deal with them.[65] In the rich lands, although some environmental policies have been successful, remedies for long-term problems are difficult because most of the causes of those problems occupy ambiguous social positions on the spectrum between good and bad. Here is the background.

Species influence one another's adaptive direction: man's best friend and dog's best feeder evolved together. All evolutionary change is coevolutionary. In an ecological niche of limited furnishings, each evolutionary advance made by any one species may be experienced as a deterioration of the environment by all its competitors.[66] On the time-compact globe, environment includes much more than natural resources: humanity now has to coevolve with an environment created by its labor, ingenuity, ignorance, and irresponsibility. Many current problems whose handling calls for "new duties" may be attributed to advances made by a group of people somewhere resulting in the deterioration of conditions for others somewhere else.

The relation between moral conduct and environmental quality was noted in 1798 by Thomas Malthus. He observed that the reproductive power of humans outruns the rate at which the earth is able to supply subsistence and concluded that unless moral behavior becomes the rule—by which he meant sexual restraints—there will always be a surplus population that will perish through hunger, war, and illness. His observations played an important role in the speculations of both Darwin and Wallace, which led them to the idea of organic evolution by natural selection.

As the historian Paul Kennedy observes in *Preparing for the Twenty-First Century*, Malthus's dire predictions failed to materialize in the nineteenth and early twentieth centuries because of the inventiveness of people in developing new resources. But this does not mean that his ideas are wrong today, when that very inventiveness has created an assault of immense proportions on the environment and when every country practices the environmental equivalent of deficit financing.[67]

Moreover, it is a psychologically and politically difficult deficit financing because the great public enemies responsible for the ecological mess and its consequences are also, or were at one time, our great friends and public servants.

The Einstein bombs—atomic and hydrogen devices based on the $E = mc^2$ relation of relativity theory—created a state of mutual terror and, through it, helped to prevent a worldwide conflagration; the deadly organisms in vials that now threaten public health were used in medical research; atomic waste comes from plants that generate electricity to satisfy innumerable different needs. The U.S. garbage that no one wants to take is made up of the odd sock, the tennis ball chewed up by the family dog, parts of the greasy outboard engine, and industrial waste left over from activities that helped to improve the quality of life. The satellites that crash like so many falling Lucifers made cyberspace operable. The present enemies of the environment were its former friends.

Surplus People

The rules of collectively approved conduct have always changed, but they used to do so gradually. Not any more. On the time-compact globe all ideas about what is right and wrong in personal or social matters have become subjects of experimentation. In the West this experimentation is feverish and in the open; elsewhere it may be feverish or cautious, underground or in the open. But there are no areas on earth where the methods and messages of received views have not been influenced by the tectonic changes in the West. The shifts reflect the acceleration of history. "The pace of change in our world is speeding up, accelerating to the point where it threatens to overwhelm the management capacity of political leadership. This acceleration of history comes not only from advancing technology, but also from unprecedented world population growth, even faster economic growth, and the increasingly frequent collisions between expanding human demands and the limits of the earth's natural system."[68] The radically increased pace of change amplifies to uncanny dimensions all earlier suggestions on population control.

In 1776 Adam Smith suggested in *The Wealth of Nations* that economy need not be a zero-sum game: my gain is not necessarily your loss. What made the nonzero-sum game possible was the mind's inventiveness applied to the unlimited resources available in the environment. His reasoning was correct for his age, social system, population density, and state of mother nature.

But that was then. By the twentieth century the incredible productivity and wastefulness of industry and commerce, combined with the revolution of expectations, had made the globe into a single finite ecological niche of vast but limited resources. In that world any group's use of nonrenewable resources, and any increase in the rate of use of renewable ones, is experienced by its competitors as a deterioration of their environment. And the competition is keen. To absorb the number of new entrants into the world's labor forces, the world's economy needs 38 to 40 million new jobs every year. This is over 100,000 new jobs every day of the year.[69] Can the social and natural environment support that many new people? To give a nasty name to a nasty situation, we might say that humanity is producing surplus people.

Bringing forth vastly more offspring than the environment can support and societies of insects, fish, birds, or people can feed, educate, and integrate has been the policy of life throughout its 3.5 billion-year history. The nasty name "surplus people" refers not to any particular number but to ever-changing conditions jointly determined by societies and by their living and inanimate environments. Human values are involved through a society's praise of having children, using all the means that imagination can suggest and skills make possible. But humans also murder people with imagination and skill. In our epoch those praising, supporting, and killing practices are undergoing radical quantitative and qualitative changes. Morality pertaining to life and death is in the process of getting reformulated.

Genocides and Epidemics

Throughout history all populations have been reduced by hunger, illness, and genocide. In antiquity massacres of whole peoples were ever-present parts of daily life, just as automobile accidents are today. The Tartars of the thirteenth century and the Turks of the sixteenth century killed or enslaved two-thirds of the population of Southeast Europe. The fourteenth-century Islamic conqueror Timur massacred over 100,000 people during his campaigns and assembled the heads of the slain in minarets. During the transatlantic slave trade, 10 million Africans were shipped to the Americas at maximized profits and minimized humaneness. In our own epoch the Turks slaughtered 800,000 Armenians; between 1917 and 1987 the Soviet government killed 54.7 million of its citizens. Early during the twentieth century the Japanese invaders of China slaughtered 20 million civilians. During World War II over 6 million Jews were systematically exterminated by the Nazis, as were half a million Gypsies. Between 1949 and 1976 in Mao's China, 34.4 million people perished in a state-sponsored famine designed to destroy the family as an institution.

With advances in science and technology, the efficiency of extermination—both of animals and of humans—has also greatly improved. On a modern pig farm south of Munich, the pigs spend their last day and night in an enclosure next to the slaughtering room so that they get accustomed to the smell of blood and the squeaks of pigs being slaughtered. So conditioned, they put up less resistance when driven to the solitary container that dumps them on the killing floor. Most of the cattle in the United States and Canada are driven to the killing floors along chutes designed by Dr. Temple Grandin, a specialist in designing chutes that make the cattle's walk to slaughter less traumatic. This is important because "adrenaline released under stress can leave soft, mushy spots in meat, a drawback in the food industry."[70] Along her "stairway to heaven" nothing will frighten the animal or make it balk until it is stunned with an electric bolt to the head.

Over the entrance of the Nazi annihilation camp in Auschwitz there was a large sign: "Arbeit macht Frei!" ("Work makes you free"). People were not certain what would happen to them until they were herded into shower rooms where poison gas issued from the showers. The German Nazis pioneered the technology of centrally directed mass murder, which they made into an art of state. Their practices anticipated the end-of-the-century problems concerning people who are judged redundant by one or another political or ideological power. R. L. Rubinstein's devastating book *The Cunning of History* is a warning that at the end of the twentieth century any group of people may be judged to be surplus and handled accordingly. In the case of the Nazis, morality was argued from a philosophy of Teutonic superiority, while on the economic side their annihilation camps supported the corporate enterprise of their war industry. Rubinstein remarks that his purpose in writing his book was "to point out that the explosive combination of surplus population, finite resources, and expanding sovereign powers of government suggest that the Nazi extermination program may yet foreshadow other exercises in the politics of total domination by future governments as they face catastrophic population problems arising out of mankind's very success of mastering nature."[71] Had it not been for Hitler's military defeat, his bureaucracy would have seen to it that information on his death camps was erased from the memory banks of computerized records. They would have survived only as uncertain tales of horror, like the story of thirty villages in the Ural mountains that ceased to appear on Soviet maps after 1958, when a nuclear dump did away with them.

The Nazis and the Bolsheviks demonstrated that a government so dedicated can inflict total domination on any selected segment of its population. The methods are at hand, should socioeconomic conditions demand and political considerations dictate their use. Consider, for instance, that in the early 1990s more than 800 million people were unemployed or underemployed around the world—in other words, unwanted because unneeded. Consider also that at the end of the millennium 13 percent of the world's population is over 65 years of age; to different degrees, these people are disposable burdens on their families. In 1991 in the United States, 70,000 old persons were abandoned by what came to be called "granny dumping." Granny dumping leaves the old and memoryless in a public place, in a variation of "the kindness of strangers" encountered in the natural history of morals (see sec. 4.3). Yet the ancient Eskimo practice of letting old people, ready to die, walk out to freeze in the frozen emptiness of the ice fields would be regarded in today's America as assisted suicide and hence a criminal act.

Consider, moreover, the trend in the United States of building jails for profit. This movement illustrates the public's unwillingness to pay for social policies that the same public loudly endorses. In the process the responsibilities for carrying out justice are delegated to the business sector, with its single-minded dedication to profit making. The report of the National Criminal Justices Commission stresses that "companies that service the criminal justice system need sufficient quantities of raw material [that is, prisoners] to guarantee long term growth" and that "the industry will do whatever is necessary to guarantee a steady supply of prisoners."[72] The prisons are experiments in disposing of surplus population profitably.

A 1997 study of state-sponsored mass killings conducted by the National Center for Policy Analysis noted that there is a "rough negative correlation . . . between the level of state killing and the real gross domestic product."[73] Government-sponsored murder, though immoral, may "nevertheless be explicable by the amoral apparatus of supply and demand." Large-scale killings exact a heavy price in lost national wealth. When the cost of "killing on the grand scale" becomes too high because the per capita productivity is high, the relative incidence of genocide declines. This analysis, concluding on the Marxist view that history is moved by economics, leaves open the question whether Genghis Khan, Stalin, Mao, or Hitler would have stopped murdering people if those people had been more productive.

A rash of newly recognized diseases also serves as healthy warnings to the master species. We have been struck by Lyme disease, Legionnaires' disease, toxic shock syndrome, and hanta viruses. Extraordinarily violent pathogens have been found in Africa and South America, such as the Ebola virus, Lassa fever, and the Marburg and Sabia viruses. Most of these plagues are new only to Western medicine: they are spread by ancient species of microorganisms that are taking advantage of the new niches in life's rich marketplace, now interconnected across the globe by human and nonhuman hosts traveling by aircraft. They are not mythical beasts with supernatural power; the spread of Lassa, Ebola, and Marburg can be interrupted by modern hygienic measures. But there is no way such measures could be taken around the world. And then there is the AIDS epidemic. It is estimated that in the United States one out of every nine adults has the precursor of the deadly disease. It is an epidemic with which even the most advanced lands are unable to deal at this time. It is estimated that 33.4 million people worldwide are infected by HIV, the human immunodeficiency virus. Other epidemics seem to be emerging continuously.[74]

"Home is the sailor, home from the sea / And the hunter, home from the hill." Homelessness is yet another method of population control because homeless people perish more quickly than those with homes. On any given night in the United States, an estimated 500,000 to 600,000 people live on the streets and in shelters.[75]

"Religion," wrote Marx, "is the sigh of the oppressed creature, the heart of the heartless world and the soul of the soulless condition. It is the opium of the people." He made his list too short. The human need to try to overcome the passage of time, for example, by reaching for or creating whatever appears permanent, has been serving as a universal opiate and is responsible for the creation of civilizations. When these opiates fail, opium becomes the religion of the people.

> *The Pool Players*
> *Seven at the Golden Shovel*
>
> We real cool. We
> Left school. We
> Lurk late. We
> Strike straight. We
> Sing sin. We
> Thin gin. We
> Jazz June. We
> Die soon.[76]

Drugs join viruses, homelessness, and violence in dealing with "surplus people."

Eros agonistes

I enter the search for a new moral framework for sexual conduct through the issue of population control.

All species control their fertility rates; mammals do so by varying the age of sexual maturity, by lactational infertility, and except for primates, by limiting the periods during which the animal is in heat. The first two are present in humans; being in heat for only limited periods is not. As a consequence, there is a continuously available libidinal energy in both sexes, ready to fire creativity and destructiveness regardless of season. The control of reproductive rates is thus transferred from a programmed biological timetable to reasoned individual conduct working under social guidance. The effort necessary to maintain that control is a source of steady conflicts between instinct and reason: the need to manage these conflicts has been one of the driving forces of human creativity and destructiveness. Novel to our epoch, however, are the dimensions of the issues of control involved: we have more people, more creativity, more destructiveness, more opportunities to make love and make hate.

As with the powers of love and hatred, the power of creating new humans has traditionally been perceived as having its source in the universe. Human sexual union has been projected on the cosmos, taking many forms. In Hinduism, for example, the lingam, a symbol of the phallus, is an object of worship; the yoni, symbol of the female sexual organ, often forms the base to the erect *lingam*. The two together represent the creativity of the universe. But conclusions drawn from a recognition of creativity vested in eros differ. Hinduism focuses on the organic; Taoism, with its yin and yang, on the principles of female and male; Christianity, on the sanctity of begetting children.

This sanctity may be represented by Paul Claudel's drama *The Satin Slipper*, where the shadows of a man and a woman, merged into a single double shadow, is seen on a wall. The man and woman who cast the double shadow have parted, however, leaving the shadow masterless "in the land of shadows." Why, asks the double shadow, "having created me, have they . . . cruelly severed me, me who am but one? Why have they carried off to the far ends of this world my two quivering halves?"[77]

This, the sacramental view of intercourse, has been rapidly fading in importance. As recreational and procreational sex is becoming easily separable in practice, eros, like Claudel's double shadow, is seeking guidance regarding how to make the two shadows separable not only in practice but also in principle.

The practice of separability is called contraception. If ignorance, poverty, dogma, or irresponsibility pushes contraception out the door, a policeman carrying a death warrant will climb through the window. Birth control will be complemented by death control, even more than it already is. Not that population control through contraception does not have its problems: a one-child policy, whether enforced or voluntary, leads to a steady increase in the relative number of old people, with an insufficient number of younger hands around to sustain the economy.[78] At their most benign, such conditions are likely to lead to the need of strict prescriptions and proscriptions of conduct. At their worst, they may lead to demands for executing people when they reach a certain age or else to the need for limited infanticide. In addition, no one knows the long-term effects of having an increasingly larger number of childless couples or of having children grow up without siblings or, in a few generations, without uncles, aunts, or cousins.

At this writing, not having children is the civilian equivalent of a soldier's dying in war: in both cases the individual's biological continuity is cut short for the benefit of the community. But having no offspring has been an unacceptable way of life through the 200-million-year history of mammals. "Look in thy glass, and tell the face thou viewest / Now is the time that face should form another. . . . / Die single, and thine image dies with thee," Shakespeare exhorted a young friend in his third sonnet. The female body evolved to deliver children; the male, to fertilize millions of eggs. The male body could not care less whether any of its sperms grow into fetuses, but the male psyche, no less than the female body and psyche, certainly does.

In Aldous Huxley's *Brave New World* contraception makes recreational sex a practical, universal sport, eliminating waiting periods and thus the demand for deferred gratification. As Brian Aldiss pointed out in his eulogy of Huxley, immediate gratification helps to preserve immaturity, which in turn reinforces superficiality.[79] This dimension of Huxley's 1932 fictional world bears uncanny resemblance to an observation that George F. Kennan made about Southern California. He wrote that

> together with all that tendency in American life which it typifies, [California] is childhood without the promise of maturity—with the promise only of a continual widening and growing impressiveness of the childhood world. And when the day of reckoning and hardship comes, as I think it must, it will be—as everywhere among children—the cruelest and most ruthless natures who will seek to protect their interests by enslaving the others; and the others, being only children, will be easily enslaved. In this way, values will suddenly prove to have been lost that were forged slowly and laboriously in the more rugged experience of Western political development elsewhere.[80]

Fortunately eros is getting reeducated. Welcoming nonreproducing persons—gays, lesbians, dedicated loners—is a part of that reeducation, as is the great increase in male impotence. Wild animals do not reproduce in captivity, nor, it seems, do men in their changing positions in the family and the revised rules of their relations to women. It is estimated that at least 20 million American men are suffering from sexual dysfunctions, including impotence.[81] Meanwhile, sexual experimentation is going on with all the ingenuity and force of armies of footloose men and women.

In a world where eros is very much alive, although agonizing, children remain the visiting waifs I showed them to be in sec. 4.3 when considering "the compassionate pilgrim." Photographs in the report of the Carnegie Task Force subtitled *Meeting the Needs of Our Youngest Children*[82] show happy, smiling, well-fed and well-dressed children, including a carefully bundled infant asleep in the arms of a homeless mother, opposite a stuffed teddy bear. The pictures are painfully incongruous with the text; they make the booklet look like the yearly report of a corporation, with illustrations praising its performance, the tables hiding some dismal details. Those tables show that 3 million children, nearly one-fourth of all American infants and toddlers, live in poverty and that one in three is a victim of physical abuse. A May 1990 fact sheet from the U.S. Department of Justice for 1988 reports about 127,100 thrown-away children (children who were told to leave home or not allowed to return or whose parents or guardians made no effort to recover them) and 438,200 children lost, injured, or otherwise missing.[83]

The State of the World's Children, 1995, a United Nations report, speaks of an underclass of undereducated and unskilled children and young people "standing beneath the broken bottom rungs of social and economic progress."[84] Improvements will not be easy because "the way forward is obstructed by political and economic vested interests, and by the politically unattractive 'pain now, gain later' nature of many of the necessary policies."[85] The children in Robert Capa's *Children of War, Children of Peace*, photographed in China and Spain in the 1930s and Europe during the 1940s, differ from their medieval cohort only in what they wear, the weapons they hold, and the man-made structures behind them, but they are equal in their expressions of hunger, pain, hatred, fright, and occasionally, hope.[86]

Childhood, as I stressed earlier, is not so much a biological phase of development as it is a socially defined state. Changes in children's literature since it first appeared in the mid-seventeenth century reflect profound changes in the conceptualization of childhood.[87] Those changes have been most dramatic during the second half of the twentieth century. Children are now shown as less and less protected from the pressures and complexities of life; they are depicted as facing serious problems without substantial adult support.

In her report on the sexual abuse of adolescent girls, Mary Pipher records a visit to a museum in New York City.

At the Whitney Biennial Art Show, I stood before a tableau entitled, "Family Romance." Four figures—a mother, father, son and daughter—stood naked in a row. They were baby doll shapes of spongy, tan material and real hair. They were all the same height and the same level of sexual development. I interpreted this work as a comment on life in the 1990's. To me it said: "There is no childhood anymore and no adulthood either. Kids aren't safe and adults don't know what they are doing."[88]

In America, with both parents working, children tend to be raised by surrogate parents and appliances: the television set, the stereo, the refrigerator, the telephone, and, in families that can afford computers, the internet.

It is reassuring that in this world of high-tech childhood, the periodic regression of humans from phenotype to genotype is still with us in the life cycle. As Winsor and Parry summed it up in *The Space Child's Mother Goose*,

> Foundations shake,
> Computers break
> And science goes be-pop,
> But baby's joy
> Is still the toy
> With foolish ears that flop.[89]

At least this remains true where children have such toys. In an unforgetta-ble photograph from 1996, three small, bare Macuxi children of Brazil are seen playing with the head of a butchered cow.[90]

A slogan of 1960s America, "Make love, not war," was a call to support the biological over the ideological. It showed good judgment: only biolog-ically fed outrage can control the mind run amok with ideas and ideolo-gies. It is here that eros—the aggregate of all impulses for which the pow-er of sex is a paradigm—drives the mind to formulate new rules of morality. By reinforming the mental, the biological helps to protect humanity from the dangers of the mind's uncontrolled imaginative powers.

Artificial Selection in Humans

Natural selection is as old as the life process, and although it results in or-ganic evolution, it has no predetermined goals. Artificial selection is recent: the domestication of animals, an example of artificial selection, has no more than a 10,000-year history. Moreover, it does have a goal: to effect such changes in animals and plants as are helpful in the struggle for human survival. Artificial selection on humans commenced when the mental de-velopment of our species first demanded and made possible the selection of mates for long-term advantages. In our epoch biotechnology makes it possible to perform such selection in vitro.

The Old Testament recounts that Sarah, Abraham's wife, was childless. To provide an offspring, she gave her husband an Egyptian slave girl and told him, "Go in to my maid; it may be that I shall obtain children by her" (Gen. 16:2). So he did and so she did. Under biblical conditions Sarah's barrenness was God's will, unappealable, but not unrepairable if one used common sense. The contemporary form of "go in to" is that of offering wombs to let. This practice replaced the traditional repair method by the use of instruments, laboratories, and scientific theories. The tent into which Abraham and Hagar adjourned is now populated with employees of the scientific, medical, and legal professions, with a minister here and there. In a commercial contract that commits a woman to produce a child, the putative parents may pay as much as $40,000, of which $10,000 might go to the mother, the rest going to the others in the tent.

In 1676 Antonie van Leeuwenhoek, the Dutch microscopist, discovered spermatozoa. In somewhat over three centuries his discovery has grown into a large trade in semen. In the United States around 11,000 physicians artifi-cially inseminate some 172,000 women each year.[91] Women who cannot produce eggs or whose eggs are defective but are able to carry a child to term pay around $5,000 for each implantation. Between $900 and $1,200 of that goes to the donor from whose body the eggs have been removed.

Shylock, a merchant of Venice, was born in the mind of Shakespeare around 1595. At an unspecified date the merchant offered to loan three thousand ducats to another merchant against the security of a pound of flesh—"to be cut off and taken," said Shylock, "in what part of your body pleaseth me." In the contemporary market of human parts it is not flesh but blood that is the most common item. In 1989 four hundred U.S. commercial centers received close to 7 million liters of blood; international blood trade is a $2 billion industry. Equally alive is the international market for body parts.[92] The machinery of genetic technology opens the possibility of selecting for culturally preferred biological traits.[93]

The practice of selling people into involuntary servitude may be as much as 4,000 years old. The laws of civilized nations prohibit the selling and buying of humans as slaves, but the institution is alive in other forms. There is a market for Asian women bought as wives or mistresses or sold into prostitution. Half a million women are annually shipped into Western Europe alone. According to United Nations estimates, "four million people throughout the world are trafficked each year, forced through lies and coercion to work against their will in many types of servitudes."[94] The Internet carries ample information about child sex rings,[95] and there is a thriving market in Africa in chattel slaves.[96]

The crudest form of artificial selection, of which preferential reproduction is a consequence, is selective death. The suffix *-cide*, from the Latin *cedere*, means "to kill." Our stores are full of herbicides, pesticides, insecticides, and machinery for suicide, homicide, and genocide. Some of these tools are desirable and are socially controlled, whereas others are not, but their availability in increasingly refined forms is obvious. Although killing mosquitoes may be a praiseworthy task, killing people is not necessarily so.

Each victim, whether killed by marauding armies or street gangs or executed in a utopian community because he has reached an age limit, will die resenting the arrogant finality of death. Would this also be the case for people born and raised in a community where death control was the morally right means for keeping the population in balance with available resources and services? In the peasant communities of Eastern Europe, pigs' lives used to be counted in months to slaughter, the way the Romans counted days to the ides and merchants advertise days to Christmas. Would counting birthdays backward from an assigned death date become as acceptable as counting them forward toward an unknown ending?[97]

Noetic time arose from a ceaseless bargaining with death. How would the absence of bargaining change the nature of noetic time? How would the texture of private and public time change if everyone knew that at the age of twenty-eight he or she would painlessly or otherwise be disposed of?

In most animal species, natural life span and reproductive capacities are closely related. As soon as an individual can reproduce, it does; soon after it loses its reproductive capacities, it dies or is devoured by its enemies. During the history of our species, the periods between sexual maturity and marriage have been increasing, permitting the young to learn more skills of mind and body. The period between the cessation of reproductive usefulness and death has also been lengthening, permitting the communication of more learned knowledge to the young. An epidemic of teenage pregnancies and much less frequent high-tech pregnancies after menopause are now bucking this trend. Their long-term effects are unknown.

The distinguished ethologist Niko Tinbergen remarked that "there are good grounds for the conclusion that man's limited behavioral adjustability has been outpaced by culturally determined changes in his social environment, and that is why man is now a misfit in his own society."[98] This mismatch is an example of a Malthusian triage caused by different evolutionary rates, mentioned earlier. The rate of organic learning (the rate at which organismic change may arise through natural selection) has been calculated to be 8 billion times slower than the rate at which the human mind can learn.[99] The number is arguable, but people can certainly learn more quickly than they can change their physiology—or at least it used to be so.

Genetic manipulation opened the way to the production of modified biological systems on demand. How soon this high-tech artificial selection on humans will become practical is an open question. Once that happens, the community, acting through its collective intelligence and manipulative skills, will have socialized not only the tools of its civilization but organismic life itself. Artificial selection on humans will then become indistinguishable from natural selection.

Responsibility for moral conduct, for the foreseeable future, remains with the person, and fortunately so, because this allows the only possible control of high-tech barbarism. It is easy to imagine ourselves as gods but difficult to shoulder the burdens of that position. Missteps can easily lead to the creation of Frankenstein's monster, with its all too human accusations: "Accursed creator! Why did you form a monster so hideous that even you turned from me in disgust?" Recently a rhesus monkey's severed head was connected by tubes and sutures to the trunk of another monkey. The head showed signs of awareness.[100]

Against such dangers the strange walker can hold out the promise of healing the sick and feeding the hungry and point to his past virtuoso achievements and to the mental satisfaction of learning more about the life process. He might also advise his opponents to keep their eyes on the doughnut and not on the hole and to start formulating moral rules to keep up with the new problems. But if the past is also a guide to the future, the new rules for artificial selection on humans will only offer guidelines to some of the ethical difficulties while introducing new, unresolvable conflicts of their own.

By Guns, Godzillas, and Computers Possessed

The Einstein bombs made large-scale warfare impractical because mutual destruction would predictably follow a first use. As a consequence, the forces of frustration shifted the locus of violence to local wars limited in size but not in savagery. These wars are supported by every land that makes or transports arms, and they are helped by the fresh pools of mercenaries as armed units are dumped on the market of lethal skills.

On the high-tech edge, all major powers possess nuclear, biological, and chemical weapons, as do several Third World countries. As I write, German companies make land mines in the form of toys that will maim the children who pick them up. On the low-tech edge, in the Ayatollah Khomeni's Iran, boys between the ages of twelve and seventeen who were officially selected martyrs wore red headbands with the words *Sar Allah*, "Warrior of God." Across the back of their shirts stood the slogan "I have the special permission of the Imam to enter heaven."[101] When ready for battle, they were roped together into groups of twenty and driven onto the mine fields or hurled against barbed wires to clear the way for Iranian troops in their war against Iraq. The Iraqis, not to be outdone, were prepared for infectious disease and biological toxin warfare.[102]

Individual initiatives for righting wrongs by force abound, especially in lands where individual initiatives are possible and the necessary material is available. Theodore Kaczynski, a Harvard-educated mathematician later dubbed the Unabomber, withdrew to a cabin in the woods of Montana and made letter bombs with which he killed a number of people who, in his view, were engaged in activities bad for humanity. He also wrote a number of manifestos and succeeded in getting them published anonymously. These texts included sensible lists of some of the problems of American society, but his solutions, floating on a Platonic view of simpler and hence presumably better times, were naïve. "There is a little bit of him in us all," declared a *New Yorker* editorial, adding that his revolt "touches a sentiment running strong in the culture."[103]

The Japanese Aum Shinrikyo cult worked in a collective and high-tech manner. The name means "the true teachings of Aum," where *Aum*—or *Om*—is a sacred syllable of Hinduism that represents important triads.[104] The group was led by a half-blind guru, Shoko Asahara, who wrote a book in 1992 entitled *Declaring Myself the Christ.*[105] He attracted a number of able university graduates by offering them life away from the iron discipline of Japanese parental authority and by cleverly mixing undigested scientific ideas with elements of religion and magic. Some initiates wore helmets festooned with wires supposedly designed to pick up the guru's brain waves. Faithful cult members kidnapped and murdered unfaithful ones and other enemies of the sect; the bodies were then reduced to dust in industrial-sized microwave ovens, high-tech versions of Hitler's incinerators. The sect had enough nerve gas to kill millions of people and planned attacks in Japan and the United States. They had a worldwide membership of 50,000 and assets over a billion dollars; they printed their own promotional material and owned a worldwide network of factories that made weapons and drugs. They also owned a radio station in Vladivostok. They collected Ebola viruses for their planned biological warfare against the Japanese government and synthesized snake venom, using instructions downloaded from the Internet. Their nerve gas attack in the Tokyo subway killed a number of people and injured thousands. In his trial Asahara maintained that his aim was to offer his followers "ultimate freedom, ultimate happiness and ultimate joy." His claim for such ultimates brings to mind a Hawaiian leaflet about an indoor shooting range that offered "The Ultimate in Gun Experience."

Eighty years earlier there was the communists' "final conflict"; later, Hitler's "final solution." Now we have the physicist's "theory of everything" and the sport called "ultimate fighting." Ultimate solutions have a bad track record.

Both Max Weber and Sigmund Freud gave convincing reasons for seeing the state as holding the monopoly on legitimate violence. For most of the last two centuries in the West that monopoly was held by the public police. During the last decades of the twentieth century, however, a new, legitimate, but nonstate police force was born in the form of an army of private law enforcement. Yet another group of armed men are working as corporate military consultants. "Since the cold war's demise," reports *Time* magazine, "there has been no end to conflicts. From Azerbeijan to Zaire, disorganized military forces need help."[106]

Godzilla was a science-fiction monster born in 1954 Japan. It was a 400-foot-tall prehistoric reptile that came back to life from the bottom of the Pacific after it received atomic radiation. The creature is not peculiarly Japanese, however, or even postatomic. It is a relative of Lewis Carroll's Jabberwock.

> Beware the Jabberwock, my son!
> The jaws that bite, the claws that catch!
> . . . . .

The Jabberwock with eyes of flame
Came whiffling through the tilgey wood,
And burbled as it came!

As with the Unabomber and the Asahara cult, there is a bit of Godzilla, alias Jabberwock, in everyone.

Our guns and godzillas are efficiently connected by electronic communication that is coded, processed, and decoded by fast abacuses known as computers. The majority of the world's population does not know how to operate computers, but they all understand when their employers run out of money, a situation recognized by computers. Eighteenth-century English romantic writers compared God to a clockmaker while allowing for clockwork devils. Considering the popular penchant for salvation through science and technology and damnation through techno-science godzillas, today we might speak of computer gods and computer devils.

The increasingly more powerful and sophisticated computers consistently prove themselves inadequate to their tasks because they are subject to a Malthusian principle: the information population grows faster than the computers that can satisfy related demands. As a result, newer software pushes out new software and hardware pushes out hardware. In addition, computer programs designed to help run large organizations, produce and distribute goods, conduct wars, or administer hospitals and jails need hundreds of thousand and even millions of lines of instructions. As this number grows, it becomes increasingly difficult to write a program without errors. All its computer power did not prevent the Pentagon from losing items valued over a billion dollars in 1984.

Early Greek theaters seated 15,000 people. The number of people who watch certain televised events may be counted in the tens or perhaps hundreds of millions; those who may be reached by radio, by the billions. Our amphitheater is a spherical stage of instant everywhere. On the Greek stage the Erinyes, the "angry ones," known to the Romans as the Furies, appeared as avenging goddesses; they were the daughters of darkness who punished insolence and the disregard of moral laws. The Furies of our age are of the same temperament, but their numbers have increased substantially because of a division of labor. There is a much larger variety of anger today because there is a much larger variety of needs and possibilities.

Our world is richly populated with the mental clones of Kaczynski, tribal copies of Aum Shinrikyo, organized crime, mercenaries, and the armed forces of nations, in addition to the many millions of solid citizens who are also by arms possessed. They speak many languages and wear different clothing, but they all bite, catch, flame, whiffle, and burble as they try to change societies from whatever they are to something else, and they all use computers. But without informed compassion, technological skills are just as dangerous as scientific knowledge.

From the Comintern to the Internet

The title of this subsection represents the current global metamorphosis, during which the moral creature, searching for stable rules of conduct, is being driven by the unresolvable conflicts of the present social systems toward a new level of incipient complexity. Whether such a new system may be created and kept viable is yet to be seen. What follows is an attempt to sketch a few dimensions of the metamorphosis as seen from the point of view of changing temporal horizons.

Early in the eighteenth century a number of thinkers who called themselves socialists became convinced that the then existing social institutions and practices could not secure equitable justice and protect people from the dislocations and misery created by the Industrial Revolution then about to get under way. In the mid-nineteenth century Eugene Pottier, a French writer, wrote "The International," a revolutionary poem expressing these thoughts. Here are its first stanza and its refrain.

> Arise, ye pris'ners of starvation!
> Arise, ye wretched of the earth,
> For Justice thunders condemnation,
> A better world's in birth. . . .

> 'Tis the final conflict,
> Let each stand his place,
> The International Party
> Shall be the human race.

The poem could be read as a hymn, no different from "Onward Christian soldiers / Marching as to war," which was written at about the same time, were it not that the International Party was a movement dedicated to the overthrow of all existing social institutions, including all churches. "The International" became the anthem of the communist movement. The principles of that movement were summed up in 1848 by Karl Marx and Friedrich Engels in their *Communist Manifesto,* which was built on the conviction that "the history of all hitherto existing societies is the history of class struggles."[107] That history, wrote these two restless Germans living in England, is approaching a crisis. "All fixed, fast-frozen relations, with their train of ancient and venerable prejudices and opinions, are swept away, all new-formed ones become antiquated before they can ossify. All that is solid melts into air, all that is holy is profaned, and man is at last compelled to face with sober senses, his real conditions of life, and his relations with his kind."[108] To achieve a utopian state on earth, they said, the correct conduct for all people must favor the proletarian movement, which is "the self-conscious, independent movement of the immense majority, in the interest of the immense majority. The proletariat, the lowest stratum of our present society, cannot stir, cannot raise itself up, without the whole superincumbent strata of official society being sprung into the air."[109]

Marx and Engels assumed that individuals' natural inclinations for caring about their fellow humans would take over and lead to the revolution's final victory. Then, goods being plentiful, governments would wither away. The assumption, implicit in their reasoning, is the idea of natural law, already discussed and laid to rest. That all humans are created equal is not a law of nature but a belief peculiar to the Christian assessment of man.

Comintern was the name of an association of communist parties called into congress by Lenin in 1919. Although its stated purpose was to promote world revolution, its chief function was to ensure Russian control over the movement. The unfolding of Lenin's plans, endorsed by the Comintern, was the seven decades of the Soviet Union. Its Communist Party claimed to be the center of protest against social injustice outside the borders of the Soviet Union, never inside. It had difficulties entering the twentieth century, however, let alone preparing for the twenty-first. Having inflicted immense suffering on its followers and foes alike, it collapsed under the burden of its social backwardness, its brutality, and the cumulative problems of a political system built on a faulty understanding of human nature.

The society that served Marx and Engels as the model for the shortcomings of capitalism was Victorian England. In the rigid class structure of its upstairs-downstairs social architecture, stability was preferred to experimentation by rich and poor alike.

Then came Stalin and Hitler. The insane enormity of perhaps 100 million political penitents paraded to misery and death kept the world's attention on the rise and fall of Soviet communism and on its shorter-lived kin and mirror, Nazi Germany. This political horror show masked the birth of profound changes in the temporal horizons of both political ideals and daily life.

The desire for stability, so esteemed by the Victorians, gave birth to a world where experimentation is preferred to constancy. The bipolarization of World War II and the cold war gave way to the conflicts of a multipolar, multicivilizational world. In that world, beneath the conflicting civilizational values, we observe national governments trying to maintain their power and the distinctness of their lands in language and customs. Sometimes they admit the homogenizing power of commerce, industry, taste, and communication, and other times they refuse to do so.

Thus, for example, Africa is a jigsaw puzzle of hundreds of different traditional tribes, with tribal allegiances often stronger than national ones. Japan has its 230,000 religious sects. The vast land of Canada has its "neverendum" because of Quebec's aspirations to have its own army, passport, and currency. The United States has aspects of a zebra, its different regions trying to get their distinct identities acknowledged at the price of decreasing the union's coherence. The United Nations is like another national government, although it is less effective than most because there are no laws that apply equally to all its members, and it lacks the power to enforce its will, assuming it ever acquires one.

Then there are the Tribal Interest Cells, or TICs, the commandos and freebooters of the time-compact globe. In its old meaning and in its current anthropological meaning, *tribe* refers to people held together by family and emotional ties. In TICs, which came into existence during the second half of the twentieth century, "tribes" are held together by fanaticism and narrow purposes. They conduct local and transnational wars underground, on the ground, and in the air in support of ethnic, religious, economic, or political goals. They serve enterprising gurus no less than crime families, petty or grand. They often advocate historically ancient causes that have emerged from their lairs, where centuries of civilizing efforts have tried to keep them.

Opposing this process of fragmentation are powerful forces promoting uniformity. In 1989 we heard Schiller's "Ode to Joy," declaring the brotherhood of man, performed at the ruins of the Berlin Wall. But such de facto vestiges of brotherhood as there are have little to do with moral convictions. They are being carried along by the forces of the global market- and workplace, the uniformity of manufacturing processes demanded by efficiency, and the shared judgments of what constitutes a desirable life. Kenichi Ohmae, a Malayasian observer of the contemporary scene, remarked that "on today's maps . . . the most salient features are the footprints cast by TV satellites, the areas covered by radio signals and the geographic reach of newspapers and magazines. . . . Political terrains . . . do not matter as much as what people know or want or value."[110]

The social agenda of Marxism in East Asia, though rooted in Christianity and in the ways of the West, was adjusted to fit Eastern cultural traditions, as occurred in the writings of Mao Tse-tung. His ideas of permanent revolution as the ethical obligation of all and conflict as a permanent way of life were planted in a soil of Confucian, Taoist, and Buddhist traditions. In *On Practice* Mao declared the need for a new philosophy, one that must be practical, scientific, democratic, and popular—that is, that addresses the masses. He could have been speaking for America, where those ideas had been made to work successfully long before the journey of China into the twentieth and twenty-first centuries ever began.

As the world enters the third millennium, the works of those who created the modern world are being synthesized into a new system of values. The forces involved and the dimensions of the task are immense.

Huntington, cited earlier, pointed out that the conflicts between Marxism-Leninism and Western liberal democracies were fleeting and superficial phenomena compared to the historical conflict between Islam and Christianity.[111] If one keeps in mind that by the year 2025 the Islamic population of the world is likely to surpass the Christian population[112] and remembers that ideologies are spread by force, conversion, and biological reproduction, it appears that the world has stormy weather ahead of it, conflicts very different from those imagined by the Comintern.

The stage on which the postcapitalist and postcommunist changes are taking place is quite different from that of Marx, Stalin, Hitler, or Mao. Let me employ one of the hallmarks of that stage to stand for all its hallmarks; let me call it "the globe of the Internet."

Internet is the name given in the early 1960s to a communication network among American laboratories. It was designed to make their cooperation possible even in the case of a nuclear attack. The Internet served as the seed of cyberspace, of which it is now only one of the many contributing parts. One of its requirements was that it remain decentralized. It still is.

From 1960 let us skip forty years. Groups of people who talk to each other through cyberspace, discussing shared interests in love and in life, how to blow up buildings or start a new religion, are said to form virtual communities. The name is pure hype. Galileo and Kepler also corresponded without having met, yet no one ever thought of calling them a virtual community. The difference is in the speed of communication, in the number of people involved, and in the shelf lives of the messages exchanged. The Galileo-Kepler correspondence is still available; it is unlikely that most of what is currently communicated through the Internet will survive the day, let alone the centuries.

Earlier I quoted George Kennan on the exaggerated American desire for privacy. That desire met its more than equal in the erosion of privacy through behavior banks, which were made possible by the same technology that built the Internet. The large business concerns and governments of wired lands hold an immense amount of liquid data on all people whose lives are within their geographical or economic domains. In the United States this data includes information on health; credit; marital status present and past; education; employment history; legal involvements; real estate ownership and use; car or boat ownership and use; travel history; the times and telephone numbers of every call made or received; the journals to which people subscribe; all purchases if charged or discounted by discount cards; bills paid by check, cash, or card; and food-shopping and eating-out habits.[113] Three CD-ROM disks with the names, addresses, and telephone numbers of 80 million Americans are available in the local library. Another CD-ROM system, called "Marketplace: Households," contains essential information on marital status, income, and buying habits of 120 million Americans.[114] All such information collected in one context can be and is being reused in friendly or hostile ways in other contexts, without the knowledge of the persons involved.[115]

In the villages of my childhood everyone knew everything about everybody—everything and then some, because imagination was always added to observation. The means of observations were small holes in the plank fences that separated backyards. They were stuffed with lamb's wool, to be removed only when you wanted to find out what your neighbors were doing. Contemporary means of gathering data unplugs all such holes.

In 1891 the theoretical jurist Jeremy Bentham proposed what he held to be an ideal prison. He called it "Panopticon" or "Inspection House." He envisaged a circular, glass-roofed structure centered on a darkened guard tower from which the guards could keep the inmates under surveillance without themselves being seen. A contemporary version of such a jail is any structure with video cameras in its nooks and crannies. Howard Rheingold, a columnist who writes on the social effects of technology, surveyed the problems of homesteading on the electronic frontier and concluded that the tightly wired globe has all the makings necessary to be turned into a contemporary form of Bentham's Panopticon in the event that such surveillance were to become useful.[116] Useful for whom? History is in the process of working out an answer.

In the words of the historian Paul Kennedy, what we are witnessing is not a new world order but a troubled and fractured planet. A society

> which desires to be better prepared for the twenty-first century . . . will have to retool its national skills and infrastructure, challenge vested interests, alter many old habits, and perhaps amend its governmental structure. But this assumes long-term vision at a time when most politicians . . . can hardly deal with even short-term problems; and it means political risk, since many of the reforms proposed would be unpopular among vested interests.[117]

The forces of change are so "far-reaching, complex, and interactive," added Kennedy, "that they call for nothing less than the reeducation of humankind."[118] That reeducation is being carried out by many teachers advocating many and different sets of values. Multinational corporations, ideologies, religions, cultures, and alliances of all kinds are shifting around for their presumptive positions in a broader order. Drug rings, mafias, and terrorist movements are doing the same, however, as are smugglers of women, children, immigrants, weapons, and body parts. People everywhere are seeking some kind of order in this disorder. The ethos that will eventually conquer the minds of people will be the one that succeeds in creating an interpretation of history and of the significance of human life on which a believable and inspiring plan for the future of humankind may be constructed.

The march toward that future will not be made to the tune of the Dies Irae, the Marseillaise, or the communist International. These turned out to have been no more than call signals of large tribes. The march is to something more elemental. We are in the middle of a new rite of time's passage. The term, it may be recalled, refers to the recognizable steps in the evolution of time itself (see pp. 38–43).

Earlier examples of time's rites of passage included the coming about of biotemporality from the integrative levels of matter and the emergence of nootemporality from the matrices of life. None of the transient structures of biogenesis or those between man and ape survive: they had to evolve rapidly into stable forms or relapse into the matrix from which they arose. If these earlier transitions are any guides, and if we are really witnessing the emergence of a new integrative level of nature, then the current transition will be a metastable one. The world will either collapse into a tribal chaos or evolve rapidly into a social system with sufficient inner controls to maintain a global present. What has been said in this section bears witness that the symptoms of such a transition, in the form of turbulent acts of creation, are all around us.

A Stained-Glass Window

The time-compact globe is so intricate that it defies any short, analytic description. For that reason it is more practical to think of it as a work of art. I propose one of Marc Chagall's stained-glass windows as a model, such as those in the chapel in Pocantico Hills, New York, or in the Frauenkirche, Zürich. Each of those windows has a network of black lines: they are the strips that hold the glass pieces together. They form line drawings that follow an artistic logic and purpose. They are called cartoons or traceries.

These lines, though intriguing, are subordinated to the many multicolored glass pieces. Their colors are sometimes vibrant and sensual, sometimes dark and brooding. They also follow a logic. They are free aesthetic agents that combine, embrace, hold, identify, and separate different surfaces. All these elements together make for a visual music of colors, shapes, and lines, announcing what the artist wanted to say about the Good Samaritan or Jeremiah.

The cartography of today's world is like one of those windows. There are black-line borders to nations and to ideological camps, which in many regions are ruthlessly guarded. They are surviving witnesses to history. The cultural and economic forces and the flow of ideas carrying their cacophony of messages are impeded but not stopped by these boundaries. The stained-glass window of the globe is awesome in its wealth, poverty, promises, and dangers. To appreciate it all, however, there must be light. For a Chagall window the light comes from outside. For humankind that light must come from within. We form a self-lighted and self-darkened stained-glass window on ourselves and our environment, with the design of the windows always in construction. In making that design, ideas about correct behavior keep on accomplishing their historical task: they whip up conflicts and through them promote changes in the preferred rules of conduct.

6.3 Malling the Beautiful

Aesthetic judgments derive from qualities of feelings mobilized by events, conditions, or processes. If these feelings are such as to make one desire their perpetuation, then their putative sources or causes are said to be beautiful; if one would prefer those feelings to be absent, then their assumed sources or causes are said to be ugly (see pp. 125–26).

If a person or even a whole civilization is quite uncertain as to what kind of feelings to endorse as desirable and what as undesirable, then distinctions between the beautiful and ugly become compromised. With that compromise, the usefulness of aesthetic judgments as collectively formulated guidelines to the management of emotions is lost. This loss is a hallmark of the contemporary arts and letters. It is a loss not of occasional greatness but of emotional belonging. Beauty as the home of the mind is being replaced by the arts and letters as malls to be visited for shopping and entertainment.[119]

The conditions behind aesthetic experience are part and parcel of the social, cultural, and economic landscapes of the time-compact globe, as are short-lived truths and conduct à la mode. Together with them they form the trinity of human values appropriate for the nascent identity of mankind.

Consistent with the nature of the aesthetic sense as first signals, the contemporary arts and letters reflect the agonizing birth of new emotional control guidelines acceptable to a multicultural, multipolar world. The words of a Maori creation myth say it well:

> The light, the light
> the seeking, the searching,
> in chaos, in chaos.

From the conception the increase,
From the increase the thought.

I will represent the travail of this birth by the lives of three men. Together they stand for the collective greatness and lowliness of our species crossing the cultural bridge that I introduced in the allegory of Brother Juniper in the introductory thoughts of this book.

Pablo Picasso (1881–1973) traveled in a world of political and social conflagration and recorded its violence in images of two and three dimensions. As a young man he hoped to create a universal art, something absolute and ultimate that would transcend all styles. His life and imagination were fired by an ever-present sexual passion; his works deconstruct biological forms into shapes ready for reassembly through new ways of perceiving man and its world. Those forms convey the pain of people forced by medieval torture into the geometries of the wheel and the rack. His men and women are human bonsai trees. In her biography of Picasso, Arianna Stassinopoulos Huffington identifies his dark bequest: "The legacy of his art has to be seen in conjunction with the legacy of our time. He brought to fullest expression the shattered vision of a century that perhaps could be understood in no other terms; and he brought to painting the vision of disintegration that Schoenberg and Bartok brought to music, Kafka and Beckett to literature. He took to its ultimate conclusion the negative vision of the modernist world."[120]

Adolf Hitler (1889–1945) traveled in the same Europe as did Picasso. He had hoped to be an artist and painted inane watercolors. In Vienna he lived in shelters for the homeless, wandering many days and nights without a roof over his head, and to earn a few schillings, he beat carpets and carried bags outside railroad stations. His visions were filled with the clash of arms, riots, and tumult. "No matter how far Germany's power might one day stretch," writes one of his biographers, "somewhere sooner or later it would come upon a bleeding, fought-over frontier where the race would have been hardened and a constant selection of the best would be taking place."[121] Capitalizing on the frustrations, fears, and hopes of his society and using his speaking skills to seduce the masses, which he often compared to "woman," he orchestrated a violent bloodletting that completed the final breakup of nineteenth-century Europe, politics, art, and all.

In 1937 the ambitions and emotions of Picasso and Hitler met in the fate of the Basque fishing village Guernica. Hitler's empire supplied the planes that savagely bombed it during the Spanish Civil War as assistance to the Spanish fascists. Picasso recorded its horrors in a stunning monochromatic painting that bears the name of the village. Hitler saw the glory of humanity in a patchwork of racist philosophy and tales of Nordic superiority;

Picasso saw the liberation of humanity from the scourge of war in a patchwork of communist ideas.

Both men tore down existing institutions and, through these destructions, forced people to revise their values. Both had insatiable hunger for power. Hitler tried to satisfy it by creating a conflagration on several continents; Picasso, by creating 20,000 pieces of art that depicted anguish, often in the presence of savage pleasure. If Picasso could not have had the endless flow of women he bedded, courted, supported, then broke and even drove to suicide, if he had been born into Hitler's Austria, with its self-important smugness, he might easily have become a tyrant bent to reduce the world to Guernica. If Hitler could not have had his followers to mold and break and send to their deaths, had he been a Spaniard who moved to France instead of an Austrian who moved to Germany, he might easily have become the creator of 20,000 pieces of art in which humans were reduced to their fragments.

Charlie Chaplin (1889–1977) and Adolf Hitler were born four days and 700 miles apart. Chaplin's father was an alcoholic, and his mother spent her days in and out of insane asylums. His early life was a dreary succession of orphanages and nights sleeping in London doorways. Other than during the last decades of his life, he was unable to form lasting relationships. But his relations to the masses was good and clear. He sensed what people wanted to see and hear and shared their beliefs of having been abused by the powers that be. His art brought forth laughter and happy smiles. Good was rewarded, bad was punished, and the right man got the right girl—or if he did not, the little tramp, as he was known, still walked into the sunset: alone, victorious in his small world, happy, free, and simple.

These three men are icons of the creative/destructive genius of twentieth-century humanity.

Picasso finalized the divorce between art and beauty. Hitler demonstrated the power of society over individuals. Chaplin showed that in spite of all things being stacked against him, the person can still keep his spirit. The arts and the letters of our epoch show the dynamics of these forces.

Aesthetic Mutations, Matings, and Funerals

Dance, I suggested earlier, is the mother lode of all arts. In a treatise on dance and drill in history, William H. McNeill notes the radical decrease of interest since World War II in folk dancing, marching bands, and choral societies. These customs at one time helped to secure coherence in social life through what he calls "muscular bonding." Bonding through rhythmic movement, which calls on visceral responses, survives as part of religious and social practices in Africa and Latin America, he writes, and as calisthenics in China, Japan, and Korea but not in the West.[122] "It is plausible to suppose that community dancing was essential to the ongoing stability of village life, upon which cities and all the works of civilization ultimately depended."[123] But the need for shared euphoria, the arousal provided by "keeping together in time," a practice that helps to define to what and with whom we belong is too deeply seated, he writes, to be eliminated.[124]

In McNeill's euphoria of muscular bonding we can recognize the ecstasy of the dance discussed in sec. 5.4 as one of the many forms of activity through which experiences of timelessness have been sought. If such experiences are unavailable in the form of village dances—often followed by copulation behind the bushes—then they are sought in drugs, sex everywhere and everywhen, religious gatherings, and political togetherness in body or by proxy. During the last decades of the century live dancing in small groups declined in importance. It gave way to highly professional and sophisticated dancing as a spectator sport seen on television and in the movies and to collective dancing of vast proportions.

On Memorial Day weekend in 1986 an estimated 5.5 million people lined up in a 4,000-mile-long chain that stretched from New York to Los Angeles. They held "hands across America" at 3 P.M. New York time, expressing solidarity with the 20 million Americans who would go hungry some time each month during that year. It was a paradigm for a national dance, rather larger than the traditional village dances. Is the next step "Hands across the Bering Sea"?

Section 5.4 suggested that just as language helps to define the cognitive self, music helps to define the affective self; when the affective self changes, so does music. The overseers of our state, wrote Plato,

> must throughout be watchful against innovations in music and gymnastics counter to the established order, and to the best of their power guard against them, fearing when anyone says that that song is most regarded among men "which hovers newest on the singer's lips," lest haply it be supposed that the poet means not new songs but a new way of song and is commending this. . . . For a change to a new type of music is something to beware of as a hazard of all our fortunes. For the modes of music are never disturbed without unsettling of the most fundamental political and social conventions.[125]

In Puccini's late nineteenth-century opera *La Bohème*, the female protagonist identifies herself in words and music. She explains that her name is Lucia but they call her Mimi: *Mi chiamano Mimi*. With that disclosure as the

Rosetta Stone that joins name and melody, the Mimi motive is established and the development of the drama can commence. What kind of music would be appropriate for a male protagonist of the postindustrial society who wants to explain that he was born Malcolm Little, his name is Hajj Malik el-Shabazz, but while he was on earth, they called him Malcolm X? Postmodern music.

Jonathan Kramer, a composer and music theorist, listed several traits characteristic of postmodern music. They all suggest strategies of egalitarian politics and experimentation in cultural preferences.[126] There is a break with tonality that parallels the break with representation in the visual arts and, because of all these breaks and experiments, there is a lack of shared musical language.

As has music, musicology itself has also become the subject of social and intellectual reimagination. Political, sexual, social analysis of music has its origins in the work of Theodor Adorno (1903–69), a German Marxist philosopher who analyzed musical styles for the purpose of revealing political leanings. Using familiar scores as his examples, he pointed to allusions to society, to the particular composer's views of himself, and to elements of endorsement or alienation. Musicologists are now trying to reinterpret musical canons so as to distance them from what is technical and formal and move them toward modes rooted in politics, economics, and sexuality. Some musicologists perceive music as a type of nonverbal politics.

Classical and recent comments on musical sound and on music in general suggest the transformation of thoughts and feelings about music during the last century and a half. This is what Wagner wrote in 1860 about emotions embedded in the music of his *Tristan und Isolde:* the music expresses "a tale of endless yearning, longing, the bliss and wretchedness of love; world, power, fame, honour, chivalry, loyalty, and friendship all blown away like an insubstantial dream; one thing alone left living—longing, longing, unquenchable, a yearning, a hunger, languishing, forever renewing itself; one sole redemption—death, surcease, a sleep without awakening."[127]

John Cage, the son of a culture with a preference for the superficial and the intellectually simple, offered a very different interpretation of the significance of musical sounds. "I imagine that as contemporary music goes on changing in the way that I'm changing it, what will be done is to more and more completely liberate sounds from abstract ideas about them and more and more exactly to let them be physically uniquely themselves. This means for me: knowing more and more not what I think a sound is but what it actually is in all of its acoustical details and then letting this sound exist, itself, changing in a changing sonorous environment."[128]

Lewis Rowell, writing about contemporary music in general, introduces several assumptions and contentions of which a single-sentence summary is that music is an unconscious mirror of temporal ideology. The following of his observations are relevant to this section:

> We are witnessing an era of temporal colonization that threatens to sweep away centuries of musical accomplishment and the residue of millennia in the precious traditional musics of the world.
>
> Musicians have only begun to realize the vast and seamless nature of the spectrum at their disposal, especially in the . . . longer spans of the temporal hierarchy.
>
> [Music] is especially apt to model the ideology of its parent culture and the attitudes of members of that culture. In this sense each musical composition and performance, as well as each literary work, can be read as a miniature creation narrative.[129]

He suggests that we are approaching a new evolutionary level of human perception "with enormous implications for the role of memory, attention, and interpretation." We may be losing our ability to follow and appreciate linear, focused narratives but gaining in our capacity to "assemble complex artistic packages out of disconnected events and perception."[130]

Long musical narratives are indeed in trouble, at least as far as popular American music goes. The causes are many: the dismantling of much of public music education; the urge to democratize the arts by eliminating aesthetic distinctions; the dominance of popular culture; and the public dislike of everything that needs an effort to be enjoyed because of the sophistication of its form or content. Glen Gass, writing about rock music, summed up how concentrating on the present affects music. The predominance of beat, he wrote, carries a "rebellious energy and its celebration of the all-consuming, combustible moment."[131]

This is what James Bakst, a historian of Russian music, wrote about musical sound with regard to what was called Soviet realism:

> Soviet realism demands that Soviet composers write music based on musical intonations, that is, intoned meanings which are supposed to be carriers of the ideological significance of Russian nationalism. . . . Musical recollections, impressions, and fragments become interwoven with life experiences, feelings, and aspirations, penetrating the artistic life and traditions of people. . . . The background of great compositions is a world of music as an activity of public consciousness: musical interjections, rhythmic intonations, popular motivic fragments, harmonic turns, and extracts of musical impressions of an epoch.[132]

A similar opinion may be found in an open letter by Joseph Goebbels, Hitler's propaganda minister, to the conductor Wilhelm Furtwängler:

Art must not only be good; it must be conditioned by the needs of the people—or, to put it better, only an art which springs from the integral soul of the people can in the end be good and have meaning for the people for whom it was created. Art in an absolute sense, as liberal democracy knows it, has no right to exist. Any attempts to further such an art could, in the end, cause the people to lose their inner relationship to art and the artist to isolate himself from the moving forces of his time. . . . Art must be good but beyond that, conscious of its responsibility, competent, close to the people, and combative in spirit.[133]

Both opinions are correct to this extent: unless art addresses its audience, it remains meaningless. But what is meaningful for me may be meaningless for you; meeting public taste must therefore allow considerable latitude. This demand is now being met by the artists of our age, people who have never heard of either Soviet realism or Herr Goebbels. They are responding to the demands of the streets, expressed in the demands of a many-dimensional marketplace. The musical corpus now includes the musics of different civilizations and ethnic groups and employs the machineries of our age, from steam hammers to computers, but tends toward the high-tech. For commercial and political reasons it tries to reach the largest variety of people, and hence it also tends toward the simple and the easy. We have New Age music that sounds dangerously like early twentieth-century moldy hotel music, and a few decades back we had Leroy Anderson's popular work "The Typewriter,"[134] which was a transcription of Bach's Toccata, Adagio, and Fugue in C major into the clatter of a typewriter.

Walt Whitman heard America sing in "myriad carols," each "singing what belongs to him and her and none else." These carols are now being heard across the country: in diners, supermarkets, trucks, elegant cars, and dentists' offices, on the telephone while one waits as well as on ghetto and suburban boom boxes. But they are not particularly varied. Most of them are carefully engineered network music, selected by specialists in mass media; they know the region where it is to be broadcast by one or another branch of the central "beat bank," a term I invented to suggest that music in the media is handled as a form of capital, to be invested for profit. Tape cassettes carry musics around the world and change the texture of life everywhere. They also promote and advertise everything from soup to nuts; they fill all niches of collective time that would otherwise be quiet. Commercials, entertainment, music, and information mix in the cacophony of an intense present.

The eighteenth-century German dramatist and critic Gotthold Ephraim Lessing condemned any attempts that would make a work of art transcend the limits of its distinctive medium: a statue is to be a statue; a painting, a painting. In the contemporary aesthetic turmoil one may still know, sometimes, the statue of a hawk from the painting of a handsaw, but the principles and techniques of art have become multimedia. Statues are now painted, paintings are made to sing, and poetry is often indistinguishable from prose, as is media reality from media fantasy. The division of art followed in sec. 5.4 has ceased to apply.

An unknown poet of the thirteenth century celebrated the arrival of summer:

> Summer is icumen in,
> Lhude sing cucu!
> Groweth seed, and bloweth med,
> And springths the wude nu,
> Sing cucu!

A well-known poet of the twentieth century protested the arrival of winter:

> Winter is icumen in,
> Lhude sing Goddamm!
> Raineth drop and staineth slop,
> And how the wind doth ramm!
> Sing Goddamm![135]

Twentieth-century Western poetry woke with a challenge to the literary conventions of the romantics. Modernism, as the movement was known, was radical and utopian. Writers, painters, architects, and theologians who wanted to break with the past communicated their enthusiasm for novelty to their audience. Ezra Pound, the author of the brilliant anger just quoted, was one of the poets dissatisfied with traditional forms of poetry, and in 1913 he founded a school of artistic expression called imagism. Imagists favored clarity, precision, and exact visual imagery (as illustrated by the stanza above), in contrast to the symbolists of the nineteenth century, who favored refined ambiguity as an expression of the indeterminate in human sensitivities. But Pound became disappointed with imagism and suggested a new movement in poetry and in the visual arts, one that would adopt the vocabulary of industrial processes. He called this movement vorticism. In 1914, in the first issue of the journal *Blast*, the vorticists declared that poetry should represent the energies of the new machine age: its images should be not pictures but forces. At the end of the twentieth century the demand for all writing to display dynamics and energy has become a common cause to readers, poets, composers, and publishers alike.

In 1909 an Italian poet, Filippo Tommaso Marinetti, promulgated the fantasy of an adolescent boy in what he called the Futurist Manifesto. Futurism, he wrote, voiced the desire

> to shake the gates of life, test the boots and hinges. [Look at] the splendor of the sun's red sword, slashing for the first time through the millennial gloom. . . . Let's break out of the horrible shell of wisdom. . . . [to] replenish the deep well of the Absurd. . . . We exalt aggressive action, a feverish insomnia . . . the moral leap . . . the punch and the slap. . . . The poet must spend himself with ardor . . . to swell the enthusiastic fervor of the primordial elements. . . . Time and Space died yesterday. We already live in the absolute, because we have created eternal, omnipresent speed. We will glorify war—the world's only hygiene—militarism . . . and scorn for woman. We will destroy the museums, libraries, academies of every kind. . . . We will sing of great crowds excited by work, by pleasure and by riot.[136]

It is uncanny how well a declaration of intent by an artistic movement anticipated the spirit of the century that was yet to follow: its love of violence and speed, its contempt for history and the intellect—unless that intellect can move the "great crowds." The great crowds materialized in Italy with fascism, in Germany with Nazism, in the Soviet Union with communism, and in China with the giant Mao celebrations. After World War II the crowds became those of the global mass markets and pop art. The feverish desire to live intensely while also disappearing in what I called the ecstasy of the crowd became joint hallmarks of the twentieth century. It is fortunate that, at least in regard to women, the manifesto proved to be less than prophetic. "Women unite, take back the night!" a slogan of the late 1990s, announces the true direction of change.

Dada means "rocking horse" in infantile French. Selecting this word to signify a philosophy of deliberate irrationality and the negation of all traditional artistic values witnesses the impotent and confused rage of the five artists who started the dada movement. It was a way for two Romanians, an Alsatian, and two Germans living in the safety of Switzerland to express their disgust with Europe and World War I. The Manifesto of Dada, composed in 1918, proclaimed their desire to be destructive and negative, to carry out a total assault on the culture.[137] Early in its history dada became associated with the technique of collages in the visual arts, including random groupings of existing or made-up words, taking any conceivable form. But the avoidance of all guidelines is itself a principle of organization. If carefully followed, it leads not to randomness but to an expression of shock and anguish about what exists (and must be avoided), which the writer or artist then conveys to his readers, viewers, and hearers. The movement helped the public to accept the idea that any object may be said to be a work of art if an artist—so judged by himself—declares it to be one. It accepts in practice what I argued in sec. 5.5 from theory, namely, that art may but need not be beautiful. But then, by what principle and by what test may a decision be made? Could a stylized pig brain that floats in singing slop ever be called artistic?

Cubism began in the Paris of 1907 as a school in the visual arts led by Picasso and Braque. The name comes from a derisive comment about their paintings' being composed of so many cubes. What the earliest examples of cubist paintings showed were fragmented objects whose different sides were seen simultaneously. One might imagine the artist turning his model or walking around it or doing so in his imagination. Alternatively, we may think of such paintings as collections of images the artist has seen at different times. This latter interpretation amounts to an extension of the boundaries of the mental present, suggesting an eotemporal mood. In their later works cubists combined fragments of various objects in collages and paintings, including written texts. Twenty-five centuries ago Plato explained how the four elements that constitute the world (fire, earth, air, and water) are constructed from triangles. Cubism was the reemergence of that cosmology, a regression to geometry that was followed by the gradual introduction of biomorphic elements.

Cubism influenced architecture, sculpting, and photography; in poetry and prose it took the form of multiple voices or images seen, heard, and remembered. The mass media themselves became a cubist studio where *papier collé* (pieces of papers torn from printed pages, showing words and figures in many colors) are thrown at the viewers, readers, and in musical form at the listeners. From the skits of the early Beatles to television, newspaper, radio, and the Internet, information is presented in bits of images and thoughts amounting to an incoherent mixture of money, murder, sports, and popular science. This type of information transfer is appropriate for a world where the attention spans of individuals have narrowed to minutes and temporal horizons to tomorrow. As for collage aesthetics, rename *papier collé* "Windows 2000" and see your World Wide Web screen.

The dadaists revolted against rationalism and art by rational and artistic avoidance of conventional patterns and coherence; the cubists manipulated the mental present and appealed (without realizing it) to the geometry of Plato's cosmology. The surrealists tried to annex the irrational by giving it more credit than it deserves. The Surrealist Manifesto, promulgated in 1924 by the French poet André Breton, shows the influence of Freud's (then recent) discovery of the unconscious processes of the mind and Breton's prompt misunderstanding of the same.

Freud saw in the unconscious functions of the mind the workings of the surviving ancestor of the mature conscious mind. He recognized in it the seat of instinctual drives necessary for maintaining the biological functions of the body and, through them, the life of the species. He observed and stressed that for society to remain continuous and creative, it is necessary to keep the instinctual drives under control. The result, if this is done, is an ever-present conflict between instinct and cultural demands. Without that conflict and its control, humans cannot do much more than parrot music and ape art (my words, not Freud's).

Instead of admitting the conflicts recognized by Freud, Breton followed the romantic tradition of Rousseau. First he mistakenly equated the manifest content of dreams with the content of the unconscious and also mistakenly equated dreams with "the disinterested play of thought." A free play of dreams, he wrote, will endeavor to solve "all the principal problems of [human] life." He believed "in the future resolution of these two states, dream and reality, which are seemingly so contradictory, into a kind of absolute reality, a surreality if one may so speak."[138] But human reality is the most advanced, most evolved way of assessing the world, and hence it is most likely to be useful in maintaining personal identity and life. All lower umwelts are hierarchical components of noetic reality; each, in itself, is poorer rather than richer than noetic reality. What Breton called "surrealism" should have been called *subrealism.*

Fortunately artistic creativity does not depend on the correctness of its psychological or philosophical interpretations. Surrealism thus granted official recognition to artistic expressions of instincts, drives, fears, and hopes in words, shapes, sounds, and colors. Artists have been following their instincts all along, but now Picasso could paint Guernica and Miró his happy abstractions without needing them to resemble the image of hell as seen by Pieter Brueghel or the image of heaven as seen by Michelangelo.

Let me backtrack to the seventh century B.C., to the island of Delos, where, at a contest for poets near a colossal statue of Apollo, one of the singers is bidding farewell to "all you maidens." Remember me, he tells them. If anyone asks, "'Whom think ye girls, is the sweetest singer that comes here, and in whom do you most delight?' Then answer, each and all, with one voice: 'He is a blind man, and dwells in Rocky Chios: his lays are evermore supreme.' As for me, I will carry your renown as far as I roam over the earth."[139] The singer is believed to have been Homer. Twenty-seven centuries later the contest for the girls and boys is still going on among very many, much lesser singers. We have street poets, the Last Poets, and the Gats; we have 200 festivals per year for "cowboy poetry," 11,000 students working for degrees in creative writing, and innumerable small poetry groups talking to themselves; we also have grunge, gansta rap, hip-hop, Snoop Doggy Dog, the Hyper-boloids and the Provi-dentals. They do at the end of the twentieth century for popular poetry and music what the Ashcan school of painters did early in it: they bring art closer to daily concerns and away from necessary kinship with beauty. Gansta rap et al. bubble up from city life, stay around, and then become moribund as other, newer beats and forms of music and poetry arise. Musical tastes now divide and are celebrated by age, sexual orientation, and ethnic background. Radio stations follow formats appropriate to the age, sex, social standing, and daily schedule of the listeners to whom the commercials are directed. Compact disks are issued by the thousands and on the average stay on the studio playlist for no more than two weeks.[140] During occasional interruptions in the investment of musical capital, listeners are reminded of ancient history, such as Bob Dylan's "Blowing in the Wind" of the 1960s and, even more ancient, "Amazing Grace," with words by a former captain in the slave trade. The family of beat banks is being pushed and shoved by vast business interests that both guide and are guided by the pushes and shoves of restless public taste.

Early visual art illustrated articulation in the discovery of the environment: the creatures on the cave walls were those our ancestors saw, fought, ate, feared, or imagined. The early artists used their hands as stencils. I can hear one of them call out: "Come, see my hands! Aren't they something?" The contemporary form of hand printing is called action painting or automatism. The artist dances, drips, drops, and maybe sings and sweats, following a presumably spontaneous desire, and then telephones his agent. In sculptures metal, gauze, canvas, wire, paper, and soiled rags are combined to make the objects and their environments merge, as artist and audience return to the undifferentiated umwelt of the infant.

The pop art of the 1950s and beyond is a celebration of the wealth of material goods available in a consumer society. A thoroughly socialized form of that art, one that responds to what people like and to the dream of the Big Rock Candy Mountain, quoted earlier, is found in the Disney towns. They carry their messages as impressively as did the cathedrals of Europe in their time. The two families of popular art contrast by their attitudes to time.

Cathedrals conveyed concern with permanence, offered the ecstasy of the chalice and that of the forest, and illustrated the conflicts native to the death-knowing, eternity-wishing mind. The Disney towns convey concern with change and motion, offer the ecstasy of the dance, and suggest that passing and conflict are unreal, that we have arrived where we should have been to begin with; we are at a happy place. The audio-animatronix hippos, horses, and people, moved by compressed air and controlled electronically, sing, talk, and dance without pause. They follow the criteria of the Disney ballets: never to require people to watch or listen to anything so long that they must expend effort to do so. The figures must be instantly legible and the disembodied voices instantly comprehensible. The marble statues of saints spoke about the continuity of history; the multimedia art of Disney towns speaks about the instant.

The film versions of these happy lands are Disney's motion pictures. Their early *Silly Symphonies* ("The Old Mill," "The Three Little Pigs") and some of their later works (*Mary Poppins*) were charming, telling, simple, and peaceful. But the makers of Disney films responded to the public appetite for spectacle and violence; they created intricate visual effects, violence, and restless movement, retaining only the demand for simplicity in the narrative.

Consider, as an example, the Disney version of *The Hunchback of Notre Dame*. It is a superbly engineered and carefully orchestrated narrative that compares with Victor Hugo's masterpiece as Clement Moore's poem "The Night before Christmas" compares with the Gospels' accounts of the Nativity. It has measured amounts of violence, flirting, hatefulness, stupidity in crowd behavior, and dignity in Quasimodo, the hunchback. The visual background is impeccable and clever. It includes dancing gargoyles and a statue of a well-nourished Virgin Mary holding her infant that reminded me of the photograph of the well-dressed homeless mother and infant I mentioned earlier.

The film brought forth severe condemnation for having "plundered high culture."[141] That the film did so is true, but its condemnation on that account is unwarranted. There is rather more than a single painting that depicts the story of Christ. Also, bypassing the irreducibly tragic aspects of life is appropriate for the mass culture industry, which at its best shows the greatness of common people.[142] An illustration of how Disney films favor this happy place, this earth, this techno-heaven, is the explanation the film offers for the origin of the name *Quasimodo*. A character explains that it means "half-formed." But the name is not that simpleminded. It comes from Peter's letter to the people of the Diaspora: "Quasi modo geniti infantes . . ."; "Like newborn babes, long for the pure spiritual milk" (1 Peter 2:2).

In sec. 5.4 I remarked that architecture, a visual art, fashions large sculptures that may be visited within and also that buildings are wombs that protect, embrace, and hold in thrall. They declare beliefs, views of the world, and attitudes to time; they also reflect the environment. With all this embarrassment of choices, twentieth-century architecture, in addition to being influenced by all the trends and schools I mentioned (and many that I did not), had its own large family of styles. Early in the century Walter Gropius recognized that architecture must draw on many other arts and crafts. To do just that, he created the idea and built the organization of the Bauhaus. The word is a play on German words and is best translated as the "House of Architecture." The Bauhaus principle of synthesizing technology, craftsmanship, and aesthetics demanded that young architects be trained in all the arts and crafts and in the humanities and be made keenly aware of socially important problems relevant to the art and science of building. The ideal had far-reaching influence: architecture today is very much a creation of the Bauhaus adapted to local tastes, needs, and material.

But the demands of building homes for an exploding population, the requirements for efficiency in industrial production, and the general demand for cheap and quickly built structures have greatly dehumanized twentieth-century architecture. It was to counter this trend that postmodernism was born in the early 1950s, the intention being to rehumanize architectural designs. In the exploding building trade, cities and suburbs became mélanges of architectural ideas and responses to the varying needs of the clientele, all changing with the changing building materials and technology. The proliferation of architectural styles, methods, and techniques, sometimes aesthetically pleasing, sometimes forbidding, and often plain ugly, have made architecture at the end of the century a laboratory in which raw needs, human ideals, and aesthetic uncertainties mix wildly.

The idea of postmodernity did not stay with architecture very long. I already mentioned it in connection with music. In the fragmented creativity of our age, the term came to be applied to everything for which it is difficult to find a niche in the flow of the history of ideas, forms, and tastes. From this perspective postmodernism is café au ersatz lait. From another perspective it is what Alexander Argyros says it is; postmodernism, he writes, "describes a world on the cusp of great horror and great leaps of imaginative freedom or more precisely, a world in which the potential of horror grows simultaneously with the potential for creativity."[143] Whether the term will ever mean anything more than the chronological location of experiments in the arts, letters, and daily living that followed modernism is yet to be seen.

After 1960 there arose a strategy of literary criticism cum philosophy called "deconstructionism," associated with the French philosopher Jacques Derrida. The movement has its roots in French intellectual and political unhappiness of the midcentury, just as, in its time, logical positivism grew from the unhappiness of Viennese intellectuals with German idealism. In its obscure jargon, deconstructionism notes that no word is an island entire of itself, that every word is a piece of the totality of the language. Words, then, are meaningless unless we know their position with respect to the totality of the language, but we cannot know the totality before knowing all its details. It follows that there is no way one can learn about reality.

That there is no one-to-one correspondence between signs and signals on the one hand and a presumed final reality on the other, as deconstructionism maintains, is hardly a new discovery. (I discussed this problem in "Reality and Its Moving Boundaries," sec. 2.1.) But the power that moves deconstructionism has little to do with the clarification of meanings. Rather, it is a way of saying "Raineth drop and staineth slop, / And how the wind doth ramm! / Sing Goddamm!" with an opaque academic accent. It is equivalent in the halls of academia to the anger expressed by American blacks who, during the 1965 race riots in Los Angeles, shouted, "Burn, baby, burn!"

The arts and letters of our age mutate and mate at a dizzying rate. Medieval styles and divisions of themes remained unchanged for several centuries; Renaissance art and literature remained stable for a few centuries; then came modernism, postmodernism, and deconstructionism. In our age there is a new style and a new art born every twenty minutes, and it is announced with fanfare each time a publisher wishes to market a new book or compact disk. The resulting mass of poems cannot be classified in stable categories of theme or style. *Stevenson's Home Book of Verse* (1912) contains some 3,500 poems grouped under a score of headings such as "The Baby," "In the Nursery," "Maidenhood," "The Man," "The Woman," and "The Conduct of Life." It would be difficult to find a current collection of poetry classed under such headings, because they are inappropriate for the end-of-the millennium society. There are no nurseries except communal ones for working mothers and fathers; there is no maidenhood to be esteemed for innocence or virginity (not that the two were ever the same); there is much poetry directed to women, but it would not be correct to separate poems by some such themes as "The Man" and "The Woman." As to conduct of life: that is left to how-to books by learned doctors. It seems impossible to find a poet or even a group of poets who could serve as icons of the end of the twentieth century because the revolt displayed in the arts has been directed against, among other targets, having such focal points at all. A contemporary collection of poetry is more likely to be arranged by the chronological order of the authors' births or alphabetically, by last names.

Allen Ginsberg, intense and concerned but without a stable spiritual core, had this to say in his essay "When the Mode of Music Changes the Walls of the City Shake."

Trouble with conventional form is it's too symmetrical, geometrical, numbered and pre-fixed—unlike to my own mind which has no beginning and end, nor fixed measure of thought (or speech—or writing) other than its own cornerless mystery. . . . plus not to forget the sudden genius-like Imagination or fabulation of unreal & out of this world verbal constructions which express the true gaiety & excess of Freedom—(and also by their nature express the First Cause of the world)—by means of spontaneous irrational juxtaposition of sublimely related facts.[144]

Reaction against the wholesale jettisoning of traditional aesthetics in poetry has been slow in coming and remains anemic. A 1995 attempt for criticism consists of forty-four essays expressing unhappiness with the "attacks on the very idea of aesthetic quality as a racist, classist, sexist conspiracy, designed to exclude minority artists from the perquisites of worldly success." What began in the 1960s as a demand for greater freedom of expression, say the authors, developed into a cult of conformity and constraints in the powerful pop culture.[145]

The United States now has a National Poetry Month, which in 1997 was also Soy Products Month. It brought forth an apologia from Robert Pinsky, poet laureate of the year, who cited in support of the celebration certain parallels between poetry and technology and spoke of poetry as a digital computer data device.[146] In turn, this brought the following comment: "Poetry is largely unread in this country not because it is poetry but because it is not very good. In its relentless insistence on issues of personal identity at the expense of humanity as a whole, American poetry followed the culture into banality. . . . When American poetry . . . ceases mumbling and speaks to the urgency of life beyond the self, it will be read again."[147]

So many have died, Gertrude Stein once said, to make verse free. As a consequence contemporary poetry is a record of random bits of emotions, compassion, and thought for which free verse is an alibi. It is encouraging, as Dana Gioia noted in his spirited *Can Poetry Matter?* that there is a revival of disciplined rhyme and meter among some young poets. The New Formalists, as they are called, "put free verse poets into the ironic and unprecedented position of being the status quo. Free verse, the creation of an older literary revolution, is now the . . . ruling orthodoxy, formal poetry the unexpected challenge."[148] Poets face the problem (as do all artists, statesmen, and philosophers) that the "proliferation of information has increasingly fragmented [the] audience into specialized subcultures that share no common frame of reference."[149]

In an introduction to her *Anthology of Modern Chinese Poetry* Michelle Yeh makes several points about the poets and poetry she reviews. Her comments are interesting because of the striking similarities between contemporary Chinese and American poetry. Poetry in contemporary China, she writes, has been marginalized. This "is not without its rhetorical, as well as ideological advantages. The autonomy that comes with marginality leaves poets alone to search for their own rules, thus not only making experimentation possible but also ensuring the intellectual and artistic distance neces-sary for engaging in a truly critical dialogue with the dominant society."[150] Whereas Westernized education in China shifted emphasis from the human-ities to the sciences and technology, modern Chinese poetry is distinguished "by its candid probing of the . . . relationships between love, beauty, truth, time, history and one's self." "Although all contemporary cultural products have been commercialized . . . the rise of mass media . . . has widened the gap between elite culture . . . and popular culture. . . . Short stories and novels, which to the Chinese are closer to popular culture, are [now] less marginally situated than poetry."[151] Here is a poem by Wang Xiaoni (b. 1955) described as an example of the poems of the Newborn Generation.

> By the lake the wind is gusty,
> Perhaps I should not have put on a skirt.
> Why does the wind make it flap?
>
> If there were no people here,
> How free I would be,
> Leaving my hair, my skirt, to the will of the wind.
>
> No, I will walk through the crowd nonchalantly,
> Why should I be afraid
> Of those eyes before and behind me?[152]

About a century ago André Gide, master of French writing and fearless in his support of individual liberty, thought that poetry is born of freedom and rule combined. No system of poetry, he wrote, can do without laws, but all poetic rules are more or less artificial. What should never be artificial is the use the poet makes of rules. The "most daring artists [were] those who felt the imperious need for struggle . . . [and] who sought the most resis-tant material and the harshest limitations. I remember . . . Michelangelo's sonnets and the tense gesture of his Moses, which was inspired, so we are told, by a flaw in the marble; and Dante's terza rima and Beethoven's rest-less search, in one of his last quartets, for the obligations of the fugue."[153] Gide would have liked Wang Xiaoni. Whether he would have liked Allen Ginsberg is uncertain.

A. C. Danto, an art critic and philosopher, remarked in *After the End of Art* that in contemporary art everything is possible: "The sense in which everything is possible is that in which there are no prior constraints on what a work of visual art can look like."[154] One consequence of this lack, as al-ready mentioned, is the radical separation between art and the beautiful. It democratizes art and permits the designation "artist" to be assigned to everyone who can create things or events that reflect wanted or unwanted feelings. It is thus that a stylized pig brain that floats in singing slop may be declared a piece of art.

In the separation of the artistic from the beautiful, in the struggle between the individual and society, and in the desire to be able to smile in the face of adversity, the Picasso-Hitler-Chaplin triad is alive.

Vibrant Instability: The High-Tech Primitive

The contemporary arts and letters make for a dizzying array of explosions. They carry much protest, much energy, fury, goodwill, and even compassion, but little or no solace. The wild and intense experimentation is worldwide. It shows vibrant instability and favors the high-tech primitive. On the time-compact globe aesthetics is preparing itself for a rearticulation of the methods used for the management of feelings. Reading contemporary poetry, seeing contemporary paintings, and listening to contemporary music all suggest painting by random numbers. The artists seem to be awaiting a new master who can order those numbers by a coherent emotional and intellectual logic.

Once upon a time there lived a steadfast tin soldier in Andersen's fairy tale by that title. He was in love with a pretty maiden. Both of them were birthday presents to a little boy. The soldier had only one leg because, when he was cast, there was not enough tin to finish him. She was cut out of paper and wore a dress of light gauze. She had two legs, but since she was a dancer, one of her legs was raised so high into the air that the tin soldier could not see it from where he was standing and supposed that she also had but one leg. That would be the very wife for me, he thought. The next day, because of the little boy's carelessness, the soldier landed in the fireplace. Whether the most horrible heat he felt came from a real fire or from the warmth of his feelings, he did not know. Then a sudden draft picked up the pretty dancer and carried her into the same fire: there she blazed up and was gone. The next morning, as the maid cleaned the fireplace, she found only a small tin heart.

Early in the twenty-first century the tin soldier, in or out of uniform, is continuously on the move. He makes and puts out atomic fires, creates or subdues tribal unrests, sells cars, informs cyberspace, markets sex, preaches homemade gospels, or drifts aimlessly, gun in hand, in the innumerable ghettos of the time-compact globe. The pretty dancer now runs with wolves (with or against men), saves others from starving, and leads corporations and countries toward things better or worse. She is getting out of the cave and kitchen and into a spacecraft, pursuing both her own and her man's primeval dreams. Or, as a sad-eyed girl child who began to menstruate only two years earlier, she holds her infant in her arms. Fate is still unpredictable, love still burns, but the venue of fairy tales has changed to urban and suburban areas and to industrial establishments. The primeval gaze that connected the soldier to the dancer now carries messages about a world where the gods have grown more powerful and life has become high-tech savage. All this and much more are reflected in contemporary art. But the evolutionary role of our aesthetic faculties remains what it has been all along. In shapes and metaphors appropriate for different social and cultural settings, those faculties generate and maintain conflicts between the world as we find it to be and the world of imagination to which art—this popular sport of mind and body—gives beautiful and ugly forms in all imaginable combinations.

OUT OF PLATO'S CAVE

Plato's theory of knowledge portrayed all things of the intelligible and visible world arranged, as it were, along a vertical line that one may imagine as connecting heaven and earth. On the top are eternal, timeless ideas or unchanging forms. They are the light of the world. Underneath them are likenesses of these ideas, such as geometrical figures drawn on a slate. Then come animals, plants, and all things made by humans. These are all temporal. The destiny of the soul is to ascend, through contemplation, from the sensible and temporal world to the timeless and intelligible one, the world of eternal truth, goodness, and beauty.

But Plato's line is upside down, because we hold precious not things timeless but things temporal.

People seek truths and hold them for dear life not because truths are timeless but because all verities are temporal and vulnerable: truths today may be lies tomorrow and lies today, truths tomorrow. People cherish the good because they know that moral judgments, though exuding the security of permanence, are subject to relentless revisions that can make today's good tomorrow's evil and vice versa. Beauty is precious not because it is eternal but, on the contrary, because a whiff of the wind can collapse those configurations of conditions by which the feelings we associate with the presence of the beautiful have been generated.

The long-term office of human values in the development of civilizations has been consistent with this understanding. Human values have never secured permanent stability. On the contrary, they have created and maintained instabilities through a family of unresolvable conflicts that make certain that human life never loses its tragic edge. It has been the task of the unbounded imaginative powers of the mind to propose solutions to those conflicts by satisfying the hunger for the true, the good, and the beautiful. Like bodily hunger, however, these mental hungers can never be permanently satisfied.

This recurring hunger then prompts a continuous reimagination of virtues in the hope that they will protect men and women from the loneliness and brutality of an unthinking, unfeeling, and amoral universe. The underlying conflicts may change their forms but remain nonetheless. As a consequence, what emerges as hallmarks of the time-knowing, value-judging creature are the living faces of hatred, the glowing eyes of love, and the insatiable hunger for knowledge.

The true home of the mind becomes not the ever-troubled present but the someday, the long ago, and the faraway, that is, those regions of human reality that cannot be visited by members of any other species. It is with the help of these imagined nonpresent regions of reality that the noetic present is continuously rebuilt. And it is the yearning for nonpresent homes that helped to create the quilt of civilizations and spurred us along an uneasy path of creative craze and destructive madness.

Although human values are unique to humans, they do of course have their ancestry. But that ancestry is to be sought not in the well-behaved dog or the duck that cares for her ducklings but in the paramecium seeking to escape a toxic dye, the migrating geese over James Bay wending their way toward better climate, and the monkey pressing its lever for food. These are different expressions of the selfsame defiance, of Hamlet's call "to take arms against a sea of troubles and by opposing, end them."

Let me represent the complex reasoning of this book by extending Plato's allegory of the cave. In the seventh book of the *Republic* Socrates speaks about a cave where prisoners were chained to the ground so that they could see only the wall in front of them. At some distance behind them a fire was burning. Between the fire and the prisoners men carried "human images and shapes of animals as well, wrought in stone and wood," which cast shadows on the cave wall. Like puppeteers, these men would talk now and then. The world of the prisoners, their universe, consisted entirely of occasionally talking shadows.

I now imagine a revolt of those slaves.

One day when the Demiurge—the craftsman, the intermediary creator of the world—came to survey the slaves he owned, he decided, for some unfathomable reasons of his own, to light his pipe. Suddenly there was a spark. To paraphrase the Johannine gospel, the darkness did not comprehend that light, but the slaves did. The shadows on the wall now showed that they were in chains. They became filled with wonder and inarticulate hope. They felt that they would never be able to rest until they found the source of the spark that gave their shadows a better resolution: they conspired, they broke their chains, they revolted. The Demiurge, hearing the commotion, lit a candle so that he might better see the world he ruled. What he saw made him retreat, keeping safely out of reach of the slaves turned wild. In the flame of the candle the people of the darkness began to discern a play of different degrees of shades, a discovery that gave them satisfaction but also increased their fury. A band of dark pilgrims, they began to ascend along the upward sloping cavern: the mind of modern man. Ignorant of specific goals, they were driven only by their inner command to reach out.

Some of them became obsessed with the idea of life after death, some drew geometrical figures on the wall, some heard harmonies, some began to inquire into the nature of the Demiurge, and others wondered about purpose in the world and in their own feelings and acts. All of them noticed that the light of the candle carried by the Demiurge came to blend with an intense patch of light that covered a small area of the distant darkness. It was toward that area that the cave dwellers marched as they began to search for the true, the good, and the beautiful. Since then, the human mind has always felt caged and has always been in revolt against the conditions in which the world happens to find itself.

The pace of the band became faster and then turned into a mad rush, because the searchers saw at the end of the darkness a surface of brilliant light that grew in size as they approached it. It had hues of blues, greens, and browns. Before they reached that opening, the Demiurge vanished, presumably on his way to Zeus to make a report. When they last saw him he was still holding his candle, but in the sunlight its flame was unnoticeable.

Stepping outside the cave, the former prisoners beheld the immensity of a world in which they were creative participants. They realized that they were naked and that they were men and women.

They stood on the ledge in front of the cave and held tightly to each other, for they knew that they were alone and that even God depended on them. Since words had failed them, they spoke through their silence. In the distance, on the top of Mount Olympus, where the earthly terminal of Plato's divided line used to be located, they saw, resting on an insignificant point, arising from a mere DNA molecule, and rising upward, a mighty exclamation mark. They noticed, however, that because of atmospheric conditions, it sometimes looked like a question mark.

Time and the Origin of Life

F ocusing on the role of time in considering the origins of life and the process of organic evolution differs from the common contemporary perspective. It directs attention to adaptation in the cyclic domain, to molecular "clock shops" that were favored by selection because their behavior fitted niches in the spectrum of the mechanical, chemical, electric, magnetic, or electromagnetic environmental cycles. I imagine the earliest forms of life as coherent molecular aggregates in coherent oscillation. They then absorbed energy, and the information carried by that energy, in whatever forms and at whatever frequencies as were available in their environments. They then transformed them into such forms of energy and information, and at such frequencies, as were useful for maintaining the continued integrity of the unit and then discarded energy and information in degraded forms. A coordinated assembly of molecular oscillators corresponding to such specifications is called a biological clock.[1]

There are reasons to believe that our nearest nonliving ancestors—biological clocks—resembled crystals.[2] What all later forms of life inherited from these unassuming forebears need not have been their physical structures or even their chemistry; rather, it could have been their Darwinian fitness in the temporal (oscillatory, cyclic) domain of the environment.[3]

These (hypothetical) primeval "clock shops" are unlikely to have been exactly identical; for that reason, the environment could exert selection pressure in the temporal domain by favoring those configurations that provided better fits to the cyclic spectrum of the surroundings.[4] Biological clocks were then bound to evolve toward increasingly more complex forms for the same reasons that made human clock makers build increasingly more complex clocks—namely, because the rich cyclic spectrum of environmental rhythms makes any clock or system of clocks, all of which serve as a model of external cycles, chronically incomplete. Each change that improves a clock's precision in modeling reveals the need for more refined tuning: this holds for both organic and manmade clocks. In addition, the increasing complexity of an oscillating system (manmade or natural) demands increasingly refined inner controls.

The history of life from the earliest molecular assemblies to our own days involved the broadening of the spectrum of biological oscillators. Contemporary species display oscillatory behavior across the immense width of twenty-four orders of magnitude; in musical measure this is seventy-eight octaves.[5]

The relevant conclusion pertains to the reasonableness of maintaining (1) that life may be identified with the capacity of coordinating cyclic process and (2) that the likely origins of life were crystal-like systems that would grow and then split.

Complexity and Its Measure

This appendix turns to certain mathematical principles of information and computation and proposes a universal measure of complexity applicable to any system, whatever the nature of its functions. First, however, I sketch some earlier attempts to define and measure complexity.

In a 1951 paper J. W. S. Pringle noted that both individual development through learning and organic evolution through natural selection lead to increasingly complex patterns of behavior.[1] He chose not to define complexity but did remark that whereas the complexity of nonliving systems remains constant, that of living organisms increases. One may refine this claim by pointing to the hidden issue of time scale. During the eons of cosmic history there arose compounds that one would intuitively label complex compared to elemental gases. But the rate of that complexification depends on passive, chance encounters and hence proceeds slowly, whereas living systems complexify as a consequence of their intentional (teleonomic) behavior and thus much more quickly.

In a frequently quoted 1962 paper on the architecture of complexity, H. A. Simon also bypassed a formal definition of complexity, saying only that it has to do with having a large number of parts that interact in non-simple ways.[2] He suggested (1) that complexity always leads to hierarchical structuring and (2) that process descriptions are more natural for complex systems than are state descriptions. The same two issues were the themes of C. H. Waddington's 1977 *Tools for Thought*.[3]

In a 1969 work John von Neumann proposed to measure complexity by "the crudest possible standards, the number of elementary parts."[4] His interest lay in determining the criteria for self-reproducing automata. In two papers P. T. Saunders and M. W. Ho argued that it is the increase in complexity that gives direction to organic evolution.[5] They also suggested that complexity be seen as a measure of the information content of the instructions required to build a system. They added that measuring the complexity of organic systems by their information content must go beyond the information content of the genome and include that of the epigenetic properties of the system.

J. T. Bonner formulated a measure of the complexity of an individual organism by equating it to the number of different types of cells composing the organism; consistently, he equated the complexity of a community to the number of different species existing in it.[6] He noted that size and complexity are positively correlated and that species with more complex members are more prone to extinction. We will encounter this second correlation again when we consider the complexification of information-driven societies.

Two other possible indices of complexity have been recommended by John Maynard Smith and Eörs Szathmary: the number of protein-coding genes and the richness and variety of morphology and behavior.[7]

In mathematics formal treatment of complexities arose in connection with issues of computability. When is a function too complex to be computed? The *Encyclopedia of Mathematics* defines complex systems as those with a "large number of interconnecting elements in mathematical logic."[8] In the same encyclopedia, hierarchical theory is defined as the classification of mathematical objects according to their complexities.[9] This definition in the domain of logic corresponds to what H. A. Simon asserted from an operational approach, namely, that hierarchical ordering is a policy of complex systems.

For reasons that will become clear later, I now turn to algorithmic information theory. An algorithm is a rule that, if repeatedly applied, leads to the construction or recognition of a new structure or process. A thirteenth-century manuscript described algorithm as "the Craft of Nombryng." That craft may involve successive logical decisions, such as in a calculus or repetitions of the same mechanical motions, as when building a brick wall.

Taking advantage of the method of algorithm, the American mathematician Gregory Chaitin formulated the notion of the algorithmic information content of a number series or set. He suggested it as an index of complexity in terms of diversity. A number standing for the minimal set of instructions necessary to construct a series, a set, or an object from its building blocks is the algorithmic information content of the series, set, or object. "In algorithmic information theory the primary concept is that of the *information content* of an individual object, which is a measure of how difficult it is to specify or describe how to construct or calculate that object. This notion is also known as *information-theoretic complexity*."[10]

Let us test the idea. Consider a series of numbers and examine them in the temporal sequence in which they come to your attention. Then, by a thought process that remains unanalyzed, determine whether the numbers are connected by a stable rule. A rule in this case is any instruction that can be used to generate that sequence of numbers and hence represent it. Here are four examples.

Example 1: "1, 2, 3, 4, 5, 6, 7, 8, 9, 10, 11, 12. . . ." A rule for constructing this series is "Start with $N = 1$ and then keep adding 1 to obtain the next member of the series." The algorithmic information content, used as a measure of the complexity of a series, is the number of elements in the formula that instructs the computer to calculate the members of the series. A suitable such formula is "$N_{next} = N + 1$," starting with $N = 1$.[11]

Example 2: "0, 3, 8, 15, 24, 35, 48, 63, 80, 99, 120, 143. . . ." The instruction that suggests itself is "$N_{next} = N^2 - 1$," starting with $N = 1$.

Example 3: "3, 1, 4, 1, 5, 9, 2, 6, 5, 3, 5, 8. . . ." Inspection fails to reveal any regularity.

Example 4: "513, 5, 13, 0.0116, −8.4957, 1, 69, 4.83, 10, 0, −256, 65.2. . . ." Here, too, inspection fails to reveal a rule.

Let us assume that each of the four series contains 3 billion members. The first two series could be represented by the short formulas shown. The third and fourth series seem random, lawless, unpredictable, and hence in a sense free. If that is the case, then the shortest way series 3 or 4 could be represented would be to write down all 3 billion digits. The first two series are said to be algorithmically compressible; the other two are not.

Someone might note, however, that the twelve numerals of example 3 are the first dozen numbers of the number π, which has been calculated to 4 billion digits. Though random by inspection, it could still be reduced to operational instructions through a suitable formula. Here is one developed by the Indian mathematician Srinivasa Ramanujan:

$$\frac{1}{\pi} = \frac{\sqrt{8}}{9801} \sum_{n=0}^{\infty} \frac{(4n)!}{(n!)^4} \frac{[1103 + 26390n]}{396^{4n}}$$

Counting the number of symbols, example 1 has a complexity of 5; example 2 has a complexity of 6. The information theoretical complexity of example 3 is more difficult to determine because it depends on the computer program used, but a reasonable figure is 70.[12] The complexity of example 4 is 3 billion: its members are completely unpredictable and hence may not be represented by anything shorter than the whole number series.

We are now ready to use the principle of algorithmic information content to help compress into a simple measure the diversity of objects that make up an integrative level. This task may be accomplished because there is an isomorphism between (1) the compression into algorithms of sets of numbers that first appear to have been randomly selected from the infinite store of numbers and (2) the compression into actual objects of sets of elementary particle-waves, objects that first appear to have randomly come about from the infinite store of potentialities resident in primeval chaos.

The compression of sets of numbers into algorithms is the work of mathematicians. The compression of the variables of physical processes into equations is the work of mathematical physics.[13] The compression of potentialities resident in absolute chaos into actual objects has been the work of inorganic and organic evolution.

If (1) we can measure the complexity of a set of numbers by the length of the shortest algorithms into which the rules of their construction may be compressed, then (2) we may also measure the complexity of an organizational level by the minimum number of distinct building blocks into which nature has compressed the infinite potentialities of primeval chaos when it constructed those integrative levels.

The process described under (1) takes place in the minds of mathematicians. This is mental learning. The process described under (2) is evolution by natural selection. This is physical and biological learning. In both processes the most parsimonious account of diversity is employed as a measure of complexity. Let us, therefore, seek numbers that represent the diversity of the building blocks of each integrative level.

The chaotic, atemporal substratum of the world comprises objects that travel at the speed of light. The set of such objects is small: the photon, the neutrino (once it is observed), and perhaps the graviton. The range 1–5 seems to be that of the diversity of the primeval chaos, though physicists have been working hard to reduce it to 1. The number 10^1 may then be assigned to that world as its index of complexity.

The next higher organizational level, the prototemporal, comprises particle-waves that travel at speeds less than that of light. The behavior of all these objects may be accounted for—at this time—in terms of six different quarks, six different leptons, and the antiparticles of each.[14] But there seem to be other objects associated with these forces of nature that hold the quarks and leptons together. If we include all those which appear in high energy interactions, their total number may be estimated to be 500.[15] This diversity may be represented by the range 10^2–10^3.

The stable constitutive objects of the macroscopic world are the chemical elements and their compounds. The 1998 *CRC Handbook of Chemistry and Physics*[16] lists over 15,000 organic compounds; *Lange's Handbook of Chem-*

istry, 3,000 inorganic compounds.[17] Diligent chemists could probably identify many others, suggesting a range of 10^4–10^6 as a reasonable one for the diversity of stable objects from which the macroscopic physical world above the quantum level has been constructed.

The classes of different building blocks from which the physical world is constructed are countable with relative ease because they comprise objects that, within their species, are indistinguishable. This is not the case for objects that make up the world of living organisms. Since no two living creatures are exactly alike, to obtain a measure of the algorithmic information content of the integrative level of life, one must count all distinct organisms that ever lived. Instead of using the type of accounting that was suitable for examples 1, 2, and 3, we must use the type of accounting that was necessary for example 4. We must estimate the total number of distinct organisms that ever lived.

For sexually reproducing species the counting of each individual as a different organism is well warranted. But just what constitutes an individual and what constitutes a society become problematic as one descends toward the simpler forms of life. Still, the kind of identity found among physical particles of the same species does not exist in the domain of life: every bacterium is in some ways different from all others of the same group.

In any event, the number of described species, sexually reproducing or otherwise, is estimated at 13,620,000; the number of species alive today is estimated at 18,375,000.[18] The number of species that ever lived is estimated at 100 million.[19]

The total number of organisms larger than insects is insignificant compared to the number of insects, hence it is enough to count insects. Among the 750,000 known insect species, there are some 10,000 species of ants. The number of ants at any instant is estimated as 10^{15} individuals.[20] Ants live for six months to a year[21] and have been around since the Paleozoic era, that is, for the last 260 million years. This leads to a head count of about 10^{23} ants that ever lived, take or leave a few trillion. But ants are vast and rare creatures compared to the microorganisms found inside each ant, guessed to be of the order of 10^9 per ant.[22] It is enough, then, to count those microorganisms. This comes to a total of 10^{29}, take or leave a few quadrillion.

Let us check the reasonableness of this number by starting again along a different tack. The total number of arthropods per hectare (ha) of soil is estimated at 2×10^9. Those above ground add another 50 percent, suggesting a figure of 3×10^9 per hectare.[23] Since the total land area of the earth is 1.5×10^{10} ha,[24] the total number of arthropods, neglecting the variability in density, is of the order of 4.5×10^{19}. Assuming that they have also been around for 260 million years, we get a total arthropod population, alive now or previously, of around 10^{28}.

The total number of microbes per hectare of land is estimated as 7×10^{18}.

If we include microbes living in ants, other arthropods, and other animals, a figure of 1.4×10^{19} microbes per hectare is reasonable.[25] For the surface of the earth this is 2×10^{29} microbes at an instant. How does one extend this synchronous figure of today diachronically to the age of microbial life? Perhaps by taking a cue from bacteria. In the life cycle of bacteria the periods of reproduction vary between fifteen minutes and sixteen hours, and bacteria existed since Devonian times, that is, for about 400 million years. I assume an average two-hour reproduction period and also a linear growth in numbers as a first approximation to a better informed weighted figure. This yields 10^{12} generations of bacteria. Assuming the same number of generations for microbes, we obtain 10^{41} as the total number of microbes that ever lived. Since this is twelve orders of magnitude above the total number of arthropods, the number of arthropods may be neglected.

The mass of the oceans is 1.4×10^{24} grams or, to first approximation, that many cubic centimeters.[26] There are an estimated 10^8–10^{10} bacterioplanktons per cubic millimeter of water. For the earth's seas this makes for 10^{32}–10^{34} bacterioplanktons. But the productive regions of the oceans are the upper 30 meters; there is hardly any productivity below 100 meters. Although the ocean area represents twice the area of the land, biological productivity on land is nearly three times that of all the oceans.[27] For this reason, I assume that the total number of planktons that ever populated the seas is less than the number of microbes and hence makes a negligible difference to the grand total.

Allowing for a considerable margin of error, the complexity range of the biotemporal world may therefore be given as 10^{40}–10^{50}.

The figures used in the calculation of organic complexity were either generally available and judged reliable (at this writing) or obtained as cited. But the responsibility for daring to carry out such a divine arithmetic is entirely that of the author. Fortunately, as will be seen later, even substantial variation from the 10^{40}–10^{50} figure would not affect the conclusion of the reasoning.

The next higher integrative level, the noetic, is the product of the minding functions of the human brain working through the body and in cooperation with other brains. Placing a number on the complexity of cultures may appear to be a hopeless task. But determining the diversity of states that the brain may occupy may not be. And surely the number of those states must be some kind of an index of the potentialities of human imagination.

Still, to seek the diversity of those states reminds one of the biblical figure of speech, the counting of the stars. Who could do so? Perhaps the Lord, because, says Psalm 147, "He determines the number of stars, he gives to all of them their names." No mortal ever actually counted all the stars one by one, but astronomers have made estimates. There are about 10^{10} galaxies,[28] with 10^9–10^{11} stars per galaxy, making for a total of 10^{19}–10^{21} stars.

Likewise, one can make an estimate of the number of possible different brain configurations.

The human brain contains an estimated 10^{10}–10^{12} neurons.[29] This happens to be on the order of the number of galaxies. But whereas the galaxies of the universe do not collectively determine a joint cosmic present—they cannot, by the provisions of special relativity theory—the neurons of the brain do define the mental present through their interactions (see sec. 2.2). Assuming that each neuron is either on or off, the upper limit of the theoretically different states possible for the human brain is on the order of $2^{12^{12}}$ or $10^{10^{12}}$.[30]

If each neuron were directly connected to all other neurons (neurons are not so connected), then this numeral would represent the theoretical upper limit of different global brain states. But each neuron is connected through its dendrites (impulse transmitters) and its axons (impulse receivers) to only 10^2–10^4 synapses.[31] This leaves a mere $10^{10,000}$ different possible configurations, which may then be thought of as that many different brain states. Brain states, one or more at a time, processed simultaneously or in meaningful order, may form an unlimited number of states of mind with their wisps of thought. Out of this unbounded store arise our fears, hopes, memories, and perceptions. Human values, then, help to select from among their fellow images those fears, hopes, memories, and perceptions that are—or promise to be—useful in maintaining personal and collective identities. The lengths of the shortest algorithms to which the selection rules may be compressed may then represent the measure of complexity of the noetic umwelt. These rules—so many different process descriptions of the brain—are explored and tested through the arts, the letters, the sciences, and the historical struggles of humankind.[32]

The human brain, being the most complex object in the known universe, cannot be modeled by anything less complex than itself. Any simpler model would lose those properties of the brain that depend on its complexity, such as the ability to construct personal identity, speak a human language, or perceive the world in terms of noetic time.

Let me now summarize the conclusions of this applied speculation based on informed guesses.

Complexity of the Integrative Levels Measured by the Diversity of Their Building Blocks

	Complexity
The chaos of radiative energy	10^1
Subatomic and atomic particle-waves	10^2–10^3
Integrative level of massive matter	10^5–10^6
Organizational level of life	10^{40}–10^{50}
The human brain and its noetic world	$10^{10,000}$

Recall the Socratic discussion of what a bee is, that is, the character in respect to which bees do not differ from one another. Similarly, we might seek the character with respect to which members of an integrative level do not differ among themselves but differ from members of other integrative levels.

They share the same range of complexities. If a diligent survey of nature turns up an object whose functions and structures are akin to no more than 10^2–10^3 other objects, then you are dealing with a subatomic or atomic particle. If you can identify in your scheme of ordering 10^{40}–10^{50} other objects whose functions and structures are akin to the one you are considering, than you are observing a living organism.

That the world of human thought is in some hard-to-define way more complex than are biological processes, which in turn, are more complex than physical processes, is a rather old idea. What is new in the conclusions of this appendix, represented by a numerical summary, is the suggestion that the ranges of the complexities of the integrative levels of nature, if defined and measured as suggested, are distinct and widely separated. This conclusion is brought forward in sec. 2.2. The conclusion that the degree of complexity of the human brain (again, if defined and measured as suggested) is some 10,000 orders of magnitude greater than that of any other structure, including the universe at large (except for other human brains), is brought forward in sec. 1.2.

Entropy: Its Uses and Abuses

F or a definition of entropy I turn to G. J. Whitrow: "The concept of entropy is a mathematical measure of the disorganization of a system.
The idea first arose as a part of the theory of heat, but a similar notion can
be associated with probability distributions of any kind."[1]

The measure of anything is a comparison expressed in numbers. The
measure of the entropy of a system is a result of a numerical comparison,
usually between two different states of organization of the same system.
Since there are many different processes to which the idea of organization
and disorganization may be applied, there are also many different ways of
defining entropy.[2]

Consider a container with two compartments separated by a wall. Each
compartment contains a different gas. Remove the wall and watch the two
noninteracting gases mix. The original condition (the two gases in two
boxes) is being replaced by a single mixture of the two that, by convention,
is judged as less orderly. If the original condition is taken to be a state of
maximum ordering, to which zero entropy is assigned, then at any later time
it should be possible to assign some nonzero entropy to the mixture of the
gases, measured in suitable units.

If the walls of the container prevent the entry of energy or information
from the outside, that container is said to be a thermodynamically closed
system. The long-term entropic behavior of a system that is thermodynamically isolated from the rest of the world is governed by a principle known

as the Second Law of Thermodynamics. There are many ways of stating that principle depending on how entropy is being measured. Common to all of them is the rule that in the long run the total entropy of a closed system can only remain constant or increase. If the closed container contains living and thinking beings, the entropic changes within are governed by the laws of the physical, biological, mental, and social worlds. Since the second law is a statistical statement, it allows for transient processes of decreasing entropy without negating the long-term increase of disorder for the container at large.

The Second Law of Thermodynamics caught the attention of the English astronomer and natural philosopher Sir Arthur Stanley Eddington (1882–1944). In that law's statement about the universality of decay Eddington perceived the physical basis of the experience of time's passage. He represented the direction of that passage by the metaphor of the arrow of time.[3]

There are yet other, different thermodynamic systems, notably, living organisms. Their spatial boundaries are defined not by a box within which they are enclosed but by their geometrical boundaries. They are said to be open because energy and information from the rest of the world may cross their boundaries. Such crossings take place whenever energy and information are called for (are needed) to maintain the continuity of the processes within.

Think next of a sheep that just died of old age. Zero entropy may be assigned to its still warm carcass as to its most highly organized state, because we know from experience that beginning with that state, the body will decay, that it will lose its organization. This is a reasonable plan even though it is uncertain at what instant the dead sheep is in its condition of maximum postmortem organization. It also involves experimental difficulties. Still, it should be possible, at least in principle, to measure the increase in the disorganization of the carcass. Eventually, after continued decay, the dust of the sheep will be indistinguishable from the dust of the shepherd.

Instead of considering a carcass, think next of a living sheep. To give any meaning to its present degree of disorganization, one must have as a reference a final and complete sheep to which zero entropy is assigned. But there is no final and complete sheep, because evolution is open-ended. The task must therefore be reversed. One has to measure the degree of organization of the present sheep with respect to one of its own less-organized states, such as when it was an embryo. But that stage is too arbitrary. Perhaps we should expand our views to organic evolution and compare the sheep's present organization to a sampling of the primeval chaos. The new variable, necessary to carry out such a comparison, is called negentropy or information.

The intermixing of the gases, with their increasing entropy, and the development (or evolution) of the sheep in terms of increasing information content (decreasing entropy) are oppositely directed changes, but they both take place in the same direction of time's experienced passage.[4]

Consider next that the notions of both closed and open systems assume an outside world from which they are—or are not—closed. How about the universe at large? Is it closed or open? Since there is nothing outside the universe, the cosmos can be neither closed nor open. Edward R. Harrison, in *Cosmology, the Science of the Universe*, explains why the entropy of the universe may be measured by the total number of cosmic photons and neutrinos and why that total number is approximately conserved. Consistently, "As we go back in time the total entropy [of the universe] remains constant."[5]

The second law applies only to systems that may become disorganized. A principle that governs decay must therefore necessarily assume some other principles that, at some time in the past, brought about order. With equal justification, Eddington's arrow may be attached to the decaying carcass no less than to the developing embryo, to the mixing of gases no less than to the creation of those separate gases out of the cosmic chaos, or to any of the entropy increasing or entropy decreasing processes of the world. Since the association is arbitrary, neither growth nor decay, neither entropy decrease nor increase, can in itself serve as the agency responsible for the passing of time.

We could reach the same conclusion without knowing anything about entropy or thermodynamics, for no arrow in itself can define a direction, whether in space or in time. Up needs down, right needs left, and decay needs growth. The cells of my body manufacture enzymes and create decay products in the same sense of time's passage.[6] The directedness of change we describe as the passage of time therefore cannot come either from decay or from growth considered in itself, because in terms of our experience they both point from past to future.

Since the experiential direction of time may be attached with equal justification to the growth or decay arrow of thermodynamics (which define each other), the sources of the experience and idea of a passage of time cannot be found in the thermodynamic behavior of the physical world. This is consistent with the absence of a definable now in the physical world, with the consequent impossibility to give meaning to a direction of time at that level, and with the constancy of the entropy of the universe. The relevant conclusion is that the physical umwelts allow for directed time but do not demand it.

A World without History: The Astral Geometry of Gauss

The origins of geometry, according to Herodotus, reach back to the ancient Egyptians, who invented it to measure land. Clement of Alexandria, a second-century Christian apologist, wrote about Egyptians who worked as *harpedonaptai,* or "rope stretchers." Rope stretching was their way of defining a straight line, that is, the shortest distance between two points. The geometry in which straight lines are defined in such an intuitively simple and obvious way is that of the Alexandrian mathematician Euclid; he lived around 300 B.C.

At the end of the eighteenth century Carl Friedrich Gauss constructed a geometry based on axioms partly different from those of Euclid. He described it as "non-Euclidean" and prophetically named it *astral geometry.* The name was intended to imply that the crucial differences between non-Euclidean and Euclidean geometry can become evident only at stellar distances (see sec. 3.2)—today we would say "intergalactic distances." I will adopt the term to identify the geometry of general relativity theory.

Gauss and, later, Georg Friedrich Riemann not only expanded the applicability of geometry to spaces with topologies different from Euclidean space: they also changed geometry from a purely logical science to one both logical and empirical. For Plato and for everyone during the two millennia after him, geometry was a science of ideal forms resident in eternity. After Riemann it became subject to experimental test. We read in a volume of interpretive essays on relativity theory that geometry is a branch of physics, "a subject to which no one has contributed more than Albert Einstein who by his theories of relativity . . . brought into being physical geometries which have supplanted the tradition-steeped a priori geometry of Euclid and Newton."[1]

If geometry is now a branch of physics, then it must have always been empirical even if it was mistakenly not so judged. If the laws of geometry may be refined by findings obtained through our senses (extended by instruments), then our minds must have abstracted the laws of geometry from sense impressions by separating in spatial orders the permanent and predictable from the impermanent and unpredictable. This is what Eddington said about our senses and astral geometry: "When we perceive that a certain region of the world is empty, that is merely the mode in which our senses recognize that it is curved no higher than the first degree. When we perceive that the region contains matter we are recognizing the intrinsic curvature of the world."[2]

The straight lines in the geometry of the universe, as understood at the beginning of the twenty-first century, are not ropes stretched between two points (be they real or imaginary ropes) but light beams. They take the place of the ropes of old because they always travel along the shortest distances between any two points in the four-dimensional manifold (space-time) of astral geometry. Our rope stretchers are laser beamers. Curvature is a variable of astral geometry that allows a degree of freedom not available in Euclidean geometry.

The master equations of general relativity theory, which use astral geometry, are known as the field equations. A shorthand for a family of these equations is $R^{\mu\nu} - \frac{1}{2}g^{\mu\nu}R = -\kappa T^{\mu\nu}$. One has to learn what the letters mean, but it is still only an equation. The righthand side speaks of the physics of 4-space in terms of energy and momenta; the lefthand side speaks of its geometry constructed from measurements along the coordinate axes used in general relativity theory. The equations are instructions for learned bookkeepers. They tell us how energy, momenta, and geometry relate. The solutions to these equations govern the fate of the universe of astral geometry. But these equations represent only physical processes. A knowledge of directed time, and with it the possibility of history, is something the physicist must bring to general relativity theory; it cannot be extracted from it.

The local worlds of the general relativistic universe are governed by special relativity theory. The master equations of that theory are called the Lorentz transformations. What do they say and not say about time?

Imagine a hefty book that contains tabulations of the exchange rates between any two currencies on the globe. It specifies so many dollars for so many English pounds, as well the rates for English pounds to yen, yen to Bangladesh taka, taka to rubles, rubles to euros, and euros to dollars. But there is nothing in the book that would tell us what is meant by *currency*.

Likewise, the Lorentz transformations tell us how to make sure that our time measurements are consistent regardless of the relative motion of the clocks used. They do not tell us what to mean by the now, the future, and the past and by time's passage. A knowledge of time must be brought to the Lorentz transformations of special relativity theory (no less than to the astral geometry of the general theory of relativity). It cannot be extracted from them.

It is this need that prompted the physicist and philosopher Michael Heller to ask why the universe has a history. "This apparently trivial question" he wrote, "opens a fascinating research field for theoretical physics."[3] He maintained that a space-time manifold (a model of the substratum of the world) may be suitable for physical processes "if and only if any of its points distinguishes between two time directions" but gives no preference to either (compare this claim with the conclusion of appendix C). Heller, citing some of his own earlier work and that of P. C. W. Davies, concluded that "for the 'arrow of time' one must look elsewhere," that is, not in the physical foundations of the world. He suggested that perhaps "some deeper non-metric level which could be called a 'pre-physics' of spacetime" might be discovered and shown to be responsible for the cosmos's having a history.[4]

The hierarchical theory of time maintains that the physical world is time orientable but is not time oriented, that it allows but does not demand a preferred direction of time. It is eotemporal.[5] If it did not allow a temporal orientation, biotemporality could not have been born. By analogy, if life had not permitted organic evolution to create a human brain, then noetic time could not have become a part of human reality.

The universe as understood in the formalism of contemporary physics does not prescribe a historical dimension to time. It has only a set of geometrical rules appropriate for the eo- and prototemporal umwelts. To these we must bring our experiential knowledge of time's passage. Once that is done, physical cosmology reports about possible alternative histories of the universe, among which astronomers will have to select the most convincing model based on observation.

The relevant conclusion is that the universe of astral geometry does not have a history describable in its own umwelt.

The Self-Scanning of the Brain

I begin with hints from the neurologist John Eccles, who drew attention to the "extraordinary problem of trying to reconcile the unitary nature of [the] conscious self with the neurological events of utmost diversity and complexity that are assumed to underlie it."[1] My suggestion is that the integrating process involves self-scanning. In support of this hypothesis I offer three independent opinions.

1. Analytically disposed psychiatrists have long maintained that consciousness oscillates between different degrees of form differentiation in the sensory inputs. In a psychological study of artistic vision and hearing published nearly half a century ago, Anton Ehrenzweig suggested that every act of visual perception recapitulates the ontogenetic development of visual motor patterns, and these patterns thus run through undifferentiated stages of dreamlike structures before they are articulated into the final images that emerge into consciousness.[2] If Ehrenzweig is correct, then conscious experience always has dreamlike aspects and may be understood as dreaming restrained by sense impressions or sense impressions enriched by dreaming.

2. Drawing on recent work by medical psychologists and much older work carried out in Würzburg, Germany, Jason Brown, a neurologist, developed what he calls the "theory of microgenesis." The word is a translation of the German *Aktualgenese*. It stands for a hypothetical neural process that consists of the unfolding of mental content through qualitatively different stages, of retracing the phylogeny of the mind as retained in the

functional and structural organization of the brain. This "unfolding" follows the growth pattern of the perceptive faculties in evolution. "For example, a visual object would begin its journey to an external perception as a two-dimensional map in the upper brain stem. There is a preliminary size and shape detection and a location in the map, but not yet an object. In the next stage, the forming object is selected through a system of personal memory. [After several steps, progressing from dreamlike to objectlike stages, there follows] the full exteriorization of object space."[3] A similar process is postulated for affects:

> they are transformed over stages, unfolding out of a hypothalamic and limbic core in relation to a small inventory of drive and motivational states. This content is selected with developing acts and objects through a neocortical phase where it fractionates, with those acts and objects, into moods, feelings, and complex affects or "affect-ideas." The transition from a few intense drives or instincts to a wider set of less intense but qualitatively richer, more distinct feelings, occurs in parallel with the specification of representations in the unfolding of the mental state.[4]

According to microgenetic theory, then, all elements of visual, auditory, or tactile perception address all levels of the mind.

3. Another theoretical mechanism for scanning and integrating the moods of temporalities may be found in the works of Gerald Edelman, cited in sec. 1.2. In a trilogy that employs late twentieth-century modes of reasoning and experimental technique in neurology, he laid out what he described as a biological theory of consciousness built on neural Darwinism.[5] The evolution of the brain for the species and its development in a person are seen as the results of internal and external selection pressures that favor some neural configurations and disfavor others, just as organic evolution favors and disfavors competing species and individuals.

Edelman describes the dynamics of interconnectedness among neuron groups as one of reentrant integration. The term seems to mean a continuous circulation of signals among many functionally segregated maps in the brain that together are responsible for each perceptual or conceptual object consciously recognized. Reentry is to be distinguished from feedback. Whereas feedback helps to maintain the equilibria of a system against perturbations, reentrant integration helps the system to remain open-ended and allows complexification.

Edelman agrees with William James and others in maintaining that consciousness is best thought of as a process. Regarding this process he distinguishes between primary and higher-order consciousness, paralleling

Freud's distinction between primary and secondary processes.[6] Primary consciousness signifies mental awareness without awareness of open futures and distant pasts and hence unaccompanied by the continuity we know as personhood. Higher-order consciousness recognizes the thinking self based "on the ability to model the past and the future."[7] Higher-order consciousness arises from the biological matrix of lower-order consciousness when intentionality expands to embrace long-term futures and relates them to memories of long-term pasts.[8]

Of the three proposals, Edelman's has been worked out in most experimental and theoretical detail.

In the self-scanning of the brain one may recognize an adaptive strategy of descents and ascents known from other phenomena, such as the life cycle and the sleep-wake cycle. The life cycle consists of a repeated development of the organism from the fertilization of the gametes to the same stage of fertilization in the next generation. In humans the ascent is from zygote to a new person; the descent is from two persons, via two gametes, to the zygote. This is a periodic regression of human life to the molecular level, out of which emerge new bodies similar to and also different from other bodies. The life cycle helps the adaptation of the species from generation to generation; its length in humans runs to the decades of the reproductive periods of men and women.

The sleep-wake state is another adaptive cycle of descent and ascent. It is a rhythmic process that turns the higher modes of reasoning on and off in twenty-four-hour cycles. Out of the cyclically recurrent noetic quiescence, new ideas for the guidance of conduct may emerge, being both similar to and different from earlier ideas. The sleep cycle helps persons to adapt to changes as day follows day.

The self-scanning of the brain, its descents and ascents, is a method of immediate adaptation. New feelings appropriate to the changing dangers and promises of the external and internal worlds are generated from instant to instant through the mobilization of aesthetic sensibilities. By "aesthetic" I mean all dualities that grow from "I like it / I dislike it." As a consequence of this scanning, all reality assessments are simultaneously present among mental functions and simultaneously interpret sense impressions.

NOTES

THE PERUVIAN LABORATORY

1. Thornton Wilder, *The Bridge of San Luis Rey* (New York: Washington Square, 1939), 6.
2. Ibid., 5.

ONE: PERSPECTIVES ON A STRANGE WALKER

1. Our ancestors forty or fifty thousand years ago were both males and females. In this book the masculine pronoun stands for humans of either sex unless the text makes clear that it refers to men. An occasional "he or she" will remind the reader of this note.

2. Sophocles, *Antigone*, tr. Elizabeth Wyckoff, in *Greek Tragedies*, ed. David Grene and Richmond Lattimore, 4 vols. (Chicago: University of Chicago Press, 1960), 1:192–93, ll. 332–34, 355–57, 359–60, 362–72.

3. Such as B. C. Goodwin, *Analytical Physiology of Cells and Developing Organisms* (New York: Academic, 1976); J. T. Bonner, *On Development* (Cambridge, Mass.: Harvard University Press, 1974); and A. T. Winfree, *The Geometry of Biological Time* (New York: Springer Verlag, 1980).

4. John von Neumann, *Theory of Self-Reproducing Automata*, ed. and completed by A. W. Burns (Urbana: University of Illinois Press, 1969), 79–80.

5. The reasoning parallels the "cost-of-reproduction" argument of J. T. Bonner. The phrase in quotation marks means that "certain secondary nonreproductive activities involve a cost, but this cost is more than compensated for by the success in producing stable and successfully perpetuating offspring" (Bonner, *On Development*, 68).

6. Plato, *Symposium*, trans. Michael Joyce, in *The Collected Dialogues of Plato*, ed. Edith Hamilton and Huntington Cairns (Princeton, N.J.: Princeton University Press, 1973), 190d.

7. Gerald Edelman, *The Remembered Present: A Biological Theory of Consciousness* (New York: Basic Books, 1989), 262–63.

8. Wallace Stegner, "The Traveler," in *Collected Stories* (New York: Wings Books, 1994), 11.

9. "Mitochondrial DNA [a molecule that mediates inheritance via the female line] from 147 people drawn from five geographic populations have been analyzed. . . . All these stem from one woman who is postulated to have lived about 200,000 years ago, probably in Africa" (R. L. Cann, Mark Stoneking, and A. C. Wilson, "Mitochondrial DNA and Human Evolution," *Nature* 325 [1987]: 31–36).

10. Steve Jones, Robert Martin, and David Pilbeam, eds., *The Cambridge Encyclopedia of Human Evolution* (New York: Cambridge University Press, 1992), 116.

11. On temporal relations in infancy from the point of view of cognitive psychology, see W. J. Friedman, "Development of Time Concepts in Children," *Advances in*

Child Development and Behavior 12 (1978): 267–98; J. T. Fraser, "Temporal Levels and Reality Testing," *International Journal of Psycho-Analysis* 62 (1981): 2–26.

12. *Webster's New International Dictionary of the English Language*, 2d ed., contains over 550,000 words. A literate person could recognize perhaps 450,000 of them as appropriate for English use and could assign correct meaning to 80,000. Wilson calculated that to possess an inborn vocabulary of 10,000 words would require 10^{14} kg of DNA (C. J. Lumsden and E. O. Wilson, *Genes, Mind and Culture: The Coevolutionary Process* [Cambridge, Mass.: Harvard University Press, 1981], 337).

13. Erick E. Lenneberg, "A Biological Perspective of Language," in *New Directions in the Study of Language*, ed. Erick E. Lenneberg (Cambridge, Mass.: MIT Press, 1966), 65–88.

14. These paragraphs are based mainly on J. T. Bonner's *Evolution of Complexity by Means of Natural Selection* (Princeton, N.J.: Princeton University Press, 1988), 198–201. See also Jones et al., eds., *Cambridge Encyclopedia of Human Evolution*, 111.

The following table, which shows data for the human brain, is from Samuil M. Blinkov and Ilya Glezer, *The Human Brain in Figures and Tables: A Quantitative Handbook*, trans. Basil Haigh (New York: Plenum, 1968), 336–37.

	Avg. volume in cm³	Avg. weight in grams	Avg. density in gr/cm³
Newborn	330	350	1.06
1 year	750	825	1.10
20 years	1200	1378	1.15
90 years	1200	1270	1.06

15. Neuron data is from E. O. Wilson, *Sociobiology: The New Synthesis* (Cambridge, Mass.: Belknap/Harvard University Press, 1975), 151–52. Data on the human brain is from Gerald M. Edelman, W. Eimar Gall, and W. Maxwell Cowan, eds., *Synaptic Functions* (New York: Wiley, 1987), 1.

16. See Gerald M. Edelman, *Neural Darwinism: The Theory of Neuronal Selection* (New York: Basic Books, 1987); Edelman, *The Remembered Present;* Edelman, *Bright Air, Brilliant Fire: On the Matter of the Mind* (New York: Basic Books, 1992). These volumes are rich in original thought but heavy in style. For an entry to Edelman's thought, the reader may wish to begin with a recent summary by G. M. Edelman and Giulio Tononi, "Neural Darwinism: The Brain as a Selection System," and continue with an exegesis of those ideas by Oliver Sacks, "A New Vision of the Mind," both in John Cornwell, ed., *Nature's Imagination* (Oxford: Oxford University Press, 1995), 78–100 and 101–21, respectively. For a slightly different perspective, see Jean-Pierre Changeux and Stanislas Dehaene, "Neural Models or Cognitive Functions," *Cognition* 33 (1989): 63–109.

17. Edelman, *Bright Air,* 5.

18. Edelman, *Neural Darwinism,* 3–4.

19. Ibid., 7.

20. Edelman, *The Remembered Present,* 287n.4 ("theologically derived" should be "teleonomically derived"; personal communication).

21. "Teleology, in its Aristotelian form, has . . . the end as immediate, 'efficient' cause. And that is precisely what the biologist . . . cannot accept. . . . What the biol-

ogist could not escape [however] was the plain fact—or rather the fundamental fact—which he must (as scientist) explain: that the objects of biological analysis are organizations (he calls them organisms) and as such, are end-directed. . . . I wanted a word that would allow me . . . to describe, stress or simply allude to . . . this end-directedness of a perfectly respectable mechanical system" (in Ernst Mayr, "The Multiple Meanings of Teleological," *Toward a New Philosophy of Biology: Observations of an Evolutionist* [Cambridge, Mass.: Harvard University Press, 1988], 63–64).

22. K. J. Friston, G. Tononi, J. N. Reeke Jr., O. Sporns, and G. M. Edelman, "Value-dependent Selection in the Brain: Simulation in a Synthetic Neural Model," *Neurosciences* 59 (1994): 229–43.

23. It is the temporal context of this idea that is new, not the idea itself. See, e.g., Leslie A. White, *The Science of Culture* (New York: Grove, 1949), 49–54.

24. See H. A. Simon, "The Architecture of Complexity," in *The Sciences of the Artificial*, ed. H. A. Simon (Cambridge, Mass.: MIT Press, 1969), 117.

25. Heinz R. Pagels, *Dreams of Reason: The Computer and the Rise of the Sciences of Complexity* (New York: Simon and Schuster, 1988), 226–28; quotation on 228.

26. Plato, *Timaeus*, trans. Benjamin Jowett, in *The Collected Dialogues*, 28a.

27. D. H. Lawrence, "Fidelity," in *The Complete Poems* (New York: Penguin Books, 1977), 476. He could have written, "The wonderful slow flowing of a golden booty."

TWO: PERSPECTIVES ON TIME AND CONFLICT

1. J. T. Fraser, "Time as a Hierarchy of Creative Conflicts," *Studium Generale* 23 (1970): 597–689, was the first attempt to suggest a universal theory of time based on the idea of a nested hierarchy of unresolvable conflicts. In *Of Time, Passion, and Knowledge: Reflections on the Strategy of Existence*, 2d ed. (Princeton, N.J.: Princeton University Press, 1990 [1975]), I summed up what I judged to be the minimal substantive material for any serious interdisciplinary study of time and identified the salient features of the theory. My *Time as Conflict: A Scientific and Humanistic Study* (Basel: Birkhäuser, 1978), explored the theory's philosophical, scientific, and humanistic background. In *The Genesis and Evolution of Time: A Critique of Interpretation in Physics* (Amherst: University of Massachusetts Press, 1982), I contrasted the conservative tradition of the study of time in physics with the study of time as it emerges from a synthesis of time-related understanding from the physical, biological, and behavioral sciences. Finally, my book *Time, the Familiar Stranger* (Amherst: University of Massachusetts Press, 1987) is a cultural vision of the experience and idea of time.

The present book is an expansion of the Founder's Lecture entitled "Change, Permanence, and Human Values," in *Time and Process: The Study of Time VII*, ed. J. T. Fraser and L. Rowell (Madison, Conn.: International Universities Press, 1992), 1–24.

Special applications and ideas of the theory have been explored in many papers, some of which will be cited as needed.

2. Letter to Hester Thrale, 21 September 1773, in *The Letters of Samuel Johnson*, ed. Bruce Redfield, 3 vols. (Princeton, N.J.: Princeton University Press, 1992), 2:78.

3. Plato, *Phaedo*, trans. Hugh Tredennick, in *The Collected Dialogues of Plato*, ed.

Edith Hamilton and Huntington Cairns (Princeton, N.J.: Princeton University Press, 1973), 78d–79a.

4. This is the essence of part 1, question 84, articles 1–8, of the *Summa Theologica* of St. Thomas Aquinas.

5. Cyrano de Bergerac, *Other Worlds,* trans. Geoffrey Strachan (London: New English Library, 1976), 47–48. The mode of the traveler's transportation is interesting. He fastened about him a quantity of bottles filled with dew. As the sun rose, the dew began to rise and transported the man to the moon, where the residents were much surprised, for he was "the first person dressed in bottles they had ever seen" (21).

6. Immanuel Kant, *Critique of Pure Reason,* ed. Norman Kemp Smith (New York: Saint Martin's, 1965), 74.

7. Thomas Hardy, *Far from the Madding Crowd* (New York: Bantam Books, 1967), 150.

8. Wallace Stevens, *Poems by Wallace Stevens,* ed. Samuel French Morse (New York: Random House, 1959), 73.

9. Ludwig Wittgenstein, *Notebooks, 1914–16,* ed. G. H. von Wright and G. E. M. Anscombe (New York: Harper and Row, 1969), 19.

10. Jakob von Uexküll, *Umwelt und Innenwelt der Tiere* (Berlin: Springer Verlag, 1921), 218–19. A good introduction to his idea of the *Umwelt Prinzip* is his paper "A Stroll through the Worlds of Animals and Men: A Picture Book of Invisible Worlds," *Instinctive Behavior,* trans. and ed. Claire H. Schiller (Madison, Conn.: International Universities Press, 1957), 5–80.

11. Horace B. English and Ava Champney English, *A Comprehensive Dictionary of Psychological and Psychoanalytic Terms* (New York: McKay, 1964), s.v. "Umwelt."

12. J. T. Fraser, "Temporal Levels and Reality Testing," *International Journal of Psycho-analysis* 62 (1981): 3–26; quotation on 4.

13. *Noetic* is from the Greek *noetikos,* "mental," related to *noein,* "to think," and *nous,* "the mind."

14. As a part of his work on the development of the human brain, discussed in sec. 1.2, Gerald Edelman described his idea of qualified realism as being "realistic and naturalistic in its assumptions, [but] by its very nature its realism is qualified and conditional. The qualifications result not only from the limits of our sensory systems but also from the nature of the selective systems and the inherent constraints on their capacity to sample from the density of world events" (Edelman, *The Remembered Present: A Biological Theory of Consciousness* [New York: Basic Books, 1989], 255).

15. Isaac Newton, *Sir Isaac Newton's Mathematical Principles of Natural Philosophy and His System of the World,* trans. A. Motte, ed. F. Cajori (Berkeley: University of California Press, 1966), book 3, "Rules of Reasoning in Philosophy," rule 4.

16. For the idea of a closed world without anything outside it, see the discussion on the finite but unbounded universe in Fraser, *Time, the Familiar Stranger,* 256–63.

17. The felicitous phrase "the first signals" is due to Hans Reichenbach; it appears in his book *The Philosophy of Space and Time* (New York: Dover, 1958), 143.

18. For a discussion of order (forms of permanence or being) arising out of pure becoming, see J. T. Fraser, "From Chaos to Conflict," in *Time, Order, Chaos: The Study of Time IX,* ed. J. T. Fraser, M. P. Soulsby, and A. Argyros (Madison, Conn.: International Universities Press, 1998), 3–19.

19. Thomas Mann, *Joseph and His Brothers,* trans. H. T. Lowe-Porter (New York: Knopf, 1976), 3.

20. A. M. Prokhov, ed., *The Great Soviet Encyclopedia* (New York: Macmillan, 1976), s.v. "Hierarchy."

21. M. Hazenwinkel, ed., *Encyclopedia of Mathematics* (Boston: Kluwer, 1995), s.v. "Hierarchy": "A classification of mathematical objects according to the complexity of their definitions."

22. "Hierarchy denotes that Occidental mode of thought which transmuted man's persistent inclination to assert order into a particular conception of the idea of the universe in terms of precisely-arranged levels of existence commonly termed 'degrees'" (Philip P. Wiener, ed., *Dictionary of the History of Ideas* [New York: Scribner's, 1968–73], s.v. "Hierarchy and Order").

23. In Joseph Needham, *Time, the Refreshing River* (London: Allen and Unwin, 1943), 233–72.

24. H. A. Simon concluded his paper "The Architecture of Complexity" (1962) by remarking that on "theoretical grounds we could expect complex systems to be hierarchies in a world in which complexity had to evolve from simplicity. In their dynamics, hierarchies have a property, near decomposability, that greatly simplifies their behavior" (near decomposability means semiautonomy). Reprinted in H. A. Simon, ed., *The Sciences of the Artificial* (Cambridge, Mass.: MIT Press, 1969), 117–18. See also Paul A. Weiss, *Hierarchically Organized Systems in Theory and Practice* (New York: Hafner, 1971); Howard H. Pattee, *Hierarchy Theory: The Challenge of Complex Systems* (New York: Braziller, 1973).

25. Plato, *Meno,* trans. W. K. C. Guthrie, in *The Collected Dialogues,* 72c.

26. Consider, for instance, the statistical (probabilistic) laws of nature. Along the evolution of causation, they first appear on the level of the particle-waves of modern physics. As a way of asserting truth, however, they may already be found in the Book of Numbers. Of a later vintage is the "political arithmetic" of Sir William Petty, a seventeenth-century economist who defined the subject as the art of reasoning by figures about matters that pertain to government (Sir William Petty, *The Petty Papers,* 2 vols. [London: Constable, 1927], 1:193–98). The contemporary science of demography, based on probabilistic truths, became formalized around the middle of the nineteenth century as the record of the mathematical study of populations, of peoples' movements, and of their physical, cultural, and moral conditions. Its methods have been adapted to epidemiology, sociology, genetics, and history, as well as to commerce, warfare, public services, and the study of history. People around the world are treated to statistical claims of truth. Its limitations derive from the necessity that members of a set about whose behavior a statistical claim is made must be assumed to be indistinguishable as far as the subject of inquiry is concerned. The introduction of distinguishability compromises the validity of statistical claims. Americans are familiar with the power of statistical predictions based on the assumption of indistinguishability among them, except as to their voting preferences, from the uncanny success of network predictions of election outcomes based on no more than a small part of the voting records.

For historical examples in the development of this science, see David Smith and Nathan Keyfitz, eds., *Mathematical Demography* (New York: Springer Verlag, 1977).

27. Fraser, "From Chaos to Conflict."

28. For a first attempt to come to grips with the nature of interfaces in a way useful for exploring the hierarchical organization of nature, see J. T. Fraser, "Time's Rites of Passage," in Fraser, *Time as Conflict*, 161–85.

29. Similar epistemic conditions are found within the physical world. Special relativity theory is primarily the law of the atemporal world; quantum theory is the law of the prototemporal world. Although special relativity theory covers aspects of quantum behavior, it is impossible to derive quantum theory from the principles of special relativity: there is no a priori bridge between the Lorentz transformations and Schrödinger's equation. Likewise, it is impossible to derive the laws governing the behavior of massive matter from quantum theory: there is no a priori connection between Schrödinger's equation and Kepler's laws.

30. W. H. Auden, "Progress?" in *Thank You Fog—Last Poems* (New York: Random House, 1974), 18.

31. Among the many proposals on how the human brain ensures the continued integrity of the self and its reasoning power, Gerald Edelman's system of reentrant cortical integration is particularly interesting and powerful. We already encountered his work in sec. 1.2. Feedback, he notes, involves connection along a fixed path and employs previous information for the purpose of control or correction. Reentry occurs in elective systems in which information is not prespecified, varies statistically in parallel channels, and is "a constructive function, not just a corrective one" (Edelman, *The Remembered Present*, 65–67).

32. J. T. Fraser, "Human Temporality in a Nowless Universe," *Time and Society* 1, no. 2 (1992): 159–73. The following remarks from various writers are relevant to the reasoning I gave:

"All the successful equations of physics are symmetrical in time. . . . The future and the past seem physically to be on a completely equal footing" (Roger Penrose, *The Emperor's New Mind: Concerning Computers, Minds, and the Laws of Physics* [New York: Oxford University Press, 1989], 302).

The "sense of Now and the so called 'passage of time' derive their meaning from aspects of reality that cannot be expressed in terms referring to spacetime, which are the terms that physicists ordinarily use" (David Park, "Brain Time and Mind Time," in *Time, Mind, and Behavior,* ed. J. A. Michon and J. L. Jackson [New York: Springer Verlag, 1985], 62).

"Although we are forced to conclude that the laws of physics do not themselves provide a time asymmetry, it is one of the most fundamental aspects of our experience that as a *matter of fact*, the world is asymmetric in time" (P. C. W. Davies, *The Physics of Time Asymmetry* [Berkeley: University of California Press, 1974], 27).

Einstein believed that there is something essential and very important about the now but that whatever it is, it lies outside the realm of science—meaning physics (see P. A. Schilpp, ed., *The Philosophy of Rudolf Carnap* [LaSalle, Ill.: Open Court, 1963], 37).

The same mistake—that of identifying science with physics—has been made by S. W. Hawking in *A Brief History of Time* (New York: Bantam Books, 1988): "The laws of science do not distinguish between the past and the future" (144), and "the laws of science do not distinguish between the forward and backward direction of time" (152).

33. What is and is not intuitively obvious is only partly an evolutionary quality of human thinking. It is also greatly a result of social conditioning embedded in the precepts of a civilization. That the earth moves is not a self-evident truth. But it is so frequently said in daily life that it is often difficult to convince students that an earth-centered view of the world may be a totally legitimate one. The reason a sun-centered model of the world is preferred is not because an earth-centered one is somehow wrong but because by assuming a sun-centered model of the planetary system we may more easily account for a large number of observations. The views of time here advocated are able to accommodate much more of what we know of the world than do the nonevolutionary views of time.

34. What follows is a technical issue.

It has been pointed out that deriving the condition of atemporality from null geodesics, which have no intrinsic metric, neglects the topological time of an inertial observer riding on a photon and hence that the decision "hinges on a philosophical issue as to the nature of time" (C. J. S. Clarke, "Point to Point," *Nature* 306 [1983]: 131). The observation is correct. The decision not to admit topology to null geodesics is made on the basis that topology (past-present-future) can acquire meaning only with the presence of life. But no living organism can ride on a photon. We can imagine ourselves so doing but cannot actually do it. The topology of time is imported into the nonmetric time of the atemporal world from the temporal world. In the language of metaphysics, the lastingness or "being" of pure becoming may be predicated only in the language of an umwelt that is eotemporal or higher, for only in such a language may "being" be given meaning.

I have elected to call the temporality at the foundations of the universe "atemporality" rather than "timelessness" to set it apart from a type of human experience that is usually, though erroneously, described as timelessness (see sec. 5.3). Formally atemporality corresponds to an empty or null set. Physically it is the temporality of absolute chaos. See Fraser, "From Chaos to Conflict."

35. For a summary review see Werner Bergmann, "The Problem of Time in Sociology: An Overview of the Literature on the State of Theory and Research on the Sociology of Time, 1900–82," *Time and Society* 1, no. 1 (1992): 81–134. "Human acts are understood not as movements in an already existing time, but as emerging events that first constitute a present with a past and future horizon." Sociology is interested not in psychological functions "but in the relationship between temporal experience and social roles" (83).

36. Anne Schullenberger Lévy, "America Discovered a Second Time: French Perceptions of American Notions of Time from Tocqueville to Laboulaye," Ph.D. diss., Department of History, Yale University, 1995, 23–24.

37. In the second edition of *The Natural Philosophy of Time* (Oxford: Clarendon, 1980), G. J. Whitrow contrasts the idea of an evolution of time along a scale of qualitatively different temporalities with the idea followed in his classical work: "The view adopted in this book . . . is that at all levels time is essentially the same, although certain aspects of it become increasingly significant the more complex the nature of the particular object or system studied" (375).

38. Fraser, *Time as Conflict*, 161–85.

39. This is as much of a surprise as was the discovery by Georg Cantor in 1873

that infinity has a structure, that not all infinite sets contain the same number of objects.

40. The evolutionary model of time "does what most genuinely innovative theories do: it does not simply refute old theories, but rather situates them within a larger, more inclusive context. By reformulating terms with which philosophy can address the issue of time, and by doing so using concepts stemming from the natural sciences, the social sciences, and the arts and humanities, [it has] done much to place the study of time on a new interdisciplinary footing that promises to solve many heretofore intransigent problems, to open the door to new research, and, with a measure of tragedy . . . to generate new, higher order problems and paradoxes" (Alexander Argyros, in *Encyclopedia of Time,* ed. S. L. Macey [New York: Garland, 1994], s.v. "Fraser, J. T."

41. Argued in J. T. Fraser, "The Problems of Exporting Faust," in *Time, Science, and Society in China and the West: The Study of Time V,* ed. J. T. Fraser, N. Lawrence, and F. C. Haber (Amherst: University of Massachusetts Press, 1986), 1–20.

42. Jean-Jacques Rousseau, *Of the Social Contract,* trans. and annotated by Charles Sherover (New York: Harper and Row, 1984), 84.

43. William Shakespeare, *Troilus and Cressida,* in *The Complete Works of William Shakespeare,* ed. W. J. Craig (London: Oxford University Press, 1962), act 3, sc. 2, l. 5.

44. Dylan Thomas, "Fern Hill," in *The Poems of Dylan Thomas* (New York: New Directions, 1971), 195.

45. Sigmund Freud, *Beyond the Pleasure Principle,* trans. James Strachey (New York: Norton, 1961), 36.

46. "Du selber machst die Zeit: das Uhrwerk sind die Sinnen: / Hemmst du die Unruh nur, so ist die Zeit von hinnen" (*Angelus Silesius: Eine Auswahl aus dem "Cherubinischen Wandersman"* [Berlin: Union Verlag, n.d.], 111).

47. St. Augustine, *The Confessions of Saint Augustine,* trans. E. B. Pusey (New York: Modern Library, 1949), book 2, sec. 14, p. 253.

48. Shakespeare, *As You Like It,* in *The Complete Works,* act 2, sc. 7, l. 26.

49. Fraser, "From Chaos to Conflict."

50. Translated by Joseph Needham in his *History of Embryology* (Cambridge: Cambridge University Press, 1959), 93.

51. Michael Polanyi, "Faith and Reason," in *Scientific Thought and Social Reality: Essays by Michael Polanyi,* ed. Fred Schwartz (New York: International Universities Press, 1974), 128–29.

THREE: THE MANY KINDS OF TRUTH

1. Alexander J. Argyros, "The Minimal Epistemological and Ontological Conditions for a Theory of Systematic Interdisciplinarity," *Philosophica* 48, no. 2 (1991): 57–74; quotation on 72.

2. Samuel Johnson, *Dictionary: A Modern Selection,* ed. E. L. McAdam (New York: Pantheon, 1964), 7.

3. John Stuart Mill, *A System of Logic,* 5 vols., ed. J. M. Robson (Toronto: University of Toronto Press, 1956), 2:679, 685.

4. For an appreciation of the psychodynamics of recoverable but generally unnoticed meanings of words, with illustrations from fifteen languages, see Theodore Thass-Tienemann, *The Subconscious Language* (New York: Washington Square, 1967). For an application of these ideas to a specialized field of knowing, see Lewis Rowell, "The Subconscious Language of Musical Time," in *Music Theory Spectrum* 1 (1979): 96–106.

5. For guidance in the Sanskrit material I am obliged to Prof. Lewis Rowell.

6. See Heinrich Zimmer, *Philosophies of India*, Bollingen Series, vol. 26 (Princeton, N.J.: Princeton University Press, 1967), 160–69.

7. Reuben Alcalay, ed., *The Complete Hebrew-English Dictionary* (Ramat-Gan, Jerusalem: Massada, 1963), s.v. "Truth."

8. *Encyclopaedia Judaica* (Jerusalem: Macmillan, 1972), s.v. "Truth."

9. The Japanese etymology brings to mind the apocryphal tradition that St. Peter was crucified head downward.

10. For these interpretations of Japanese and Chinese equivalents of *truth* I am indebted to Prof. Masaki Miyake, of Meiji University, Tokyo; Prof. David Loy, of Bunkyo University, Chigasaki; Prof. Nathan Sivin, of the University of Pennsylvania at Philadelphia; and Dr. Jack W. Chen, of the University of Michigan. I am solely responsible for mistakes introduced through my attempts to combine and consolidate their careful remarks.

11. St. Augustine, "On Free Will," in *Augustine: Earlier Writings*, ed. and trans. J. H. S. Burleigh (Philadelphia: Westminster, 1953), 154.

12. Ibid., 190.

13. Johannes Kepler, *Gesammelte Werke*, ed. Walter von Dyck and Max Caspar, 20 vols. (Munich: C. H. Beck'sche Verlagsbuchhandlung, 1938–75), 8:30n.8, 6:223.

14. Ibid., 6:219.

15. Albert Einstein, "Autobiographical Notes," in *Albert Einstein, Philosopher-Scientist*, ed. P. A. Schilpp (New York: Tudor, 1949), 7.

16. Benjamin Gal-Or, *Cosmology, Physics, and Philosophy* (New York: Springer Verlag, 1981), 40. Gauge fields are associated with particles that carry the forces of nature. "Salam's elementary particles" is an alternative way of saying "gauge fields."

17. Nathan Sivin, "Why the Scientific Revolution Did Not Take Place in China— or Didn't It?" *Chinese Science* 5 (1982): 60.

18. Max Weber, *Protestant Ethics and the Spirit of Capitalism*, trans. Talcott Parsons (New York: Scribner's, 1904), 249n.145.

19. The correspondence on astral geometry may be found in Carl Friedrich Gauss, *Gesammelte Werke*, ed. Martin Brendel, 14 vols. (Berlin: Springer Verlag, 1910), 8:177–82, 10 (part 2): 31–35.

20. Karen Wynn, "Addition and Subtraction by Human Infants," *Nature* 358 (27 Aug. 1992): 749–50.

21. Konrad Lorenz, "Kants Lehre vom aprioristischen in Licht gegenwärtigen Biologie," *Blätter für Deutsche Philosophie* 15 (1941): 94–125.

22. This sketch of the development of number knowledge and the self follows those by J. H. Flavell, P. H. Miller, and S. A. Miller in their *Cognitive Development*, 3d ed. (Englewood Cliffs, N.J.: Prentice-Hall, 1993), 100–130 (number skills), 204–8 (selfhood). For guidance in this matter I am indebted to Prof. Richard A. Block.

23. Odd numbers, represented by "one," were said to have had "masculine virtue and [were] proper to the Celestial Gods." Even numbers were "indigent and imperfect, and Female" (*Pythagoras: His Life and Teachings, Being a Photographic Facsimile of the Ninth Section of the 1687 Edition of "The History of Philosophy," by Thomas Stanley* [Los Angeles: Philosophical Research Society, n.d.], 524).

24. Thass-Tienemann, *The Subconscious Language*, 15–16 and passim. There are cultures in our own days whose languages use counting based on two; see the delightful chapter "The Counter Culture" in J. D. Barrow, *Pi in the Sky: Counting, Thinking, and Being* (Oxford: Clarendon, 1992).

25. Baruch Spinoza, *Ethics*, trans. Samuel Shirley (Indianapolis, Hackett, 1992), proposal item 44, "On the Nature and Origin of Mind."

26. Baruch Spinoza, *Improvement of Understanding* (Washington, D.C.: M. Walter Dinn, 1901), 3.

27. Immanuel Kant, *Kant's Inaugural Dissertation and Early Writings on Space*, trans. John Handyside (LaSalle, Ill.: Open Court, 1929), sec. 3, para. 14, item 5.

28. Kepler had to defend this degrading of perfection and eternity. In a 1605 letter to the Danish astronomer Longomontanus he wrote, "You accused me of having sinned with my 'ovals,' . . . yet you hold the ancients faultless for their 'spirals' [epicycles and helices used to describe planetary orbits]. If my ovals are a cartful of dung, the spirals of the ancients are whole stables full of dung" (Kepler, "Briefe," in *Gesammelte Werke*, 15:141–42).

29. From Russell's *Introduction to Mathematical Philosophy* (New York: Macmillan, 1919); reprinted in *The Basic Writings of Bertrand Russell, 1903–1959*, ed. R. E. Egner and L. E. Denonn (New York: Simon and Schuster, 1961), 175.

30. Consider as an example the liar's paradox, attributed to Moiletus, a fourth-century B.C. Athenian philosopher:

A man asserts, "I always lie." He is either telling the truth or lying. If he is telling the truth, then his claim is lie. If he is lying, then his claim is true. It follows that the truthfulness of the proposition "I always lie" is undecidable.

Russell would rephrase the claim by introducing a hierarchical structuring. "There is a proposition which I am affirming [he called this a first-order proposition] and which is false [this is a second-order proposition]" ("Mathematical Logic as Based on the Theory of Types" [1908], reprinted in Bertrand Russell, *Logic and Knowledge* [New York: Macmillan, 1956], 59–102; quotation on 61). In other words, he removed the self-referential quality of the claim "I always lie" by introducing a new, higher-order observer entitled to remark that the claim of the first-order proposition is false.

For background see Morris Kline's masterful *Mathematics: The Loss of Certainty* (New York: Oxford University Press, 1980), 216–44.

31. John von Neumann, *Theory of Self-Reproducing Automata*, ed. and completed by A. W. Burns (Urbana: University of Illinois Press, 1969), 47–48, 51.

32. His method was one of arithmetization. Gödel reduced formal logical axioms (which one may mistrust) to arithmetic ones (which one can trust because people trust numerals). He then defined the different variables and operations in terms of numbers and carried out his arguments in the form of calculations that were ultimately changed back to conclusions in metamathematical language. See the

thirty-two-page introduction by R. B. Braithwaite to Kurt Gödel's book *On Formally Undecidable Propositions of "Principia Mathematica" and Related Systems,* trans. B. Meltzer (Edinburgh: Oliver and Boyd, 1962).

33. Kline, *Mathematics,* 228.

34. John Fowles, *Mantissa* (Boston: Little, Brown, 1982), 149.

35. The emergence of the unpredictably new in nature must be sharply distinguished from the degrees of statistical unpredictability that govern prototemporal processes. Among the canonical forms of causation, statistical unpredictability is a hallmark of the most primitive lawfulness that arose from the Big Bang (see the subsection on probabilistic truth), whereas the unpredictably new is a "feed-through," as it were, from the ever-present absolute chaos at the foundations of the universe (see the subsection on the atemporal world of pure becoming).

36. From Einstein's 1921 lecture entitled "Geometry and Experience." It appeared as part 2 of his *Sidelights on Relativity,* trans. G. B. Jeffery and W. Perrett (London: Methuen, 1922), 28.

37. This view of the creation and usefulness of number lends substance to L. E. J. Brouwer's idea of intuitionism, developed early in the twentieth century. The term stands for the belief that the elements of mathematics arise from the contrast between current awareness and past experience. Obviously this demands the human sense of time (see his "Consciousness, Philosophy, and Mathematics," in *Proceedings of the Tenth International Congress of Philosophy,* 2, ed. E. W. Beth, H. J. Pos, and J. H. A. Hollak [Amsterdam: North Holland, 1949], 1235–49).

There is usually a difference between what one anticipates and what happens, sometimes an immense difference. The conflicts so generated are part and parcel of the existential tensions of life. It is these tensions that may be decreased through the use of numbers. Count the heads of those you love; if in the evening the number is the same as it was in the morning, sleep will be sweeter.

38. Kline, *Mathematics,* 277.

39. In Ernest Jones, *The Life and Work of Sigmund Freud,* 2 vols. (New York: Basic Books, 1953), 2:419.

40. J. R. Lucas, "Minds, Machines, and Gödel," *Philosophy* 36 (1961): 112–27.

41. In Isaac Newton, *Sir Isaac Newton's Mathematical Principles of Natural Philosophy and His System of the World,* trans A. Motte, ed. F. Cajori (Berkeley: University of California Press, 1966), xiii.

42. *English Hymnal,* no. 104. The idea is much older: it is that of Psalm 148.

43. Joseph Needham, *Science and Civilization in China,* vol. 2, *History of Scientific Thought* (Cambridge: Cambridge University Press, 1956), 582–83; but see the whole chapter, "Human Law and the Laws of Nature in China and the West," 518–83.

44. Discussed in J. T. Fraser, "The Problems of Exporting Faust," in *Time, Science, and Society in China and the West: The Study of Time V,* ed. J. T. Fraser, N. Lawrence, and F. C. Haber (Amherst: University of Massachusetts Press, 1986), 1–20.

45. In quantum theory there is "no mention of particles or orbits; gone is anything that can be described as a process in space and time. Instead, the electron is an entity that produces certain effects, nothing more. It is more like a verb than a noun. It is hard to describe the new formalism without ascending to technicalities, but its most characteristic feature is that the numbers it uses to designate the phys-

ical states of an atom are whole numbers. Nothing varies continuously as the position of a moving particle does; everything jumps, but not in the space and time we know" (David Park, *The How and the Why: An Essay on the Origins and Development of Physical Theory* [Princeton, N.J.: Princeton University Press, 1988], 318).

46. Shakespeare, *Macbeth*, in *The Complete Works of William Shakespeare*, ed. W. J. Craig (London: Oxford University Press, 1962), act 1, sc. 3, ll. 58–70. The insecurity of our species in the face of "imperfect speakers" is evident in a mistrust of conditions that are likelihoods rather than certainties. "When I was a child / world was better spot / some things were so / some things were not. / Now that I'm a man / things have changed a lot / some things nearly so / some things nearly not" (from the Rodgers and Hammerstein musical play *The King and I*).

47. See J. T. Fraser, "From Chaos to Conflict," in *Time, Order, Chaos: The Study of Time IX*, ed. J. T. Fraser, M. P. Soulsby, and A. Argyros (Madison, Conn.: International Universities Press, 1998), 3–19. This paper locates deterministic chaos in the evolutionary history of time and causation and traces the evolution of predictability from the primeval chaos of pure becoming.

48. See the relevant sections in H.-O. Peitgen, Hartmut Jürgens, and Dietmar Saupe, *Chaos and Fractals: New Frontiers of Science* (New York: Springer Verlag, 1992).

49. G. S. Kirk and J. E. Raven, *The Presocratic Philosophers* (Cambridge: at the University Press, 1975), 294–95.

50. For a summary of contemporary views on the paradox of the flying arrow, see G. J. Whitrow, *The Natural Philosophy of Time*, 2d ed. (Oxford: Clarendon, 1980), 190–200.

51. Albert Einstein, "The Foundation of the General Theory of Relativity" (1916), in H. A. Lorentz, A. Einstein, H. Minkowski, and H. Weyl, *The Principle of Relativity* (New York: Dover, 1923), 113.

52. The conventional measure of motion is velocity, defined as $v = s/t$, where s is the distance traveled during an interval t of time: so many kilometers per hour. The relativistic measure of motion is the ratio v/c, a dimensionless number, where v is the speed of an object with respect to the observer measuring it. The symbol c is a constant of nature—the speed of light—which is the same numeral for all locations in the universe and all observers, whether they themselves are moving along a straight line or doing somersaults. The new number for the speed of a car traveling at 100 km/hour (as I would measure it, standing along a road), is 0.000 000 009; for a rifle bullet it is 0.000 003. The measure of the speed of the earth with respect to the galaxy at large is 0.000 1.

53. For a delightful and clear summary of quarks and other particles, see Park, *The How and the Why*, 363–71.

54. P. C. W. Davies, *The Forces of Nature* (Cambridge: Cambridge University Press, 1979), 215.

55. That life itself originated in silicon clay, with the silicon later replaced by carbon in a "genetic takeover," has been suggested and discussed by Graham Cairns-Smith in *Genetic Takeover and the Mineral Origins of Life* (Cambridge: Cambridge University Press, 1982).

56. Ernst Mayr, *Toward a New Philosophy of Biology: Observations of an Evolutionist* (Cambridge, Mass.: Harvard University Press, 1988), 45.

57. "Breaking the symmetry" is a phrase often used in writings about time in physics, whence it was copied by other disciplines. But the term is seldom if ever explained. It was borrowed from mathematical physics, where *symmetry* describes the extent to which phenomena remain invariant (in terms of the equations describing them) under changes of the system. Absolute chaos is said to have perfect symmetry because it is completely lawless from all conceivable points of observation. As regularities (forms of permanence or being) emerge during inorganic evolution, such as the coming about of particles from radiation and, later, the formation of massive matter from particles, mathematical physics speaks about the breaking of symmetries.

58. T. S. Eliot, "Burnt Norton," in *Four Quartets* (New York: Harcourt, Brace, and World, 1971), 16.

59. On logic that depends on the direction of time, see J. T. Fraser, "Time and the Paradox of Unexpected Truth," *XIV Internationale Kongress für Philosophie*, Akten 4 (1968): 395–401.

60. Here I represent the thought of S. G. F. Brandon. His writings may be entered through *Creation Legends of the Ancient Near East* (London: Hodder and Stoughton, 1963); see "The Dawning Concept of Creativity," 1–13.

61. In a review of J. P. King's book *The Art of Mathematics* (New York: Plenum, 1992), the reviewer remarked that King "shares physicist Eugene Wigner's puzzlement over the 'unreasonable effectiveness' of mathematics. This puzzlement puzzles me. Not only is the Universe mathematically structured, it is made entirely of mathematics. Matter consists of fields and their particles, which are not made of anything except equations. What is so mysterious about the application of these equations to a Universe from which our minds, in turn made of mathematics, originally extracted them?" (*Nature* 358 [2 July 1992]: 28–29).

62. Immanuel Kant, *On History*, Lewis White Beck (New York: Bobbs-Merrill, 1963), 11.

63. G. W. F. Hegel, *Philosophy of History*, J. Sibree (New York: Dover, 1956), 457.

64. Here are examples of facts that changed when hypotheses changed.

— In Christian chronology Christ was born in A.D.1, until nineteenth-century high criticism revised the theoretical framework. Henceforth he was born in 4 A.D.

— The facts that led to the collapse of the Roman Empire have never been settled to everyone's satisfaction. Those "facts" have been changing with the interpreter.

— Until the Copernican theory, planets followed epicyclic orbits.

— The details of the assassination of John F. Kennedy will continue to give rise to different hypotheses and with them different interpretations of facts until people tire of the affair.

See also the discussion of terms, including "facts" of history, in Arnold Toynbee, *The Study of History XII* (Oxford: Oxford University Press, 1964), 229–35.

65. Leonard Krieger, *Time's Reasons: Philosophies of History Old and New* (Chicago: University of Chicago Press, 1989).

66. Sophocles, *Antigone*, tr. Elizabeth Wyckoff, in *Greek Tragedies*, ed. David Grene and Richmond Lattimore, 4 vols. (Chicago: University of Chicago Press, 1960), vol. 1, ll. 611–13.

67. Krieger, *Time's Reasons*, 52.

68. Ibid., 10.

69. Ralph Waldo Emerson, "Circles," in *Essays by Ralph Waldo Emerson, First Series* (Boston: Houghton Mifflin, 1903), 302.

70. Huw Price, *Facts and Functions of Truth* (New York: Blackwell, 1989), 4. Price gives an answer in terms of the functions of truth in the linguistic community.

FOUR: GOOD AND EVIL

1. I am following the definition of "historical times" suggested by E. J. Bickerman in his essay "The Ancient Near East," in *The Columbia History of the World*, ed. J. A. Garrat and Peter Gay (New York: Harper and Row, 1972), 49–94.

2. Ludwig Feuerbach, *Principles of the Philosophy of the Future*, trans. M. H. Vogel (Indianapolis: Bobbs-Merrill, 1966), 71.

3. Thomas Mann, *Joseph and His Brothers*, trans. H. T. Lowe-Porter (New York: Knopf, 1976), 3.

4. "The time of origin of reality [the time when a particular event is believed to have taken place] has a paradigmatic value and function; that is why man seeks to reactualize it periodically by means of appropriate rituals. . . . The periodic reactualization of the creative acts . . . *in illo tempore* constitutes the sacred calendar" (Mircea Eliade, *The Sacred and the Profane: The Nature of Religion* [New York: Harper and Row, 1961], 85).

5. T. S. Eliot, "Little Gidding," in *Four Quartets* (New York: Harcourt, Brace, and World, 1971), 51; these words are engraved on Eliot's tomb.

6. Bronislav Malinowski, "Magic, Science, and Religion," in *Science, Religion and Reality*, ed. Joseph Needham (New York: Braziller, 1955), 23–88.

7. Rudolf Otto, *The Idea of the Holy: An Inquiry into the Non Rational Factor in the Idea of the Divine and Its Relation to the Rational*, trans. J. W. Harvey, 2d ed. (Oxford: Oxford University Press, 1957).

8. S. G. F. Brandon, *History, Time, and Deity* (Manchester: Manchester University Press, 1965); see also his "Time and the Destiny of Man," in *The Voices of Time: A Cooperative Survey of Man's Views of Time as Expressed by the Sciences and by the Humanities*, ed. J. T. Fraser, 2d ed. (Amherst: University of Massachusetts Press, 1981), 140–57.

9. S. G. F. Brandon, *Man and His Destiny in the Great Religions* (Manchester: Manchester University Press, 1962), 384–85.

10. Hesiod, "Works and Days," in *The Homeric Hymns and Homerica*, trans. H. G. Evelyn-White (Cambridge, Mass.: Harvard University Press, 1967), 145.

11. Plato, *Timaeus*, trans. Benjamin Jowett, in *The Collected Dialogues of Plato*, ed. Edith Hamilton and Huntington Cairns (Princeton, N.J.: Princeton University Press, 1973), 29a.

12. Ibid. 30a.

13. On this point see John Gunnell, *Political Philosophy and Time* (Middletown, Conn.: Wesleyan University Press, 1968), 15.

14. Plato, *Republic*, trans. Paul Shorey, in *The Collected Dialogues*, 608e.

15. Plato, *Phaedo*, trans. Hugh Tredennick, in *The Collected Dialogues*, 67 and passim.

16. Anne Fremantle, ed., *The Papal Encyclicals in Their Historical Context* (New York: New American Library, 1963), 298.

17. According to whispered tradition known to me from childhood, Saint Joseph was a carpenter who made crosses for the Romans. This age-old hearsay is woven into Nikos Kazantzakis's *Last Temptation of Christ*, trans. P. A. Bien (New York: Simon and Schuster, 1960).

18. D. H. Lawrence, *The Rainbow* (New York: Modern Library, 1915), 264–65.

19. Immanuel Kant, *Foundations of the Metaphysics of Morals*, trans. Lewis White Beck (New York: Liberal Arts Press, 1959), 39.

20. Jeremy Bentham, *An Introduction to the Principles of Morals and Legislation* (New York: Doubleday, 1961), 7.

21. Joseph Needham, "Science and China's Influence on the World," in *The Legacy of China*, ed. Raymond Dawson (Oxford: Oxford University Press, 1964), 234–308; quotation on 307–8.

22. See Kristofer Schipper and Wang Hsiu-huei, "Progressive and Regressive Time Cycles in Taoist Ritual," in *Time, Science, and Society in China and the West: The Study of Time V*, ed. J. T. Fraser, N. Lawrence, and F. C. Haber (Amherst: University of Massachusetts Press, 1986), 185–205.

23. Both quotations from Lao-tzu, *Tao-te Ching*, trans. D. C. Lau (London: Penguin Books, 1983), nos. 8 and 66.

24. S. G. F. Brandon, *A Dictionary of Comparative Religions* (New York: Scribner's, 1970), s.v. "Ethics."

25. The use of numbers in the chronology of Hindu theology demonstrates the insignificance of passage. The life of the Brahma is 100 Brahma years, each with 360 Brahma days. During each Brahma day Vishnu, the preserver and protector of the world, winks 1,000 times in his dream. Each time his eyelid opens, a universe appears and lasts for 12,000 divine years. As he closes his eyes, the universe vanishes. Each divine year consists of 360 human years. Multiplying it together, this amounts to $155{,}520 \times 10^9$ human years for a Brahma lifetime. When Vishnu's dream ends, the lotus in which he reposes closes and one Brahma lifetime ends. As Vishnu's dream resumes, the lotus once again opens and the new Brahma begins its mission. This numerical exercise helps to negate time by eternity.

26. Brandon, *Man and His Destiny*, 301–34.

27. Mircea Eliade, *Cosmos and History* (New York: Harper and Row, 1959), 12.

28. Charles Darwin, *"The Origin of Species" and "The Descent of Man"* (New York: The Modern Library, n.d.); see esp. 471–95 but also the related chapters. The following quotation is on 472.

29. Ibid., 484.

30. Ibid., 473.

31. Ibid., 489.

32. Ibid., 495.

33. In James Paradis and G. C. Williams, eds., *"Evolution and Ethics," with New Essays on Its Victorian and Sociobiological Context* (Princeton, N.J.: Princeton University Press, 1989), 107.

34. Ibid., 62.

35. Ibid., 109.

36. Ibid., 53.

37. Ibid., 111.

38. Ibid., 117.

39. Sociobiology defined its concern as the comparative study of social organization and behavior in animals and man inferred through an understanding of the
genetic basis of evolutionary biology. Sociobiologists search for all those aspects of
behavior by which an individual, of whatever species, increases its reproductive
fitness by taking advantage of the society of which it is a member. The goal is to
identify the manner in which the genotype (the genetic makeup of the fertilized
egg) develops into a phenotype (such as the human body) that behaves as a member of a society. As general reference, see E. O. Wilson, *Sociobiology: The New Synthesis* (Cambridge, Mass.: Belknap/Harvard University Press, 1975).

40. For a critique, see J. T. Fraser, "Temporal Levels: Sociobiological Aspects of a
Fundamental Synthesis," *Journal of Social and Biological Structures* 1 (1978): 339–55.

41. "Perfect societies, if we can be so bold as to define them as societies that lack
conflict and possess the highest degree of altruism and coordination, are most likely
to evolve where all members are genetically identical" (Wilson, *Sociobiology*, 314).

42. Since an altruistic animal usually loses something in the process—food, advantages, or even life—the following question arises: how did such behavior evolve?
How was it selected for and how is it maintained, considering that natural selection
favors the fittest? An answer comes from neo-Darwinism, which replies that although
natural selection works on the individual, it ultimately targets the genetic traits
shared by all members of a species. To improve the genotype, natural selection works
on the phenotype. If the target of selection is enlarged to include the genes of kith
and kin, an individual may enhance the evolutionary success of the group by sacrificing itself for the benefit of others. An example is provided by the sterile worker castes in colonial invertebrates. Why should a nonreproducing individual preferentially survive and its caste flourish? The answer is that by doing what they do
(work), even though they do not reproduce, they help to maintain certain genetic
traits that they themselves carry and that are served by their conduct.

43. Wilson, *Sociobiology*, 380.

44. Ibid., 380. This entomological model of ethics has been criticized for favoring political conservatism through a form of social Darwinism. The opposite is the
case: it has political affinity with the communism of a human anthill rather than
with obdurate individualism.

45. Kobo Abé, *The Woman in the Dunes* (New York: Vintage Books, 1964), 51.

46. Martin C. Raff, "Social Controls on Cell Survival and Cell Death," *Nature* 356
(2 Apr. 1992): 397–400.

47. Leviticus 17:14.

48. The reader may wish to look at Tenniel's drawing of the Mad Hatter's tea party
in *Alice in Wonderland*. The glirarium has been turned into a teapot into which the
Mad Hatter and the March Hare are trying to insert the Dormouse, head first.

49. Mosleh Od-din Sa'di, *Gulistan; or, the Rose Garden of Sa'di*, trans. Edward Re-
hatsek (New York: G. P. Putnam, 1965).

50. Plato, *Symposium*, trans. Michael Joyce, in *The Collected Dialogues*, 192d–93b.

51. "If a male is about to spend considerable time and effort in helping his mate

to rear the young he ought to (in evolutionary terms) check carefully that the young carries his genes. . . . The female herself is not necessarily averse to infidelity" (John Krebs, "Suspicious Husbands," *Nature* 262 [15 July 1976]: 177).

52. Wilson, *Sociobiology*, 560.

53. Ibid., 562.

54. D. H. Lawrence, *The Complete Poems*, ed. Vivian de Sola Pinto and Warren Roberts (New York: Penguin Books, 1977), 363.

55. "Die hohe Seele, die sich mir verpfändet, / Die haben sie mir pfiffig weggepascht. / Bei wem soll ich mich nun beklagen? / Wer schafft mir mein erworbnes Recht?" (The noble soul that pledged itself to me, was craftily snatched from me. To whom may I now complain? Who would restore to me what I lawfully own?) (Johann Wolfgang Goethe, *Faust*, part 2, ll. 11830–33).

56. *Tao-te Ching*, no. 6, in Joseph Needham, *Three Masks of the Tao: A Chinese Corrective for Maleness, Monarchy, and Militarism in Theology* (London: Teilhard Centre, 1979), 14; translation by Needham.

57. W. B. Yeats, "Crazy Jane Talks with the Bishop," in *The Collected Poems of W. B. Yeats* (New York: Macmillan, 1956), 255.

58. D. B. Dickson, *The Dawn of Belief: Religion in the Upper Paleolithic Southwestern Europe* (Tucson: University of Arizona Press, 1990), 197.

59. "Trust not their life, and respect not their labour. For better is one that feareth God than a thousand ungodly children" (Eccl. 16:1–4).

60. Plato, *Laws*, trans. A. E. Taylor, in *The Collected Dialogues*, 721c.

61. On this point see Angus McLaren, *A History of Contraception from Antiquity to the Present Day* (London: Basil Blackwell, 1990).

62. Here is an unrefined version of a well-known Mother Goose rhyme: "There was an old woman and she lived in a shoe, / She had so many children she didn't know what to do; / She crumm'd 'em some porridge without any bread; / And she borrowed a beetle, and she knoc's 'em o' the head" (a beetle is a heavy wooden hammer) (W. S. Baring-Gould and Cecil Baring-Gould, *The Annotated Mother Goose* [New York: Bramhall, 1962], rhyme 87).

63. Barbara Tuchman, *A Distant Mirror: The Calamitous 14th Century* (New York: Ballantine Books, 1978), 49–53; see also Bette P. Goldstone, "Views of Childhood in Children's Literature over Time," *Language Arts* 63, no. 8 (1986): 791–98.

64. Tuchman, *A Distant Mirror*, 50, 52.

65. John Boswell, *The Kindness of Strangers: The Abandonment of Children in Western Europe from Late Antiquity to the Renaissance* (New York: Pantheon, 1988).

66. Ibid., 432.

67. Ibid., 113.

68. Ibid., 238–39. The practice reminds one of the Turkish Janissaries, who were Christian children kidnapped by the Turks during their rule of southern Europe, indoctrinated as Moslems, prevented from marrying, and then organized into a ruthless fighting force.

69. Ricardo J. Quinones, *The Renaissance Discovery of Time* (Cambridge, Mass.: Harvard University Press, 1972), 17; see also his article in *Encyclopedia of Time*, ed. S. L. Macey (New York: Garland, 1994), s.v. "Renaissance."

70. Boswell, *Kindness of Strangers*, 432. The extensive literature on child abandon-

ment, no less than the motif of child abandonment in fiction, demonstrates a fear well grounded in reality.

71. Ibid., 433–34.

72. Gerard Piel, "West Is Distant Mirror to China's Infant Death," letter to the editor, *New York Times*, 27 January 1996.

73. The ideal of natural law must be distinguished from the definition of the sense of justice. What I claim is that every human has a sense of justice but—an important "but"—there is no agreement on what specific deeds are right or wrong.

74. See Joseph Needham's brilliant essay "Human Law and the Laws of Nature," in *Technology, Science, and Art: Common Ground* (London: Hatfield College of Technology, 1961), 3–27.

75. Arthur Koestler, *Darkness at Noon*, trans. Daphne Hardy (New York: Modern Library, 1941), 257.

76. In John Chapman, ed., *Theatre '56* (New York: Random House, 1956), 149.

77. Jorge Luis Borges, *Selected Poems, 1923–1967*, ed. N. T. Di Giovanni (New York: Dell, 1972), 120–23.

78. Carl von Clausewitz, *On War*, ed. and trans. Michael Howard and Peter Paret (Princeton, N.J.: Princeton University Press, 1984), 87.

79. John Laffin, *Brassey's Battles: 3,500 Years of Conflict, Campaigns and Wars from A-Z* (London: Brassey Defence Publishers, 1986). This dictionary, as do many others of related purpose, records the earliest known battle as being the (first) battle of Megiddo in 1479 B.C., signaling the establishment of the Egyptian empire in Asia. That battle survives in the word *Armageddon*, "the hill of Megiddo."

80. Gabriel Schreiber, Sofia Avissar, Zeev Tzahor, and Numrod Grisaru, "Rhythms of War," *Nature* 352 (1991): 574–75.

81. For a general survey see John Keegan, *A History of Warfare* (New York: Knopf, 1993).

82. Barbara Tuchman, *The March of Folly* (New York: Knopf, 1984), 384, 387.

83. Sigmund Freud, *The Standard Edition of the Complete Psychological Works*, ed. James Strachey, 24 vols. (London: Hogarth, 1964), 22:197–215.

84. Clausewitz, *On War*, 75.

85. Freud, *Standard Edition*, 22:205.

86. Ibid., 22:209.

87. Ibid., 22:211.

88. Wilson, *Sociobiology*, 254.

89. Ibid., 255.

90. Vera Brittain, *Testament of Youth* (El Cerrito, Calif.: Seaview Books, 1980), 291–92.

91. For an image of this phase, see Kathe Kollwitz's engraving "The Carmagnole" and its caption in J. T. Fraser, *Of Time, Passion, and Knowledge: Reflections on the Strategy of Existence*, 2d ed. (Princeton, N.J.: Princeton University Press, 1990 [1975]), 392–93.

92. I am following the definition of cultural process proposed by E. B. Tylor in *Primitive Culture*, 2 vols. (New York: Harper and Row, 1958), 1:1.

93. Fraser, "Temporal Levels," 339–55. By *linguistic inertia* is meant "the tendency of language and, by extension, the tendency of the total human communication

network, including art and artifact, to resist change in the direction of the cultural process" (350).

94. Joseph Vining, *The Authoritative and the Authoritarian* (Chicago: University of Chicago Press, 1986), 90–91.

95. Sigmund Freud, *Civilization and Its Discontents*, trans. James Strachey (New York: Norton, 1962), 81.

96. Tertullian, *Tertullian*, trans. Rudolph Arbesmann, Sr. Emily Joseph Daly, and Edwin A. Quain (Washington, D.C.: Catholic University of America Press, 1950), 125 (apologeticum 50).

97. As a young boy I was regularly a horrified yet willing witness to the slaughtering of the year's family pig a few days before Christmas. Since I personally knew the pigs from the day they were born, I could hear in their desperate squeals a call to their mother and to me, their friend, who had forsaken them.

It is a custom among Greek fishermen who spear octopuses to tear or gouge out the eyes before killing them underwater. It is my guess that this is their way of preventing those intelligent animals from looking at their murderers with accusing eyes. The custom is akin to that of placing a bag on the heads of people to be executed so that the executioner will not have to live with the memory of accusing looks. This speculation is consistent with the high degree of innervation of the brain for the reading of facial features.

98. Yeats, "Into the Twilight," in *Collected Poems*, 56.

99. T. H. Clutton-Brock and G. A. Parker, "Punishment in Animal Societies," *Nature* 373 (1995): 209–16.

100. Steven A. Frank, "Mutual Policing and Repression of Competition in the Evolution of Cooperative Groups," *Nature* 377 (1995): 520–22; see also the editorial comments on this article in the same issue, 478.

101. James Russell Lowell, "The Present Crisis," in *The Poetical Works of James Russell Lowell* (Boston: Houghton Mifflin, 1890), 68.

102. Both communism and nazism were Platonic in their idealism, taking on themselves the task of defining ultimate moral values. But the "final conflict" of the communist International or the "final solution" of Hitler's Germany did not turn out to be final.

103. Isabel Allende, *The Infinite Plan* (New York: HarperCollins, 1993), 379.

FIVE: THE BEAUTIFUL AND THE UGLY

1. W. B. Yeats, "The Cat and the Moon," in *The Collected Poems of W. B. Yeats* (New York: Macmillan, 1956), 164.

2. S. G. F. Brandon, *History, Time, and Deity: A Historical and Comparative Study of the Conception of Time in Religious Thought and Practice* (Manchester: Manchester University Press, 1965), 15–18.

3. Homer, *The Iliad*, trans. A. T. Murray (Cambridge, Mass.: Harvard University Press), ll. 478–617.

4. Plato, *Symposium*, trans. Michael Joyce, in *The Collected Dialogues of Plato*, ed. Edith Hamilton and Huntington Cairns (Princeton, N.J.: Princeton University Press, 1973), 201d.

5. Ibid., 210b–11c.

6. Aristotle, *Poetics*, trans. Ingram Bywater, in *The Basic Works of Aristotle*, ed. Richard McKeon (New York: Random House, 1941), 1148b.

7. Ibid., 1450b–51a.

8. Plotinus, *Plotinus: The Six Enneads*, trans. Stephen McKenna and B. S. Page (Chicago: Encyclopedia Britannica, 1952), 1st ennead, sixth tractate.

9. St. Augustine, *The City of God*, trans. Marcus Dods (New York: Random House, 1950), book 11, sec. 18.

10. St. Augustine, *On Free Choice of the Will*, trans. A. S. Benjamin and L. H. Hackstaff (Indianapolis: Bobbs-Merrill, 1964), 74.

11. The transition of taste in that age has its own literature. See "The Aesthetic Sentiment," chapter 20 of J. Huizinga, *The Waning of the Middle Ages* (New York: Penguin Books, 1976), 264–72.

12. Leonardo da Vinci, "Notebooks," in *The Literary Works of Leonardo da Vinci*, ed. J. P. Richter, 2 vols. (London: Phaidon, 1970), 2:242.

13. Thomas Hobbes, *Hobbes's Leviathan, Reprinted from the Edition of 1651* (Oxford: Clarendon, 1967), part 1, chap. 2, p. 14.

14. This is the essence of the long, searching reflections that make up the first and second books of Immanuel Kant's *Critique of Judgment*, trans. J. H. Bernard (New York: Hafner, 1966), 37–202.

15. Friedrich Schiller, *Aesthetic and Philosophical Essays*, 2 vols., trans. N. H. Dole (Boston: Nicolls, 1902), 1: no. 26.

16. Leo Tolstoy, *What Is Art?* trans. Aylem Maude (Oxford: Oxford University Press, 1930), 221–24.

17. George Santayana, *The Sense of Beauty* (New York: Dover, 1955 [1896]), 52.

18. John Dewey, *Art as Experience* (New York: Putnam's, 1980), 288–89.

19. Benedetto Croce, *Aesthetic*, trans. Douglas Ainslie (New York: Macmillan, 1909), chap. 1.

20. Susanne K. Langer, *Feeling and Form: A Theory of Art* (New York: Scribner's, 1953), 40.

21. Lewis Rowell, *Music and Musical Thought in Early India* (Chicago: University of Chicago Press, 1992), 328.

22. Ibid., 336.

23. "The mouth is the primary organ of knowledge for the sucking infant. The infant displays the impulse to introject everything it wants to know. It gives the baby the first orientation to the outside world. . . . No wonder that [the] sense perceptions of taste, smell, touch, smoothness, and warmth became fused and charged with emotions and, in the course of cultural development, drifted a long way from their primary concrete reference toward highly abstract and [even] spiritual concepts" (Theodore Thass-Tienemann, *The Subconscious Language* [New York: Washington Square, 1967], 72).

24. Rowell, *Music and Musical Thought*, 336.

25. Hajime Nakamura, *The Ways of Thinking of Eastern People* (Honolulu: East-West Center Press, 1964), 352; see also his "Time in Indian and Japanese Thought," in *The Voices of Time: A Cooperative Survey of Man's Views of Time as Expressed by the Sciences*

and by the Humanities, ed. J. T. Fraser, 2d ed. (Amherst: University of Massachusetts Press, 1981), 77–91.

26. Donald Keene, "Japanese Aesthetics," in *Philosophy East and West* 19 (1969): 291–306; read also the four comments on that paper, 307–26.

27. Lewis Rowell, "*Ma:* Time and Timing in the Traditional Arts of Japan," in *Dimensions of Time and Life: The Study of Time VIII,* ed. J. T. Fraser and M. P. Soulsby (Madison, Conn.: International Universities Press, 1996), 166.

28. R. V. Alatalo and Johanna Mappes, "Tracking the Evolution of Warning Signals," *Nature* 382 (22 Aug. 1996): 708–9.

29. Plato, *Republic,* trans. Paul Shorey, in *The Collected Dialogues,* 606d. These are the puritanical opinions of an aristocrat whose views on sexual passions must surely appear reprehensible to latter-day puritans. Consider his ideas about the origins of sexuality: "But the woman who is a slice of the original female is attracted by women rather than by men . . . while men who are slices of the male are followers of the male, and show their masculinity throughout their boyhood by the way they make friends with men, and the delight they take in lying beside them and being taken in their arms" (*Symposium,* 191e).

30. Jean-Jacques Rousseau, *The Confessions of Jean-Jacques Rousseau,* trans. W. C. Mallory (New York: Tudor, 1928), 8.

31. Charles Darwin, *"The Origin of Species" and "The Descent of Man"* (New York: Modern Library, n.d.), 448.

32. For instance, in hatred or anger animals often uncover their teeth, signaling that they are ready to bite. Sneering in humans is an analogous behavior: it involves the retraction of the lips and the exposing of the teeth. "The expression of a half-playful sneer graduates into one of great ferocity when, together with a heavily frowning brow and fierce eye, the canine tooth is exposed" (Charles Darwin, *The Expression of Emotions in Man and Animals* [Chicago: University of Chicago Press, 1965 (1872)], 248). An illustration on page 249 shows the frown of a woman suggesting that she is herself ready to bite or at least do the next socially acceptable thing.

33. In the evolution of the body new structures usually replace their earlier forms. The forms of our bones closely resemble those of our early human ancestors, but our leg bones are fourteen inches long, whereas theirs were eight inches long. Since it is not possible to have a leg bone that is both fourteen and eight inches long, we have only the currently standard model.

34. P. D. MacLean, "On the Origin and Progressive Evolution of the Triune Brain," in *Primate Brain Evolution,* ed. E. Armstrong and D. Falk (New York: Plenum, 1982), 291–316.

35. See J. T. Fraser, "The Many Dimensions of Time and Mind," in *Time and Mind: Interdisciplinary Issues: The Study of Time VI,* ed. J. T. Fraser (Madison, Conn.: International Universities Press, 1989), 1–14.

36. In making time measurements in the primitive simplicity of the physical world, the identities of the clocks are clear. It is the clock on the wall against the rate of crystallization in a beaker; it is the revolution of the stars against an atomic clock. The principles of comparison that connect two clock readings involved in measuring time are also clear: they are the laws of nature.

Consider, for instance, two identical clocks purchased in the local hardware store. If they are in relative motion or in different gravitational fields, they will show different amounts of elapsed times between the same two events. Which clock is right? If we know the principle (law of nature) that conjoins the readings, and if what they show corresponds to what that principle predicts, then they can both be right.

From the nonliving let us step up to the living. We learned that every living organism is a clockshop of billions of clocks kept coordinated in the organic present. These clocks can get out of step with each other in innumerably many ways. Some of them, then, may be said to be fast or slow with respect to some others. The principle of nature that holds the oscillators together in a coherently functioning system and makes the comparison among the oscillators of an organic system meaningful is the life process. Dysrhythmia among the clocks is usually manifest as illness; complete loss of coherence (the loss of stable relationships among the clocks) leads to death.

37. On the experience of "timelessness" seen from the psychoanalytic point of view, see Jacob A. Arlow, "Disturbance of the Sense of Time: With Special Reference to the Experience of Timelessness," *Psychoanalytic Quarterly* 53 (1984): 13–37; see also Arlow, "Time as Emotion," in *Time and Mind*, ed. Fraser, 85–96.

38. M. P. Soulsby, "Order and Disorder: Creating Temporality in Literary Experience," in *Time and Process: The Study of Time VII*, ed. J. T. Fraser and L. Rowell (Madison, Conn.: International Universities Press, 1993), 205–16; quotation on 213.

39. Courtesy of Prof. Argyros.

40. Nikos Kazantzakis, *Zorba the Greek*, trans. Carl Wildman (New York: Simon and Schuster, 1966), 72.

41. Albert Einstein, *The World as I See It* (London: John Lane at the Bodley Head, 1935), 124.

42. Joachim Fest, *Hitler* (New York: Harcourt Brace Jovanovich, 1974), 323.

43. St. Augustine, "On Free Will," in *Augustine: Earlier Writings*, ed. and trans. J. H. S. Burleigh (Philadelphia: Westminster, 1953), 118.

44. St. Augustine, *On Music*, trans. R. C. Taliaferro, in *The Fathers of the Church*, 4 vols. (New York, CIMA, 1947), 4:172.

45. See J. T. Fraser, "The Art of the Audible 'Now,'" *Music Theory Spectrum* 7 (1985): 181–84. See also Albert Mayr, Antonello Colimberti, and Gabriele Montagano, eds., *L'ascolto del tempo: musiche inaudibili e ambiente ritmico* (Florence: (mp)x2, 1995); and Dietrich Ebert, "Gehen, atmen, Herzschlag: von musikalischen und biologischen Rhythmen," in *Von Rhythmen und Eigenzeiten*, ed. Martin Held and K. A. Geissler (Stuttgart: S. Hirzel, 1995), 55–66.

46. David Epstein, "On Musical Continuity," in *The Study of Time IV*, ed. J. T. Fraser, N. Lawrence, and D. Park (New York: Springer Verlag, 1981), 185. In a later work, *Shaping Time: Music, the Brain, and Performance* (New York: Schirmer, 1995), Epstein asks, "How can musical symbol, as structure, be joined to affective state?" (471). Through the mechanism by which affect is controlled and shaped. "Those mechanisms extend beyond musical structure. They encompass the nervous system . . . with its functions, propensities, and tendencies to relate to periodicity, coupled oscillations, and other aspects of timing—the physical substrata of musical timing in its broadest sense" (481).

47. From Kramer's comments on the moods of time, as defined in the hierarchical theory of time, in Jonathan Kramer, *The Time of Music: New Meanings, New Temporalities, New Listening Strategies* (New York: Schirmer, 1988), 375–97.

48. Lewis Rowell, "Music as Process," in *Time as Process: The Study of Time VII,* ed. J. T. Fraser and L. Rowell (Madison, Conn.: International Universities Press, 1993), 143.

49. *Zangetsu* (Morning Moon), by Kinto Minezaki, suggests the *ecstasy of the forest.* Its melody, for traditional Japanese ensemble of koto, shamishen, shakuhachi, and female voice, is infused with the eotemporal atmosphere of the country dawn. One may also think of the orchestral introduction to Benjamin Britten's opera *Peter Grimes.* It is a metaphor for the quiet contemplation of the infinity of the sea stretching out to merge with the sky.

Maurice Ravel's *Bolero* is a brilliant orchestral tour de force, a seamless unit of hypnotic crescendo over a single repeated rhythmic pattern, surely a musical image of the *ecstasy of the dance,* with that of the forest to come.

The orchestral introduction to Richard Strauss's opera *Der Rosenkavalier* is a vivid description of the *ecstasy of the bower.* The listener may detect both male and female orgasms transformed into music and will hear a postcoital languor on which the curtain rises to find Marschallin and young Octavian in bed.

A Teutonic version of Creation may be detected in the orchestral prelude to Richard Wagner's opera *Das Rheingold.* The Rhine River wells up from its primordial sources to carry, with irresistible force, both gods and godlike men and women toward their preordained fall. The music conveys a sense of a reality where time has no direction. The reader may extend this list indefinitely.

For guidance to these examples I am indebted to Professor Lewis Rowell; see his *Thinking about Music: An Introduction to the Philosophy of Music* (Amherst: University of Massachusetts Press, 1983), esp. 246–48.

50. A good entry to the twenty-seven-century-old science of interpreting the temporal organization of poetic language may be had through the article on prosody in Alex Preminger and T. V. F. Brogan, eds., *The New Princeton Encyclopedia of Poetry and Poetics* (Princeton, N.J.: Princeton University Press, 1993), s.v. "Prosody."

51. D. H. Lawrence, "Poetry of the Present," *The Complete Poems,* ed. Vivian de Sola Pinto and Warren Roberts (New York: Penguin Books, 1977), 181–82.

52. Ibid, 182–83, 184–85.

53. Walt Whitman, *Complete Poetry and Selected Prose and Letters,* ed. Emory Holloway (London: Nonesuch, 1938), 182.

54. Walt Whitman, "Song of Exposition," in ibid., 101.

55. Maya Angelou, "On the Pulse of the Morning," *The Complete Collected Poems of Maya Angelou* (New York: Random House, 1994), 270.

56. Chinese poetic forms have an uninterrupted history of over three thousand years. The earliest form, called *shih* and still popular, consists of lines of four characters (as seen) with rhymes at the end of even-numbered lines (as heard) (Burton Watson, ed. and trans., *The Columbia Book of Chinese Poetry: From Early Times to the Thirteenth Century* [New York: Columbia University Press, 1984], 12–13, 373–75). See also Wu-chi Liu and Irving Yucheng Lo, *Sunflower Splendor: Three Thousand Years of Chinese Poetry* (New York: Anchor Books, 1975). Here are the first eight lines of a

2,500-year-old song, with each line consisting of four characters. The translation attempts to reflect the denseness of the Chinese language in general and of its poetry in particular by offering, in all but one of the lines, only four words per line.

> Kuan-kuan, the ospreys.
> On the river's isle.
> Delicate, a good girl:
> A gentleman's fit mate.
> Long and short, duckweeds.
> Fetch some—left and right.
> Delicate, a good girl.
> Waking, sleeping: seek her.

This poem appears in Wai-lim Yip, trans. and ed., *Chinese Poetry: Major Modes and Genres* (Berkeley: University of California Press, 1976), 49; *kuan-kuan* is the cry of the bird.

During the later Han (the first two centuries A.D.) a government office was set up to collect folk songs. Poetry in its collection was often of irregular form, but as the centuries passed, the office came to prefer lines with five or seven characters. Between the seventh and tenth centuries arose the "regulated verse," which was a *shih* with eight lines, with demands for parallelism and restrictions on rhymes.

Japanese poetry, thirteen hundred years old, has retained its family ties to the older poetic literature of China, except that it lacks meaningful rhymes, because all Japanese words end in one of five simple vowels. The oldest Japanese verse form is the *tanka*, or short poem, consisting of five lines of thirty-one syllables (words, characters) grouped as 5–7–5–7–7. From the thirteenth century on, the *haiku* of seventeen syllables became the most popular form; it declined in popularity through the centuries but reemerged during the late nineteenth century (see Kenneth Yasuda, *The Japanese Haiku* [Rutland, Vt.: Tuttle, 1971]; Harold Stewart, ed. and trans., *A Chime of Windbells: A Year of Japanese Haiku in English Verse* [Rutland, Vt.: Tuttle, 1969]).

57. See George Ford's essay "Dickens and the Voices of Time," *Nineteenth Century Fiction* 24, no. 4 (Mar. 1970): 428–48.

58. Charles Dickens, *Bleak House* (New York: J. A. Hill, n.d.), 1.

59. Michael Holquist, "From Body-Talk to Biography: The Chronobiological Bases of Narrative," *Yale Journal of Criticism* 3, no. 1 (1989): 1–25; quotation on 21.

60. Ibid., 19.

61. Ibid., 32.

62. A scholarly guide to Tsvetaeva's life and work, itself a work of poetic prose, is Olga Peters Hasty's *Marina Tsvetaeva's Orphic Journey to the Worlds of the Word* (Evanston, Ill.: Northwestern University Press, 1996).

63. Alexander Argyros, *A Blessed Rage for Order: Deconstruction, Evolution, and Chaos* (Ann Arbor: University of Michigan Press, 1991), 309.

64. Ibid., 322.

65. Soulsby, "Order and Disorder," 205–16.

66. W. W. Bird, ed., *George Grey's Polynesian Mythology* (Christchurch: Whitcombe and Tombs, 1954), 2.

67. The poem, in this form, is from Stephen Bertman's *Doorways through Time* (Los Angeles: Tarcher, 1986), 39. It is Bertram's sensitive rewriting of two prior translations that, in turn, were translations from W. Max Müller's *Die Liebespoesie der alten Ägypter* (Leipzig, 1899) of the Harris papyrus, now in the British Museum. For guidance in this matter of ancient beauty and intriguing provenance, I am indebted to Prof. Stephen Bertram.

68. In Shakespeare's *Pericles* (in *The Complete Works of William Shakespeare*, ed. W. J. Craig [London: Oxford University Press, 1962], act 4, sc. 6, l. 145) a bawd (a madam) and a servant named Boult are discussing Marina, daughter of Pericles.

> Bawd: Boult, take her away; use her at thy pleasure; crack the glass of her virginity, and make the rest malleable.
> Boult: An if she were a thornier piece of ground than she is, she shall be ploughed.

69. Paul Ricoeur, *Time and Narrative*, 3 vols. (Chicago: University of Chicago Press, 1984–88), 1:ix.

70. Metaphors are necessary constituents not only of the language of the literary arts but also of the sciences. As our umwelt expands through the use of instruments and mathematical reasoning, we encounter objects, events, and processes to which nothing in sensory experience does or could correspond; these alien furnishings of reality can be designated only through metaphors. We have particles that are said to spin though they do not spin, objects that are said to be particles or waves though they are both at the same time, and other objects identified by their colors although they could not possibly have colors.

71. Jacob A. Arlow, *Psychoanalysis: Clinical Theory and Practice* (Madison, Conn.: International Universities Press, 1991), 160.

72. Terence Hawkes, *Metaphor* (London: Methuen, 1972), 59.

73. Octavio Paz, *The Bow and the Lyre: The Poem. Poetic Revelation. Poetry and History*, trans. Ruth L. C. Simms (Austin: University of Texas Press, 1973), 3–4.

74. The essay, which is an introduction to his *Lyric Ballads*, may be found in William Wordsworth, *The Prose Works of William Wordsworth*, ed. W. J. B. Owen and J. W. Smyser, 3 vols. (Oxford: Clarendon, 1974), 1:141.

75. R. Adolphs, D. Tranel, H. Damasio, and A. Damasio, "Impaired Recognition of Emotion in Facial Expressions Following Bilateral Damage to the Human Amygdala," *Nature* 372 (1994): 669–72. See also the editorial on that report, "Faces, Fear, and the Amygdala," 613–14.

76. Stephen Jay Gould, "Church, Humboldt, and Darwin: The Tension and Harmony of Art and Science," in *Frederic Edwin Church*, ed. Franklin Kelly (Washington, D.C.: National Gallery of Art, 1989), 94–107; quotation on 100.

77. Franklin Kelly, "A Passion for Landscape: The Paintings of Frederic Edwin Church," in *Frederic Edwin Church*, ed. Kelly, 32–75; quotation on 32.

78. Étienne Gilson, *Painting and Reality* (New York: Meridian Books, 1959): 123–24.

79. J. D. Ormeland, *Michelangelo's Sistine Ceiling: A Psychoanalytic Study* (Madison, Conn.: International Universities Press, 1989), 131.

80. Ibid., 144.

81. Dreaming is not limited to the faculty of sight: Homer heard his dreams. See H.-J. Schumann, "Phänomenologische und psychoanalytische Untersuchung der Homerischen Träume," *Acta Psychotherapeutica Psychosomatica et Orthopaedagogica* 3 (1955): 205–19. This theme is discussed in "Homer, Borges, and Time," the foreword to the Braille edition of my *Time, the Familiar Stranger* (Stuart, Fla.: Triformation Braille Service, 1989).

82. Ormeland, *Michelangelo's Sistine Ceiling*, 61. Note the twenty naked male adolescents, the *ignudi*, of the Sistine ceiling.

83. Paul G. Bahn, "Age and the Female Form," *Nature* 342 (1989): 345–46.

84. Ferguson starts with equations of three-dimensional connected surfaces of complex variables, selects ranges of variables, and displays the behavior of the functions in computer-generated images. He then selects from the many resulting displays those he finds aesthetically pleasing. The final object relates to the underlying mathematics in the way some plant structures relate to Fibonacci numbers, except that these objects are the products of not natural but artificial selection. See Haleman Ferguson and Claire Ferguson, *Mathematics in Stone and Bronze* (Erie, Pa.: Meriden Creative Group, 1994). (The dedication of the book is worth noting: "To our seven sometime hours of unbridled passion become seven lives of living love.")

85. E. H. Gombrich, "Moment and Movement in Art," *Journal of the Warburg and Courtland Institutes* 27 (1964): 293–306; quotation on 296.

86. Van Deren Coke, *The Painter and the Photograph: From Delacroix to Warhol* (Albuquerque: University of New Mexico Press, 1972).

87. Edward Steichen, *The Family of Man* (New York: Museum of Modern Art, 1955).

88. "Two Lives: Georgia O'Keefe and Alfred Stieglitz—a Conversation in Paintings and Photographs," exhibit at the Phillips Collection, Washington, D.C., December 1992–April 1993.

89. Marta Braun, *Picturing Time: The Work of Etienne-Jules Marey* (Chicago: University of Chicago Press, 1992). Although the book focuses on Marey, three-quarters of it deals with the late nineteenth-century technique and art of making still pictures of moving objects and then displaying them so as to create impressions of motion.

90. This phenomenon is known as flicker fusion. It was first reported by the English philologist and physician Peter Mark Roget, remembered for *Roget's Thesaurus*. The phenomenon is species specific. For humans the boundary is at about eighteen images per second. For the fighting fish it is thirty frames per second, minimum. This fish is so combative that it attacks its own image in a mirror. If the image is visually chopped at about thirty times a second or less, the fish stops attacking it (G. A. Brecher, "Die Entstehung und biologische Bedeutung der subjektiven Zeiteinheit des Momentes," *Zeitschrift für Vergleichende Physiologie* 18 (1932): 204–43.

91. Ingmar Bergman, *"Persona" and "Shame,"* trans. Keith Bradfield (New York: Grossman, 1972), 145.

92. Aristotle, *Poetics*, 1450a.

93. Jacqueline de Romilly, *Time in Greek Tragedy* (Ithaca, N.Y.: Cornell University Press, 1968), 11.

94. The literary scholar S. L. Macey expressed a widely held opinion when he

wrote that "there is a remarkable absence of great tragic drama between the 5th century B.C. Athens and the Renaissance England of Elizabeth I" (Macey, "The Relationship between Our New Sense of Time and Our Sense of an Ending in Tragedy," in *The Study of Time IV*, ed. J. T. Fraser, N. Lawrence, and D. Park [New York: Springer Verlag, 1981], 94–102; quotation on 95).

95. This is in Dante's *Di vulgari eloquentia* ("On the vernacular tongue"), in *Le opere di Dante Allighieri*, ed. E. Moore and Paget Toynbee (Oxford: nell Stamperia dell' Università, 1924), 392–93.

96. Geoffrey Chaucer, "Words of the Host to the Monk," *Canterbury Tales*, trans. into modern English by Neville Coghill (London: Penguin Books, 1971), 206.

97. Roger L. Cox, *Between Earth and Heaven: Shakespeare, Dostoievski, and the Meaning of Christian Tragedy* (New York: Holt, Rinehart and Winston, 1969), 238.

98. See Arthur Schopenhauer, *The World as Will and Idea*, 3 vols., trans. R. B. Haldane and J. Kemp (New York: Dover, 1966), 2:433 and passim, vol. 2.

99. Friedrich Nietzsche, *"The Birth of Tragedy" and "The Genealogy of Morals,"* trans. Francis Golffing (New York: Doubleday, 1956), 9–10.

100. Susanne K. Langer, *Feeling and Form: A Theory of Art* (New York: Scribner's, 1953), 356.

101. Ibid., 335.

102. Both from Alfred Lord Tennyson's "In Memoriam A. H. H.," in *The Norton Anthology of English Literature*, 4th ed., 2 vols. (New York: Norton, 1979), 2:1146, 1148 (no. 56, l. 15; no. 50, l. 7).

103. Erwin Panofsky, "Et in Arcadia ego: On the Conception of Transience in Poussin and Watteau," in *Philosophy and History: Essays Presented to Ernst Cassirer*, ed. R. Klibansky and H. J. Paton (Oxford: Clarendon, 1936), 222–54. The essay was later revised and appeared as chap. 7, "Et in Arcadia ego: Poussin and the Elegiac Tradition," of Panofsky's *Meaning in the Visual Arts* (New York: Doubleday, 1955), 295–320.

104. Panofsky, "Et in Arcadia ego," 225.

105. Ibid., 227.

106. Ibid., 224.

107. Wallace Stevens, *The Palm at the End of the Mind: Selected Poems and a Play by Wallace Stevens*, ed. Holly Stevens (New York: Vintage Books, 1972), 6.

SIX: THE GLOBAL LABORATORY

1. Literature contains many marvelous examples describing the quirks of the social present. Here are two of them.

Thomas Hardy's *Tess* is the story of a woman victimized by one man's lust, by poverty, and by social hypocrisy. She is condemned to be hanged for having murdered the man who raped her. The morning of her execution her sister and the sister's lover walk away from the courthouse. "Though they were young, they walked with bowed heads. . . . Upon the cornice of the tower a tall staff was fixed. Their eyes were riveted on it. A few minutes after the hour had struck, something moved slowly up the staff and extended itself upon the breeze. It was a black flag. . . . The two speechless gazers bent themselves down to the earth, as if in prayer, and remained thus a long time. . . . As soon as they had strength, they arose, joined hands again, and went on" (Thomas Hardy, *Tess of the D'Urbervilles: A Pure Woman* [New York: New American Library, 1980], 419).

William Styron has been fascinated by the uncanniness that may surround the realization of simultaneity among uncorrelated events. Sometimes it suggests the presence of providence; sometimes, that of inscrutable evil. Here the narrator of *Sophie's Choice* recalls one of her remarks. "'The day I arrived in Auschwitz,' I heard her say behind me, 'it was beautiful. The forsythia was in bloom.' . . . I was eating bananas in Raleigh, North Carolina, I thought, thinking this not the first time since I had known Sophie, yet perhaps the first time in my life aware of the meaning of the Absurd, and its conclusive, unrevocable horror" (William Styron, *Sophie's Choice* [New York: Bantam Books, 1980], 567).

2. A 1996 example: shown on the left, preparations in Washington, D.C., for the president of the United States to deliver his State of the Union message to Congress. On the right, people gathered in Los Angeles to learn how many millions of dollars a man who murdered his wife will have to pay to her family.

3. "I coined the word 'cyberspace' in 1981 in one of my first science fiction stories and subsequently used it to describe something that people insist on seeing as a sort of literary forerunner of the Internet. This being so, some think it remarkable that I do not use E-mail" (William Gibson, *New York Times Magazine*, 14 July 1996, p. 31).

4. Jorge Luis Borges, *Labyrinths* (New York: New Directions, 1964), 55, 52.

5. Esther Dyson, George Gilder, Jay Keyworth, and Alvin Toffler, "A Magna Carta for the Knowledge Age," *New Perspectives Quarterly*, no. 11 (Fall 1994): 26–37; quotation on 27.

6. *World Holiday and Time Guide*, 77th ed. (N.p.: J. P. Morgan, 1995).

7. Murray Melbin, *Night as Frontier: Colonizing the World after Dark* (New York: Free Press, 1987).

8. Within the four time zones of the continental United States, Massachusetts fishermen work at night. The people who staff hospitals also work at night, as do those who process the checks deposited during the day; bakers have traditionally worked at night, but never before have so many people needed or made bread; food deliverers of all kinds work at night, as do stock traders who handle billions of dollars; and there are the brigades of cleaning people who come at midnight to bury the garbage of all kinds of working places. Prostitutes, police, and a goodly number of individuals in the criminal justice system are at work during the night, as are the people who control the media and the government. For a very readable and interesting treatise on night work, see Kevin Coyne, *A Day in the Night of America* (New York: Random House, 1992).

9. As an example related to the use of computers in psychotherapy, see Larissa MacFarquhar, "Point and Click," *The New Republic*, 8 April 1996, pp. 14–16. To make psychotherapy cheaper, a computer package was "designed to help unsophisticated clinicians draw up the kind of plans that pass muster with . . . managed care assessors." The consequence is a complete revamping of psychotherapy favoring short-term objectives.

10. George Steiner, "Books in an Age of Post-Literacy," *Publishers Weekly*, 24 May 1985, pp. 44–48. For a later assessment of the book, updated but in agreement with

his earlier views, see "Ex Libris: A Love Letter Written to Reading," *The New Yorker,* 17 March 1997, pp. 117–19.

11. Daniel J. Boorstin, *The Republic of Letters,* ed. John Y. Cole (Washington, D.C.: Library of Congress, 1989), 65–66.

12. Doreen Carvajal, "Americans Buy Books. Foreigners Buy Publishers," *New York Times,* 10 August 1997, p. 4. See also, by the same writer, "Read Faster; Today You Are Already Another 166 Books Behind," *New York Times,* 24 August 1997, p. E1.

13. Robert MacNeil, "Is Television Shortening Our Attention Span?" *Phi Kappa Phi Journal,* Fall 1987, pp. 21–23.

14. "Evolution of Attention," *Science News,* 3 January 1998, p. 11, which reports on the work of a group at the National Institute of Health. See also Stephen Bertman, "Cultural Amnesia: The Role of Memory in America's Future," *Vital Speeches of the Day* 61, no. 19 (15 July 1995): 602–6. See also his *Hyperculture: The Human Cost of Speed* (Westport, Conn.: Praeger, 1998). On the same theme, see David Shenk, *Data Smog: Surviving the Information Glut* (San Francisco: Harper Edge, 1996), 36.

15. James Reston, "The Decline of History," *New York Times,* 5 May 1985.

16. William Blake, "Milton, Book the Second," in *Blake: Complete Writings,* ed. Geoffrey Keynes (Oxford: Oxford University Press, 1972), 481.

17. Paul Alkon, "Alternate History and Postmodern Temporality," in *Time, Literature, and the Arts: Essays in Honor of Samuel L. Macey,* ed. Thomas Cleary (Victoria: University of Victoria, 1994), 65–85; quotation on 65.

18. David Lowenthal, *The Past Is a Foreign Country* (Cambridge: Cambridge University Press, 1985).

19. Tom Engelhardt, "The Morphing of the American Mind," *New York Times,* 24 December 1994.

The following names are copyrighted by Games Workshop, Ltd.: "Blood angel space marines," "Predator annihilator," "Cadian shock troops," "Khorne berzerker champions," and "Tyranids with lash whip or with venom canon."

20. Francis Fukuyama, *The End of History and the Last Man* (New York: Free Press, 1992).

21. Paul Valéry, *History and Politics,* trans. D. Foliot and J. Mathews (New York: Pantheon, 1962), 372.

22. Mary Shelley, *Frankenstein; or, the Modern Prometheus* (New York: Penguin Books, 1983), 52.

23. Joseph Needham, "The Roles of Europe and China in the Evolution of Oecumenical Science," *Advancement of Science* 24 (1967–68): 1–15.

24. Samuel P. Huntington, *The Clash of Civilizations and the Remaking of World Order* (New York: Simon and Schuster, 1996), 57. See also Huntington, "If Not Civilizations, What?" *Foreign Affairs* 72, no. 3 (1993): 22–29.

25. See, for instance, Anwar Ibrahim, "A Global Convivencia vs. 'The Clash of Civilizations,'" *New Perspectives Quarterly* 14, no. 3 (1997): 31–43.

The concept of culture can annoy some people. The Nazi playwright Hannst Johst is the author of a remark broadly endorsed by his fellow believers: "When I hear the word, 'culture,' I reach for my revolver."

26. J. R. Durant, G. A. Evans, and G. P. Thomas, "The Public Understanding of Science," *Nature* 340 (1989): 11–13. On one of the many unpalatable side effects

of this ignorance, see P. W. Huber, *Galileo's Revenge: Junk Science in the Courtroom* (New York: Basic Books, 1991).

27. Christopher P. Toumey, *Conjuring Science: Scientific Symbols and Cultural Meanings in American Life* (New Brunswick, N.J.: Rutgers University Press, 1996).

28. Anne Schullenberger Lévy, "America Discovered a Second Time: French Perceptions of American Notions of Time from Tocqueville to Laboulaye." Ph.D. diss., Department of History, Yale University, 1994.

29. Ibid., 21.

30. Ibid., 279–80.

31. There are 13 churches of the Vedanta Society, 30,000 Jewish temples, 11,000 Evangelical Lutheran churches, 20,000 Roman Catholic churches, and 900 Old Order Amish groups; there are the Quakers, the Shakers, the Bickertonians, the Swedenborgians, the Church of Scientology, the Moon sects, Children of God, Krishnaivas, the Nation of Islam, and the Divine Light, as well as other religious groups of Native American, Latin American, Asian, and African origins. There are 1,840 full-time religious radio and television stations. After people move to a new town, they often "shop for a church." They may join the Albanian Orthodox church or groups of snake handlers, the Church of Baptized Holiness or Weaver Mennonites, or perhaps the Shiloh True Light Church or the Sanctuary of the Master's Presence. There are at least a hundred groups whose spiritual interests focus on flying saucers; they assign to them the role that angels used to play. There are witchcraft cults, ritual magic churches, neopagans, and gay religions (see J. Gordon Melton, ed., *The Encyclopedia of American Religions*, 2 vols. [Wilmington, N.C.: McGrath, 1978]).

There is a now a journal, *Nova Religio*, devoted exclusively to the study of "alternative, emergent and new religious movements and communities" (from a 1997 announcement).

32. Harvey Cox, *Fire from Heaven: The Rise of Pentecostal Spirituality* (Reading, Pa.: Addison-Wesley, 1995), 304.

33. Such as, for instance, the volumes for which Robert John Russell serves as the general editor. All these volumes are jointly published by the Vatican Observatory–Vatican City-State and the Center for Theology and the Natural Sciences, Berkeley, Calif. They include R. J. Russell, W. R. Stoeger, and G. V. Coyne, eds., *Physics, Philosophy, and Theology: A Common Quest for Understanding* (1988); R. J. Russell, Nancey Murphy, and C. J. Isham, eds., *Quantum Cosmology and the Laws of Nature* (1993); and R. J. Russell, Nancey Murphy, and A. R. Peacocke, eds., *Chaos and Complexity* (1995).

34. Scott Macmillan and Jennifer Bricken, "Celtic Mass for the Sea," Marquis Classics (tape), ERAC 149.

35. Peter Steinfels, "Female Concept of God Is Shaking Protestants," *New York Times*, 14 May 1994, p. 8. See also Gustav Niebuhr, "Lay Women of Faith Seek Joy on a Journey," *New York Times*, 27 January 1997, p. 10.

36. Michel Chevalier, *Lettres sur l'Amérique du nord* (1836), quoted in Lévy, "America Discovered," 171–74.

37. Jane Katz, "The Joy of Consumption," *Regional Review of the Federal Reserve Bank of Boston* 7, no. 1 (1997): 12–17.

38. Jeremy Rifkin, *The End of Work: The Decline of the Global Labor Force and the Dawn of the Post-Market Era* (New York: Putnam's, 1994), 197.

39. Harry McClintock, "Big Rock Candy Mountains," quoted by Wallace Stegner in *Where the Bluebird Sings to the Lemonade Springs: Living and Writing in the West* (New York: Penguin Books, 1992), epigraph.

40. In Lévy, "America Discovered," 217.

41. Rifkin, *The End of Work*, 172–80.

42. "In America," *New York Times*, 27 January 1997, p. A17.

43. In Lévy, "America Discovered," 184.

44. M. T. Jacobs, *Short-Term America: The Causes and Cures of Our Business Myopia* (Boston: Harvard Business School Press, 1991), 12.

45. Lévy, "America Discovered," 190.

46. George Kennan, *Sketches from a Life* (New York: Pantheon, 1989), 207.

47. "The Business Homeless," *New York Times*, 8 March 1998.

48. Lévy, "America Discovered," abstract.

49. Ibid., 283.

50. L. F. Kohl, *The Politics of Individualism: Parties and the American Character in the Jacksonian Era* (New York: Oxford University Press, 1989), 148; quoted in Lévy, "America Discovered," 202.

51. Chevalier, letter concerning "symptoms of revolution," quoted in Lévy, "America Discovered," 203.

52. Ibid., 205.

53. James Reston, *New York Times*, 23 November 1963, p. 1.

54. "The profession is becoming a business. . . . It's not a calling any more" (member of a task force of the Boston Bar Association quoted by John Ellement in "Many Lawyers Wonder Whether the Joke Is on Them," *The Boston Globe*, 14 August 1997, p. A1). For detailed comments, see Walter K. Olson, *The Litigation Explosion* (New York: Dutton, 1991).

55. Steven R. Donziger, ed., *The Real War on Crime: The Report of the National Criminal Justices Commission* (New York: HarperCollins, 1996), xvii.

56. Ibid., 37.

57. Ibid., 68.

58. Joseph Tainter, *The Collapse of Complex Societies* (Cambridge: Cambridge University Press, 1988).

59. John LeCarré, *Our Game* (New York: Ballantine Books, 1995), 312.

60. Lévy, "America Discovered," 189.

61. Kennan, *Sketches from a Life*, 43.

62. William J. Bouwsma, "Anxiety and the Formation of Early Modern Culture," in *After the Reformation*, ed. Barbara C. Malament (Philadelphia: University of Pennsylvania Press, 1980), 215–46.

63. Ibid., 244n.79. She is quoting Ari Kiev, an anthropologist.

64. Kennan, *Sketches from a Life*, 132.

65. See the special sixteen-page report "Dirt Poor: A Survey of Development and the Environment," *The Economist*, 21 March 1998.

66. This is the essence of the "Red Queen hypothesis" of Leigh Van Valen, "A New Evolutionary Law," *Evolutionary Theory* 1, no. 1 (1973): 1–30.

67. Paul Kennedy, *Preparing for the Twenty-First Century* (New York: Random House, 1993).

68. L. R. Brown, "The Acceleration of History," in *State of the World 1996: A World-watch Institute Report on Progress toward a Sustainable Society,* ed. Linda Stark (New York: Norton, 1996), 3.

69. Kennedy, *Preparing,* 27.

70. Anne Raver, "Qualities of an Animal Scientist: Cow's Eye View and Autism," *New York Times,* 5 August 1997, p. C1.

71. R. L. Rubinstein, *The Cunning of History: The Holocaust and the American Future* (New York: Harper and Row, 1975), 86. In his introduction to Rubinstein's book, William Styron writes about the American reader's general lack of a sense of history coupled with a vacuous unawareness of evil. Rubinstein's work seems to have supplied some of the background to William Styron's novel *Sophie's Choice,* a brilliant mapping into an easily understandable plot and characters of what Rubinstein describes in the language of a historian.

72. Donziger, *Real War on Crime,* 87.

73. G. W. Sully, excerpts from a report entitled "Murder by the State," in "Genocide Is Bad for the Economy," *New York Times,* 14 December 1997.

74. "Addressing Emerging Infectious Disease Threats: A Prevention Strategy for the United States" (Atlanta, Ga.: Center for Disease Control and Prevention, 1994).

75. "Homelessness," GAO/HEHS-94-98 (Washington, D.C.: U.S. General Accounting Office, 1994), 1.

76. Gwendolyn Brooks, "We Real Cool," in *The Norton Anthology of Literature by Women,* ed. S. M. Gilbert and Susan Gubar (New York: Norton, 1985), 1855.

77. Paul Claudel, *The Satin Slipper* (New Haven, Conn.: Yale University Press, 1931), sc. 13, p. 126.

78. It is predicted that life expectancy in Japan will continue to rise and birth rates there will continue to decline. It is estimated that by 2050 the Japanese working population will be 55 million, which is barely half the total population. See David Swinbanks, "Japan's Demography Poses Questions for Old and Young Alike," *Nature* 385 (30 January 1997): 379.

79. Brian Aldiss, "Cultured Tour of the Ineffable," *Nature* 370 (4 August 1994): 337.

80. Kennan, *Sketches from a Life,* 150.

81. Andrew Kimbrell, *The Masculine Mystique* (New York: Ballantine Books, 1995), 8.

82. Carnegie Task Force, *Starting Points: Meeting the Needs of Our Youngest Children* (New York: Carnegie Corporation, 1994).

83. U.S. Department of Justice, Office of Juvenile Justice and Delinquency Prevention, "Fact Sheet on Missing Children," May 1990.

84. James P. Grant, *The State of the World's Children, 1995* (Oxford: Oxford University Press for UNICEF, 1995), 2–3.

85. Ibid., 43.

86. Robert Capa, *Children of War, Children of Peace,* ed. Cornell Capa (New York: Little, Brown, 1991).

87. The history of children's literature may be entered through Bette P. Goldstone's "Views of Childhood in Children's Literature over Time" and its bibliography, *Language Arts* 63 (1986): 791–98.

88. Mary Pipher, *Reviving Ophelia: Saving the Selves of Adolescent Girls* (New York: Ballantine Books, 1994), 79–80.

89. Frederick Winsor and Marian Parry, *The Space Child's Mother Goose* (New York: Simon and Schuster, 1963), no. 37.

90. "In Brazil, Indians Call on Spirits to Save the Land and Its Riches from Miners and Ranchers," *New York Times,* 21 June 1996, p. A6.

91. "The Human Body Shop," *Washington Post,* 1 July 1990.

92. Organ trafficking markets thrive on the Indian subcontinent, on the Arabian Peninsula, and in Southeast Asia. In India a healthy kidney fetches upward of $1,500; a cornea, $4,000. Persian Gulf Arabs will pay as much as $50,000 for a kidney. According to Jim Hogshire, author of *Sell Yourself to Science,* a heart can go for about $20,000 on the world black market. Blood is worth $120 a pint, and a liver can fetch up to $150,000 a slice (because a partial liver will regenerate itself). Bone marrow sells for $10,000 a quart. See E. P. Nash, "What's a Life Worth?" *New York Times Magazine,* 14 August 1994.

93. Consider, for instance, the Human Genome Diversity Project. It proposed to collect DNA samples from 500 of the surviving 5,000 different indigenous ethnic groups and, with their aid, help to map the history of diversification in humans. The U.S. Department of Commerce has filed patent claims for cell lines taken from indigenous people on the Solomon Islands. A representative of that group remarked, "We don't view our genes as protein actions ready to be interpreted; for us genes are sacred." A proponent of the project argued that the findings could show that we are all of common origins (very likely to be true), and hence, he added with the naïveté of a cloistered scientist, this would reduce racism. A Paiute Indian representative remarked that showing common origins among people threatens the mythologies of human origins that differ from those held by the dominant world culture ("Genetic Diversity Proposal Fails to Impress International Ethics Panel," *Nature* 377 [5 October 1995], 373). See also Philip Kitcher, *The Lives to Come: The Genetic Revolution and Human Possibilities* (New York: Simon and Schuster, 1996). For a short introduction, see "Junior Comes Out Perfect," *New York Times Magazine,* 29 September 1996, pp. 124–26.

94. "Traffickers' New Cargo: Naive Slavic Women," *New York Times,* 11 January 1998, p. A1.

95. Seth Schiesel, "On Parole and out of Cyberspace," *New York Times,* 5 January 1997.

96. Howard W. French, "The Ritual Slaves of Ghana: Young and Female," *New York Times,* 20 January 1997, p. A1.

97. Hardy, *Tess of the d'Urbervilles,* 114. Tess thinks about her deathday as she reflects on her birthday: "She suddenly thought one afternoon, when looking in the glass at her fairness, that there was yet another date, of greater importance to her than those [of her birthdays]: that of her own death, when all these charms would have disappeared; a day that lay sly and unseen among all the other days of the year, giving no sign or sound when she annually passed over it; but not the less surely there."

98. Niko Tinbergen, "On War and Peace in Animals and Man," *Science* (1968): 1411–18; quotation on 1415.

99. Stafford Beer, *Decision and Control* (New York: Wiley, 1967), 364. See also Hans Kalmus, "The Measurement of Biological and Social Changes," in *The Study of Time III*, ed. J. T. Fraser, N. Lawrence, and D. Park (New York: Springer Verlag, 1978), 237–68.

100. M. W. Brown, "From Science Fiction to Science: The 'Whole Body Transplant,'" *New York Times*, 5 May 1998.

101. Terence Smith, "Iran: Five Years of Fanaticism," *New York Times Magazine*, 12 February 1984.

102. "A Sick Inventory," *The Economist*, 12 April 1997, p. 80.

103. D. J. Kevles, "E Pluribus Unabomber," *The New Yorker*, 14 August 1995, pp. 2–5.

104. *Om* is composed of three sounds *a–u–m*. They represent earth, air, and heaven, as well as the three Hindu gods, Brahma, Vishnu, and Shiva, and the three Vedic scriptures, Rg, Yajur, and Sama.

105. Murray Sayle, "Nerve Gas and the Four Noble Truths," *New Yorker*, 1 April 1996, pp. 56–71.

106. "Soldiers for Sale," *Time*, 26 May 1997, pp. 42–43.

107. Karl Marx and Friedrich Engels, "Manifesto of the Communist Party," in *Introduction to Contemporary Civilization in the West: A Source Book*, 2 vols. (New York: Columbia University Press, 1947), 2:415–35; quotation on 2:416.

108. Ibid., 2:418.

109. Ibid., 2:425.

110. Kenichi Ohmae, "China and the 600,000 Avon Ladies," *The New Perspectives Quarterly* 12, no. 1 (Winter 1995). See also Ohmae, *The End of the Nation State* (New York: Free Press, 1995).

111. Huntington, *The Clash*, 209.

112. Ibid., 66.

113. James Gleick, "Big Brother Is Us," *New York Times Magazine*, 29 September 1996, pp. 130–33.

114. Howard Rheingold, *The Virtual Community: Homesteading on the Electronic Frontier* (Reading, Mass.: Addison-Wesley, 1993), 293. See also Roger Rosenblatt, "Who Killed Privacy? The Right to Know Everything about Everybody," *New York Times Magazine*, 31 January 1993, pp. 24–28.

115. A current catalog of Hugo Dunhill Mailing Lists, Inc., lets anyone purchase printed labels, or label data on disk, by the millions. You may have mailing labels for households with incomes over $125,000 per year: 190,000 for New York State, 50,000 for Michigan, 240,000 for California, and 9,000 for South Dakota. Or you may choose millionaires: 217 for Vermont, 64 for Wyoming, 5,500 for Connecticut, and over 14,000 for New York. You may have attorneys by specialties and then by state or video, computer, or data processing companies, retailers, and distributors. You may purchase lists to target plant physiologists (2,600), hazardous material executives, organizations using nuclear material, or corporate big business executives, as well as churches, museums, and home owners. Income ranges are listed by ZIP codes, which they follow fairly well.

Computerized election forecasts based on less than 10 percent of election returns, using demographic data, are usually correct, making one wonder why elections are necessary.

116. Rheingold, *The Virtual Community,* 176–300.

117. Kennedy, *Preparing,* 344–50.

118. Ibid., 339.

119. "The word *beauty* is a little embarrassing; there is something old-fashioned about it, like a country girl wearing her mother's dress. It is precisely for this reason that I shall use it rather than the much cooler and more stylish term, the *aesthetic*" (Fred Turner, *Beauty: The Value of Values* [Charlottesville: University Press of Virginia, 1991], 1).

120. Arianna Stassinopoulos Huffington, *Picasso: Creator and Destroyer* (New York: Simon and Schuster, 1988), 473.

121. Joachim C. Fest, *Hitler* (New York: Harcourt Brace Jovanovich, 1974), 608.

122. William H. McNeill, *Keeping Together in Time: Dance and Drill in Human History* (Cambridge, Mass.: Harvard University Press, 1995), 151.

123. Ibid., 153–54.

124. Ibid., 156–57.

125. Plato, *Republic,* trans. Paul Shorey, in *The Collected Dialogues of Plato,* ed. Edith Hamilton and Huntington Cairns (Princeton, N.J.: Princeton University Press, 1973), 424b–c.

126. These are the traits he identified: (1) the breakdown of barriers between highbrow and lowbrow musical idioms; (2) a lack of concern for structural unity; (3) use of historically or culturally remote sounds; (4) refusal to accept the distinction between elitist and populist styles; (5) avoidance of totalizing forms (e.g., not allowing an entire piece to be tonal or serial or cast in a prescribed form); (6) inclusion of quotations of or reference to many traditions; (7) acceptance of contradictions; (8) distrust of binary oppositions; (9) inclusion of fragmentation and discontinuities; (10) presentation of multiple meanings and multiple temporalities; (11) the location of meaning and structure more in the listeners than in scores, performances, or composers; (12) and the embrace of chaos (adapted from Jonathan Kramer, "Music and Postmodernism: Some Observations and Some Responses," in *Aflame with Music: 100 Years of Music at the University of Melbourne,* ed. Brenton Brodstock et al. [Melbourne: Centre for Studies of Australian Music, 1996], 411).

127. The words are those of Wagner from his program notes for the performance of the prelude in Paris, 25 January 1860. My source is Daryck Cooke, *The Language of Music* (New York: Oxford University Press, 1987), 187–88.

128. Quoted in Michael Nyman, *Experimental Music: Cage and Beyond* (New York: Schirmer Books, 1974), 42.

129. Lewis Rowell, "Music as a Source for Cultural Intuitions of Time," paper read at a 1990 seminar on time in New Delhi (private communication).

130. Ibid. A sweeping change is now taking place in our attitude toward music and its perception, Rowell writes. We are moving from a text-obsessed period toward a period "in which readers and listeners will be invited—perhaps even impelled—to perceive in a more active, selective, and critical way, instead of passively registering and responding to the artistic data presented to them."

131. Glen Gass, in *Encyclopedia of Time*, ed. S. L. Macey (New York: Garland, 1994), s.v. "Music, Rock."

132. James Bakst, *A History of Russian-Soviet Music* (New York: Dodd, Mead, 1962), 286–87.

133. *Berliner Lokalanzeiger*, 11 April 1933, quoted in Lewis Rowell's *Thinking about Music: An Introduction to the Philosophy of Music* (Amherst: University of Massachusetts Press, 1983), 224.

134. BMG Classics 0926-48048-2.

135. Ezra Pound, "Ancient Music," in *Personae: The Collected Short Poems of Ezra Pound* (New York: New Directions, 1971), 116.

136. Filippo Tommaso Marinetti, "Futurist Manifesto," in *Poems for the Millennium: The University of California Book of Postmodern Poetry*, ed. Jerome Rothenberg and Pierre Joris (Berkeley: University of California Press, 1995), 196–98.

137. See the section on dada in ibid., 289–341; quotation on 289.

138. André Breton, "Manifesto of Surrealism," in ibid., 468.

139. In *Hesiod, the Homeric Hymns and Homeridae*, Loeb Classic Library, 1954, p. 336.

140. Details from Mr. Jack Camarda, of radio station WEBE, Fairfield, Connecticut.

141. Paul Goldberger, "Cuddling up to Quasimodo and Friend," *New York Times*, 23 June 1996, p. B1.

142. The Disney organization may take encouragement from Allen Ginsberg, poet of the Beat Generation. In a 1966 essay on the nature of poetic writing, he defended his mode of writing against academic criticism: "Squares shut up & learn or go home" (Allen Ginsberg, "When the Mode of Music Changes the Walls of the City Shake," in *The Unity of Literature*, ed. Michael Alssid and William Kenney [Boston: Addison-Wesley, 1968], 318).

143. Alexander Argyros, *A Blessed Rage for Order: Deconstruction, Evolution, and Chaos* (Ann Arbor: University of Michigan Press, 1991), 326.

144. Allen Ginsberg, "Mode of Music," 318.

145. Hilton Kramer and Roger Kimball, eds., *Against the Grain: The New Criterion on Art and Intellect at the End of the Twentieth Century* (Chicago: Dee, 1995), xi, 74.

146. Robert Pinsky "The People's Verse," *New York Times*, 10 April 1997.

147. "Poetry's Sorry State," letter, *New York Times*, 13 April 1997.

148. Dana Gioia, *Can Poetry Matter? Essays on Poetry and American Culture* (Saint Paul, Minn.: Graywolf, 1992), 31.

149. Ibid., 246–47.

150. Michelle Yeh, ed. and trans., *Anthology of Modern Chinese Poetry* (New Haven, Conn.: Yale University Press, 1993), 1.

151. Ibid., xxiv–xxxv.

152. Wang Xiaoni, "Holiday, Lakeside, Reverie," in ibid., 213.

153. André Gide, "Metric and Prosody," in *Imaginary Interviews*, trans. Malcolm Cowlry (New York: Knopf, 1945), 118–24; quotation on 123.

154. Arthur C. Danto, *After the End of Art: Contemporary Art and the Pale of History* (Princeton, N.J.: Princeton University Press, 1996), 149.

APPENDIX A

1. The reader may enter the literature of biological clocks through J. T. Fraser, *Time, the Familiar Stranger* (Amherst: University of Massachusetts Press, 1987), 112–46; and S. L. Macey, *Time: A Bibliographic Guide* (New York: Garland, 1991), which lists some 550 citations under the heading "Chronobiology." The number of related citations in the data bank PASCAL for 1973–1995 approaches 10,000.

2. Joseph Needham, writing about mesoforms (systems found between successive stable levels of integration), noted that between the living and nonliving realms the crystalline represents the highest degree of organization (Needham, "Integrative Levels: A Revaluation of the Idea of Progress," in *Time, the Refreshing River* [London: Allen and Unwin, 1943], 233–72). See also Needham, *Order and Life* (Cambridge, Mass.: MIT Press, 1968), 158 and passim. J. D. Bernal called for a generalized crystallography as the key to the biology involved in the origins of life (Bernal, *The Origins of Life* [Cleveland: World, 1967], 192–94; Bernal, *The Physical Basis of Life* [London: Routledge and Kegan Paul, 1951], 34–39). A. G. Cairns-Smith carried these arguments further by maintaining that the ancestors of life were, in fact, crystalline structures that stood in for the later DNA-RNA-protein system of modern biochemistry. See Cairns-Smith, "Beginnings of Organic Evolution," in *The Study of Time IV*, ed. J. T. Fraser, N. Lawrence, and D. Park (New York: Springer Verlag, 1981), 15–33; Cairns-Smith, *The Genetic Takeover and Mineral Origins of Life* (Cambridge: Cambridge University Press, 1982). On some later, related thought, see E. W. Prohofsky, "The DNA as a Kind of Solid," *Nature* 317 (1985): 197.

3. J. T. Fraser, "Time and the Origin of Life," in *Dimensions of Time and Life: The Study of Time VIII*, ed. J. T. Fraser and M. P. Soulsby (Madison, Conn.: International Universities Press, 1996), 3–18. See also A. T. Winfree, *The Geometry of Biological Time* (New York: Springer Verlag, 1980); box E, p. 115, provides a rapid entry into the phenomenon of spontaneous synchronization, but it must be read in the context of the section entitled "Communities of Clocks," 388–94.

4. The early Precambrian environment, during which life was born, was rich in cyclic processes but would be judged unfriendly by later forms of life. The days were eighteen hours or shorter, the atmosphere was mostly hydrogen, and the surface of the earth was bathed in ultraviolet radiation. Natural radioactivity was strong, and there were continuous electric discharges and hosts of obscure phenomena, such as sonoluminescence. The ground continuously shook, boulders rolled, and the earth vibrated at many frequencies.

5. The fastest-ticking clocks are the molecules of the body, such as those of the skin, that respond to ultraviolet light at 10^{16} Hz. Retinal cells respond to light between 10^{15} and 10^{14} Hz. Photosynthetic processes that capture light energy and change it into forms of energy useful in the synthesis of organic compounds involve cyclic reactions with periods of 10^{-12} seconds. Periods of insect wing beats range between 10^{-4} and 10^{-3} seconds, whereas vocal sounds in animals and people are spread between below 100 Hz to 20,000 Hz—that is, they have periods between 10^{-5} and tenths of a second. Periods of neural signals are between 3 and 10 seconds. The most quickly growing bacteria reproduce every 600 seconds, and cells divide at rates from 10^3 to 10^5 seconds. All living organisms, probably down to the genes, display

circadian periods (just below 10^5 seconds); hundreds of thousands of species show lunar periods of about 10^6 seconds and circannual rhythms of 10^7 seconds; and there are bamboos that flower every 13 to 17 years, that is, with a period around 10^8 seconds.

APPENDIX B

1. J. W. S. Pringle, "On the Parallels between Learning and Evolution," *Behavior* 3:174–215.

2. H. A. Simon, "The Architecture of Complexity," *Proceedings of the American Philosophical Society* 106:467–82.

3. C. H. Waddington, *Tools for Thought* (London: Jonathan Cape, 1977).

4. John von Neumann, *Theory of Self-Reproducing Automata*, ed. and completed by A. W. Burns (Urbana: University of Illinois Press, 1969), 79–80.

5. P. T. Saunders and M. W. Ho, "On the Increase in Complexity in Evolution," *Journal of Theoretical Biology* 63 (1976): 375–84; Saunders and Ho, "On the Increase of Complexity in Evolution II," *Journal of Theoretical Biology* 90 (1981): 515–30.

6. Issues related to complexity in biology first appeared in J. T. Bonner's book *On Development* (Cambridge, Mass.: Harvard University Press, 1974), 65–126. Fourteen years later they became the central theme of his *Evolution of Complexity by Means of Natural Selection* (Princeton, N.J.: Princeton University Press, 1988). With regard to different trends in evolution, Bonner sees complexification as the result of selection for an increase in the diversity of the parts of an organism (a division of labor) simultaneous with a collateral increase in the sophistication of the control systems necessary to ensure coherence. (The reader may recognize in the concept of coherence the demands for the definition of the organic present.) The two trends together lead to a refinement of organic functions manifest in the differentiation of cell types. The diversity among the cells may then serve as an index of complexity of an organism.

7. John Maynard Smith and Eörs Szathmáry, "The Major Evolutionary Transitions," *Nature* 374 (1995): 227–32.

8. M. Hazenwinkel, ed., *Encyclopedia of Mathematics* (Boston: Kluwer, 1995), s.v. "Complex systems."

9. Ibid., s.v. "Hierarchical theory."

10. G. J. Chaitin, "Algorithmic Information Theory," in *Encyclopedia of Statistical Sciences*, ed. Samuel Kotz and N. L. Johnson, 8 vols. (New York: Wiley, 1982), 1:38–41. See also his "Randomness and Mathematical Proof," *Scientific American* 232, no. 5:47–52.

11. This formula takes it for granted that the person or computer following the instructions knows how to handle temporal relationships of the before/after type.

12. This is the number of symbols in the program for calculating by the Ramanujan formula written in Octave, a mathematically oriented language. I am indebted to Mr. David Felsenthal for writing the program. Those interested may note with well-deserved amazement that in three iterations the series converges to twenty-three significant digits.

13. For an entry into discussions pertaining to the equations of science as exam-

ples of compressibility in nature, see Michael Heller's "Chaos, Probability, and the Compressibility of the World," in *Chaos and Complexity*, ed. R. J. Russell, Nancey Murphy, and A. R. Peacocke (Berkeley, Calif.: Center for Theology and the Natural Sciences, 1995), 107–21.

14. Quarks are structural units from which other particles are formed. They are kin to the five geometrical forms—the five regular solids—Plato used to represent the four elements and their relationships.

15. A few decades ago the number of known elementary objects (particle-waves) could be easily listed and unambiguously counted. At the end of the century the listing of such objects and the identification of their properties takes up 708 pages of a special issue of the *Physical Review D* ("Review of Particle Properties," *Physical Review D: Particles and Fields*, 3d ser., 54, part 1 [1 July 1996]). The numeral in the text—500—is a ballpark figure of what has been called the "particle zoo."

16. David R. Lide, ed., *CRC Handbook of Chemistry and Physics*, 78th ed. (Boca Raton, Fla.: CRC, 1997).

17. John A. Dean, ed., *Lange's Handbook of Chemistry*, 13th ed. (New York: McGraw-Hill, 1988).

18. The two figures are from V. H. Heywood, ed., *Global Biodiversity Assessment* (Cambridge: Cambridge University Press, 1995), 118 and 202.

19. E. O. Wilson, "The Current State of Biological Diversity," in *Biodiversity*, ed. E. O. Wilson (Washington, D.C.: National Academy Press, 1988), 5. See also Michael L. Rozenzweig, *Species Diversity in Space and Time* (Cambridge: Cambridge University Press, 1995), 3.

20. Wilson, "The Current State," 7.

21. Laurent Keller and Michel Genoud, "Extraordinary Lifespan in Ants: A Test of Evolutionary Theories of Ageing," *Nature* 389 (1997): 958.

22. I assumed that an average ant is 10 mm^3 and an average microorganism (bacteria and viruses) is 10^{-3}–10^{-9} mm^3. Microorganism size is taken from a table in Bonner's *Evolution of Complexity*.

23. Prof. David Pimentel, private communication.

24. C. W. Allen, *Astrophysical Quantities* (London: Athlone, 1955), 106.

25. Prof. David Pimentel, private communication.

26. Allen, *Astrophysical Quantities*, 106.

27. Prof. David Pimentel, private communication.

28. Allen, *Astrophysical Quantities*, 244. The number of particles in the universe has been estimated as 10^{81}.

29. Gerald M. Edelman, W. Eimar Gall, and W. Maxwell Cowan, eds., *Synaptic Functions* (New York: Wiley, 1987), 1. Blinkov and Glezer give 10^{10}–10^{18} neurons (Samuil M. Blinkov and Ilya Glezer, *The Human Brain in Figures and Tables: A Quantitative Handbook*, trans. Basil Haigh [New York: Plenum, 1968], 201–2).

30. Paul Churchland refines the type of calculation I gave here. Instead of calculating conditions with neurons on or off, he allows for ten different strengths of connections and obtains a figure of $10^{10^{14}}$; see his book *The Engine of Reason, the Seat of the Soul: A Philosophical Journey into the Brain* (Cambridge, Mass.: MIT Press, 1995), 4–5.

31. Edelman, Gall, and Cowan, *Synaptic Functions*, 1.

32. Under the sponsorship of the National Center for Ecological Analysis and Synthesis in Santa Barbara, California, thirteen ecologists and economists joined forces to estimate the annual value of the services that the earth's ecosystem provides. "We have estimated the current economic value of 17 ecosystem services for 16 biomes, based on published studies and a few original calculations. For the entire biosphere, the value (most of which is outside the market) is estimated to be in the range of US$16–54 trillion ($10^{12}$) per year, with an average of US$33 trillion per year. Because of the nature of the uncertainties, this must be considered a minimum estimate. Global gross national product is around US$18 trillion per year" (Robert Costanza et al., "The Value of the World's Ecosystem Services and Natural Capital," *Nature* 387 [15 May 1997]: 253–60).

The estimates and figures I offer belong in the same category of calculations, except that they are rooted in natural science.

APPENDIX C

1. Paul Edwards, ed., *The Encyclopedia of Philosophy* (New York: Macmillan, 1972), s.v. "Entropy."

2. Specific formulations of entropy principles exist for such diverse systems or quantities as steam tables, transfer of messages along radio links, learning behavior of rats, population pressure, and the economics of commodity production. There is no single unit or even physical dimension of entropy that would be common to these different uses.

3. A. S. Eddington, *The Nature of the Physical World* (Ann Arbor: University of Michigan Press, 1958), 69, 79, 101.

4. Information theory uses entropy as a measure of directed change through sleight-of-hand, namely, a particular representation of the future. It postulates an ensemble of possible future events and determines current entropy in terms of the probabilities associated with each. This approach has proved useful in handling messages in languages whose statistical properties are known but has little usefulness for calculating the entropy of a living sheep because the statistical properties of sheep yet to evolve are not known.

5. Edward R. Harrison, *Cosmology, the Science of the Universe* (Cambridge: Cambridge University Press, 1986), 356.

6. See an analogous elaboration of this point in Huw Price, "A Point on the Arrow of Time," *Nature* 340 (20 July 1989): 181–82; and Price, "Cosmology, Time's Arrow, and That Old Double Standard," in *Time's Arrows Today*, ed. S. Savitt (Cambridge: Cambridge University Press, 1994), 66–94. See also Price's "Chaos Theory and the Difference between Past and Future," in *Time, Order, Chaos: The Study of Time IX*, ed. J. T. Fraser, M. P. Soulsby, and A. Argyros (Madison, Conn.: International Universities Press, 1998), 155–62.

APPENDIX D

1. H. P. Robertson, "Geometry as a Branch of Physics," in *Albert Einstein: Philosopher-Scientist*, ed. P. A. Schilpp (New York: Tudor, 1949), 332.

2. A. S. Eddington, *Space, Time, and Gravitation* (New York: Harper Torchbooks, 1959), 190.

3. Michael Heller, "The Origins of Time," in *The Study of Time IV*, ed. J. T. Fraser, N. Lawrence, and D. Park (New York: Springer Verlag, 1981), 90–93.

4. "The essential point is that even if the physical world is not *time oriented*, one should ascribe to it a property of being time *orientable*—the possibility that it *could be* time oriented (e.g. by the temporality of our mind)" (Michael Heller, "Why Does the World Have a History?" *The Astronomy Quarterly* 5, no. 19 [1986]: 177; emphasis added). We may expand the parenthetic remark to "by the temporalities of life, the human mind, and society."

5. Since an expanding universe in forward-moving time (to use accepted terms) is empirically indistinguishable from a collapsing universe in backward-moving time, an interesting conclusion of the eotemporality of the universe is that the Big Bang and the Big Crunch (of the expanding-collapsing model) are one and the same event.

APPENDIX E

1. John Eccles, *The Brain and the Unity of Conscious Experience* (Cambridge: Cambridge University Press, 1965), 35.

2. Anton Ehrenzweig, *The Psycho-analysis of Artistic Vision and Hearing* (New York: Braziller, 1965), 189.

3. Jason W. Brown, *Self and Process: Brain States and the Conscious Present* (New York: Springer Verlag, 1991), 7.

4. Ibid., 149–50.

5. Gerald M. Edelman, *Neural Darwinism: The Theory of Neuronal Selection* (New York: Basic Books, 1987); Edelman, *The Remembered Present: A Biological Theory of Consciousness* (New York: Basic Books, 1989); Edelman, *Bright Air, Brilliant Fire: On the Matter of the Mind* (New York: Basic Books, 1992).

6. Doing so is appropriate to the dedication of Edelman's *Bright Air:* "To the memory of two intellectual pioneers, Charles Darwin and Sigmund Freud."

7. Edelman, *Bright Air,* 167.

8. Edelman, *The Remembered Present,* 287–88.

J. T. FRASER, founder of the International Society for the Study of Time, is the author of *Of Time, Passion, and Knowledge* (1975), *Time as Conflict* (1978), *The Genesis and Evolution of Time* (1982), and *Time, the Familiar Stranger* (1987); the editor of *The Voices of Time* (1968); and the senior editor of the nine volumes in The Study of Time series (1972–   ). Acknowledged to be the world's foremost authority on the interdisciplinary study of time, he has published numerous articles in professional periodicals and has lectured extensively on the study of time. He has also taught courses and conducted seminars at the Massachusetts Institute of Technology, Mount Holyoke College, the University of Maryland, and Fordham University.

Typeset in 10/12.5 New Baskerville
with New Baskerville display
Designed by Copenhaver Cumpston
Composed at the University of Illinois Press
Manufactured by Maple-Vail Book Manufacturing Group

University of Illinois Press
1325 South Oak Street
Champaign, IL 61820-6903
www.press.uillinois.edu